Hegel and the Philosophy of Nature

SUNY Series in Hegelian Studies
William Desmond, editor

Hegel and the Philosophy of Nature

edited by Stephen Houlgate

State University of New York Press

Published by
State University of New York Press, Albany

Printed in the United States of America

For information, address State University of New York Press,
State University Plaza, Albany, N.Y. 12246

Production by Marilyn Semerad
Marketing by Anne M. Valentine

Library of Congress Cataloging-in-Publication Data

Hegel and the philosophy of nature / edited by Stephen Hougate.
p. cm. — (SUNY series in Hegelian studies)
Includes bibliographical references (p.) and index.
ISBN 0-7914-4143-1 (hardcover : alk. paper). — ISBN 0-7914-4144-X (pbk. : alk. paper)
1. Hegel, Georg Wilhelm Friedrich, 1770–1831—Contributions in philosophy of nature. 2. Philosophy of nature. I. Houlgate, Stephen. II. Series.
B2949.N3H43 1998
113'.092—dc21 98-34335
CIP

Contents

Abbreviations vii

Introduction xi
Stephen Houlgate

1. The Very Idea of the Idea of Nature, or Why Hegel Is Not an Idealist 1
William Maker

2. The Logic of Hegel's *Philosophy of Nature*: Nature, Space and Time 29
Edward Halper

3. Space, Time and Matter: Conceiving Nature Without Foundations 51
Richard Dien Winfield

4. Hegel's Geometric Theory 71
Lawrence S. Stepelevich

5. How to Save the Phenomena: Meaning and Reference in Hegel's Philosophy of Nature 97
Brigitte Falkenburg

6. On Hegel's Early Critique of Kant's *Metaphysical Foundations of Natural Science* 137
Kenneth R. Westphal

7. Hegel's Appropriation of Kant's Account of Teleology in Nature 167
Daniel O. Dahlstrom

8. How Final Is Hegel's Rejection of Evolution? 189
Errol E. Harris

9. Hegel's Nature 209
Donald Phillip Verene

10. Hegel's Worm in Newton's Apple 227
Mauro Nasti De Vincentis

11. The Ontological Foundations of Hegel's Dissertation of 1801 257
Olivier Depré

12. Framing Hypotheses: Numbers in Nature and the Logic of Measure in the Development of Hegel's System 283
Cinzia Ferrini

Bibliography 311

About the Contributors 341

Index 345

Abbreviations

The following abbreviations have been used for works by Hegel and Kant referred to frequently in this volume.

Hegel

GW	G.W.F. Hegel, *Gesammelte Werke*, Rheinisch-Westfälische Akademie der Wissenschaften & Hegel-Archiv der Ruhr-Universität Bochum (Hamburg: Felix Meiner, 1968–).
Werke	G.W.F. Hegel, *Werke in zwanzig Bänden*, edited by E. Moldenhauer and K.M. Michel (Frankfurt am Main: Suhrkamp Verlag, 1969–).
DOP	G.W.F. Hegel, *Dissertatio philosophica de orbitis planetarum. Philosophische Erörterung über die Planetenbahnen*, translation, with introduction and commentary by W. Neuser (Weinheim: Acta Humanoria VCH, 1986).
Phän.	G.W.F. Hegel, *Phänomenologie des Geistes*, edited by J. Hoffmeister (Hamburg: Felix Meiner, 1952).
Phän. (*GW*, **9**)	G.W.F. Hegel, *Phänomenologie des Geistes*, edited by W. Bonsiepen and R. Heede, *Gesammelte Werke*, Vol. 9 (Hamburg: Felix Meiner, 1980).
Miller, *Phen.*	*Hegel's Phenomenology of Spirit*, translated by A.V. Miller (Oxford: Oxford University Press, 1977).

Logik (*GW*, **11**)	G.W.F. Hegel, *Wissenschaft der Logik. Erster Band: Die Objektive Logik (1812/1813)*, edited by F. Hogemann and W. Jaeschke, *Gesammelte Werke*, Vol. 11 (Hamburg: Felix Meiner, 1978).
Logik (*GW*, **12**)	G.W.F. Hegel, *Wissenschaft der Logik. Zweiter Band: Die Subjektive Logik (1816)*, edited by F. Hogemann and W. Jaeschke, *Gesammelte Werke*, Vol. 12 (Hamburg: Felix Meiner, 1981).
Logik (*GW*, **21**)	G.W.F. Hegel, *Wissenschaft der Logik. Erster Teil: Die Objektive Logik, Erster Band: Die Lehre vom Sein (1832)*, edited by F. Hogemann and W. Jaeschke, *Gesammelte Werke*, Vol. 21 (Hamburg: Felix Meiner, 1985).
Logik (*Werke*, **5**)	G.W.F. Hegel, *Wissenschaft der Logik I. Erster Teil: Die Objektive Logik, Erstes Buch*, edited by E. Moldenhauer and K.M. Michel, *Werke in zwanzig Bänden*, Vol. 5 (Frankfurt am Main: Suhrkamp Verlag, 1970).
Logik (*Werke*, **6**)	G.W.F. Hegel, *Wissenschaft der Logik II. Erster Teil: Die Objektive Logik, Zweites Buch. Zweiter Teil: Die Subjektive Logik*, edited by E. Moldenhauer and K.M. Michel, *Werke in zwanzig Bänden*, Vol. 6 (Frankfurt am Main: Suhrkamp Verlag, 1970).
Logik (Lasson)	G.W.F. Hegel, *Wissenschaft der Logik*, edited by G. Lasson, 2 Vols (Hamburg: Felix Meiner, 1971).

Miller, *Logic*	*Hegel's Science of Logic*, translated by A.V. Miller (Atlantic Highlands, NJ: Humanities Press International, 1989).
EL (1830)	G.W.F. Hegel, *Enzyklopädie der philosophischen Wissenschaften im Grundrisse (1830). Erster Teil: Die Wissenschaft der Logik mit den mündlichen Zusätzen*, edited by E. Moldenhauer and K.M. Michel, *Werke in zwanzig Bänden*, Vol. 8 (Frankfurt am Main: Suhrkamp Verlag, 1970).
Wallace, *EL*	*Hegel's Logic: Being Part One of the Encyclopaedia of the Philosophical Sciences (1830)*, translated by William Wallace (Oxford: Clarendon Press, 1975).
EN (1830)	G.W.F. Hegel, *Enzyklopädie der philosophischen Wissenschaften im Grundrisse (1830). Zweiter Teil: Die Naturphilosophie mit den mündlichen Zusätzen*, edited by E. Moldenhauer and K.M. Michel, *Werke in zwanzig Bänden*, Vol. 9 (Frankfurt am Main: Suhrkamp Verlag, 1970).
Miller, *PN*	*Hegel's Philosophy of Nature: Being Part Two of the Encyclopaedia of the Philosophical Sciences (1830)*, translated by A.V. Miller (Oxford: Clarendon Press, 1970).
Petry, *PN*	G.W.F. Hegel, *Philosophy of Nature*, edited and translated by M.J. Petry, 3 Vols (London: George Allen and Unwin, 1970).

Kant

GS	*Kants Gesammelte Schriften* (Königlich Preußische [now Deutsche] Akademie der Wissenschaften, Berlin: G. Reimer [now De Gruyter], 1902–).
KdrV	I. Kant, *Kritik der reinen Vernunft*, *Kants Gesammelte Schriften*, Vols. 3, 4 (Königlich Preußische [now Deutsche] Akademie der Wissenschaften, Berlin: G. Reimer [now De Gruyter], 1902–).
Prol.	I. Kant, *Prolegomena zu einer jeden künftigen Metaphysik, die als Wissenschaft wird auftreten können*, *Kants Gesammelte Schriften*, Vol. 4 (Königlich Preußische [now Deutsche] Akademie der Wissenschaften, Berlin: G. Reimer [now De Gruyter], 1902–).
MAdN	I. Kant, *Metaphysische Anfangsgründe der Naturwissenschaft*, *Kants Gesammelte Schriften*, Vol. 4 (Königlich Preußische [now Deutsche] Akademie der Wissenschaften, Berlin: G. Reimer [now De Gruyter], 1902–).
KdU	I. Kant, *Kritik der Urteilskraft*, *Kants Gesammelte Schriften*, Vol. 5 (Königlich Preußische [now Deutsche] Akademie der Wissenschaften, Berlin: G. Reimer [now De Gruyter], 1902–).

Introduction

Stephen Houlgate

G.W.F. Hegel's *Philosophy of Nature*, which forms the second part of his *Encyclopedia of the Philosophical Sciences* (1817, 1827, 1830), has long been the object of ridicule and disdain. Karl Popper famously mocked Hegel's account of sound and heat in *The Open Society and its Enemies* (first published in 1945); and one hundred years earlier (in 1844) the biologist, Matthias J. Schleiden, dismissed the entirety of the *Philosophy of Nature* as a "string of pearls of the crudest empirical ignorance" consisting of little more than "miserable criticism and excerpts put together without judgment."[1] As a result of such uncompromising condemnation, all that the name "Hegel" has signified to many during the last century and a half is an arrogant and ignorant German philosopher who denied evolution and who (in 1801) "proved" *a priori* that there could only be seven planets just as the asteroids were being discovered between the orbits of Mars and Jupiter. Jacob Bronowski, speaking to a television audience of millions in the 1970s in his series, *The Ascent of Man*, mentioned nothing at all about Hegel *except* the latter's "proof" that there can be no eighth planet, and felt moved to confess that he "specifically detest[s]" Hegel, in part no doubt because of the latter's infamous "proof."[2] It seems that for many the only redeeming feature of Hegel's philosophy of nature is that (unlike Schelling's) it failed to exercise any significant influence whatsoever over practicing natural scientists.[3]

Herbert Schnädelbach has pointed out that ever since the early to mid-nineteenth century Hegel's *Philosophy of Nature* has been regarded by scientists as precisely the kind of work from which serious students of nature should seek to distance themselves. After 1830, he notes, scientific consciousness in Germany was distinguished by regular attacks on Romantic and Idealist nature-philosophy as a whole. But Hegel's nature-philosophy in particular was generally regarded as a horrible example of the aberrations of philosophical speculation, and was taken as a motive for affirming that it was now finally time to leave philosophy in general well alone and to pursue the advance of science.

For nineteenth-century scientists (and for historians), the rejection of Hegel thus had "paradigmatic significance."[4] It is clear, then, that one of the reasons why Hegel's *Philosophy of Nature* has met with so much ridicule is that modern science has so often defined itself explicitly against Hegel.

The problem is that the rejection of Hegel's *Philosophy of Nature* as the product of a scientifically ignorant mind by so many scientists and philosophers has itself all-too often been based on a profound *ignorance* of Hegel's philosophy and its relation to nature and science. Too few have been willing to approach Hegel with the sympathy and understanding they (quite properly) accord to Kant, and too many have been prepared, without reading anything of Hegel's work, simply to follow the injunction of Popper and his nineteenth-century forebears not to take Hegel "too seriously."[5] It is, however, now being recognized by a small but growing number of Hegel scholars and philosophers of science that Hegel was neither ignorant of, nor indifferent to, natural science, as is often claimed, but was in fact deeply knowledgeable about the science of his day.[6] We have learned that Hegel drew intelligently on the work of, amongst others, Lagrange and Cauchy in mathematics, Cuvier and Hutton in geology, and Berthollet and Pohl in chemistry.[7] Indeed, Michael Petry has shown that even the few definite scientific mistakes Hegel made invariably have a highly respectable source in the scientific literature of the time (according to Petry, Hegel's claim that "*ammonia* ... has a metallic base in *ammonium*," for instance, is almost certainly based on a paper by Sir Humphry Davy).[8] Parts of Hegel's *Philosophy of Nature* may indeed be outdated or just plain wrong, and his philosophical language may well continue to create problems for those who are not trained in his philosophy. However, what is becoming more and more apparent, through the work of scholars like Petry, is that those who simply dismiss Hegel as ignorant about science or as a charlatan are blinding themselves to one of the richest and most sophisticated philosophical accounts of the natural world ever produced. For, in fact, as Petry points out, "the 'Philosophy of Nature', far from being an arbitrary and irresponsible exposition of partially understood subject matter, is a sensitively structuralized, deeply informed and infinitely rewarding assessment of the whole range of early nineteenth-century science."[9]

Hegel's *Philosophy of Nature* is clearly not intended to be a work of straightforward natural science itself, but to be a work of *philosophy* in the manner of Aristotle's *Physics* or Kant's *Metaphysical Foundations of Natural Science.* It does not simply offer the results of empirical research and observation (or of mathematical analysis), but seeks to provide an account of the ultimate *conceptual* structure of nature. Hegel thus does not just provide a philosophy of science in the manner of a Popper, Kuhn or Lakatos (Gerd Buchdahl notes that "to the modern Anglo-Saxon scholar, there appears to be a curious lack of concern with epistemological issues [in Hegel]").[10] He offers a metaphysical account of the very structure of nature itself, of what nature itself ultimately *is*.

Nevertheless, Hegel makes it clear, not only that the insights of philosophy must coincide with those of natural science, but also that the philosophy of nature must actually draw on the discoveries of natural science in presenting its philosophical conceptions of space, time, matter, and so on. In this sense, for Hegel, "philosophic science presupposes and is conditioned by empirical physics" (and the other sciences).[11]

It should be noted, however, that there is by no means universal agreement amongst Hegel scholars on the precise nature of the relation between philosophy and natural science in Hegel's *Philosophy of Nature*. Some argue that the structure or skeleton of the *Philosophy of Nature* is developed purely conceptually, but that the flesh, as it were, is derived from empirical observation and scientific experimentation and analysis. On this view, Hegel is led to the very idea of nature by the *Science of Logic*, develops the conceptual structure of nature *a priori* from the initial determination of nature as abstract externality, and then "maps" natural phenomena as described by science on to the various conceptual determinations that arise. Discoveries in science are thus understood and evaluated in the light of a conceptual account of nature which is developed *a priori*. Others argue, however, that scientific discoveries themselves condition, and perhaps even determine, the development of Hegel's conceptual account of nature. On this view, the procedure of Hegel's philosophy is not to map natural phenomena on to an *a priori* conceptual structure, but to provide a flexible conceptual framework which organizes in an intelligible way, and is wholly *relative* to, the scientific knowledge of a given time, and which changes with future scientific discoveries. Passages can be cited from Hegel's *Philosophy of Nature* in favor of each of these interpretations, but, as yet, it has not been definitively determined which, if either, is more correct.[12] One of the major tasks facing those who concern themselves with Hegel's *Philosophy of Nature* continues, indeed, to be to work to resolve this central issue.

The essays in this collection, written by internationally recognized Hegel scholars from the USA, Britain, Italy, Germany, and Belgium, deal with a wide array of topics: Hegel's alleged idealism, his account of space and time, his conception of geometry, his critique of Kant's *Metaphysical Foundations of Natural Science* and indebtedness to Kant's *Critique of Judgment*, his critique of Newtonian science, his concept of evolution, his notion of *Aufhebung*, and his theory regarding the orbits of the planets around the sun. Some essays concentrate on Hegel's writings on the philosophy of nature from the early Jena period (1801) rather than on the text of the *Encyclopedia Philosophy of Nature* itself. Each of these essays, however, makes a distinctive contribution towards furthering our understanding of the relation between philosophical concepts and natural science in Hegel's philosophy of nature as a whole. The essays do so by falling broadly into two groups. On the one hand, several of the essays focus specifically on the conceptual structure of nature as Hegel understands it and seek to clarify its relation to the structure of pure thought set out in the *Science of Logic*. On the other hand, several of the essays examine in detail Hegel's relation to the sciences, in particular Newtonian physics, modern geometry, and neo-Darwinian biology. No single interpretation of Hegel's philosophy of nature emerges from the essays; nor, indeed, do all the contributors agree on whether the structure of the philosophy of nature is determined *a priori* by self-determining reason or *a posteriori* by the findings of the sciences of Hegel's day. What does emerge clearly from this collection, however, is that the philosophy of nature cannot be understood in isolation from Hegel's speculative logic and that anyone seeking to establish the precise role played by the sciences in the philosophy of nature can only do so by simultaneously establishing the precise role played by speculative logic. Similarly, it becomes clear that, whether the insights of Hegel's philosophy of nature are to be understood as founded on, or as merely coincident with, the findings of natural science, Hegel was scientifically literate and made penetrating and insightful criticisms of specific sciences, in particular of Newtonian physics and Enlightenment biology. Indeed, two contributors suggest that Hegel's philosophy of nature also contains important criticisms of modern neo-Darwinism. The essays in this collection thus all confirm that, far from being irrelevant to, or having been simply surpassed by, nineteenth- and twentieth-century scientific developments, Hegel's philosophy of nature has always had, and continues to have, great significance for the natural sciences and our understanding of the natural world.

In 1970 M.J. Petry produced his ground-breaking English edition of Hegel's *Philosophy of Nature* and demonstrated just how subtle and well-informed that work is. Since then there have appeared at least four major collections of essays designed to promote the serious study of Hegel's nature-philosophy: *Hegel and the Sciences*, edited by R.S. Cohen and M.W. Wartofsky (Dordrecht: Reidel, 1984); *Hegels Philosophie der Natur: Beziehungen zwischen empirischer und spekulativer Naturerkenntnis*, edited by R.-P. Horstmann and M.J. Petry (Stuttgart: Klett-Cotta, 1986); *Hegel und die Naturwissenschaften*, edited by M.J. Petry (Stuttgart: Frommann-Holzboog, 1987); and *Hegel and Newtonianism*, edited by M.J. Petry (Dordrecht: Kluwer, 1993). The essays collected together in the present volume reflect the wide variety of work that continues to be done by scholars from North America and Europe in the 1990s to deepen our understanding of the historical importance and enduring scientific relevance of Hegel's philosophy of nature.

In the opening essay of the collection, "The Very Idea of the Idea of Nature, or Why Hegel Is not an Idealist," William Maker offers a vigorous defense of Hegel's *Encyclopedia Philosophy of Nature* against the familiar charge that it is metaphysically idealistic. Maker argues that, contrary to popular belief, Hegel does not deny the existence of an independently given nature or conceive of nature as a mere product of thought, but proceeds rather from the conviction that thought and nature are radically *non-identical*. Furthermore, Maker contends that Hegel is led to this conviction by the philosophical requirement of systematicity. Hegel's *Logic* sets out the process of thought's systematic and autonomous self-determination; and, according to Maker, if such self-determining thought is to become fully determinate, it must *limit* itself. But it can only limit itself, we are told, by conceiving of itself as bounded by what is radically other than itself—that is, by the realm of sheer givenness, externality and non-self-determination that constitutes *nature*. Systematic philosophy must conceive of nature as other than thought, therefore, in order to conceive of thought itself as a distinctive and complete domain of logical self-determination. Maker goes on to show that, precisely because it recognizes nature to be genuinely other than systematic thought, Hegel's *Philosophy of Nature* has to acknowledge that specific contingent features of nature lie beyond the reach of *a priori* philosophy and can only be discovered by empirical observation. Far from seeking to supplant empirical science, therefore, Hegel's systematic philosophy of nature *necessarily* accords an indispensable and independent role to such science.

In his essay, "The Logic of Hegel's *Philosophy of Nature*," Edward Halper offers an alternative account of the relation between the *Science of Logic* and the *Philosophy of Nature*. In his view, the transition from pure logic to nature is effected not by conceiving of logical thought as limited by its other, but rather by conceiving of the logical "Idea" *itself* as immediate and external to itself. The realm of nature, for Halper, is thus simply the absolute Idea together with a further logical determination, namely, immediate being. In the latter part of his essay, Halper then argues that the transitions in the *Philosophy of Nature* result from the complex interplay between the absolute Idea and its further determination (unlike the transitions in the *Logic* which are the result of the simple self-determination of the individual logical categories). By showing in this way that nature is constituted by a new and distinctive "totality" of logical determinations that is not found in the *Logic* itself, Halper aims to demonstrate that nature is systematically derived from logical determinations by Hegel, but is not reducible to the determinations of logic as such. Despite clear differences between his approach to the *Philosophy of Nature* and that of William Maker, it is thus evident that he, too, like Maker, is endeavoring to explain how nature can be both different from, and intelligible to, thought.

In "Space, Time and Matter: Conceiving Nature Without Foundations," Richard Dien Winfield also considers the relation between Hegel's speculative logic and philosophy of nature. If Hegel's philosophy of nature is not simply to take for granted what it must prove, Winfield argues, it must articulate the structure of nature without appealing to anything assumed to be given in reality. This means that the idea of natural determinacy from which the philosophy of nature begins must emerge from an account of logical determinacy in general which is itself presuppositionless and self-determining. However, the philosophy of nature must at the same time provide categories of nature that go beyond purely logical categories. Like Halper, therefore, Winfield maintains that Hegel can make use of nothing but self-determining logical categories in his derivation of the minimal determination of nature, and yet must employ those logical categories in such a way that they comprise a new determination that remains clearly distinct from each one of them. Furthermore, Winfield maintains, the philosophy of nature must itself proceed by passing from its starting point—the self-externality of logical determinacy, or space—to further structures of nature which incorporate nothing other than what has already been determined, but which at the same time comprise something irreducible to their antecedents. Space must thus be determined independently of time; time must require nothing but space for its determination; place and motion must require nothing but space and time for their determination; and the sheer formality of space, time, place and formal motion must alone serve to account for matter.

In Lawrence Stepelevich's essay, "Hegel's Geometric Theory," attention is turned from the method employed in the *Philosophy of Nature* to the relation between Hegel's philosophy and modern geometry. According to Stepelevich, the opening of Hegel's *Philosophy of Nature* presents a "geometry of reason" which not only recognizes the modern distinction between "pure" and "physical" geometry, but presents speculative grounds for their mediation. From a Hegelian perspective, Stepelevich maintains, the difference between the "logical" or "pure" point of Hilbert's geometry and the "physical" point of Max Born's empirical geometry is that the latter is the dialectically or speculatively articulated conclusion of the former. Moreover, in so far as Hegel's "geometry of reason" is not tied to a spatial metric expressed exclusively as *either* a "pure" *or* "physical" geometry, it can provide speculative support for both non-Euclidean and Euclidean geometry. Stepelevich further emphasizes the importance of Hegel's contribution to geometric theory by pointing out that he anticipated not only Carnap's critique of Kant's theory of geometry, but also Minkowski's claim that space and time are united, Einstein's view that space and its geometry is logically prior to physical mass and gravitational force, and Riemann's geometry of "constant positive curvature."

In her essay, "How to Save the Phenomena," Brigitte Falkenburg considers the relation between Hegel's *Philosophy of Nature* and empirical science, focusing in this case on Newtonian physics. Her main concern is to clarify how empirical science relates to natural phenomena and how Hegel's philosophy of nature relates both to these phenomena and to the concepts of empirical science itself. Falkenburg argues that Hegel shifts from the extensional view of scientific concepts espoused by Newton (in which concepts refer to classes of individual entities) to a non-extensional view of scientific concepts (in which concepts refer to law-like structures in nature or to natural kinds). Furthermore, she contends that the concepts of Hegel's own philosophy of nature do not refer directly to entities in nature, but correspond rather to the concepts of empirical science. In other words, Hegel's philosophy of nature begins, not with nature itself, but with concepts supplied by science (in particular physics) and organizes the contents of such concepts into an adequate system of natural kinds in accordance with the categories of the *Science of Logic*. But, if the philosophy of nature presupposes the concepts of physics in this way, then it obviously cannot be a wholly *a priori* theory of nature as some have claimed. Falkenburg's study of Hegel's understanding of the meaning and reference of scientific and philosophical concepts thus leads her to the conclusion that Hegel's philosophy of nature is far more dependent on empirical science than is often recognized.

Hegel's criticisms of Kant's philosophy are often regarded as failing to hit their intended target. However, in his essay, "On Hegel's Early Critique of Kant's *Metaphysical Foundations of Natural Science*," Kenneth Westphal sets out to show that one specific criticism made by Hegel in 1801 of Kant's theory of nature is in fact far more significant than has hitherto been recognized. In his *Differenzschrift* Hegel claimed that, for Kant, forces are either purely ideal or transcendent and that "the only construction of phenomena that he [Kant] can allow is mathematical, not dynamical."

Westphal contends that Hegel is right, and he undertakes a close and detailed analysis of Kant's *Metaphysical Foundations of Natural Science* (1786) to show why. Westphal's main argument is that Kant's "phoronomic" analysis of the mathematics of motion does not justify the "dynamical" claim it is intended to justify that "matter fills a space ... by a special moving force." In his view, this clearly establishes Hegel's point that the only *valid* construction of phenomena Kant can offer remains a merely *mathematical* one. Westphal points out that by 1800 Kant had himself come to acknowledge that dynamical principles and the concept of force they employ cannot be constructed on a purely mathematical basis. Indeed, Kant saw that the mathematical expression of forces itself presupposes dynamical forces, because those forces are necessary for the means of measurement through which alone their mathematical relations can be determined. According to Westphal, this problem profoundly undermines Kant's claim to be able to provide a proper rational *foundation* for a physics of the real world, based purely on principles drawn from the *Critique of Pure Reason* together with the concept of motion. It thus paves the way for Hegel's alternative conception of philosophy as itself rooted in, and in dialectical relation with, the empirical sciences.

In his essay "Hegel's Appropriation of Kant's Account of Teleology in Nature" Daniel Dahlstrom continues to focus on the relation between Hegel and Kant, in this case pointing to the central importance of Hegel's reading of the *Critique of Judgment* for the development of his speculative metaphysics. Dahlstrom notes that, in Hegel's eyes, Kant's account of inner purposiveness in nature is nothing short of a disclosure of what Hegel understands by the "Idea." However, for Hegel the concept of purposeful organization is not merely a regulative one, but is an ontological category characterizing the status of organic entities themselves quite apart from their relation to a potential observer. Dahlstrom goes on to stress that, despite this difference, Kant and Hegel both agree that organic behavior can only be rendered intelligible by means of the concept of *purpose*. Both thus endorse the thesis that organic processes are irreducible to physico-chemical processes. Dahlstrom points out that this commitment to the teleological explanation of organic behavior conflicts with the more recent, neo-Darwinian commitment to the idea of random mutation generated by chance and mechanistic necessity alone. Yet, Dahlstrom also notes that recent research into a strain of the E. coli bacterium suggests that in certain circumstances this bacterium can in fact adapt its DNA "purposefully" to its environment, and that genetic mutation is thus not always random. For Dahlstrom, this opens the possibility that contemporary biology might have more to learn from Kant and Hegel than is often assumed.

The possibility of a Hegelian challenge to modern neo-Darwinism is also envisaged by Errol Harris in his essay, "How Final Is Hegel's Rejection of Evolution?" Hegel is well-known for his rejection of evolution. However, Harris argues that what Hegel sought to reject were primarily the inadequate theories of biological development known to him at the time: preformation (the belief that a miniature version of the mature creature was encapsulated in the original germ and in the course of time grew in size to become the mature organism) and epigenesis (the idea that the germ-plasm was simple protoplasm which gradually differentiated itself into the embryo and then grew larger to attain adult form). Furthermore, in so far as Hegel rejected the idea that *species* were transformed one into another, he was simply following other noted scientists of his day, such as Linnaeus, Haller, Bonnet and Cuvier. In spite of its apparently anti-evolutionary bias, however, Harris argues that Hegel's dialectical philosophy is in fact profoundly *evolutionary* in character and indeed anticipates certain modern biological concepts, such as the recent Gaia hypothesis that the earth is an organic whole. Harris acknowledges that Hegel would have rejected the modern, Darwinian assumption that species originate solely as a result of an accumulation of chance variations giving selective advantage. However, like Dahlstrom, Harris points out that there is now evidence to suggest that not all genetic mutation is in fact random, but that some may well be induced by pressures within the organism to maintain its integrity in its specific surroundings. This change of outlook promises a theory of evolution based on the nature of, and nisus towards, the whole; and, according to Harris, if such a theory, with sound scientific credentials, had been available to Hegel in the early nineteenth century, there is little doubt that he would have embraced it with alacrity.

In his presidential address, "Hegel's Nature," Donald Phillip Verene returns to the problem of the transition from the *Science of Logic* to the *Philosophy of Nature* and asks what it means for Hegel to claim that the Idea freely goes forth as nature. Verene prefaces his discussion of the move from the *Logic* to the *Philosophy of Nature* by looking back to the *Phenomenology* remarking that there consciousness lives in the ambiguity of two objects: what is "for it" and what is "in itself." Each stage of the *Phenomenology* is predicated on the belief that this ambiguity can be resolved, but this belief is an illusion and in the attempt to resolve the ambiguity consciousness simply passes over into more complex ambiguity. In Verene's view, the moves from the *Phenomenology* to the *Logic* and from the *Logic* to the *Philosophy of Nature* are also marked by an "unresolved twoness": there is no real *transition* in either case, but rather free acts of "doubling up." The key to the free release of the Idea into nature thus lies not in any mysterious movement of *Aufhebung*, but rather in the constant doubling of one-to-one relationships—one self freely going forth into another and another. Taking his cue from Schiller's poem, *Die Freundschaft*, (mis)quoted by Hegel at the end of the *Phenomenology*, Verene refers to such doubling as *friendship*. In Verene's view, therefore, there is not so much a smooth transition of the Idea into nature at the end of the *Logic*; rather the Idea *befriends* nature.

In the final three essays of the collection, we turn to Hegel's 1801 *Dissertation on the Orbits of the Planets*. This dissertation is a sorely neglected text, but, according to Mauro Nasti De Vincentis, it contains a highly significant criticism of Newton's generalized areal law which deserves to be taken seriously. Newton's areal law states that, when one body is in orbit around another (fixed central) body, the line drawn from the orbiting body to the central body—the "radius vector"—describes equal areas in equal times, hence these areas are proportional to the times. However, according to Hegel, what is actually *proven* by Newton in the *Principia* is that the orbital *arcs*, as well as the areas, are proportional to the times. But, of course, if this is this case, then Newton in fact proves—absurdly—that all orbits must be circular, since a circular orbit is precisely one in which equal orbital arcs are described in equal times. Guided by Hegel, Nasti De Vincentis examines Newton's original proof closely and ascertains that, although certain qualifications need to be added, Hegel's criticism is highly astute. Nasti De Vincentis points out that, as it stands, Newton's proof proves the areal law for *polygonal* arcs, but does not soundly prove that what holds for polygonal arcs also holds for the corresponding *finite curvilinear orbital* arcs. Since the differences between polygonal arcs and curvilinear orbital arcs can be ignored when the orbital arcs are *infinitesimally small* (i.e. non-finite), Newton's proof *can* be considered valid in the case of such infinitesimal orbital arcs. Furthermore, if certain other conditions are also specified, Newton's proof does successfully establish in this case that the areas only and *not* the arcs are proportional to the times. However, Newton's proof cannot be considered to be sound in the case of *finite* curvilinear orbital arcs of a determinate magnitude, even though it is clear that Newton intends his proof to be valid of such finite orbital arcs. According to Nasti De Vincentis, it is when Newton's proof is taken—incorrectly, but in accordance with Newton's intentions—to be valid of *finite* orbital arcs, that not only the areas swept through by the radius vector, but also the orbital *arcs* described by the moving mass point, are proven to be proportional to the times of describing them. It is in this case, therefore, that, just as Hegel contended, Newton's proof has the absurd conclusion that all the arcs must be equal in equal times and the orbit must be circular. Nasti De Vincentis notes that modern proofs of Newton's areal law have been developed which avoid this problem, but that Hegel's criticism (which is derived from one made by the French Jesuit, Louis-Bertrand Castel) remains an important criticism of Newton's original proof.

Hegel's *Dissertation on the Orbits of the Planets* has long been ridiculed and scorned (by writers such as Jacob Bronowski) because it is there that Hegel offered what he took to be a rational explanation for the supposed absence of any planet between Mars and Jupiter just at the time the asteroid Ceres was being discovered. In his essay, "The Ontological Foundations of Hegel's Dissertation of 1801," Olivier Depré sets out to understand what led Hegel to commit his error and argues that Hegel is not by any means as guilty of mindless "apriorism" as has often been claimed. Towards the end of the eighteenth century a group of scientists, guided by an arithmetical series of numbers known as the "Titius-Bode Law," committed themselves to looking for a planet between the orbits of Mars and Jupiter. Hegel regarded this law as nonrational and inexact, and suggested that an alternative *exponential* series, inspired by Plato's *Timaeus*, would be much more rational and would account for the gap between Mars and Jupiter. Depré notes that, although Hegel would probably have heard reports that a minor planet had been discovered precisely where he thought there should be a gap, he would not have had any reason at the time he was writing to regard the existence of this minor planet as anything more than conjecture. His motivation for preferring the exponential series was thus not only that it was more rational, but also that it corresponded more closely to what he took to be the currently *known* empirical facts. Indeed, from Hegel's point of view, it was actually the scientists looking for a planet between Mars and Jupiter on the basis of a merely arithmetical series who were guilty of apriorism. Moreover, Depré points out that, although Hegel was wrong not to take the reports of the discovery of Ceres more seriously, he was actually right not to trust the Titius-Bode law, as the discovery of Neptune in 1846 would later demonstrate. Depré concludes by arguing that Hegel's critique of Newton in his dissertation is motivated by precisely the same desire to provide a rational, rather than merely quantitative, account of nature and its laws.

In the first edition of his *Encyclopedia* (1817), Hegel acknowledged that the attempt made in his 1801 dissertation to find a law governing the distance of the planets from the sun was unsatisfactory. However, in the second and third editions of the *Encyclopedia* (1827, 1830), Hegel omitted any such criticism—indeed omitted all mention—of his dissertation. In her essay, "Framing Hypotheses," Cinzia Ferrini considers the significance of this later omission and concludes that it reflects an important change, occurring between 1817 and 1827, in Hegel's philosophical understanding of the relation between reason and empirical numbers in nature. Ferrini argues that in the 1817 *Encyclopedia* (and in the first edition of the *Science of Logic* on which it is based) Hegel understood the actual empirical numbers in nature to fall outside the scope of physical law and thus not to be determinable by reason. On this basis, Hegel had to regard as fundamentally misguided his earlier efforts in his dissertation to find a rational law governing the empirical distances of the planets from the sun. However, in the 1827 and 1830 editions of the *Encyclopedia* (and in the second edition of the *Science of Logic* with which they are closely connected), Hegel held the view that empirical numbers in nature can be captured *an sich* by reason. From this perspective, he would still have to acknowledge the specific error he made in 1801, but he would no longer have to reject out of hand the very attempt to find a rational law governing the empirical distances of the planets from the sun. By paying subtle attention to an apparently insignificant omission made by Hegel in the second and third editions of the *Encyclopedia*, Ferrini thus uncovers a radical shift that occurred between 1817 and 1827 in Hegel's fundamental understanding of the relation between reason and mathematics and between reason and the empirical world.

Hegel's philosophy of nature has for too long been dismissed as "mystifying cant" by those who should—but unfortunately do not—know better. The essays in this collection serve to remind us just how powerful and perceptive that philosophy actually is. The essays were first presented under the title "Hegel and the Philosophy of Nature" at the Thirteenth Biennial Meeting of the Hegel Society of America, which was held at The Catholic University of America in Washington, D.C. from September 30 to October 2, 1994. I would like to thank Michael Baur for helping with the organization of that conference, and DePaul University, Chicago and the University of Warwick for supporting the preparation of this volume. Special thanks go to Pauline Wilson for completing the task of putting the manuscript into camera-ready copy with such grace and ease.

Notes

1. K.R. Popper, *The Open Society and its Enemies* (1945), 2 Vols (London: Routledge, 1966), **2**: 28; M.J. Schleiden, *Schelling's und Hegel's Verhältnis zur Naturwissenschaft* (1844), edited by O. Breidbach (Weinheim: VCH, Acta Humaniora, 1988), Schleiden Nachdruck, p. 60.

2. J. Bronowski, *The Ascent of Man* (London: BBC, 1973), p. 360.

3. Schleiden Nachdruck, p. 61.

4. H. Schnädelbach, *Philosophy in Germany, 1831-1933*, translated by Eric Matthews (Cambridge: Cambridge University Press, 1984), pp. 76-7.

5. Popper, **2**: 28.

6. Gerd Buchdahl, for example, speaks of Hegel's "formidable breadth of knowledge." See G. Buchdahl, "Hegel's Philosophy of Nature and the Structure of Science," in *Hegel*, edited by M. Inwood (Oxford: Oxford University Press, 1985), p. 110.

7. See, for example, the essays by M. Wolff, T.H. Levere, M.J. Petry and H.A.M. Snelders in *Hegels Philosophie der Natur. Beziehungen zwischen empirischer und spekulativer Naturerkenntnis*, edited by R.-P. Horstmann and M.J. Petry (Stuttgart: Klett-Cotta, 1986).

8. *Hegel's Philosophy of Nature*, edited by M.J. Petry, 3 Vols (London: George Allen and Unwin, 1970), **1**: 51 and **2**: 204. (Hereafter Petry, *PN*, **1**: 51.)

9. Petry, *PN*, **1**: 60.

10. Buchdahl, p. 111.

11. Petry, *PN*, **1**: 197.

12. See Petry, *PN*, **1**: 224 [ll. 8-13] and **2**: 12 [ll. 8-11], which could be taken as supporting the first—*a priori*—interpretation, and Petry, *PN*, **1**: 197 [ll. 11-13] and **1**: 201 [ll. 33-6], which could be taken as supporting the second—*a posteriori*—interpretation.

1

The Very Idea of the Idea of Nature, or Why Hegel Is Not an Idealist

William Maker

If we speak of 'what is living and what is dead' in Hegel, it is probably safe to say that nowadays, nothing is more dead than Hegel's philosophy of nature.[1] I shall examine and question this diagnosis, contending that the *Philosophy of Nature* has been subject to a premature burial.

The Problem

While the expression 'philosophy of nature' may not be in vogue, it is nonetheless true that, since Hegel's time, philosophers have continued to speak about nature and our knowledge of it in a wide variety of ways. So what is it about Hegel's treatment of this topic that invites dismissal? Many have concluded that Hegel's overall philosophical method—his systematic approach—led him into a metaphysical idealism which is patently incompatible with an acceptable view of nature and how we know it. Thus, just what Hegel sees as the distinctive mark of truth and superiority in his philosophy—its systematic character—appears to be what renders the *Philosophy of Nature* problematic. Before examining the justice of this view, we need to see why systematicity as Hegel construes it may seem to entail metaphysical idealism.

Hegel claims that the scientific character of his system consists in the strictly immanent self-determination of its categories. According to him, the system is "absolute"—it articulates unconditional, universal, and necessary truth—because it is radically autonomous and self-contained: lacking any external foundations, what comes to be established in it is unequivocally true because fully self-grounded, not conditionally dependent on anything outside of the system which stands in need of further legitimation or accounting.[2] In conceiving truth in this manner Hegel makes a radical break with the philosophical tradition, for this systematic approach means that we must abandon the view that truth can be founded upon some already given determinacy. Instead we must see that truth which is demonstrable and legitimatible is truth construed as self-determination.

It is not hard to see why a philosophy claiming systematicity may be taken to be metaphysically idealistic, especially when we take into account the fact that a major part of the system is a *Realphilosophie*. For, if the system is autonomous and self-contained, and is so because it is not grounded in any given determinacy but rather generates all determinacies from within, we must ask the seemingly fatal question: How can this philosophy speak about the real unless it makes the notorious reduction or identification of reality and thought which Hegel is widely recognized as having made?[3] Doesn't systematicity engender an absolute, metaphysically idealistic identity philosophy of the most egregious and outdated form? How can a philosophy which claims to have all of its determinacies self-generated, and in a strictly immanent fashion, address the real unless the real is taken to be identical to, or a product of, or is otherwise derivative from and dependent upon, philosophical thought?

In line with current fashion in Hegel scholarship, we may not take this purported idealism to be a necessarily fatal problem as regards his social and political philosophy. Society and culture are areas of reality which, unlike nature, we can more readily regard as quasi-idealistic. In many respects, they are our creations, bearing the marks of the human mind and will. So, we might say, even a philosophy which makes the mistake of seeing all of reality as ideal will likely get some things right in these domains. But this popular piecemeal approach, which allows that Hegel's social and political philosophies may contain some truth despite the suspect character of his larger systematic claims, does not seem workable with the *Philosophy of Nature*.[4] Hasn't it become clear, at least since the downfall of Hegel and the British Idealists, that the givens of nature are the final authority against which all theoretical claims must be checked? Doesn't the success of the natural sciences demonstrate that we more closely approximate truth when we have effaced as far as possible the marks of the mind from our account? Isn't it obvious that all legitimate philosophical talk of nature must not only acknowledge the importance of the empirical sciences and work to incorporate their results (as Hegel does) but must also—against Hegel—take these results as determinative and authoritative for philosophy?[5] In short, isn't it obvious that *a priori* knowledge of nature can have no serious advocates? Since systematicity requires that both form and content follow solely from the immanent self-determination of the concept, the contemporary conviction that nature, as an apprehended given, must be finally authoritative for all possible knowledge of nature would seem to preclude Hegel's approach—unless we begin already with the fatal idealistic conviction that thought and reality are one, in which case thought's self-determination could be regarded as synonymous or isomorphic with the given determinations of nature.

So, if we are to make a case for the worth of the *Philosophy of Nature* as a whole, and as more than just an historical curiosity, we must either accept and defend it as metaphysically idealistic, or provide a systematic reading of it which indicates how that charge can be avoided. (More than the *Philosophy of Nature* is at stake here. If the system's account of nature cannot be defended, then Hegel's whole systematic approach cannot be defended, since a break in developmental continuity violates systematicity, and we must dismiss his idea of philosophy, if not all of his substantive claims.)

My aim is to defend the *Philosophy of Nature* by denying that it is metaphysically idealistic. I shall argue the following points: (1) Hegel's claims about systematicity—about strict immanence, self-determination, and self-containedness—are not only incompatible with, but require us to *reject*, the received view of his philosophy as a metaphysically idealistic *Identitätsphilosophie* which dismisses the facticity of the given and absorbs all otherness and finitude into thought. In defending this view I shall argue that Hegel explicitly rejects the conceptual underpinnings of metaphysical idealism: He neither denies the genuine existence of an independently given nature, nor conceives of given nature as a product of thought, nor identifies thought and nature. On the contrary: Hegel originates the *Philosophy of Nature* with the notion of the radical *nonidentity* of thought and nature, holding that thought and nature do not even resemble one another, that they quite literally have nothing in common (and that only when first conceived in this fashion can nature be properly understood philosophically). Put positively, my first thesis is that it is just *because of* the requirements of systematicity that Hegel recognizes and conceptualizes the radical and consummate otherness of nature and thought, and works, on the basis of this recognition, to develop a philosophy which can think finitude and givenness without fetishizing them.

(2) I shall further contend that only when nature is conceived systematically can metaphysical idealism be avoided. A philosophical consideration of nature which *fails* to fulfil the demands of systematicity (which purportedly led Hegel to idealism) will in fact be genuinely idealistic in the pejorative, metaphysical sense.

What then of the truism that Hegel is an idealist, and a self-described one at that?[6] Careful distinctions need to be drawn. We should say that, consistent with his systematic approach, Hegel is a *methodological* idealist. He regards autonomous reason, strictly self-determining thought to be the only mode of philosophically justifiable cognition. And he is a *critical* idealist in the sense that he thinks a system of autonomous reason can articulate the truth about reality—albeit critical, rather than descriptive truth.[7] But I shall argue that these commitments to methodological and critical idealism neither follow from nor entail *metaphysical* idealism, understood as the thesis that reality is thought or thought-like, or is a derivative or product of thought. In fact, I shall show that they are thoroughly incompatible with it.

By way of explaining and defending these points I shall first argue that Hegel's whole project is rooted in and pervaded by a concern with avoiding metaphysical idealism. When we recognize how he does this, we can begin to appreciate how the *Philosophy of Nature* can speak about nature in an *a priori* fashion without being metaphysically idealistic.

Hegel's Refutation of Idealism

Hegel's refutation of metaphysical idealism is a salient feature of what, according to him, systematic science presupposes: the rejection of the opposition of consciousness.[8] The elimination of consciousness as a foundation for philosophy is also a rejection of metaphysical idealism because we can only make sense of any version of idealism in so far as we hold fast to the fixed and irreducible distinction between thought and object definitive of consciousness: Idealism asserts that we can establish that what is seemingly other than thought is fundamentally identical with, or similar to thought, or that it shares a form or structure in common with thought, and is thus (in virtue of this sameness or similarity) knowable by thought. Any demonstration of this identity (or similarity or isomorphism) between thought and its other requires the ineliminable assumption that thought and the other are and remain determinate and distinguishable in some sense, for we can only demonstrably identify what we can meaningfully distinguish. However, as Hegel asserts in the *Science of Logic*, the *Phenomenology* culminates not in the identity of thought and object, but rather in their complete collapse into an indistinguishable indeterminacy which offers no determinate residue whatsoever.[9] Thus, one common basis for charging Hegel with metaphysical idealism—the erroneous notion that the system begins with the assertion of a determinate, established identity (or identity-in-difference) of thought and being—requires us to interpret the system and its *Realphilosophie* from the very standpoint he not only explicitly rejects, but also regards as antithetical to systematic philosophy. That is to say, in order to read the system as metaphysical idealism we must remain committed to the perspective of consciousness, for we must hold that, as philosophical thought, the system does what consciousness claims to do, only better. To see the system as propounding metaphysical idealism we must read it as *representing* (albeit better than consciousness can) what is given, as *describing* (albeit better than consciousness can) what appears. This reading, however, is only intelligible if we remain committed to consciousness's definition of truth—as descriptive representation—as the ineliminable definition and benchmark. But not only is abandoning consciousness required for entering systematic philosophy, Hegel also insists again and again that representation and description are not, finally, philosophically viable modes of truth (and that only when this is recognized is true philosophy possible).[10] Indeed, Hegel reiterates his rejection of idealism at the very opening of the *Philosophy of Nature* when he describes *avoiding* metaphysical idealism as the paramount task for all thought about nature. No one who was asserting that thought and nature are identical or similar would outline the problem he aims to avoid in the following way:

> In thinking things, we transform them into something universal; but things are singular and the Lion as Such does not exist. We give them the form of something subjective, of something produced by us and belonging to us, and belonging to us in our specifically human character, for natural objects do not think and are not presentations or thoughts.

No metaphysical idealist could assert that what he aims to avoid is

> mak[ing] Nature, which is an Other than we are, into an Other than she is ... transform[ing] things into universals, or mak[ing] them our own ... [for] as natural objects they are supposed to have a free, self-subsistent being. This, therefore, [allowing natural objects their "free, self-subsistent being"] is the point with which we are concerned in regard to the nature of cognition—this is the interest of philosophy.[11]

Yet even if Hegel's many attacks on the adequacy of *Verstand* and representation render a popular reading of the *Philosophy of Nature* untenable, in showing that metaphysical idealism's claims to descriptive superiority are not in accord with Hegel's understanding of his project, they do not resolve the issue. Even if we allow that Hegel intended to reject the standpoint of consciousness and metaphysical idealism, we can still contend nonetheless that what he attempts to do in the *Philosophy of Nature*—provide *a priori* knowledge of nature—is possible only if metaphysical idealism is viable, and further, that the finitude of consciousness indicates that it is not. So defending the *Philosophy of Nature* requires showing how it provides a kind of *a priori* knowledge of nature that is viable. How can the *Philosophy of Nature* be said to have anything to say about nature if it is systematic—if it neither derives its determinations from given nature nor claims that nature is thought or thought-like? After indicating how this is possible—how Hegel recognizes the facticity of given nature without reducing it to thought and also without violating systematicity—I will move on to my further claim that only the systematic approach to nature avoids metaphysical idealism.

Nature Immaculately Conceived

As I have briefly outlined, Hegelian systematicity requires strictly immanent self-determination, and such self-determination is consequent upon rejecting the model of consciousness. The question of how this initial self-determination takes place in the *Logic* cannot concern us.[12] What must concern us is how such a process as strictly self-determining—as systematic—can somehow go beyond itself to address the real as nature. This move would seem to force systematic philosophy onto the horns of a dilemma. Either systematic philosophy can abjure metaphysical idealism and accept the cognitive authority of nature as something given to thought. (Testifying to this recognition, philosophy would determine its account of nature—and not merely coordinate it—in accordance with apprehended givens, with the results of the empirical sciences. But this means sacrificing systematicity, autonomous self-determination.) Or, systematic philosophy can deny the radical otherness of nature as a given and proceed with its immanent account, preserving systematicity. (But this means embracing metaphysical idealism.) What I shall now do is explain why this is a false dilemma, why acknowledging genuine otherness in the form of the radical givenness of nature is not incompatible with Hegel's methodological but nonmetaphysical idealism.

The salient point here is that it is precisely because of systematicity—immanence—and not in spite of it, that the *Philosophy of Nature* avoids metaphysical idealism. This occurs because the *Logic*'s initial articulation of radical self-determination itself requires an intrasystemic recognition and conceptualizing of *radical* otherness: that is, the recognition of an other which is not, in its determinate content, a derivative, reducible product of thought, a quasi-other, despite the fact that this content *is* articulated in and by thought. First, why does the process of logical self-determination require the conceptualizing of such an other? Second, how is it that this other is radically other, not a derivative of thought, even though, as a concept of systematic philosophy, it is generated by thought? How is the system's concept of nature not metaphysically idealistic in terms of what it says about the nature of nature, while being methodologically idealistic in terms of the origin and the manner of the constitution of this concept of nature?

(1) In so far as the logical process of autonomous self-determination is to reach an immanently generated completeness, a thorough *self*-articulation of *self*-determination, it must complete itself by limiting or circumscribing itself. A completing limitation is necessary because what is being articulated is self-determination: the domain of logical self-determination must be fully determinate, complete; if what it articulates is to be self-determined, it can't omit any features of *this* mode of determination. Additionally, this completion must be a self-*limitation*, it must involve thought thinking what is radically other than

itself, for if such an other is not conceptualized the completeness of logical self-determination cannot be guaranteed. We can only be sure that logical self-determination is truly complete by moving on to something else. But just the thinking of a radical other which the systematicity of methodological idealism requires necessitates that metaphysical idealism is abjured. If the limiting other is, in its determinate content as the concept of nature, anything less than a genuine other to self-determining logical thought, logic would not be fully determinate as self-determining, there would be no final definiteness to its domain. If nature were conceptualized as only a quasi-other, in the manner of metaphysical idealism, logical thought would not have completed itself but would pass on into a bad infinity. If the content of nature is conceptualized as being thought-like, or as a derivative product of thought—as though thought had no genuine limit—there would be no truly distinctive and complete domain of logical self-determination, and consequently no 'self' to self-determination. Self-determination without limit cannot finally be self-determinate at all. (In fact, just the developmental problematic of determination in terms of a quasi-other is what is thematized, and revealed as necessarily incomplete, in the logic of essence.) So, only if strictly self-determining logical thought conceptualizes what is genuinely other than itself can it be said to fully determine itself as thoroughly constitutive of the domain of strict self-determination. Additionally, since this completing limitation is required in and by logical thought, it is immanent; no constitutive appeals to nature as an apprehended given are, or need to be, made.[13] Speaking generally, the mode of logical self-determination must complete itself by a process of self-transformative transcendence, an *Aufhebung*: A different domain of determinacy and a different mode of determination must emerge just in order that logic can be complete and completely determinate in its own right.

(2) But how is it that this other whose conceptualization is immanently required, is genuinely other? What can genuinely other mean in systematic thought? Would not any

other, just in being thinkable, be a mere derivative? We may be able to understand why systematic thought would require such an other, without being convinced that it can conceptualize it in an immanent fashion. Does not systematicity inevitably entail reductionism? Doesn't Hegel's methodological idealism lead to metaphysical idealism? Are not immanence and genuine otherness, finitude, radically incompatible? For how can access to a genuine other be made without leaving the domain of systematic thought, without returning to finite consciousness for real data about the given in its givenness? A thorough reply to these questions will require explaining why the latter alternative cannot make the given as given accessible to thought.

Before taking up that crucial issue, we need to see just how, in coming to think the other of logic as nature, nature is conceptualized, how it attains a determinate content that is manifestly nonidealistic. I will reconstruct the move to nature to show that, while the *concept* of nature is "the Idea in the form of otherness,"[14] this does not mean that we think of nature as being an idea or even like an idea, but rather just the opposite. I want to show that in the *Philosophy of Nature* the content of the concept of nature is immanently and explicitly determined initially as not being thought or thought-like, as not being a derivative of thought, and that this is just what it means first of all to think the Idea in the form of otherness. More concretely, I want to show that, in its initial specification as externality, nature is thematized by Hegel as givenness and is thus recognized as genuinely other in an immanent but still nonreductive fashion.

Consistent with its unity of form and content, the subject matter articulated in logic by a process of self-determination has been the very nature of self-determination itself. Having run through a process of self-determination in which the nature of self-determination is the substantive content being developed, the completeness of this stage of self-determination necessitates the conceptualizing of a mode or type of determinacy which is not conceived, in its substantive content, its determinate character, as self-determining at all. We think nature then by thinking the idea of a domain of determinacy which is determinate—and thoroughly so, in its own right—but not at all self-determining. How is that to be done—how are we to get a handle on what 'not self-determining' means—if we have been enmeshed in the thinking of self-determination and if systematicity precludes determinative reference to anything outside the system? The answer to that question lies in understanding why nature is more specifically determined as *externality*. And accounting for externality will also indicate how the move to nature amounts to a systematic recognition of *givenness* as radically other, a self-induced acknowledgement, by systematic, infinite thought, of the existence of something which lies beyond its purview. In other words, Hegel does just what his postmodernist critics claim he does not and cannot do. How?

Externality and an immanent recognition of givenness can be seen to emerge as follows: We are attempting to think the determinate character of a domain of determinacy which is not thought, not self-determining. In the *Logic*, we came initially to conceive self-determining determinacy by rejecting the idea that all possible determinacy must be minimally determinate as *given* to conscious awareness.[15] So, minimally speaking, the antithesis to self-determining determinacy, logic's radical other, would be a domain of sheer given determinacy. This domain of determinacy needs to be conceived for logical self-determination to complete itself, but, methodologically speaking, it cannot be conceived either by returning to the purview of consciousness and what it might actually find given, or even by a formal reference to the nature of consciousness as that for which there is a domain of givenness.[16] Either of these moves would violate systematic immanence; the resources for conceptualizing what is other than logic can only come from logic. The second move would additionally plunge the system into the Kantian transcendental problematic. Recall Hegel's remarks quoted earlier: we want to conceive nature as it is in its own right, not just as it appears to us. What we find then in the *Philosophy of Nature* is that sheer 'givenness for' or 'difference from', now conceived without determinative reference to the nature of what it might *be* for, now conceived just in its own right, is a domain of 'being for' which is just that and nothing else. Nature is initially nothing but a domain of determinacy which is what it is as being everywhere 'for', with no other determinacy present; nature is sheer 'for-ness' as capable of subsisting in this determinacy without reference to anything else. Now if we are to think this domain so that we omit mention of explicit 'being *for*' as such (since that must connote 'a *something* for which'), we can conceive this domain as self-subsisting outsideness, in short, as externality.[17] Externality is conceived as that which is as always 'different from', where there is not already a determinate other 'from which' this determinacy is different.[18] Such a domain of subsisting outsideness may be more specifically determined, as coordinated with our empirical concepts, as space.[19] How, more specifically, is externality "the Idea in the form of otherness"? We may think externality as the Idea in otherness if, in conceptualizing the Idea as the consummation of logical self-determination, we make the requisite return to reconsider the initial mode of logical self-determination in the logic of being.[20] There, at the very start of logical self-determination, no determinacy is capable of being determinatively distinguished from its other. Now, to think this mode of determinacy 'in otherness' is precisely to think of a domain of determinacy capable of sustaining determinate difference, a domain of sheer stable differentiation: externality.

Since nature is conceived *just as* externality and thus without constitutive reference to any determinacy 'for which' nature is, systematic thought has come to think of a domain of determinacy which is not self-determining determinacy but which is determinate, and which has been conceived as being determinate in and for itself. As conceived without reference to anything 'for which' it might appear, nature has been thought precisely as that which is what it is independently of any conscious mind and thus this conception of nature is thoroughly nonidealistic. In sum, since externality has emerged as the antithesis to a domain of thought which was itself conceived without reference to any determinations save its own, and since externality emerges as that determinacy which is what it is in the absence of any reference to consciousness (or any other determinacy), we can say that systematic thought has begun to conceive of nature in its character as a "free, self-subsistent being."

The Superiority of Systematic Philosophy of Nature

But what about the issue mentioned previously: how can a philosophy which refuses to surrender to given nature as actually apprehended make the claim to be providing the philosophically superior account of nature? Isn't it obvious that in order to know nature as it is we must renounce systematicity and turn to nature as it is given to us, as actually apprehended? While we might say that Hegel has allowed the idea of what is other than thought to emerge determinatively, isn't the only true way to recognize and grasp otherness to allow it literally to determine thought? The Hegelian response is to indicate that attempting to think nature in that fashion must in fact lead to some form of metaphysical idealism. If we are to recognize and think nature on the basis of apprehended data, we must, in some fashion or another, either explicitly or implicitly, transform that which we take to be other than thought into thought or into something thought-like. How so? If nature is to be thought as determinate and as other than thought, it must have some determinate attributes which are not those of thought. (Hegel claims that thought in and of itself can think the general nature of these attributes, while noting that nature as apprehended has many characteristics which lie beyond those thinkable in systematic philosophy.) But if we turn to apprehended givens to supply these attributes we must, in order to render nature knowable, implicitly or explicitly assume that there is some feature (or features) of sameness or similarity between thought and the given, or we must impose them. And this idealizing must occur even if this similarity is only a similarity of form, or if given nature's knowability is attributed to a receptivity of nature to thought, or of thought to nature. If we turn to the given but *refrain* from idealizing it by refusing to assume or impose the similarity necessary to render cognition explicable, the given will be inaccessible and will thus be an indeterminate unknowable which is finally indistinguishable from thought. Furthermore, if we do idealize in order to incorporate the given, once we assume or impose such sameness or similarity, we can no longer claim to know nature as it is, but only as it appears to us, and we are again forced to think of nature itself as an indeterminate unknowable. So if we try to turn to the given without idealizing it, or if we deliberately make it accessible by idealizing it, given nature as what it is in its own right remains inaccessible, a *Ding an sich* which is ultimately indistinguishable from thought, and we are thereby left firmly within metaphysical idealism. Thus part of what it means to say that the *Philosophy of Nature*'s account of nature is critical (is a variety of critical idealism) is that it is superior to descriptive accounts of nature as it appears, just because any descriptive account, whether commonsensical or scientific, must be metaphysically idealistic to some degree.

So critical idealism rejects the cognitive authority of apprehended givens for philosophy not by denying the existence of such givens, but as a consequence of conceptualizing the genuine, ineluctable *otherness* of givenness to thought and its recalcitrant resistance to complete comprehension by consciousness. Critical idealism conceptualizes this otherness as genuinely and irreducibly other by refusing, as it goes about the business of articulating the determinate character of the other, to construe it in the metaphysically idealistic manner, as an other *for* consciousness. As we saw, construing the other in the latter manner finally must lead to its indeterminate indistinguishability from thought. Hegel's critical idealism avoids reducing the other to a mere adjunct or derivative of consciousness. Thus, rather than denying the finitude of consciousness and the sheer impenetrable otherness of given nature, as postmodernists claim, Hegel's philosophy is based on an acknowledgement of them. Hegel's critics are thoroughly mistaken in charging him with propounding a idealistically reductive absolutism.

The empirical sciences cannot escape, but they can ignore, the problem of idealizing in so far as they do not attempt to substitute for philosophy, and in so far as their account of nature is supplemented by the proper philosophical one. Since they rest on unjustified assumptions—since they account neither for the necessity of their methods nor their objects, but take both as given—the empirical sciences can rest content with turning to the given and affording knowledge of nature as it appears, that is, as it is conditioned by the particular conceptual assumptions, the paradigms, they happen to operate with.[21] But if we are to proceed philosophically, such that our knowledge is not relative, but unconditioned, we cannot turn to the given as determinative even in our cognition of nature. For paradoxically, as we have seen, turning to given evidence in the attempt to think nature forces us, in any final philosophical defense of this nonsystematic approach, to hold that the given *as such* is unknowable, and as unknowable, finally indistinguishable from thought itself. So, Hegel says: If we wish to recognize and think what nature is as a genuine, ineliminable, and irreducible other to thought, the only way to do this—to genuinely and adequately recognize this otherness—is by attempting not to incorporate, include, or bring this other *into* thought, but rather to think just what it must mean for there to be such a domain of *external* determinacy. Systematic *a priori* thought is better capable of conceptualizing the nature of nature as a given than is descriptive thought which derives its determinacies from the given, since, as we have seen, descriptive thought must idealize the given to render it cognizable. And systematic thought can better conceptualize nature as given, not because it claims that the given is thought or thought-like, but just because it refuses to make that claim.

Both in terms of method and content, this approach to nature is able to conceive nature nonidealistically, as what it is in its own right. Because this thinking process has been itself constituted without any determinate presuppositions, because it has come to determine what self-determining thought is without already contrasting this domain with some given determinate other, it is subsequently capable, methodologically speaking, of thinking its other—nature—in the same fashion, as what *it* is in *its* own right. Methodologically, because systematic thought in logic has determined itself in a manner which is free of other, extraneous determinations, it can then, in the *Philosophy of Nature*, consider the nature of something other than itself in a similar fashion: in such a way that, as conceptualized, nature is not already invested with thought's determinate character in an illicit fashion. Having first determined what self-determination as such is in logic, systematic thought is capable of thinking what it means for there to be an other domain of determinacy which attains to and constitutes its own determinate character. Only systematic philosophy's methodological idealism is capable of *thinking* given nature as such. Rather than leading to metaphysical idealism, it is systematicity which makes its avoidance possible.

Furthermore, because the *content* of the concept of nature in systematic philosophy is thought as radically other, this thinking of nature can conceptualize those aspects of nature which comprise this otherness without transforming them immediately into thought-like things, and in this sense it can also be said to think nature in its own right. For example, systematic philosophy can and does make intelligible the contingency of nature, its sheer alogicality, and the multiple and superfluous character (from a logical point of view) of many of its random, unconnected, and unnecessary determinations.[22] Because the systematic philosophy of nature can indicate why nature as other than thought must be determined in this fashion (since it has thematized and thought through the nature of givenness as such), it is a critical account of nature in yet another sense.[23] Not in the metaphysical sense that it says what nature should be if it were ideal, but rather in the sense that the systematic philosophy of nature can go beyond nature in its apprehended givenness, not to describe it, but to explain *why* nature as it is given has those general features of givenness such as contingency. Empirical thought, thought which attends to the given as given, must impose its ideal, conceptual form on the given, and thus, while it may recognize, it cannot attend adequately to, what it must *ignore* in imposing that ideal form: the general characteristics of nature as not like thought at all. Empirical science cannot explain these general features of nature because they are incompatible with its idealistic method which involves the incorporation of the given into thought. But systematic philosophy of nature can and does conceptualize just these features, accounting for why nature appears as it does.[24]

On the one hand, as Hegel notes, empirical thought which attends to the given as given can provide an actual descriptive account of these things, but it cannot at the same time sort out what it brings as thought to the given and what the given contributes, since it is always in some ineluctable way shaping the given to fit thought.[25] On the other hand, however, systematic thought in and of itself alone cannot account for the specific ways in which given nature concretely manifests the general features of givenness as such.[26] (Here the *Philosophy of Nature* depends on the results of empirical research, and could certainly be updated in regard to the empirical coordinates of its systematic determinations.)[27] Nor can the *Philosophy of Nature* ordain that they must appear, since what actually appears is dependent upon the many contingencies of nature and of human observation, such as opportunity, proper instrumentation, etc.[28] As Hegel notes, the *Philosophy of Nature* cannot deduce Herr Krug's pen.[29] In these respects this philosophy of nature is remarkably anti-aprioristic. But, since it has conceptualized what givenness, naturality, is, systematic philosophy can articulate what its general features are. And, once empirical thought has indicated how apprehended nature may display these features, the *Philosophy of Nature* may then account for why given nature, as it actually happens to appear, does have them.[30] Since empirical thought must be guided by the given as it does appear, it cannot venture into that issue.[31] (For example, were empirical thought to attempt to explain the necessity of the contingency of given nature—say, the fact, as Nancy Cartwright has indicated, that the laws of physics lie, and can only be approximations—empirical science would have to move beyond the given fact of this contingency and so violate its own methodological strictures.)[32] So while systematic thought is philosophically superior, it and empirical science complement one another; as Hegel says, they consider the same object from different points of view.[33]

But isn't there still a residual problem of idealism? Doesn't the *Philosophy of Nature* still 'read' thought into nature? For while we might say that nature is first thought as radically other in being thought as externality, can't we also say that subsequent developments in the *Philosophy of Nature* indicate that nature comes to be thought as taking on more and more of the character of self-determining thought? This misdescribes what takes place in the *Philosophy of Nature*, both in terms of its method and content. For one thing, the determinations which emerge in the *Philosophy of Nature* emerge immanently, not by using the logic as some kind of form or model imposed on a given content.[34] As nature is initially thought as thoroughly unlike—as the antithesis of—pure self-determining thought in the *Logic*, we can expect that, in thinking through this concept of nature to its full determinacy, determinacies which are gradually determined as increasingly other than sheer externality will appear. Just as logically self-determining thought required thinking *its* other, conceiving nature will require thinking an other to its initial determinacy. Since this is the other to externality in its immediacy, we can expect this other neither to be logical self-determination, nor externality, but to emerge as the increasing attainment of what is determinate in externality to greater degrees of independent self-subsistence. Being determinate in its own right in the domain of nature consists in the emergence of more determinate modes of independent self-subsistence, the emergence of *things*. (Externality as space is that domain in which determinacies can be—subsist—as over against one another.) But note: 'determinate in its own right' in the *Philosophy of Nature* means independent self-subsistence. This is not at all what 'determinate in its own right' meant for self-determining logical thought, for logic's determinacies were not at all self-subsistent vis-à-vis one another. Thus, the *Philosophy of Nature* is not the embodiment or instantiation or concretizing of logical form, because what was distinctive about that form in logic—the inextricable interconnectedness and the mutual determination of its determinacies—is precisely what is not found in nature.

Furthermore, as Hegel observes, nowhere in nature as such do we find real self-determination.[35] As achieved in the domain of the given, self-determination is freedom, which requires thought and the kind of liberation from nature which involves transforming and taking possession of it, and this is only found when we get to spirit.[36] But what about spirit's appearance in the system? Is that not indicative of an emergent metaphysical idealism? No. As the overriding activity of systematic thought is the activity of determining self-determination in all its manifold guises, the system moves as a whole in the direction of fully determinate self-determination, in the direction of spirit and freedom. But this is not because we know already that this is what given reality truly is, but because philosophically cognizable truth is self-determination, and must be completely conceived as such. So we move as a whole in systematic *Realphilosophie* from nature to spirit not because there is some organic, spiritually evolutionary development in given nature—Hegel explicitly and properly rejects this form of metaphysical idealism[37]—but just because nature is so unlike self-determining thought but is nonetheless being conceptualized in the system of self-determining thought. As called upon methodologically to completeness, the system must think the full range and nature of self-determination. It cannot stop at nature.

So, by starting out with the antithesis of the thesis of metaphysical idealism, Hegel articulates a philosophy of nature which avoids metaphysical idealism and which provides an *a priori* account of nature, not as it is given in all its specificity (as that must fall beyond systematic thought), but in terms of delineating and accounting for the general features of givenness as such. Since these are features that thought which turns to the given cannot grasp as such, this *a priori* account is a necessary complement to empirical science. While the *concept* of nature which the *Philosophy of Nature* articulates is, as a concept of systematic philosophy, a thoroughly immanent product of thought, what it recognizes and articulates is the notion that, in being determined as what it is, nature must not be thought of as a product of thought or as thought-like. What we must do is distinguish carefully the systematic process through which the concept of nature comes to be thought in the *Philosophy of Nature*—a process which is consummately idealistic—from what this concept asserts about the nature of nature—which is consummately anti-idealistic. When we do that, we can see that Hegel's *Philosophy of Nature* avoids the metaphysically idealistic pitfalls of descriptive accounts and can explain features of nature to which such accounts cannot do justice. When we also consider that Hegel's account emerges in a systematic philosophy which has provided a full legitimation of the conditions of its own possibility, we can further appreciate why his *Philosophy of Nature* remains philosophically superior and indispensable.

Notes

1. Hegel notes the problematic status of the philosophy of nature even in his own times. See G.W.F. Hegel, *Enzyklopädie der philosophischen Wissenschaften im Grundrisse (1830). Zweiter Teil: Die Naturphilosophie mit den mündlichen Zusätzen*, edited by E. Moldenhauer and K. Michel, *Werke in zwanzig Bänden*, Vol. 9 (Frankfurt am Main: Suhrkamp Verlag, 1970), Einleitung, Zusatz, p. 9; *Hegel's Philosophy of Nature: Being Part Two of the Encyclopaedia of the Philosophical Sciences (1830)*, translated by A. V. Miller (Oxford: Clarendon Press, 1970), Introduction, Addition, p. 1. (Hereafter cited as *EN* [1830]; Miller, *PN*.)

2. G.W.F. Hegel, *Enzyklopädie der philosophischen Wissenschaften im Grundrisse (1830). Erster Teil: Die Wissenschaft der Logik mit den mündlichen Zusätzen*, edited by E. Moldenhauer and K. Michel, *Werke in zwanzig Bänden*, Vol. 8 (Frankfurt am Main: Suhrkamp Verlag, 1970), §§213, 9, 12, 14, 17, 41 Zus., 52

Zus., 77, 232, 238 Zus.; *Hegel's Logic: Being Part One of the Encyclopaedia of the Philosophical Sciences*, translated by William Wallace (Oxford: Clarendon Press, 1975). (Hereafter cited as *EL* [1830]; Wallace, *EL*.) Also see G.W.F. Hegel, *Wissenschaft der Logik I. Erster Teil: Die Objektive Logik*, edited by E. Moldenhauer and K. Michel, *Werke in zwanzig Bänden*, Vol. 5 (Frankfurt am Main: Suhrkamp Verlag, 1970), p. 16; *Science of Logic*, translated by A. V. Miller (Atlantic Highlands, NJ: Humanities Press International, 1989), p. 27 (hereafter cited as *Logik* [*Werke*, **5**]; Miller, *Logic*), and G.W.F. Hegel, *Phänomenologie des Geistes*, edited by E. Moldenhauer and K. Michel, *Werke in zwanzig Bänden*, Vol. 3 (Frankfurt am Main: Suhrkamp Verlag, 1970), pp. 65-6; *Phenomenology of Spirit*, translated by A.V. Miller (Oxford: Oxford University Press, 1977), p. 44.

3. See, for example, Michael Rosen, *Hegel's Dialectic and Its Criticism* (Cambridge: Cambridge University Press, 1982), p. 174: " ... Idealism's characteristic difficulty [is], namely, the need to give an account of the relationship between empirical and transcendental realms. The problem is resolved by Hegel's Absolute Idealism because the transcendental subject is, in fact, an absolute one, which itself generates the empirical. Transcendental and empirical, mind and nature, are not heterogeneous but emerge as 'moments' in a unified process; the problem of how one realm is 'constituted on' another is left behind when we operate in the element of Thought." Charles Taylor identifies Hegel as an absolute idealist and asserts that "Absolute idealism means that nothing exists which is not a manifestation of the Idea, that is, of rational necessity." See *Hegel* (Cambridge: Cambridge University Press, 1975), p. 110.

R. G. Collingwood claims that Hegel has the "idealistic view of nature" which asserts "that mind makes nature: nature is, so to speak, a by-product of the autonomous and self-existing activity of mind," *The Idea of Nature* (London: Oxford University Press, 1945), p. 7. According to Errol Harris, nature is "an actual and substantial form of mind's self-manifestation"; "the philosopher of Nature ... sees Nature as implicit or potential mind." See *The Spirit of Hegel*, (Atlantic Highlands: Humanities Press, 1993), pp. 100, 133; also see pp. 101 and 115. Also see Dieter Wandschneider, "Nature and Dialectic of Nature in Hegel's Objective Idealism," *Bulletin of the Hegel Society of Great Britain* 26, (Autumn/Winter 1992): 30-51. In *Hegel's Idealism* (Cambridge: Cambridge University Press, 1989) Robert Pippin gives, but does not endorse, a good brief overview of Hegel as a metaphysical idealist. The reading I am presenting is not, however, Pippin's Kantian account of Hegel's idealism.

4. This piecemeal approach probably has its origins in Marx. Also see Taylor, *Hegel*, p. 538ff. Pippin discusses this view in *Hegel's Idealism*, pp. 4-5, and also endorses it, pp. 259-60. Karl Ameriks discusses it in "Recent Work on Hegel: The Rehabilitation of an Epistemologist," *Philosophy and Phenomenological Research* 52, 1 (March 1992): 177-202.

5. "Our procedure consists in first fixing the thought demanded by the necessity of the Notion and then in asking how this thought appears in our ordinary ideas," *EN* (1830), §254 Zus.; Miller, *PN*, p. 29. Hegel's views on the differences—and the relationship—between systematic philosophy and the empirical sciences are developed in detail in the Introduction to the *Encyclopedia Logic*. Philosophy "must necessarily be in harmony with actuality and experience" (*EL* [1830], §6; Wallace, *EL*, p. 8), but this does not mean accepting experience as determinative, for even experience can distinguish "the mere appearance, which is transient and meaningless, from what in itself really deserves the name actuality" (*EL* [1830], §6; Wallace, *EL*, p. 8), and "existence is in part mere experience, and only in part actuality" (*EL* [1830], §6; Wallace, *EL*, p. 9). Philosophy "does not in the least neglect the empirical facts contained in the several sciences, but recognizes and adopts them: it appreciates and applies toward its own structure the universal element in these sciences, their laws and classifications, but besides all this into the categories of science it introduces, and gives currency to, other categories" (*EL* [1830], §9; Wallace, *EL*, p. 13). Philosophy "cannot, like them [the sciences], rest the existence of its objects on the natural admissions of consciousness, nor can it assume that its method of cognition, either for starting or continuing, is one already accepted"; " ... philosophy will be satisfied with nothing short of showing the existence of its objects, as well as their nature and qualities. Our original acquaintance with them is thus discovered to be inadequate," (*EL* [1830], §1; Wallace, *EL*, p. 3). In the *Philosophy of Nature* Hegel asserts "Not only must philosophy be in agreement with our empirical knowledge of Nature, but the origin and formulation of the Philosophy of Nature presupposes and is conditioned by empirical physics. However, the course of a science's [the philosophy of nature's] origin and the preliminaries of its construction are one thing, while the science itself is

another. In the latter, the former can no longer appear as the foundation of the science, here the foundation must be the necessity of the Notion," *EN* (1830), §246 Anm.; Miller, *PN*, p. 6. See also *EL* (1830), §134 Zus.; Wallace, *EL*, p. 190.

6. See *EL* (1830), §160 Zus.; Wallace, *EL*, p. 223, and *Logik* (*Werke*, **5**), pp. 172-3; Miller, *Logic*, pp. 154-5. On *Logik* (*Werke*, **5**), p. 172; Miller, *Logic*, p. 155, Hegel asserts that idealism denotes the proposition that "*das Endliche [ist] nicht als ein wahrhaft Seiendes anzuerkennen*," "the finite is not to be acknowledged as truly existing." This is consistent with what I discuss as Hegel's critical idealism. See *EL* (1830), §§6, 142; Wallace, *EL*, pp. 8-9, 201-2.

7. See especially *EL* (1830), § 6; Wallace, *EL*, pp. 8-9, where Hegel makes clear that the fact that something exists and is apprehended does not mean that it is actual and true in the systematic meaning of these terms.

8. "These views on the relation of subject and object to each other express the determinations which constitute the nature of our ordinary, phenomenal consciousness; but when these prejudices are carried out into the sphere of reason as if the same relation obtained there, as if this relation were something true in its own self, then they are errors the refutation of which throughout every part of the spiritual and natural universe is philosophy, or rather, as they bar the entrance to philosophy, must be discarded at its portals"; "But the liberation from the opposition of consciousness which the science of logic must be able to presuppose lifts the determinations of thought above this timid, incomplete standpoint and demands that they be considered not with any such limitation and reference but as they are in their own proper character, as logic, as pure reason," *Logik* (*Werke*, **5**), pp. 37-8, 45, cf. p. 43; Miller, *Logic*, pp. 45, 51, cf. p. 49.

9. *Logik* (*Werke*, **5**), pp. 66-9; Miller, *Logic*, pp. 68-70.

10. For example, see *EL* (1830), §§6, 142 Zus.; Wallace, *EL*, pp. 8-10, 201-2.

11. *EN* (1830), §246 Zus.; Miller, *PN*, pp. 7-8.

12. See my essay, "Beginning," in *Essays on Hegel's Logic*, edited by George di Giovanni (Albany: SUNY Press, 1990), pp. 27-43.

13. Hegel rules out such appeals while recognizing that, in terms of its formulation, the *Philosophy of Nature* involves taking the

results of the empirical sciences into account (see note 5). I will argue subsequently that nature's first determination as externality is immanently conceived, but that it can also be coordinated with the empirical representation of space.

14. *EN* (1830), §247; Miller, *PN*, pp. 13-14.

15. See "Beginning."

16. In ruling out the latter option this interpretation is importantly different from Klaus Hartmann's non-metaphysical interpretation of Hegel ("Hegel: A Non-Metaphysical View," in *Hegel: A Collection of Critical Essays*, edited by Alasdair MacIntyre [New York: Doubleday, 1972]), as well as those of his disciples such as Alan White (*Absolute Knowledge: Hegel and the Problem of Metaphysics* [Athens, Ohio: Ohio University Press, 1983]) and David Stern ("The Immanence of Thought: Hegel's Critique of Foundationalism," *The Owl of Minerva* 22, 1 [Fall 1990]: 19-33).

17. *EN* (1830), §§252-3; Miller, *PN*, pp. 25, 28.

18. Conceiving externality systematically requires that externality be conceived as what it is in such a way that we think its determinacy as being itself constituted without determining reference to logic, to self-determination, just because systematic thought has shown that nature must be thought as being what it is in the complete absence of self-determination. Hegel is asking us to think what it means for nature to be determinate in its own right and not in virtue of some likeness with or some relation to thought. Nature is, after all, logic's radical other. Of course the activity of so conceiving nature involves a methodological reference to the already constituted domain of logical self-determination: it is only in virtue of this procedural demand that nature is thinkable immanently and as that domain in which logical determination does not take place. Only because we know what logical self-determination involves can we think a mode of determination which is not logical. But this methodological reference to logic (that "nature is the idea in the form of otherness") does not amount to the claim that logical determinacies are somehow or in some form present in nature as an actually apprehended given, as though Hegel was claiming that natural things "really are" just ideas. I quoted Hegel above as explicitly denying this and as indicating it as the pitfall he aims to avoid. While the concept of nature as a concept of systematic

philosophy is constituted by thinking the idea in otherness, in thinking that we see that nature as a given is not in any way, shape, or form an idea or like an idea at all.

19. *EN* (1830), §254; Miller, *PN*, p. 28.

20. Hegel specifically calls for this return in the addition to the last section (§ 244 Zus.; Wallace, p. 296) of the *Encyclopedia Logic*: "We have now returned to the notion of the Idea with which we began. This return to the beginning is also an advance. We began with Being, abstract Being; where we now are we also have the Idea as Being; but the Idea which has Being is Nature."

21. "Philosophy misses an advantage enjoyed by the other sciences. It cannot like them rest the existence of its objects on the natural admissions of consciousness, nor can it assume that its method of cognition, either for starting or for continuing, is one already accepted," *EL* (1830), §1; Wallace, *EL*, p. 3. According to Hegel, in the empirical sciences "the beginnings are in every case data and postulates, neither accounted for nor deduced" and thus "necessity fails to get its due," *EL* (1830), §9; Wallace, *EL*, p. 13.

22. *EN* (1830), §250; Miller, *PN*, pp. 22-3.

23. " ... Nature in its manifestations does not hold fast to the Notion. Its wealth of forms is an absence of definiteness and the play of contingency; the Notion is not to be based on them, rather it is they which are to be measured by the Notion," *EN* (1830), §341 Zus.; Miller, *PN*, p. 299.

24. Philosophy "gives their [the empirical sciences'] contents what is so vital to them, the freedom of thought—gives them, in short, an *a priori* character. These contents are now warranted necessary, and no longer depend on the evidence of facts merely, that they were so found and so experienced. The fact as experienced thus becomes an illustration and a copy of the original and completely self-supporting activity of thought," *EL* (1830), §12 Anm.; Wallace, *EL*, p. 18.

25. "The fact is, however, that the principal charge to be brought against physics is that it contains much more thought than it admits and is aware of ... ," *EN* (1830), Einleitung, p. 11; Miller, *PN*, p. 3. In this respect Hegel anticipates the contemporary philosophers of science T. S. Kuhn and Paul Feyerabend.

26. "The dignity of science must not be held to consist in the comprehension and explanation of all the multiplicity of forms in

Nature; we must be content with what we can, in fact, comprehend at present. There is plenty that cannot be comprehended yet; this is something we must grant in the Philosophy of Nature," *EN* (1830), §268 Zus.; Miller, *PN*, p. 62. See also *EN* (1830), §354 Zus.; Miller, *PN*, p. 359.

27. "The Philosophy of Nature takes up the material which physics has prepared for it empirically, at the point to which physics has brought it, and reconstitutes it, so that experience is not its final warrant and base. Physics must therefore work into the hands of philosophy, in order that the latter may translate into the Notion the abstract universal transmitted to it, by showing how this universal, as an intrinsically necessary whole, proceeds from the Notion," *EN* (1830), §246 Zus.; Miller, *PN*, p. 10. "Here, as throughout the whole of the Philosophy of Nature, all that we have to do is to substitute for the categories of the Understanding the thought-relationships of the speculative Notion, and to grasp and determine the phenomenon in terms of the latter," *EN* (1830), §305 Anm.; Miller, *PN*, p. 154.

28. "For philosophy it is a matter of complete indifference which bodies manifest magnetism. ... all this is no affair of the Notion," *EN* (1830), §312 Zus.; Miller, *PN*, pp. 166-7.

29. *EN* (1830), §250 Anm.; Miller, *PN*, p. 23.

30. *EL* (1830), §12 Anm.; Wallace, *EL*, p. 18.

31. "In empirical science, any statement as to what color or heat etc., is, cannot be based on the Notion but must depend on their modes of origin. These modes are, however, extremely varied," *EN* (1830), §320 Anm.; Miller, *PN*, p. 196.

32. Nancy Cartwright, *How The Laws of Physics Lie* (Oxford: Oxford University Press, 1983).

33. *EN* (1830), §246; Miller, *PN*, p. 6.

34. Space prevents a full exposition of this topic. Hegel deals with it, in his consideration of the theoretical and practical modes of cognition, both at the end of the logic (see the *EL* [1830], §§224 and 225; Wallace, *EL*, pp. 283-4) and briefly, almost in passing, at the opening of the *Philosophy of Nature* (in the Einleitung, *EN* [1830], p. 13; Miller, *PN*, p. 4).

35. See *EN* (1830), §§248 Zus., 275 Zus.; Miller, *PN*, pp. 18-19, 288.

36. *EN* (1830), §248; Miller, *PN*, p. 17.

37. *EN* (1830), §249; Miller, *PN*, p. 20.

2

The Logic of Hegel's *Philosophy of Nature*: Nature, Space and Time

Edward Halper

The philosophy of nature is the most difficult portion of Hegel's system. Besides the extensive scientific development since Hegel's time—far beyond what he could have imagined—there has always been skepticism about his conceptual grasp of the science of his own era. His notion of a systematic conceptual development would seem to be at odds with the way that natural science actually developed and his accounts of one concept's "passing over" into another are, of all the parts of his system, perhaps least instructive for grasping the development or content of scientific concepts. Indeed, a conceptually complete system is strikingly at odds with what the contemporary world values most about science: its power to grow and correct itself, sometimes radically. This essay will address the seeming irrelevance of Hegel's *Philosophy of Nature* to modern science, but not by showing that Hegel's concepts are important to scientific practice. What really needs explaining is why he would think that a purely conceptual system could constitute genuine scientific knowledge of nature. Ironically, on this issue, it seems to me that the greatest obstacles to appreciating Hegel's *Philosophy of Nature* are internal questions about its character as a conceptual system, and it is such questions that I shall pose and consider here. My contention is that seeing how to resolve these problems will put us in a position to see that Hegel is himself addressing the most persistent of all objections to his system: how there could be a philosophical treatment of nature. That is to say, the objection made to Hegel's system of nature is the very difficulty he himself addresses: the indifference or externality of nature to conceptual determination. I shall return to this point in the final section of this paper. For now, the internal problems.

First, though Hegel's *Philosophy of Nature* belongs to a conceptual system that is supposed to be both self-contained and self-generating, many scholars persist in speaking of its categories as if they were merely *logical* categories applied to some new non-conceptual content or were merely concepts imported from the science of his day.[1] But a fully systematic development could admit of nothing imported from outside. In an idealism like Hegel's, there is nothing non-conceptual to which concepts could be applied. The problem for us is, thus, how the philosophy of nature could belong to an idealist conceptual system.

A second, closely connected problem is how to understand the concepts of the philosophy of nature. What, in particular, distinguishes the categories of nature from those of logic? Philosophy of nature comes after logic in Hegel's system, but it is puzzling how there could be another branch of the system after logic reaches its pinnacle in the absolute idea. How could there be new non-logical categories? Either conceptual development beyond the absolute idea is impossible, or such development would seem to produce new *logical* categories. This difficulty could be resolved by adding some non-logical content to the categories of logic to generate the categories of nature. But, again, the addition of something external would undermine the system's idealism and its self-containment. The categories of nature must thus be, on the one hand, distinct from those of logic and, on the other, generated from logical categories. But even if there were somehow a new category after absolute idea, why would it not remain a logical category?

A third problem with philosophy of nature is how the categories of nature transform themselves into new categories. I have argued elsewhere that the categories of logic are transformed by processes of self-relation: Hegel shows that particular categories are themselves instances of the conceptual content they contain, but this self-determination adds new content to the category and so transforms it into another category.[2] The process differs for different categories, and differs significantly in different spheres; but it allows logical concepts to be generated without introducing additional non-logical content. Are the processes that transform the categories of nature into new categories the same as those that transform the categories of logic? If categories of nature were also transformed by self-determination, then, in this respect, too, they would not differ from logical categories, and the philosophy of nature would either be a branch of logic or altogether superfluous. If, on the other hand, the process of development of the categories of nature does *not* involve self-determination, it is hard to see how it could be self-contained and not rely upon additions from outside the system. In short, in respect of both their character and the process of their development, the categories of nature either reduce to those of logic or undermine the systematic and idealistic character of Hegel's philosophy.

Logic and Philosophy of Nature

The best way to understand how philosophy of nature can be systematic is to resolve the second and third problems. Let me, thus, begin with the second problem, the character of the categories of nature and their difference from those of logic. Discussing the culmination of logic, absolute idea, in the final pages of the *Science of Logic*, Hegel characterizes it as both the product of the entire preceding conceptual development[3] and as a concept that contains this development within itself.[4] (These are, respectively, its form and content.) What makes absolute idea the culmination of logic is that, unlike other categories, it does not transform itself into a new concept; and the reason for this is that it already contains its own transformation. In other words, because the absolute is a self-unfolding of all the categories, transformation does not affect it; its nature is transformation. In Hegel's terminology, the content of the absolute idea is the "method" of its conceptual transformations, but the totality of this "method" is also the distinctive character of absolute idea, its form; hence, absolute idea's content is identical with its form. Once the conceptual development that constitutes logic reaches absolute idea, it immediately begins to unfold again. Thus, logic completes itself by returning to itself:

Hegel's image of the absolute idea is a circle that includes the whole of logic.[5] This image conveys the closure of logic, a closure that makes it puzzling how the system can contain other parts.

Yet, ironically, it is also the recognition of logic as a kind of circle that Hegel thinks makes the other portions of the system possible.[6] Though his discussion of the emergence of the sphere of nature is somewhat obscure, it seems that the basis for this sphere lies in the same distinction within absolute idea that Hegel draws upon to assert its completion: that between its form and content. Again, the content of absolute idea is the conceptual transformations between all the logical categories, and its form is just its character as a particular category. Absolute idea is the culmination of logic in so far as its form is identical with its content; that is, in so far as its individuality is just the totality of the transformations of all categories. However, it is also a category that is distinct from all other logical categories: it is a single universal that differs from the logical categories contained within it and from their complex conceptual development. In this latter respect, absolute idea is indifferent and external to the processes of conceptual unfolding that constitute logic. It is precisely this *externality* of absolute idea's form from its content that defines the realm of nature.[7] So it is that absolute idea, in being just what it is, is also something else. Alone among all the logical categories, absolute idea does not develop; it is its own self-unfolding. Yet this self-unfolding that is its content can be distinguished from the concept it defines, a concept that is external to its own content. It is the very closure of logic that opens the possibility for a treatment of nature.

This account is entirely consonant with Hegel's well-known image of the system:

> [S]cience exhibits itself as a *circle* returning upon itself, the end being wound back to the beginning, the simple ground by the mediation; this circle is moreover a *circle of circles*, for each individual member as ensouled by the method is reflected into itself, so that in returning to the beginning it

> is at the same time the beginning of a new member. Links of this chain are the individual sciences [of logic, nature and spirit], each of which has an *antecedent* and a *successor*.[8]

In the absolute idea's returning to itself, it completes a circle that is both itself and something else.

What is this other? It is important to see that it is not a *new* logical category, but an additional logical category. As Hegel puts it,

> The Idea, namely, in positing itself as absolute *unity* of the pure Notion (*Begriff*) and its reality and thus contracting itself into the immediacy of *being*, is the *totality* in this form—*nature*.[9]

In other words, the conceptual development that constitutes the content of the absolute idea along with the simple immediate (category of) being that constitutes its form comprise together a "totality" that defines the realm of nature. This form of the absolute idea does not merge with it to engender a new, more complex category—there is no further logical development beyond absolute idea. We are not dealing with a new logical category, but with a plurality of logical categories, a "totality." The category of nature consists of two constituent logical categories, absolute idea and its determination, being. The constituents remain indifferent to each other and thus comprise an irreducible composite.

This is an extraordinarily simple idea, but one looks hard to find it expressed anywhere in the literature. Again, the absolute idea that completes logic turns back upon itself, and this simple self-identity makes it an instance of the category of being. But the being that absolute idea acquires in returning to itself, that is, in being what it is, remains distinct from the being (the first logical category) that belongs to its unfolding. This acquired being is added to absolute idea, and the result is two categories yoked together: this is nature. In being what it is, absolute idea is something else—a being—and this being remains distinct from and indifferent to it. This explains how the completion of the circle that constitutes logic is also the beginning of the circle that constitutes nature.

It may seem odd to speak of logic's first category, being, as a predicate, but all Hegelian categories are both subjects and predicates. Or, better, they are completely general conceptual determinations that could characterize anything, including themselves. This possibility of applying categories to themselves and to other categories is crucial if the system is to be self-contained.

A composite of two logical categories, the idea of nature adds nothing to logic. As we saw, the new determination, being, stands outside the conceptual development that is the absolute idea. Though being and absolute idea are both external to each other, it is the externality of being that Hegel seems to have in mind when he characterizes nature as externality in the *Philosophy of Nature* (*EN* [1830], §247); for it is the *determinations* of absolute idea that have the characteristics of space and other natural categories, as we will see. The emphasis in the *Philosophy of Nature* is always on absolute idea's determination rather than absolute idea, and it is easy to see why. Since absolute idea is already fully determined, anything that is added to the totality of it and its determination could only be a determination of its determination. Thus, a determination of the concept of nature could only transform being, the determination of absolute idea. Indeed, we could expect this determination to be transformed into nothing and then into becoming, and the entire sequence of the *Logic* to repeat itself. With many qualifications, this is what we see in the *Philosophy of Nature*. In characterizing the concept of nature as absolute idea determined as a being, Hegel contrasts it with the absolute idea with no determination. Hence, the determination of absolute idea is not only simple being but also the negation of being: nothing. As such, nature becomes a determinate being (*Dasein*) (§248). In its initial stages, then, the development of the concept of nature is the development of its determination, and, as we will see more clearly shortly, this development parallels the opening moves of the *Logic*.

It is important to remember that Hegel is not dealing with logical categories here. Nature is not the category of being, but being attached to absolute idea, and the presence of this latter component is important not only to distinguish logical and natural categories, but also, as we will see, for the latter's transformations. According to my interpretation, just as logic is the self-unfolding of the categories, so, too, nature is the beginning of a kind of second-go-round of the same concepts, now with absolute idea attached to them. The rest of Hegel's system completes this second coming, as it were.[10]

This distinction between logical and natural categories provides a solution to the second of the three problems mentioned above, and the account advanced here also resolves part of the first problem: since nature includes no new categories beyond what logic makes available, there is no need to import any non-conceptual content into the system or to give up its self-containment. The new realm emerges from conjunctions of already developed logical categories.

Categories of Nature

Thus far I have focused mainly on the transition to nature that Hegel presents in the final pages of the *Science of Logic*. It is time now to look for evidence for this account in the *Philosophy of Nature*. Since Hegel never worked out this portion of his system in detail, we are forced to rely on the often sketchy *Encyclopedia*. In this section I shall show that the account of nature just derived from the *Logic* can also be found in the *Philosophy of Nature*. This understanding of the realm of nature helps to explain what would otherwise seem to be only scattered remarks on the concept of nature that open the second part of Hegel's *Encyclopedia*.

Paragraphs 245 and 246 both emphasize the presence of the concept (*Begriff*) in nature. In the former, Hegel claims that the concept is immanent (*immanent*) in nature;[11] in the latter, he speaks of nature as a self-determined concept.[12] These characterizations would seem incompatible; for if the concept is "immanent in nature," then nature is *more* than just the concept, and it is wrong to identify nature with the concept. However, the characterizations become intelligible when we reflect on the end of the *Logic*. The concept that is both immanent in nature and self-determined can only be the concept taken over from the preceding stage of the system, from logic. That concept is, of course, the absolute idea. Nature, as we have seen, is just absolute idea in its immediacy, that is, absolute idea determined as a being. Thus, absolute idea is at once merely immanent in nature and, in so far as it is nature's content, identical with nature; it manifests itself in nature and constitutes nature.

On the other hand, nature is not simply absolute idea, but this idea with an additional determination. As I said, since absolute idea is already complete in itself, any additional determination would be external to it. So it is that Hegel insists in §247 that nature is characterized by its externality. The idea of nature contains two components that remain external to each other. As Hegel says in §248, the determination of the concept is isolated from it, though the concept remains present as "something inward."[13] Significantly, in the remark that accompanies this section, he refers to the determination as "being"; the concept determined can only be the absolute idea.

This conception of the idea of nature makes intelligible Hegel's preliminary account of the development of nature in §§249-52. In §249, he calls nature a "system of stages, one arising necessarily from the other … not generated *naturally* out of the other but only in the inner idea which constitutes the ground of nature." The "inner idea" is, again, absolute idea, and Hegel's point is that it is successively determined by other categories and that these determinations spring from it rather than from each other. Thus far, absolute idea has been determined as an "immediate being."[14] Yet, this scarcely does it justice. The determination's inadequacy to the concept it is supposed to express constitutes the basis of an inner dynamic.[15] To characterize absolute idea simply as an immediate being is to falsify it. Absolute idea is, rather, different from this determination. It is better grasped without any determination, but to grasp it as such is to determine it as nothing. In so far as absolute idea is and is not its determination, it is a determinate being (*Dasein*). I think it significant that Hegel refers to nature as a determinate being in §248 while distinguishing the concept from its determinations. These initial determinations consist of the opening categories of the *Logic*. As we will see, the determinations are not generated from each other as in the *Logic*; rather they arise from absolute idea. In respect of absolute idea they are necessary; in relation to each other, the determinations are contingent "properties" (§250).

It is clear that characterizing absolute idea as a determinate being is only slightly more adequate than characterizing it as a being. The conceptual development within the sphere of nature aims to overcome this externality and generate a determination adequate to the absolute idea. What is needed is a determination that would match the idea. Moreover, any determination that would remain external to the idea would fail to capture its all encompassing character. To overcome this externality, the determination must belong to the idea; it must be a determination that the idea gives to itself. To give itself its own determination and remain what it is defines the logical category of concept (*Begriff*).[16] If nature posits its determination as what it is in itself, and then returns to itself; it will overcome externality. But this movement would at once determine it as belonging to spirit (§251). Thus, the truth of nature lies in the next realm of the system, spirit. It is in respect of this end that Hegel marks off the divisions of nature in §252. He describes them as moments of the concept: universal, particular, and individual (see also §252 Zus.). Though Hegel uses these categories in his treatment of nature, most often it is categories from the earlier portion of the *Science of Logic*, the Objective Logic, that he draws on to do the conceptual work of the *Philosophy of Nature*. Since nature consists of the absolute idea with its additional determination, and since the absolute idea is a concept, Hegel is entitled to speak of the idea of nature as a concept. It is only the additional determinations of that concept, not the idea of nature as a whole, that belong to the categories of Objective Logic.

Though Hegel clearly uses logical categories to characterize the categories of nature, deciding which logical category defines a category of nature is not always easy. He identifies space as a universal characterized only by its self-externality, its self-otherness (§254 Anm.); and time he calls the negativity of this otherness, a being that is "for itself" (§257). Otherness is one of the logical categories of the sphere of determinate being. Hegel characterizes time as the transition from being to nothing and from nothing to being, that is, as becoming, the category that precedes the logical sphere of determinate being (§§258, 259). The synthesis of space and time yields the categories of place and motion, both of which are defined as transitions or becomings of space into time and time into space, that is, as negations of negations (§§260, 261). Similar characterization as negation of negation defines the last logical categories of the sphere of determinate being, finite and infinite,[17] though Hegel does not mention them in this portion of the *Philosophy of Nature*. Thus, the first section of Mechanics would seem to employ the logical categories of the sphere of determinate being, roughly in their logical sequence.

The categories of the remaining two portions of Mechanics are characterized through the next set of logical categories, those of the sphere of being-for-self. Thus, in the second portion matter is a being-for-self (§§262, 263 Zus.),[18] a body is a one (§264), and the relation between bodies is repulsion (§268). The third portion of Mechanics, Absolute Mechanics, focuses on gravity, and the interaction of attractive and repulsive forces, clearly drawing on the logical categories of the third portion of being-for-self. If all this is right, then the categories of the first division of nature are defined with, or at least correspond to, the logical categories of the spheres of determinate being and being-for-self.

Though well supported by the text, there is at least one apparent problem with this association of logical and natural categories. According to the proposed alignment, space and time are instances of determinate being. But Hegel insists, in his remark to §254, that space is *not* a quality but pure quantity.[19] The reason, he explains, is that unlike the *Logic* where the first determination is "abstractly First and immediate," the first determination of nature is "a Being already essentially *mediated* within itself, an external- and other-being." What he apparently means is that since the first determination of nature is a determination of a concept, the absolute idea, it cannot be simply immediate but must be distinct from this concept, and precisely such a distinction, with the independence and indifference of its moments to each other, is the mark of the quantitative.[20] With these two moments so distinguished, nature is space, and in its totality the idea of space is a quantity because its two moments, absolute idea and determinate being, are indifferent to each other. In other words, the entire idea is a quantity because one of its constituents is a determinate being.[21] It is not contradictory for Hegel to say that categories of nature *as wholes* are quantities and that they are defined with categories from the logic of quality.

This reasoning shows some of the complexity possible in categories that are defined quite simply. Recalling an earlier point, I can add that the idea of nature also includes determinations from its other constituent, the absolute idea. Thus, as noted, Hegel refers to it as a concept and uses the categories of concept, universal, particular, and individual. Logical categories from concept, quality, and quantity provide Hegel with rich conceptual material with which to develop the idea of nature. His resulting discussion is often confusing, but the account offered here shows why it is legitimate to use categories from all three spheres.

Logical categories can be applied to experience or to the world, but if the categories are to receive a systematic and self-contained development, they should be applied to themselves. In the *Logic*, the application of categories to themselves generates new logical categories. Yet such an application of categories need not do so. Thus, the idea of space, absolute idea that is also a determinate being, is an instance of the category of quantity, but it is neither the logical category of quantity nor a new logical category. It is not identical with the category of quantity because quantity does not exhaust its nature, just as, a person has a size without being a quantity. The idea of space is not a new logical category because the categories that do define it do not constitute a unity: categories of nature consist of ununified pluralities of logical categories. The natural categories, at least the first group, as I have shown here, are constituted from the logical categories. They add nothing logically, but they present rich new pluralities of logical categories some of whose internal relations Hegel explores in the *Philosophy of Nature*. Significantly, the externally related constituents of natural categories mirror the externality that defines them.

Natural Transformations

The processes of transformation between logical categories are developed in the *Logic*. Since the categories of nature are composed of logical categories, we need to ask whether the transitions between natural categories are effected by the same processes of reasoning as those between logical categories. Are the transitions between natural categories logical transitions, effected by self-determination, or are they dialectical processes peculiar to the natural realm?

My account of the opening sections of Hegel's *Philosophy of Nature* suggests an answer to this question. Logic, the beginning of Hegel's system, can work only with being and what emerges from it. Thus, the determination of logical categories by logical categories is the only possibility. In the sphere of nature, though, the fully determined absolute idea is present and receives a further logical determination. This logical determination can itself be further determined, and the result is, of course, still another natural category. As we have seen here, it is important in the generation of the second determination that the first determination both be other than the absolute idea and fail to express it fully. The interplay between the two moments of natural categories, that is, between the absolute idea and its determination, constitutes a dimension not present in logic. Exploiting the difference between these moments, Hegel can develop a dialectic of nature that differs from the dialectic that generates logical categories, a dialectic based upon otherness. To understand how it works let us look closely at the transitions between the opening categories of nature.

The first particular category of nature is space. This is, I have argued here, the absolute idea determined as a determinate being. Now the determination is not divided further; it has no differentia within. Hence, it is all alike (§254). However, it is distinguished from the concept (namely, the absolute idea). The determination is, then, at once indifferent within itself and different from the concept (§255). In being indifferent, space is different from its notion, absolute idea. In other words, the determination, determinate being, contains within itself no differentiation, and just this lack of difference makes *it* different from the other component of the concept of space, the absolute idea which is differentiated in itself. If, though, absolute idea's determination differs from it, then that determination is not absolute idea but its negation. Hence, the concept of space contains, as it were, its own negation, its essential difference from the absolute idea.

This first negation of space is the negation of its "differenceless self-externality." The determination that characterizes absolute idea cannot be all alike. The negation of "being all alike" is a determination of space. It cannot be a determinate place because there is nothing else, no other determinate thing, from which it would differ. Conceptually, the negation of space, the negation of being everywhere the same, is a particular determination of space, a point.[22] However, the point fares no better as a determination of the absolute idea than does space. In so far as the point is other than the idea, it also negates the idea; and, consequently, its expression of the absolute idea is also the negation of itself. This second negation adds additional content to the point. Thus, the negated point has more conceptual content than the point, and much more content than space. Hence, the negation of point, the double negation of space, cannot be space. But in so far as it negates the particular determination of space (the point), it is spatial. Without explanation, Hegel identifies it with the line. But the line remains other than the idea it is supposed to express; hence, to determine the absolute idea as a line is also to recognize it as other than the line, as the negation of the line. Again, this cannot be the point or space; Hegel just identifies it as bounded space, or figure.

These last conceptual moves come rather too quickly in the text. It is not clear, on conceptual grounds, that there should be successive negations of space or that they should be identical with line or figure. Nor is it clear that, once begun, the process should terminate at figure—Hegel's assumption of three dimensionality is particularly grating to those who have become accustomed to talk of multidimensional spaces. There is clearly a conceptual development that is omitted from the tersely argued *Encyclopedia* version of the *Philosophy of Nature*. Nevertheless, Hegel's main point is well-founded: there remains an insurmountable otherness between the concept, that is, the absolute idea, and the determination of determinate being that expresses it; and the more that we try to distinguish the concept from this determination as something other, the more we determine it as other and the more ways in which its otherness comes to be expressed. Ironically, the attempt to distinguish absolute idea from its determination results in new determinations of it—but determinations of the same sort, namely, determinations of otherness, spatial determinations.

This possibility of continuous otherness is precisely the concept of time. Space determines itself as point, line, and figure; the successive determination is also a successive negation, a continuous passing away. This self-negating otherness is time. The difference between space with its determination and time is that whereas the former preserves the determinations "next to each other," time is the succession of determinations. As Hegel notes, time is the negativity of spatial determinations (§257 Zus.). Time is the other side of the process of spatial determinations.

Since the determinations of space are continuously self-negating, time is something whose being lies in its non-being (§258). The self-negating character of time makes it possible to distinguish what has already been negated (past) from what remains (future). Yet, the very same character renders any such distinction meaningless; for in so far as time is continuously self-negating, all its moments are alike (§259). Thus, it has just the character of space. That is to say, time, determined through itself, is space.

This identity of space and time is what Hegel terms "place" (§260). Since, though, space and time are continuously self-determining, they are also continuously reconstituted: this change of place is motion. Conceptually, motion is the *process* of determination that continues as space and time negate themselves; it is the otherness of their identity, place. The latter, being itself other than motion, persists through the continual negation of space and time. This determination of place as persistent (in a peculiar way) is just what Hegel terms "matter" (§261). Matter, in this sense, is simply the fullness of place in space and time, a fullness that is constituted by quantity itself. As Hegel explains in a note, these abstract determinations become concrete and real by being further determined.

In sum, the first categories of nature emerge through a dialectical development that follows from the otherness of absolute idea and its determinations. Though Hegel is not always as clear as he could be, the present section shows that these first categories do emerge in a rigorous way. Whereas the development of the categories of logic proceeds by *self-relation*, that is, by showing that a category is an instance of itself, the first categories of nature develop in virtue of their internal otherness, their *self-otherness*. Hence, philosophy of nature has its own characteristic mode of dialectic distinct from the dialectic of logic.

To show that the first categories of nature are derivable through a rigorous reasoning process does not, of course, prove that the rest are as well. Nor can we predict in advance the system's entire conceptual development: the reapplication of logical categories to the absolute idea is, by no means, wooden or mechanical. Still, the preceding shows that a systematic development of philosophy of nature is possible in principle. And it relies on the otherness that Hegel declares to be fundamental to this realm. More developed logical determinations will generate more developed natural categories.

Externality and Nature

It remains to consider why otherness, that is, externality, should be fundamental to the realm of nature. To say that externality is not widely recognized as a problem in natural philosophy or philosophy of science would be an understatement. Hence, it is not surprising that Hegel's concern to overcome it in his *Philosophy of Nature* has not aroused great interest. The fact that philosophy of science is so often dominated by empiricists and their heirs has, I suggest, rather obscured the issue. Some historical remarks can help us put it into context.

Recall that what Aristotle called "science" consisted of grasping the essential nature of a genus and demonstrating the attributes that belonged to the genus in virtue of that nature. Because the principle of knowledge, the generic nature, resided in a genus, little or nothing could be said about interactions among different genera. Medieval thinkers, supposing that all such interactions were guided by a just and benevolent deity, opened up the possibility of knowledge of the entire world and of all its distinct genera as constituting an organic whole.[23] The laws governing these interactions resided in God's mind. Philosophers in the modern period removed the immediate effects of divine agency and tried to find the laws of nature in nature itself. This created enormous ontological problems; a history of their treatment would be a history of modern philosophy. Current discussions of this period often pose its central metaphysical problem as the relation of mind and matter, but what was the reason for modern philosophers' interest in this problem? Their assumption was that the laws of nature must be rational and intelligible but that what they govern, matter, is something of a completely different nature. How could something intelligible, a rational law, govern the interactions of material things?

It was, I suggest, concern to account for the relation of laws and matter that motivated much modern metaphysics. Descartes insisted that any law we could think clearly and distinctly must correspond to matter, and Spinoza also advanced a kind of correspondence between thought and matter, albeit a different one. Leibniz located laws in matter; but in so far as each bit of matter contains all the laws, no law could govern the interactions between distinct bits of matter, nor could any bit of matter account for its interactions with other matter. Thus, Leibniz had to give up on the possibility of interactions among different bits of matter; instead matter acts in pre-established harmony. Empiricists did not solve the problem; they reacted against the rationalists' solutions by noticing that science could get along without solving it.

The point of all this is that throughout the modern period the laws governing nature were understood to be ontologically distinct from the material they governed. This is, I suggest, Hegel's problem of otherness. It manifests itself quite clearly in the first categories of natural philosophy: space and time are determinations that are most distinct from the rational principles of thought, the content of absolute idea. Yet, Hegel insists that it is just such rational principles that generate space and time. The *Philosophy of Nature* aims to show that the rational principles are not outside of nature but somehow present within it. It is only if we could grasp the laws as existing within nature that we would be justified in regarding those laws as laws of nature. Laws that existed within nature would not be "other."

Aristotle's principles of nature lack otherness, but they are species essences that, as noted, do not account for interactions among species. A law that resided in any one bit of matter could not account for its interactions with other bits of matter. The law would somehow have to reside in all matter. The idea expressed by some contemporary physicists that the laws of physics were fixed in the first micro-seconds after the big bang avoids the externality of having laws outside of matter, but because these laws stem from chance arrangements of matter, they remain, to some extent, external. Hegel's aim in overcoming externality is to understand the laws of the universe to belong to what they govern. This question, how is the law related to what it governs?, is fundamental for any understanding of nature. If philosophers do not pursue this question, it is only because they doubt that we can truly grasp nature. Law is, of course, the logical component of nature; the absolute idea that is brought from logic into the realm of nature is the conceptual analogue of all laws of nature. The determinations that philosophy of nature adds to this logical component are the material constituents of nature. Though the material determinations are external to law/idea and initially inadequate, they are successively determined until they come closer to expressing the idea. In this overcoming of externality, Hegel shows the possibility that thought about nature might genuinely express nature, and so answers the chief objection against him: nature admits of a conceptual treatment only if it contains reason, and this is precisely what *Philosophy of Nature* shows. Yet, ironically, in overcoming externality, in showing nature as the expression of laws or, equivalently, the determination as an expression of the absolute idea it determines, Hegel must determine the determination as the idea's own expression. In this case the determination the absolute idea receives would belong not to the logical realm of being, but to concept; and the complex of idea and the determination it gives itself would belong to spirit. So it is that in overcoming externality, thought passes over to the realm of spirit.

Notes

1. After making (well justified) fun of remarks made by earlier commentators on the relation of logic and the rest of the system, M. J. Petry, *Hegel's Philosophy of Nature*, 3 Vols (London: George Allen and Unwin, 1970), **1**: 40-1, describes his own view of the relationship: "The categories of the 'Logic' ... are an integral part of [natural and spiritual] phenomena, and yet, on account of their

greater simplicity, universality or generality, and on account of the complexity relationships in which they stand to one another as categories, they have to be regarded as constituting a distinct sphere and as demanding treatment in a distinct discipline" (**1**: 42). This is true enough, but our expectation that Petry will explain the complexity of nature is frustrated. He only notes that the logical categories of measure and rule have manifold applications and then claims that there is a correspondence between the categories of logic and the "levels" of nature (**1**: 42-3). Space is the first of the latter, he claims, "simply because it was the least complex level recognized in the natural science of his day" (**1**: 46). Apparently, Petry also sees the *Philosophy of Nature* as some sort of application of logic and he gives up on its being a genuine system. But what are the "natural phenomena" to which logical categories are applied? What additional components make them more complex than the logical categories? Despite Petry's term, "level," these additions must clearly be conceptual. Yet, how could they be conceptual but non-logical?

M.J. Inwood, *Hegel* (London: Routledge & Kegan Paul, 1983), pp. 350-1, is right to reject this thinking as unsupported by the text. However, he himself is unable to explain Hegel's account at the end of the *Logic* of the transition from logic to nature; he ascribes it to "confusion" on Hegel's part (pp. 378-9). Though he goes on to discuss Hegel's arguments for the transition, he takes these from other parts of the system; consequently, they do not respect the system's integrity. Nor, indeed, does much of the rest of his discussion. Inwood's concern with whether "the world corresponds to [Hegel's] system" (p. 379) is a throwback to the notion of application he wishes to reject; for what is "the world" besides the totality of concepts?

2. See my "Self-Relation in Hegel's *Science of Logic*," *Philosophy Research Archives* 7 (1981): 89-133. See also my discussion in "Hegel and the Problem of the Differentia," in *Essays on Hegel's Logic*, edited by George di Giovanni (Albany, New York: SUNY Press, 1989), esp. pp. 196-202.

3. G.W.F. Hegel, *Wissenschaft der Logik II. Erster Teil: Die objektive Logik, Zweites Buch. Zweiter Teil: Die subjektive Logik*, edited by E. Moldenhauer and K.M. Michel, *Werke in zwanzig Bänden*, Vol. 6 (Frankfurt am Main: Suhrkamp Verlag, 1969), p. 550; A.V. Miller, *Hegel's Science of Logic* (London: George Allen & Unwin, 1969), p. 825. (Hereafter cited as: *Logik* [*Werke*, **6**], p. 550; Miller, *Logic*, p. 825.)

4. *Logik* (*Werke*, **6**), pp. 552, 568-9; Miller, *Logic*, pp. 827, 839-40.

5. *Logik* (*Werke*, **6**), pp. 570-1; Miller, *Logic*, pp. 841-2.

6. *Logik* (*Werke*, **6**), p. 571; Miller, *Logic*, pp. 841-2.

7. *Logik* (*Werke*, **6**), p. 573; Miller, *Logic*, p. 843.

8. *Logik* (*Werke*, **6**), pp. 571-2; Miller, *Logic*, p. 842. There is another reference to philosophy as a circle of circles in the *Zusatz* that opens the *Encyclopedia*'s treatment of nature: G.W.F. Hegel, *Enzyklopädie der philosophischen Wissenschaften im Grundrisse (1830). Zweiter Teil: Die Naturphilosophie. Mit mündlichen Zusätzen*, edited by E. Moldenhauer and K. M. Michel, *Werke in zwanzig Bänden*, Vol. 9 (Frankfurt am Main: Suhrkamp Verlag, 1970), p. 10; A. V. Miller, *Hegel's Philosophy of Nature* (Oxford: Clarendon Press, 1970), p. 2. (Hereafter cited as: *EN* [1830]; *Werke*, **9**: 10; Miller, *PN*, p. 2.)

9. *Logik* (*Werke*, **6**), p. 573; Miller, *Logic*, p. 843.

10. Is still another circle possible? It would be conceptually more complex and richer than the system Hegel develops. Perhaps the derivation of Herr Krug's pen (*EN* [1830], §250; *Werke*, **9**: 35n.; Miller, *PN*, p. 23) awaits such a third coming.

11. *EN* (1830), §245; *Werke*, **9**: 13; Miller, *PN*, p. 5.

12. *EN* (1830), §246; *Werke*, **9**: 15; Miller, *PN*, p. 6.

13. *EN* (1830), §248; *Werke*, **9**: 27; Miller, *PN*, p. 17.

14. *EN* (1830), §248 Anm.; *Werke*, **9**: 27-8; Miller, *PN*, p. 17.

15. "Starting therefore from the externality in which the concept at first exists, its progress is ... a bringing of immediate and external existence, which is inadequate to itself, to subjective unity, to being-within-self," *EN* (1830), §251 Zus.; *Werke*, **9**: 37; Miller, *PN*, p. 25 (translation slightly modified).

16. *Logik* (*Werke*, **6**), pp. 273-5; Miller, *Logic*, pp. 600-2.

17. G.W.F. Hegel, *Wissenschaft der Logik I. Erster Teil: Die objektive Logik, Erstes Buch*, edited by E. Moldenhauer and K.M. Michel, *Werke in Zwanzig Bänden*, Vol. 5 (Frankfurt am Main: Suhrkamp Verlag, 1969), p. 162; Miller, *Logic*, p. 147. (Hereafter cited as: *Logik* [*Werke*, **5**], pp. 162; Miller, *Logic*, p. 147.)

18. In a remark on matter (*EN* [1830], §262 Anm.; *Werke*, **9**: 61; Miller, *PN*, p. 45), Hegel directs readers to his remark on Kant's treatment that appears in the *Logic* among the categories of being-

for-self (*Logik* [*Werke*, **5**], pp. 200-8; Miller, *Logic*, pp. 178-84), further supporting the categorial alignment proposed here. In the *Logic* the remark comes at the end of being-for-self because it criticizes Kant's definition of matter through the last categories of this sphere. Its counterpart is appropriately placed after Hegel's own definition of matter with the first category in this sphere.

19. *EN* (1830), § 254; *Werke*, **9**: 42; Miller, *PN*, p. 29. See also *Logik* (*Werke*, **5**), pp. 214-15; Miller, *Logic*, p. 189. Besides treating space and time as pure quantities, Hegel also mentions the logical categories of continuous and discrete quantity in the remark on time; *EN* (1830), §259 Anm.; *Werke*, **9**: 52-4; Miller, *PN*, pp. 37-9.

20. Hegel defines quantum by the indifference and externality of the determinateness and the something that it determines; *Logik* (*Werke*, **5**), p. 209; Miller, *Logic*, p. 185. In nature, the something that is determined is the absolute idea.

21. For example, Hegel speaks of space as a concept that contains differences (*EN* [1830], §255; *Werke*, **9**: 44; Miller, *PN*, p. 30), but he adds that its difference is qualitative (*EN* [1830], §256; *Werke*, **9**: 44; Miller, *PN*, p. 31), by which he means that the difference, namely, otherness, belongs to quality, the first large grouping of logical categories.

22. Though he does not adopt the scheme I propose here, Dieter Wandschneider, *Raum, Zeit, Relativität. Grundbestimmungen der Physik in der Perspektive der Hegelschen Naturphilosophie* (Frankfurt: Vittorio Klostermann, 1982), p. 48, also refers to categories of determinate being, notably limit, to characterize the point.

23. Michael Foster's article, "The Christian Doctrine of Creation and the Rise of Modern Science," *Mind* (1934): 446-68, remains valuable.

3

Space, Time and Matter: Conceiving Nature Without Foundations

Richard Dien Winfield

The Problem of Conceiving Nature Without Foundations

Before the juggernaut of scientific achievement and the positivism it fostered, the philosophy of nature has fallen into such disrepute that any thought of rehabilitation seems hopelessly quixotic. Systematic philosophical inquiry into nature has been banished into the limbo of antiquarian scholarship, supplanted by a philosophy of science for whom nature is either the construct of contingently given conceptual schemes or an entirely empirical object equally beyond the grasp of pure reason.

This virtual extinction of the philosophy of nature is not, however, simply a result of the rise of empirical science as a vaunted paradigm of knowledge. It equally reflects the daunting demands that a philosophy of nature makes upon reason. The full challenge of these demands first becomes evident in the aftermath of Hegel's critique of metaphysics and transcendental argument. No longer can it be denied that if reason is to conceive nature systematically three hurdles must be conquered:

First, nature must be determined without appealing to anything assumed to be given in reality. If, instead, the philosophy of nature proceeds upon a voyage of discovery, offering assurances of encountering certain categories embodied in what it finds immediately at hand, the objectivity of its "findings" and the accuracy of the "descriptions" applied to them will always be uncertain. Only a radical departure from reliance upon the given can possibly save the philosophy of nature from the clutches of such doubt.

Secondly, nature must not be conceived by appealing to given frameworks of reference, linguistic practices, conceptual schemes or any other structures of cognition that reputedly determine what nature must be to count as an object of knowledge. Any such transcendental constructions of nature fall prey to charges of idealism, where, on the one hand, the determining cognitive structures always stand in need of critique to overcome their own dogmatic assertion, and on the other hand, any resulting construct of nature remains indistinguishable from a subjective/intersubjective stipulation, relative to some assumed framework of reference.

Thirdly, while direct reference to the given and transcendental constitution need to be avoided, the philosophy of nature must still somehow provide categories of nature that go beyond the ideal self-identity of logic's thinking of thought. Otherwise, the conception of nature will simply recapitulate logic, without capturing the difference by which nature can be distinguished from categories. Yet how can nature be conceived by thought and be given a content distinct from thought without reverting to metaphysical assurances about the given or to transcendental constructions of a nature receiving its law from the understanding, language or other privileged conditions of knowing?

Hegel poses the problem with stark acuity at the end of the *Science of Logic* by characterizing the gaining of access to the philosophy of nature as a free development of the totality of logical determinacy (the Absolute Idea), whereby it arrives at self-externality.[1] This notoriously perplexing formulation presents the emergence of natural determinacy as the outcome of a presuppositionless development of determinacy in general that relies upon no reference to what is given in reality nor to any determining structures of knowing. By characterizing the threshold of nature as the self-externality of logical determinations in their totality, Hegel's formulation moreover seeks to arrive at a minimal determination of nature that, on the one hand, makes use of no resources other than the logical categories that have arisen from indeterminacy without assumption, and yet, on the other hand, employs these categories so that they comprise a determination that remains distinct from every last one of them.[2] The difference of nature, by which it is irreducible to thought, is accordingly a pure difference, a difference defined in terms of nothing but thought itself. Hegel has here indicated that since no other resources can be admissibly introduced, the totality of thought can stand distinguished from something other than itself, something more than mere categories, only by arriving at its own totality related to itself as an other. Although each side of the relation may well add nothing to logical determinacy, their relationship, that of self-externality, involves more than either logical totality or any of its component features. The self-externality of the logical totality has this irreducible character simply because it succeeds in incorporating and qualifying in its entirety the whole from which it emerges, without appeal to any illicit extraneous terms.

Yet if the self-externality of the totality of determinacy provides the minimal threshold of something non-categorial, it no more comprises a defining principle of nature than the indeterminate category of being serves as a first principle guiding the development of determinacy that begins from it. If Hegel's project, the project of a fully self-responsible, non-arbitrary philosophy, is to be fulfilled, then the philosophy of nature must treat its starting point, the self-externality of logical determinacy, as simply the most elementary component of all further dimensions of nature, presupposed by every one without itself incorporating anything else of nature. Otherwise, this putative starting point fails to be the minimal constituent of natural determinacy, signifying that other unaccounted for contents have been allowed to play a role in nature from the outset.

This prescription imposes an exigence that extends throughout the toils of the philosophy of nature, and indeed, beyond to all further parts of the system of philosophy. In moving from the initial category of natural determinacy to further structures of nature, the conceptualization of nature must always arrive at new terms that incorporate nothing other than what has already been determined and yet comprise something irreducible to their antecedents. Only by following this path of determinate negation, where the difference between successive determinacies resides in incorporating former terms so as to be other to them, can reliance upon arbitrary stipulation be avoided. Accordingly, what will then certify that the ensuing development is valid is how the subject matter turns out to be nothing but the totality incorporating the determinations that have successively comprised its self-development. In that case, what nature is cannot be detached from the categories determining its self-constitution.

These radical demands of a systematic conception of nature provide a preliminary guide for understanding and evaluating Hegel's initial efforts to determine nature in the opening arguments of his philosophy of nature. There, he begins with space, determined as the immediate self-externality of determinacy,[3] and proceeds to time, motion and matter. Should space come first, as Hegel maintains, followed by time, motion and matter, and should each have the determinations Hegel ascribes to them?

Space as the Minimal Determinacy of Nature

Space will deserve the honor of being that with which the philosophy of nature should begin, provided that 1) its own determinacy involves nothing else that is natural and 2) that everything else in nature will involve spatial determinacy. The first consideration can be addressed directly, whereas the second ultimately requires anticipating the entire constitution of nature.

The difficulty of conceiving space resides precisely in the unparalleled elementarity it must possess as the prospective first and most minimal element of nature. Hegel identifies space simply in terms of self-externality, ascribing to spatial extension little else but a continuity whose differentiation is entirely formal and ideal.[4] Since no factor of nature can be employed to determine space, if space is to be the minimal feature of nature, Hegel departs from the metaphysical approach, canonically followed by Aristotle in his *Physics*,[5] of defining space in terms of place, where existing bodies and their spatial interrelations are presupposed. As Kant recognized, such an approach begs the question by relying upon spatial determinations (e.g. the extension of individual bodies as well as the spatial relations between them) to account for space.[6] Yet, whereas Hegel grants that space is a pure form of externality, lacking any real individual spatial entities within itself, he departs from Kant by conceiving this pure formality to involve no reference to forms of intuition or any other presupposed cognitive structure.[7] Although in the subsequent *Philosophy of Mind*, Hegel will allow for space, as well as time, to figure as a pure form of intuition,[8] he recognizes that consciousness involves a self-consciousness of a spatio-temporally situated self,[9] which accordingly presupposes space, time and a body of its own within an independently existing nature as a precondition for its own reflection.[10] Moreover, since determining space in reference either to different bodies and their places or to determinate perspectives in the world would take space for granted, distinctions of relative and absolute space cannot enter in at this juncture. Space as such is simply one and unbounded.

As Hegel consistently indicates, the only interruptions in space's infinite continuity are purely ideal points. Points of space are ideal in that their negation of extension cannot rest upon any real thing in space, since space per se cannot be determined by bodies and their relations without falling into a vicious circularity. This leaves no point distinguishable from any other, for each figures in just the same manner as a way station in the continuity of extension. What bounds each point as its spatial other is another point in exactly the same situation, possessing nothing in itself or in its relations to others distinguishing it from its counterparts.[11] Consequently, the point, as the discrete element in space's continuity, generates a line, where one point after another cannot help but pass into identity with the point contiguous with it. Since, moreover, the resulting line is just as indistinguishable from the edge of space it terminates, space's internal differentiation into point and line entails planes, whose own analogous similitude fills the continuity of space with the unbounded extension of spatial dimensions, which are equally indistinguishable from one another.[12] It makes little difference whether height, length and breadth be construed in Euclidean space or in a non-Euclidean space,[13] whose use of curvilinear axes already presupposes the two and three-dimensionality defined by straight lines.[14] In each case, what a dimension is identified as is a matter of indifference, since every one can substitute for the others without altering its internal or external relations.[15]

Be it situated as a point on a line, a line on a plane, or a plane within spatial dimensions, each "here" accordingly remains utterly identical to every other, comprising, as Hegel puts it, merely the possibility of a determinately identifiable place[16] Other differentiating factors must be introduced if any here is to become an actual place, abidingly distinguishing one space from another, and therewith establishing the resources for contrasting relative and absolute space.[17] Yet what are such real spatially individuating factors and how are they to be accounted for without arbitrary assumptions?

Hegel's own solution is perplexing at first glance. If one follows the course of his argument and the order of constitution in which categories are introduced and determined, the spatial individuation of place arises out of a unity of space and time, which itself first requires that time be accounted for following space.

Time as the Truth of Space

The treatment of time as the conceptual successor of space involves two complementary claims: 1) that space is determined independently of time and 2) that time requires space and nothing but space for its own determination.

The first claim is already confirmed by how the determination of space as sheer extension, i.e. immediate self-externality, involves nothing but the continuity of ideal points, whose passage into lines, planes and all-encompassing dimensions proceeds apart from any temporal differentiations.

Yet, how time can follow from space appears inscrutable, if not preposterous, on several grounds. On the one hand, the very abstractness of space seems to offer hardly anything with which temporality could be constituted. On the other hand, although time may well presuppose no other natural factors in its own process, how the passage of past, present and future requires space is hardly evident. The familiar appeal to motion as a basis of time may employ changes in place, but since such changes comprise motion only in conjunction with temporal alteration, motion must be derivative from, rather than constitutive of, time.

Accordingly, the temptation is great to treat space and time as two independently given factors, each as inexplicably basic as the other, and only externally connected in motion.[18] Kant, for example, initially appears to grant time an equiprimordiality with space not only by describing it without reference to space as a pure form of intuition in its own right, but by identifying it as the form of inner experience, which seems to operate without space at all. Of course, in his Refutation of Idealism, Kant later acknowledges how internal time consciousness is predicated upon external spatial experience to the degree that temporal duration can be experienced only if consciousness can reidentify something enduring as an objective backdrop for the subjective succession of its own representations.[19]

How can time be predicated upon space, however, if space and time are to be determined in themselves without reference to a structure of cognition whose own individuality ultimately depends upon being an embodied standpoint, already ordered in space and time?[20]

Hegel's answer is brutally simple: time follows from space in so far as time is what space becomes.[21] With spatial continuity involving a negation of extension in the point, which no less extends into other points, whose encompassing line both terminates and extends into adjacent lines, forming planes and dimensions, space exhibits an inherent contradiction: wherever spatial limits occur in the constitutive continuity of extension, they become external to themselves, transgressing the boundary that separates them from what they demarcate. They thus cancel their own discrete character on which space's expanse itself depends.[22] For if points, lines and planes cannot hold themselves apart, externality collapses. Yet, as continuous, space must involve both the differentiation of point, line and plane as well as their self-transgression. Hegel claims that time consists in just this ongoing self-transcendence endemic to space.[23]

If this is the case, then space directly generates time as a qualification of itself and time inherently refers to space by being that wherein extension and its negation are at one.

Yet why should the process of space count as time?

To begin with, it might appear that the ceaseless self-transcendence of spatial differentiation is no more than the negation within space whereby points, lines and planes comprise the intra-spatial terminations of extension. If space as a whole transcends itself, however, the negation in question cannot fall within space, as a merely spatial limit. In this sense time can count as the self-transcendence of space in its entirety, for the differentiation between space at one moment and at another is that whereby space as a whole is external to itself. That differentiation goes beyond any distinguishing between points and lines and planes that is internal to space. Instead, it comprises a negation of space in which space stands in relation to its other, where that other is defined in terms of nothing but the totality of space posited as external to itself. Since each differentiated space is subject to the same self-externalization by which each spatial now is immediately supplanted by another, time's negation of space is ongoing. In this way, time becomes determined by relying upon no other resource than space and yet achieves irreducibility to spatial differentiation. Time is, in other words, the self-externality of immediate self-externality, just as space is the self-externality of logical determinacy.

Consequently, time cannot be determined independently of space, for it is nothing but the process whereby space is differentiated from itself. Each halt of this process is the entirety of space, where all spatially connected "heres" get further subsumed under the determination of "now," setting them external to space at the next moment.

At every juncture, the mere self-externality of space provides nothing other than this abstract difference of space transcending itself, where each successive space has nothing in its own spatial character to distinguish it from its counterparts, which themselves immediately pass over into an otherwise indistinguishable spatiality, which undergoes the same self-transcendence. Only when real motion enters in, requiring matter and its differentiation into bodies in space, can spatial configurations at one moment be actually distinguished from those at another. Since, however, motion presupposes the passage of time, time itself cannot involve a self-externality of space relying upon the movement of bodies to distinguish space from itself at different moments. Moreover, matter and its diremption into bodies must itself be constituted, which hardly can occur on the basis of space alone.

Owing to the absence of any such real differentiation as bodies in motion could provide, time's process is just as continuous as the intra-spatial differentiation of extension.[24] Nothing real separates one now from another except the externality of space at this moment to an otherwise indistinguishable space at another moment. The differentiation of one moment from another is thus nothing but the self-externality of space in its entirety. Accordingly, just as space as a whole perennially becomes self-external, so time continually consumes its own moments, immediately supplanting one now with another equally straddling past and future. Whereas space surmounts its internal boundaries by continuing into other points, lines and planes that remain external to one another, time cancels each moment that comprises the other or negation of its predecessor, allowing Hegel to characterize time in terms of a negation of the negation or self-relating negation.[25] As this self-devourer, time never exists as anything more than space, just as space never is without subjecting itself to time, acquiring a transient presence arisen from the past and succumbing to the future.

Lacking any further real differentiation of one temporal moment from another, time is as abstract and ideal as space,[26] equally comprising a mere form of nature, awaiting the concretizations that further natural factors could bring. Once more, this very formality leaves no room for injecting the very concrete distinctions between objectivity and subjective consciousness that Kant will add by treating time as a pure form of subjective intuition.[27] When consciousness takes its place in the world, all its intuitions may well be temporally ordered, but this hardly reduces time itself to nothing but a fixture in the mind.

Nevertheless, the preceding basic determinations of time as the outcome of space appear to be flatly contradicted by the temporality of internal consciousness, wherein representations follow one another in time in a sphere presumably devoid of extension. If indeed we have representations before and after one another without setting space external to itself, time can hardly involve, let alone issue from, space. Yet if the sequence of representations involves no reference to space, how is their succession distinguishable from a purely logical ordering? Kant's appeal to a spatial backdrop in his Refutation of Idealism reflects this inability to keep temporal succession from collapsing into logical succession when space is not incorporated into the determination of time.

Indeed, it is time's constitutive reference to space that permits the sequence of the *categories* of space and time to be, like that of all categories in the philosophy of nature, a merely conceptual ordering. The move from point to line to plane is not temporal in character because it itself involves no continuous differentiation of spatial backdrops. A hopeless paradox would, of course, arise if the transition from space to time were temporal, rather than categorial, for then the very emergence of time would be preceded by a passage of time.[28]

The Determination of Motion and Matter from the Unity of Space and Time

Precisely because time incorporates space as a constitutive factor in the perennial movement of the future into the present and the present into the past, time itself involves a space-time continuum in which each spatial point is no less situated at a moment in time. By so uniting the here and now, time provides the resources for distinguishing "heres" by their different times and for distinguishing different times by their different "heres." Moreover, time's joining of here and now permits a point in space to retain its position over time and thereby be a temporally enduring point, distinguishable from others. Hegel appropriately calls the immediate unity of space and time, "place," in so far as it provides a concrete space-time location sufficient to provide a positive existence for differences of both time and space.[29] Without any connection to temporal moments, each point in space is indistinguishable from its counterparts, just as each moment in time is indistinguishable from its successors without any tie to a particular here. With the joining of place, however, time can have a determinate duration and space can have determinate locations that persist, instead of disseminating themselves into indifferently juxtaposed points.

Moreover, with place providing enduring, reidentifiable points in space, as well as a positive existence for the passage of time, motion and its counterpart, rest, become determinable. With identifiable spatio-temporal locations, the ideal self-transcendence of point into line and line into plane can be tied to the succession of temporal moments, constituting motion as the double-sided becoming where time transpires in terms of a succession of different places and space extends itself in terms of the sequence of time.[30]

Although the particular spatio-temporality of place provides the resources for determining the presence and absence of motion, movement and rest remain wholly ideal since nothing is available to distinguish moving from stationary points except a wholly external and arbitrary reference to other points that incorporates them into some trajectory in time. By themselves, space, time and place provide no basis for connecting one point rather than another to its adjacent counterparts, making one motion more actual than any other possible alternative. Consequently, the possibility of time embodying itself in a succession of different places and of space having identifiable places in time remains completely formal. For this very reason, as Hegel observes,[31] each place immediately passes over into another place, otherwise indistinguishable from itself, generating formal motion, just as each point passes over into adjacent points to generate a line.

What can overcome the ideality of motion and the formality of place in space-time is, of course, matter, differentiated into a plurality of bodies determinately occupying space in motion and at rest. Yet how are matter and its bodies to be accounted for on the basis of the only legitimate resources at hand: space, time, place and formal motion? The difficulty of this problem might appear to be easily escapable by simply removing the restriction to such meager constituents. However, what other natural factors could possibly be appealed to that do not themselves already involve matter?

The logical account of determinate being faced the analogous difficulty of having to constitute determinacy without employing any factors that are already determinate. Determinacy could accordingly only consist in a unity of being and non-being, for any other solution would beg the question by using determinacy, which is precisely what is in question.[32]

To avoid a similar vicious circularity, matter must be constituted without any material factors. Consequently, the very ideality and formality of space, time, place and formal motion qualify them as resources in nature that can serve to account for matter. Yet how can the immateriality of space, time, place and formal motion become constitutive of the basic materiality incorporated in all further dimensions of nature?

Hegel's answer is as simple and confounding as his parallel solution to the emergence of determinate being in logic: just as determinacy arose as the unity of being and non-being issuing from the internal collapse of coming to be and ceasing to be in becoming, so matter is determined as the unity of place and motion that arises from the internal collapse of motion's passing away and regeneration of space in time and time in space.[33] In motion, the passage of time presents itself spatially as the move from one place to another, where time continually reverts to space, while space simultaneously differentiates its extension in a temporal succession, extinguishing itself into time. Just as what becomes is something, as a paralyzed unity of being and non-being, so what moves is matter, as a unity of space and time where a determinate extension persists, brought along by time in its passage through space. Place, the spatial now, becomes united with motion to the extent that the temporal succession of time *both* renders place external to itself (as passing into another place which passes on into another, and so forth), and retains the self-identity of place along this trajectory of ongoing self-transcendence. In other words, a determinate, reidentifiable space travels along the trajectory of motion.

In so doing, two constitutive features of matter are exhibited: the occupancy of a determinate space and the enduring character of that occupancy through change of place in time. These coordinate aspects of matter depend upon both space and time for their constitution. If, instead, occupancy of a determinate space were instantaneous rather than enduring, materiality would vanish, just as it would if occupancy of a determinate space did not persist over change of place. For this reason, matter must exist in time, as well as in place, and be movable.

Whereas the movability of matter presupposes its spatio-temporality, it might be thought that the existence of matter in time and space need not be tied to movability. After all, why could not all motion be external to matter, as simple mechanics might be thought to presume, not only allowing for inertia, but allowing for matter or, at least, some matter to be immovable? In that case, motion would either be an inexplicable accident or the result of a mover beyond matter. What precludes the immovability of matter, however, are not the problems of such ramifications, but rather the inability to distinguish matter from mere space if matter cannot maintain its extension while changing its place. This persistent occupancy of space during motion is a key element in any dynamic conception of matter, which conceives of material extension in terms of moving force and thereby conceives matter and motion as ineluctably connected.

Not surprisingly, Hegel adopts such a dynamic conception of matter, further determining matter as a unity of attractive and repulsive force. In so doing, he follows Kant, with the qualification that Hegel jettisons reference to conditions for the experiencing of objects as well as eliminates the external relation in which Kant leaves the forces of attraction and repulsion in matter.[34] Reference to the framework of experience cannot be tolerated since it takes for granted cognitive structures that themselves presuppose a subject bodily existing in the world. The forces of attraction and repulsion cannot be treated as independent, separately given aspects of matter because the dynamic materiality they constitute cannot involve one without the other. As Hegel points out in his critique of Kant in the account of one and the many in the *Science of Logic*,[35] attractive force operates only in so far as what is attracted has not collapsed into a single point, but remains self-repelling, whereas repulsion operates only in so far as what is repelled has not dispersed to infinity, but retains a self-attraction resisting its dispersal. Consequently, if matter occupies a determinate space through moving forces, those moving forces must involve both attraction and repulsion.

If, however, the coeval operation of attraction and repulsion permits matter to occupy space by excluding similarly exclusive material, it threatens to coalesce into an endless homogeneous expanse of matter. This would result in all the conundrums of Descartes' equation of matter and extension,[36] wherein degrees of density become a mystery and the possibility of actual motion is eliminated, since the space that matter "leaves" or "enters" might just as well be occupied.

Matter can only uphold its own durable and reidentifiable occupation of space in time if, as Hegel's argument suggests,[37] matter constitutively possesses a center of gravity, allowing matter to be differentiated into a plurality of real bodies, whose attraction and repulsion as discrete masses is mediated by an independent unity of attraction and repulsion holding each body together as something in itself in its relation to others. This minimal play of gravity provides, as Hegel aptly puts it,[38] the substance of each body, maintaining internal cohesion and independence from its counterparts during motion and rest, as well as compression and expansion. Gravity does so, as would be required, by employing nothing but attraction, repulsion and the relations of space and time that they incorporate. For when attraction and repulsion are combined, preventing the collapse of matter into a single point, attraction figures as gravity, drawing matter to a center that matter's own repulsion prevents it from attaining.[39]

Hence, gravity is not external to matter, but the immediate result of the combination of attractive and repulsive force basic to material being. Moreover, since possessing a center of gravity renders matter a real unit, forming a body able to interact as such with others,[40] the differentiation of matter into bodies is equally inherent in material nature. Furthermore, by providing the minimal independence and discreteness of individual bodies, whereby bodies can act upon and resist one another, gravity equally entails the elementary relations of external mechanical motion: pressure and impact.[41]

Avoiding appeals to the given or transcendental constructions, Hegel has here succeeded in being a midwife to the concept of nature, presenting the self-emergence of its primary determinations: space, time, motion and matter. If the philosophy of nature is to regain respectability, it must follow this path of conceiving nature without foundations, leaving behind the fast and loose adventures of its metaphysical and transcendental past. Only then will the

Einsteins of tomorrow have something more to hang their theories on than the latest absence of conflicting observation.

Notes

1. G.W.F. Hegel, *Wissenschaft der Logik, Zweiter Band: Die Subjektive Logik (1816)*, edited by F. Hogemann and W. Jaeschke, *Gesammelte Werke*, Vol. 12 (Hamburg: Felix Meiner, 1981), p. 253; G.W.F. Hegel, *Science of Logic*, translated by A.V. Miller (Atlantic Highlands, NJ: Humanities Press, 1989), p. 843. (Miller's translation hereafter cited as: Miller, *Logic*, p. 843.)

2. In so doing, Hegel seeks to obey the two fundamental requirements of any immanent categorial development: 1) that each advance to a new category relies upon nothing other than what has already been established, and 2) that each advance nevertheless achieves its own irreducible identity through that means. Such an advance can only occur if categories entail their own determinate negation.

3. G.W.F. Hegel, *Enzyklopädie der philosophischen Wissenschaften im Grundrisse (1830). Zweiter Teil: Die Naturphilosophie mit den mündlichen Zusätzen*, edited by E. Moldenhauer and K. Michel, *Werke in zwanzig Bänden*, Vol. 9 (Frankfurt am Main: Suhrkamp Verlag, 1969), §252; G.W.F. Hegel, *Philosophy of Nature*, edited and translated with an introduction and explanatory notes by M.J. Petry, 3 Vols (London: George Allen and Unwin, 1970), **I**: 217. (Hereafter cited as: *EN* [1830], §252; Petry, *PN*, **1**: 217.)

4. Hegel, *EN* (1830), §254; Petry, *PN*, **1**: 223.

5. Aristotle, *Physics*, Book IV, Chapter 4, 210b35 ff.

6. I. Kant, *Kritik der reinen Vernunft, Kants Gesammelte Schriften*, Vols. 3, 4 (Königlich Preußische [now Deutsche] Akademie der Wissenschaften, Berlin: G. Reimer [now De Gruyter], 1902–), A23/ B38; *Critique of Pure Reason*, trans. by Norman Kemp Smith (New York: St. Martin's Press, 1965), p. 68. (Hereafter cited as *KdrV*, B38; Kemp Smith, p. 68.)

7. Hegel, *EN* (1830), §254 Amn.; Petry, *PN*, **1**: 223.

8. G.W.F. Hegel, *Enzyklopädie der philosophischen Wissenschaften im Grundrisse (1830). Dritter Teil: Die Philosophie des Geistes mit den mündlichen Zusätzen*, edited by E. Moldenhauer and K. Michel, *Werke in zwanzig Bänden*, Vol. 10 (Frankfurt am

Main: Suhrkamp Verlag, 1969), §418; G.W.F. Hegel, *Philosophy of Mind*, translated by William Wallace and A.V. Miller (Oxford: Clarendon Press, 1971), p. 159.

9. In this way, Hegel foreshadows aspects of P.F. Strawson's argument in *Individuals* (New York: Routledge, 1990), with the qualification that Strawson remains committed to a transcendental construction of nature. As a result, Strawson is plagued by the difficulty of upholding the primacy of our conceptual scheme in defining the reality given to us while acknowledging how our awareness is itself predicated upon the spatio-temporality of our being in the world.

10. For this reason, Augustine's account of time as a mental projection begs the question. Indeed, Augustine's own argument makes this clear in so far as he must presuppose the duration and temporal ordering of mental representations in order to give his constructions of past, present and future in terms of memory, attention and expectation. See Saint Augustine, *Confessions*, translated by R.S. Pine-Coffin (Harmondsworth: Penguin Books, 1979), Book XI, sections 27-8, pp. 275-8.

11. Hegel, *EN* (1830), §254 Zus.; Petry, *PN*, **1**: 224.

12. Hegel, *EN* (1830), §254 Zus.; Petry, *PN*, **1**: 224.

13. Eva T. Brann gives a telling argument that in so far as only Euclidean geometry permits "the preservation of shape across variations of size," our imagination, for which imaging similarity is essential, must operate in terms of Euclidean space. See Eva T. Brann, *The World of The Imagination* (Savage, Maryland: Rowman and Littlefield, 1991), p. 604.

14. Hegel points out that curvilinear lines are derivative of straight lines, since curved lines involve two dimensions. See Hegel, *EN* (1830), §256 Zus.; Petry, *PN*, **1**: 227.

15. Hegel, *EN* (1830), §255; Petry, *PN*, **1**: 225.

16. Hegel, *EN* (1830), §254 Zus.; Petry, *PN*, **1**: 224.

17. As Hegel points out, relative space involves the determinate spaces of bodies, whereas absolute space is the sheer abstractness of space, as it extends with indifference to every body within it (Hegel, *EN* [1830], §254 Zus.; Petry, *PN*, **1**: 225).

18. Hegel points out that space and time are ordinarily taken to be completely separate, so that space is given by itself and then, in an

unrelated move, time is “also” to be found. See Hegel, *EN* (1830), §257 Zus.; Petry, *PN*, **1**: 229.

19. Kant, *KdrV*, B275-B279; Kemp Smith, pp. 245-7.

20. This is the question that escapes, and cannot help but escape, such transcendental thinkers as Strawson and Heidegger who conceive the conditions of knowing as a subjective being-in-the-world.

21. Hegel, *EN* (1830), §257; Petry, *PN*, **1**: 229.

22. To paraphrase Hegel in paragraph 260, space is the contradiction of indifferent juxtaposition and continuity devoid of abiding difference (Hegel, *EN* [1830], §260; Petry, *PN*, **1**: 236).

23. Hegel, *EN* (1830), §257 Zus.; Petry, *PN*, **1**: 229.

24. Hegel, *EN* (1830), §258 Anm.; Petry, *PN*, **1**: 229.

25. Hegel, *EN* (1830), §257 Zus.; Petry, *PN*, **1**: 229.

26. Hegel, *EN* (1830), §258; Petry, *PN*, **1**: 229.

27. Hegel, *EN* (1830), §258 Anm.; Petry, *PN*, **1**: 229.

28. Similar difficulties trouble Augustine in considering the temporality of creation.

29. Hegel, *EN* (1830), §260 Zus.; Petry, *PN*, **1**: 236.

30. Hegel, *EN* (1830), §261; Petry, *PN*, **1**: 237.

31. Hegel, *EN* (1830), §261; Petry, *PN*, **1**: 237.

32. For an analysis of this constitution of determinate being, see Richard Dien Winfield, *Overcoming Foundations: Studies In Systematic Philosophy* (New York: Columbia, 1989), chapter 3, “Conceiving Something Without Any Conceptual Scheme,” pp. 55-75.

33. Hegel, *EN* (1830), §261; Petry, *PN*, **1**: 237.

34. For Kant’s account, see I. Kant, *Metaphysische Anfangsgründe der Naturwissenschaft, Kants Gesammelte Schriften*, Vol. 4 (Königlich Preußische [now Deutsche] Akademie der Wissenschaften, Berlin: G. Reimer [now De Gruyter], 1902–), pp. 496-535; Immanuel Kant, *Metaphysical Foundations of Natural Science*, translated by James W. Ellington, in Immanuel Kant, *Philosophy of Material Nature* (Indianapolis: Hackett, 1985), Second Chapter, “Metaphysical Foundations of Dynamics,” pp. 40-94.

35. G.W.F. Hegel, *Wissenschaft der Logik, Erster Teil: Die Objektive Logik, Erster Band: Die Lehre Vom Sein(1832)*, edited by F. Hogemann and W. Jaeschke, *Gesammelte Werke*, Vol. 21 (Hamburg: Felix Meiner, 1985), pp. 166-72; Miller, *Logic*, pp. 178-84.

36. R. Descartes, *Principles of Philosophy*, Part II, sections 4, 11, in *The Philosophical Writings of Descartes*, translated by J. Cottingham, R. Stoothoff, and D. Murdoch, 2 Vols (New York: Cambridge University Press, 1985) **1**: 224, 227-8.

37. Hegel, *EN* (1830), §265 Zus., and §266 Zus.; Petry, *PN*, **1**: 248, 251.

38. Hegel, *EN* (1830), §262 Anm.; Petry, *PN*, **1**: 242.

39. Hegel, *EN* (1830), §262 Zus.; Petry, *PN*, **1**: 242.

40. Hegel, *EN* (1830), §266 Zus.; Petry, *PN*, **1**: 251.

41. Hegel, *EN* (1830), §265 Zus.; Petry, *PN*, **1**: 248.

4

Hegel's Geometric Theory

Lawrence S. Stepelevich

At the conclusion of the first section of his lectures on the philosophy of nature, Hegel did something quite unusual for him—he predicted the future. In his words,

> I have set down here only the rudiments of a rational procedure in the comprehension of the mathematical and mechanical laws of Nature. ... This standpoint, I know, is ignored by professional astronomers; but a time will come when this science will require for its satisfaction the philosophical notion.[1]

The time did come, and less than a century after Hegel's death.

In the first decades of the twentieth century, mathematical physicists, who hitherto had relied upon the intuitions of ordinary consciousness regarding spatial metric, suddenly found themselves faced with a problem of their own making—a problem brought about by their own demands for ever-more refined observational techniques. Specifically, certain astronomical measurements, such as the perihelion advance of the planet Mercury, could not be explained in Newtonian terms. In fact, the attempt to do so actually generated an incorrect description of the planet's behavior.[2] The inability of Newtonian theory to explain the perihelion advance of Mercury not only created difficulties for astronomers, but in so far as the eighteenth-century mathematician Euler had conclusively demonstrated that Newton's First Law depended upon the assumptions of Euclidean space,[3] it followed that the very foundation of classical Euclidean geometry itself was threatened. And so it was that by the end of the first decade of the twentieth century a new "non-Euclidean" geometry had become the metric of the new physics. (That such a geometry once seemed unimaginable is evidenced by the fact that one of the first to develop non-Euclidean geometry and the one who gave it its name, Karl Friedrich Gauss [1777-1855], a contemporary of Hegel, had, out of fear of ridicule, concealed his innovative work from his own colleagues.) In this new non-Euclidean metric, the classical, or Newtonian-Euclidean understanding of space as an absolute container of invariable magnitudes was, if not completely discarded, only retained as the basis for a special metric that did not take into account factors introduced by the General Theory of Relativity.

When these radical changes in previous conceptions of space and its measurement were introduced, a need was felt to re-examine the philosophic grounding of these hitherto lightly examined categories. This need for the "philosophical notion" was mainly felt among European scientists, who began by re-examining Kant's treatment of time and space. The reason for this seems less philosophical than geographical, as Neo-Kantianism, at least in German academic centers, was the dominant philosophical school during the latter half of the nineteenth and the early part of the twentieth century.[4]

However, Kantianism soon proved to be unsatisfactory. Its structure was so co-relative with the principles of Euclidean geometry and Newtonian physics that it not only could not serve as a support for the new physics, but even proved itself to be an impediment to the latter.[5] As the geometrician Bonola observed, "the acceptance of the Non-Euclidean Geometry was delayed by special reasons, such as ... the Kantian conception of space which was then in the ascendant."[6]

In this regard, it now seems that there has long been a covert alliance between the followers of Gauss and Hegel, an alliance at least based upon their shared rejection of Kant's geometric theory. As an example, here, following Gauss, is Rudolf Carnap's criticism of Kant's reliance upon intuition as the basis of geometric axiomatics:

> Geometry provided Kant with one of his chief examples of synthetic *a priori* knowledge. His reasoning was that if the

> axioms of geometry (by which he meant Euclidean geometry—no other geometry was available in his time) are considered, it is not possible to imagine the axioms as not true. For instance, there is one and only one straight line through two points. Intuition, here, gives absolute certainty. [7]

Almost a century and a half before Carnap's criticism, Hegel had set forth an identical critique:

> It was the singular opinion of Kant's that the definition of the *straight line* as the shortest distance between two points is a synthetic proposition, since my *concept* of *straight* involves nothing of quantity, but only a quality. In this sense, every definition is a synthetic proposition. What is defined, *the straight line*, is at first [primarily] only intuition or figurative conception (§256 Anm.).

Here, for both Carnap and Hegel, Kant's unquestioning reliance upon intuition as the basis for geometric axiomatics simply confused concrete appearance with abstract logic. But Kant, resting upon his own conditioning epistemology, was satisfied that Euclidean geometry was the absolute geometry of intuited space, since it derived its necessity from the *a priori* character of that space.

On his side, Kant had the advantage of tradition. For almost twenty-two centuries of mathematical history, Euclidean geometry, despite revision and question, had endured as the exemplar of a science that granted both truth and certainty. In so far as Euclidean geometry, before Einstein, had accorded with all the requirements of pre-Einsteinian physics, it had the prestige of not only being theoretically certain, but empirically true.

However, long before post-Einsteinian physics was empirically forced to set aside Kantianism, Hegel had already done so. Hegel was particularly critical of Kant's unspeculative formalism in regard to the natural categories of space and time. In his view, it allowed Kant simply to avoid a fundamental discussion of the categories. Certainly, Kant does treat of space and time, but, as Hegel says,

> What the nature of time and space is, it does not occur to the Kantian philosophy to inquire. To it, what space and time are in themselves does not signify "What is their Notion," but "Are they external things or something in the mind?"[8]

In short, Kantianism does not—nor, given its epistemological limitations, could it—discuss the nature of space and time *per se*. In this, Kant somewhat resembles Newton, who in his *Principia*, rather blandly noted that "I do not define time, space, place, and motion, as being well known to all."[9]

According to such as Bertrand Russell[10] and David Hilbert, Kant's lack of reflection not only led to his unquestioning reliance upon the absolute character of Euclidean space and Newtonian physics, but prevented him from making a fundamental distinction between two forms of geometry. Rudolf Carnap, repeating Russell's and Hilbert's critique, terms the two forms of geometry mathematical or pure geometry and physical or empirical geometry. The distinction between these two forms of geometry is understood as a condition *sine qua non* for the articulation of post-Newtonian physics. In Carnap's mind, Kant's failure to distinguish the two geometries was shared by "almost all nineteenth-century philosophers." In his words:

> Mathematical geometry is *a priori*. Physical geometry is synthetic. No geometry is both ... Once this distinction between pure and physical geometry is understood, it becomes clear how Kant's belief, and the beliefs of almost all nineteenth-century philosophers, involved a fundamental confusion between two fields of quite different character.[11]

Certainly Carnap and others would not have confused Hegel with Kant had they merely read Hegel's brief presentation of the nature of space which introduces the

Philosophy of Nature, the second part of the *Encyclopedia of the Philosophical Sciences* (§§254-6). Had they done so with some care, they might have noticed that Hegel's philosophy might even provide a basis for satisfying the need they felt for the revision of their philosophical notions. Given this possibility, this essay will submit that Hegel not only recognized the modern distinction between so-called "pure" and "physical" geometry, but presented speculative grounds for their mediation. In sum, Hegel's geometric theory comprehends what the logic of the understanding has sundered into two exclusive geometries, one developed from an abstract logical content, the other deriving its content from the concrete contingencies of sensuous intuition. This will suggest that Hegel's theory, in so far as it is not tied to a spatial metric expressed exclusively as either a "pure" or a "physical" geometry, can thereby provide speculative support for both Euclidean and non-Euclidean geometry.

For mathematicians, the final acceptance of a radical distinction between "pure" and "physical" geometry was at first resisted. In time, it was hailed as a great advance. Hegelians would be expected to understand that mathematics, as a science of the understanding, as a *Verstandeswissenschaft*, would logically advance to the expression of its immanent contradictions. But if this division of geometry into Euclidean and non-Euclidean might be taken by Hegelians as vindicating Hegel's logic, for mathematical physicists it meant the somewhat embarrassing relinquishment of their earlier claims to universal and absolute truth. After Einstein, claims to any absolute truths based upon a universal and absolute geometry had to be surrendered. At present, unlike their Newtonian and Euclidean predecessors, mathematical physicists seem less comfortable in making truth-claims; or, as Henri Poincaré observed in this regard, "Experience ... tells us not which is the truest geometry, but which is the most *convenient*."[12] This replacement of absolute truth by relative convenience signals the end of both the pride and the innocence of early mathematical physics. From the perspective of Hegelian historical logic, perhaps too romantically expressed, the age of Newtonian/Euclidean physics was indeed an age wherein the unreflective innocence of the understanding, a Faustian innocence, led inexorably to its own fall. Even to this day, that there might actually be a meta-geometry along the lines suggested by Hegel, one which might serve to mediate the one-sided abstractions of pure and physical geometry, seems unknown to physicists. For example, Carnap speaks with approval of the strict dichotomy that Einstein placed between the two. As Carnap writes:

> One of the clearest, most precise statements of this distinction [between pure and physical geometry] was made by Einstein at the close of a lecture entitled "Geometry and Experience." Einstein spoke of 'mathematics', but he meant geometry in the two ways that it can be understood. "So far as the theorems of mathematics are about reality," he said, "they are not certain." ... "And so far as they are certain," he continued, "they are not about reality."[13]

In this context it might not be too cryptic to say that the whole of Hegel's philosophy is intended to resolve this Cartesian distinction between reality and certainty. Carnap describes pure or mathematical geometry as saying

> nothing at all about the world. It says only that, if a certain system of relations has certain structural properties, the system will have certain other characteristics that follow logically from the assumed structure. ... Physical geometry, on the other hand, is concerned with the application of pure geometry to the world. Here the terms of Euclidean geometry have their ordinary meaning. A point is an actual position in physical space.[14]

Pure geometry begins, as Hilbert's axiomatic geometry, with merely a "positing" without empirical referent, and develops itself *purely* in accord with the rules of the logic of the understanding, with a pure logic of consistency. There is nothing in it that needs physical verification, although, at the same time, there is nothing in it which resists physical verification.

Distinct from this purely logical geometry is the geometry of "the world"—a physical geometry which finds its premise in the empirical order of time-space. The logic of this empirical or physical or "real" geometry is not articulated, as is that of pure geometry, from abstract premises, but rather is reflectively derived from sensuous intuitions. In the words of Max Born,

> The objects of the geometry which is actually applied to the world of things are thus these things themselves regarded from a definite point of view. A straight line is by definition a ray of light, or an inertial orbit, or the totality of the points of a body regarded as rigid which do not move when the body is turned about two fixed points, or some other physical something.[15]

Now, for Hegel, geometry, in its widest sense, is "a science of the understanding ... a science of space" (§259 Anm.) and as such, "Geometry ... is not a philosophical science" (§255 Anm.). This *Wissenschaft des Verstandes*, this "science of space," is fundamentally different from what I would term Hegel's "speculative geometry," which is a philosophy of metric space, a geometry of reason. Unlike this philosophical geometry, the geometry of the understanding, in Hegel's view, rests upon fixed and unexamined axiomatic givens, framed within the first principles of the understanding. This geometry is the articulation of a consistently derived set of theorems which rest upon given axioms. The exclusive rules of the understanding, found in the principles of identity and non-identity, dictate the articulation of this "science of the understanding." In regard to this Hegel notes that

> The science of geometry sets out to find what determinations follow when certain others are presupposed. The main object is then that the presupposed and derived determinations should form a single developed totality. The

> cardinal propositions of geometry are those where a whole is postulated, and this is expressed in terms of its determinate elements (§256 Zus.).

This general definition is in accord with those given by contemporary geometricians. As one observed, the science founded by Euclid, in regard to its "logical format, ... has served as the prototype of all modern deductive systems constructed by the *axiomatic* or *postulational* method."[16] Here, geometry gains its necessity, not from its axiomatic formulations, but only in so far as its determinate elements logically follow upon the given propositions. Geometry as a science of the understanding cannot violate the principle of non-contradiction, and must be consistent in its determinations. This standard holds true for *any* geometry deserving of the name—whether the axioms from which it proceeds are pure or based on sensuous intuition. As the well-known contemporary geometrician, H.S.M. Coxeter, notes, "Each of these geometries, Euclidean and non-Euclidean, is *consistent*, in the sense that the assumptions imply no contradiction."[17]

This consistency, cast as the avoidance of contradiction, is the unmistakable mark of a geometry based upon the logic of the understanding, a logic that finds its sureties in the fixity and exclusiveness of its definitions. However, in 1931 the search for a complete and consistent *pure* geometry was brought to a sudden and unexpected end. Until that time, the geometry of Hilbert, in the words of the physicist John Barrow, "had been steadily producing small collections of proofs that appeared to advance them inexorably towards the formalists' goal of capturing all of mathematics in their logical web."[18] However, in 1931 the young mathematician, Kurt Gödel, demonstrated that no axiomatic system could prove itself to be consistent. An examination of Gödel's proof will reveal that he himself is locked entirely within the understanding's logic of consistency, wherein the false infinite sets a limit to all fixed definitions. Along this line, it might be of interest to note Barrow's somewhat shrill tone as he ended his observations regarding the unsettling effect of

Gödel's theory upon mathematicians: "Gödel's theorem not only demonstrates that mathematics is a religion, but shows that mathematics is the only religion that can prove itself to be one!"[19]

On the side of *physical* geometry, any certitudes that it might have claimed were put to final rest even before Gödel had ended the optimistic course of pure geometry. In 1927 Werner Heisenberg established the so-called "Indeterminacy Principle." It held that it is impossible to determine at the same time both the position and the velocity of an electron. For Carnap, in so far as "the essentially nondeterministic character of quantum mechanics rests upon the principle of indeterminacy," then the principle put an end to the absolute metric claims of prior physical theories. In his words, "Classical physicists were convinced that, with the progress of research, laws would become more and more exact, and that there is no limit to the precision that can be obtained in predicting observable events. In contrast, the quantum theory sets an insuperable limit."[20] It might be of interest for Hegelians to note that the famous physicist, Hans Reichenbach, in an attempt to avoid the theoretical impasse brought about by a logic that could only deal in the either/or of the understanding, suggested that another logic be employed. Suggestively Hegelian, he offered a "three-valued logic" which would interpose the category of "indeterminate" between the otherwise exclusive poles of the true and the false.[21] Perhaps, as Hegel might have suggested, it is now time for both pure and physical geometricians to consider a consistency other than that imposed by the abstract and external "either/or" logic of the understanding.

This other consistency is that of speculative *reason*, the necessitated course of dialectical logic. This speculative consistency is evidenced in the process by which reason presses the exclusive definitions of the understanding beyond their one-sided positivity into a comprehensive unity with the very opposites generated by these definitions. In this speculative unity, the true infinite includes both finite and non-finite rather than excluding one from the other. As absolutes of the abstract understanding, neither pure nor physical geometry can, as both Gödel and Heisenberg have shown, stand alone. The central event in the history of geometry was the abrupt overthrow of its paradigm, Euclidean geometry, by the advance of its own methodology. What had for centuries existed as the undisturbed claimant to an absolute and universal knowledge of spatial metric abruptly found itself sundered into two abstract geometries, one based upon axiomatic certitudes divested of any sensuous content, and the other upon the uncertainties of the sensuous world. If a reconciliation of these geometries is to be found, then it is only to be found in a speculative geometry comprehending both the necessity of pure logic and the contingencies of the physical world. I would maintain that the "rudiments" of this rational procedure are to be found in Hegel's philosophy.

The first signs of what we now term Hegel's "speculative geometry" appeared in his unpublished and incomplete *Geometrische Studien* of 1800.[22] The *Studien* were written less than a year before Hegel applied for a position at Jena, and would have served as a preparation for his inaugural dissertation, *De orbitis planetarum*.

Of particular interest in these *Studien* is Hegel's critical discussion of Euclid's Fourth Postulate. This so-called "congruency postulate" intends to demonstrate that if any three elements of a triangle are given, the other three elements will, of necessity, also be determined. At the time Hegel prepared his critique of this proposition, others had already criticized its proof, because it had, by requiring the superimposition of one triangle upon another, assumed that geometric figures could be moved without changing their size or shape. However, neither Hegel nor the influential non-Euclidean mathematician, Felix Klein, chose to criticize Euclid's "congruency postulate" on the usual grounds that superimposition of one triangle upon another might affect the dimensions involved.[23] Moreover, whereas Klein actually went on to develop his own subsequent geometric theory on the basis of the Fourth Postulate, Hegel used the postulate to illustrate how Euclid's demonstration actually leads thought away from the speculative comprehension of triangularity. That Hegel considered his critique of the fourth proposition to be of value is seen in his repeated use of that proposition as an example of what a geometrician should not do, a specific example which he employs not only in his Jena lectures[24], but in his *Science of Logic* [25] as well as in his *Philosophy of Nature* (§256 Zus.).

Hegel's critique of Euclid's effort to prove the congruency postulate not only afforded him the opportunity to define the nature of geometry, but to distinguish between the "Notion" of a geometric figure, in this case the triangle, and its "outer [external] reality" (§256 Zus.). His clearest statement of the way he employs his critique of Euclid's congruency postulate is found in the *Science of Logic*:

> Euclid's first propositions about triangles deal only with *congruence*, that is, *how many* parts in a triangle *must be determined*, in order that the *remaining* parts of one and the same triangle, or the whole of it, shall be *altogether determined*. The comparison of *two* triangles with one another, and the basing of congruence on *coincidence* is a detour necessary to a method that is forced to employ *sensuous coincidence* instead of the *thought*, namely the *determinateness* of the triangles. ... [T]hese theorems themselves contain *two* parts, one of which may be regarded as the *Notion*, and the other as *reality*, as the element that completes the former into reality. That is to say, whatever completely determines a triangle, for example two sides and the included angle, is already the whole triangle for the *understanding*; nothing further is required for its complete determinateness; the remaining two angles and the third side are the superfluity of reality over the determinateness of the Notion.[26]

In this passage, the relation between the certitude of the understanding and the "detour [*Umweg*]" through sensuousness into physical geometry becomes clear. On one side, the determinations of the understanding dominate, on the other, the intuited "superfluity of reality"—this contingent latter element being, as pure geometricians might say, "unnecessary" for the necessitated course of axiomatic thought.

To recall Einstein's remarks about the antithetical character of certainty and reality, it might be said that the certainty of pure geometric theory deductively advances from its axiomatic foundations towards the uncertainties of real experience, towards a possibly "mistaken" reality, and that physical geometry inductively falls back from this reality to the certainties of pure geometry. Both paths of thought, deductive and inductive, meet at the nexus of space-time, but neither can pass beyond that point. Pure geometry, such as developed from Hilbert's infinitely dimensional space, ends where physical geometry begins; and physical geometry, such as developed from Minkowski's world-lines, ends where pure geometry begins. The fixity and invariancy of geometric constructions is required by the understanding and is the basis of pure geometry. Confronting this understanding is that which Hegel terms the inchoate "asunderness of the sensuous itself."[27]

In so far as the *Encyclopedia*, of which the *Philosophy of Nature* is the second part, expresses the triadic articulation of the Absolute Idea in the forms of logic, nature, and spirit, it would be expected that the development of all three parts of the *Encyclopedia* would bear genetic resemblances one to another. Hegel himself drew attention to this.[28] In this case, the well-known introductory logical triad of being-nothing-becoming finds itself restated as the natural triad of space-time-motion.[29] The indifference of "pure being" in nature is reflected in the "mediationless indifference" of space (§254), and its abstract opposite, "nothing" is transformed into the "self-relating negation" of time (§257 Zus.). In this context, just as becoming is the first concrete category of logic, "the first concrete thought," so motion is the first concrete actuality of nature, the real consequence of the dialectical conjunction of the abstractions of space and time.[30] In themselves, time and space are merely the abstracted moments of motion following upon the reflective activity of understanding.

Space, as the "pure being" of nature, is the logical initiation of extensional being, that which is other than the intensional being of pure logic. Space is "the abstract *universality of Nature's self-externality*, self-externality's mediationless indifference" (§254). However, space has this indifferent [*gleichgültig*] character only when taken abstractly, on the initiating level of universal "otherness." When it is sensuously *intuited*, in its mediated form as expressed physical mass, it is presented as tri-dimensional. This physical matter, in the form of physical mass, is analogous to the logical category of determinate being, or *Dasein*. Tri-dimensionality is the first, and so indeterminate, expression of physical mass, and it is only at the immediate sensuous level that this triadic expression exists. As consistent non-Euclidean multidimensional geometries have developed, the "naturality" of tri-dimensional space is now taken to hold only for concrete apprehension, for image-thought, and not for the abstract reflections of pure geometry. Now it might seem that Hegel would have found this intuitive tri-dimensionality to be a confirmation of his own triadic interests. But he did not. Physical geometry, resting as it did upon the deliverance of intuition, could only assume those dimensions—not prove them. As Hegel observed:

> In so far as it is not a philosophical science, geometry may assume *the universal determinations of space* as its object, and it is not to be demanded of it that it should deduce the necessity of the three dimensions of space (§255 Anm.).

Intuitive tri-dimensionality is not derived from the concept of space. Indeed, spatial difference encountered in experience is merely a

> superficial and a completely empty difference. The reason, therefore, why it cannot be said how *height*, *length*, and *breadth* differ from each other is that these dimensions only *ought* to be different, but that they *are* not yet differences [*aber noch keine Unterschiede* sind] (§255 Zus.).

In sum, the quantitative dimensions of height, length, and breadth are merely different, not qualitatively determined. In other words, the sensuously apprehended three dimensions of space are *conceptually indifferent* one to another, and characterized by Hegel as "ganz bestimmungslose drei *Dimensionen.*"[31] There is no essential distinction between height, length and breadth other than that which is *desired*, that which *ought* to make a difference. The indeterminate directions of tri-dimensionality are thus derived from a desire to posit an operative space, just as the science of geometry is initiated by the positing of a "here," in its abstract form as an element in the understanding, as a "point"—a point which, in its actual physical expression, is a "place."

At the beginning of Hegel's *Philosophy of Right,* his *Philosophy of Nature*, and *Phenomenology of Spirit*, there is no prior specification or qualification of "desire," of what "ought to be." This intensional movement, as initially opposed to and determining the extensional, is merely, in Hegel's term "absolutely free will."[32]

In principle, then, Hegel's speculative geometry begins not with intuitive tri-dimensionality, nor "by saying nothing about the world," but rather with the *free positing* of the "point." The "point" is taken as the first qualitative negation of the merely quantitative and indeterminate self-externality of the concept of space. The point is defined as "the *negation* of space itself, because this is immediate *differenceless* self-externality. ... [T]he negation is the negation of *space*, i.e. it is itself spatial" (§256). For Hegel, the point is thus only "in" space as the first specification of space as such.

Now, pure geometry establishes the point as a purely definitional entity, quite apart from intuited space. Physical geometry, on the other hand, takes the point as if it were *in* space, as a specification of a *given* indeterminate space. Nevertheless, the note of negativity in regard to the relation of the point to space to which Hegel draws attention appears in both pure and physical geometry. In pure geometry the "point" is merely defined consistent with the geometry in question and is regarded as only a specification of an unspecified geometric context. In physical geometry it is regarded as a specification of a specified geometric context—of a "real" or given space.

It is of interest to compare the definitions of a "point" as set forth in the opposing views of pure and physical geometry. The geometrician Richard Swineburne defines the point as understood by physical geometry:

> Physical geometry interprets the terms of physical space in their normal sense. Thus it interprets the term 'point' as a very, very small place, such as could be occupied by a material object, very, very small in diameter compared with the distances from other material objects with which we are concerned.[33]

In this case, "concern" seems to be Swineburne's criterion of placement. Now, just as it is desire which intends the "here" of sense-certitude, so Hegel's "positing" of the "point" upon the undifferentiated expanse of space is also an expression of will or interest. However, the difference between Hegel and Swineburne is that Swineburne's definition of a point as understood by physical geometry rests entirely upon the spatial *intuitions* of material objects. In this case, the conception of a "point" does not initiate a *logically* generated geometry but rests upon the actual and prior presence of tri-dimensional physical mass. Nevertheless, for both Hegel and Swineburne, a "point" can be placed at will and so is an intended place.

On the side of "pure" geometry, such as that of Hilbert, the question of giving a definition to a point is simply left unspecified—although whatever definition it is given must be consistent with the other definitions of the geometry, and the "point" must be the first element. In Swineburne's text: "The basic element of pure geometry is the point, a term usually left undefined."[34] Or again, as a commentator upon Hilbert's system noted: "The unavoidable use of undefined terms leaves us free to assign to the words 'point,' 'line,' 'plane,' any meaning consistent with the axioms to be stated."[35] In a manner of speaking, the point is to be nowhere.

It would not be surprising here to find that Hegel's systematic approach to this "basic element," the geometric point, avoids fixing upon either side of the definitional dilemma while yet retaining the immanent truth of both. On the one hand, "it is not permissible to speak of *points in space*, as if they constituted the positive element of space" (§254 Anm.). On the other hand, it is nevertheless the case that a point is a qualified negation of indifferent physical dimensionality—and to that extent is "physical" or "real." A point, as a "here," as a referent, would lose that spatial significance if taken merely as an unqualified *ens rationis*. However, in so far as a point, taken according to its initial abstract meaning, is only negatively related to the actual externality of space, it is to that extent not located within intuited space and hence is a "logical" entity. From a Hegelian perspective, the difference between the "logical" or "pure" point of Hilbert's geometry and the "physical" point of Max Born's empirical geometry is that the latter is the dialectically or speculatively articulated conclusion of the former. That is, the physical point, the "here," which is a place, can be understood as the natural concretization of the progressing logic of reason which, from the abstract premise of the "pure" point, advanced to a conclusion which was the formation of actual physical mass. To know that one is in a "place" and to be able thereby to construct a physical geometry reflective of that placement requires the presence of self-consciousness. But this consciousness, as reason, comprehends that that which confronts it as a consistent actual world is *itself* a logical result. As Hegel has it, *"Was vernünftig ist, das ist wirklich; und was wirklich ist, das ist vernünftig."* For the Hegelian, this adage holds as good for geometry as it does for political theory.

From its initial intensionality, the "pure" point, in accord with its own immanent negativity, its "self-sublating" (*sich aufhebend*) character, immediately displaces itself as a linear moment. However, it is not that with the generation of the line two exclusive geometric elements are given—the point and the line—but rather that the line is the further self-negation of the point. In terms of physical geometry a line might be termed, a "displaced point." The logic of linearity follows the same path as punctuality, and so displaces itself into the plane. This, in its turn, is displaced into the enclosing surface, which "divides off and separates a distinct part of space." The dialectic of abstract geometrical self-displacement reaches its conclusion and truth in time, wherein the fully developed manifold of spatial figurations is displaced *in toto*. Each element or figure is a moment of nature's negative logic of incremental self-externalization. This articulation of space through its various geometric qualifications or figurations to the threshold of time is set forth in one concise paragraph, a paragraph which concludes Hegel's direct study of geometry and space:

> The difference of space [as opposed to merely quantitative dimensional difference] is, however, essentially a determinate, qualitative difference. As such, it is (a) first, the negation of space itself, because this is immediate *differenceless* self-externality, the *point*. (b) But the negation is the negation of *space*, i.e., it is itself spatial. The point, as essentially this relation, i.e. as sublating itself, is the *line*, the first other-being, i.e. spatial being, of the point. (c) The truth of other-being is, however, negation of the negation. The line consequently passes over into the plane, which, on the one hand, is a determinateness opposed to line and point, and so surface, simply as such, but, on the other hand, is the sublated negation of space. It is thus the restoration of the spatial totality which now contains the negative moment within itself, and *enclosing surface* a *single* whole space (§256).

Hegel's systematic unfolding of the pure geometric moments leading from space to time is unique in the history of geometry. However, it can be added that in treating the category of space before that of time, Hegel is in agreement with the general view of most theoretical physicists.[36] Other approaches to the ordering of these elements, even when they are defined, take them simply as independent constructs requiring the application of an external logic, generally mathematical, to render them interdependent. This seems to be the function of matrix algebra.[37]

In 1908 Hermann Minkowski profoundly influenced the course of modern physics by introducing the idea of the "world-line." In introducing this idea, Minkowski sounds quite Hegelian:

> The views of space and time which I wish to lay before you have sprung from the soil of experimental physics, and therein lies their strength. They are radical. Henceforth space by itself, and time by itself, are doomed to fade away into mere shadows, and only a kind of union of the two will preserve an independent reality.[38]

However, that time and space were not disjoined, and that both were actual only in their union, was stated by Hegel long before Minkowski. In Hegel's words, "In pictorial thought space and time are taken to be quite separate: we have space and *also* time; philosophy fights against this 'also'" (§257 Zus.).

The difference between the two is that Minkowski has only provided a more adequate measure of physical events, a refinement of physical geometry. He did not propose, as Hegel did, that space itself generated time, and that time, in its turn, reflected back upon space in the form of enduring matter. In regard to the so-called "fourth dimension"—usually credited to Minkowski—it is, as Moritz Schlick noted, only the introduction of time as a factor affecting metric considerations, and not the introduction of another quasi-spatial reality.[39]

The category of time not only concludes the syllogism of space, but the logic of pure geometry as well. From the moment that time is introduced, motion, duration, and physical mass emerge, and with this the whole actuality of physical reality. Motion ensues, and when motion ensues, so does matter; and with matter emerges the full actuality of physical reality. The truth of space and time is confirmed in the intuition of sense and the exercise of physical geometry.

In the passage beyond the abstract categories of space and time, the further self-unfoldings of extensional reality are first revealed in the category of place, then in motion, then in matter. In the interplay of space and time,

> their unity is manifested only as a movement of transition of the one into the other. But it is precisely the result which enunciates their ground and truth. What persists is the equality-with-self into which time has retreated; this is space. ... The point exists here in its truth. ... This unity of Here and Now is Place (§260 Zus.).

Indeed, it is not merely the physical place, the enduring concrete point, which exists within the interplay of space-time, but all of the other actual spatial directions, linear or curved, which provide the shapes of physical geometry. What, from the side of pure geometry, were axiomatic abstract figurations, are, from the moment in which the categories of space and time interact, returned to intuition as concrete extensions, actual physical vectors. Were it here possible, it would be of interest to examine Hegel's treatment of circular motion, which, as self-referential gyroscopic rotation,[40] suggests Riemann's geodesic geometry of "constant positive curvature."[41] For Hegel,

> It is in circular motion that the necessary paralysis [i.e., the metric fixation of space-time in geometric thought] of these dimensions is first posited in space. Circular motion is the spatial or subsistent unity of the dimension of time (§261 Zus.).

This circular motion as "motion extinguished within itself" considered as self-centered rotational mass might well provide a speculative link between Riemann's geometry and Einstein's General Theory. The metric link alone is found in Einstein's employment of Riemann's geometry, in which the closed geodesic circle replaces the Euclidean flat plane. This metric substitution enabled Einstein to establish his General Theory of Relativity. Before this, physicists were forced to accept the Newtonian gravitational theory and its inexplicable premise of action at a distance; after Einstein they were able to describe gravitational effects in the less mysterious form of geometric fluctuations of space. In sum, with both Einstein and Hegel, the category of space and its geometry is logically prior to that of physical mass and gravitational force.

In conclusion, I will add that Hegel's geometric theory, when understood as expressing itself in the Riemannian grounding of force in geometry[42], might well provide a philosophical basis for that most recent of recent physical theories, the so-called "superstring" theory of matter. In this, the ever-elusive particle of particle physics, the so-called "point-particle," is not taken to be a particle, but a harmonic fluctuation, "about 100 billion billion times smaller than a proton."[43] As one of its advocates asserts, it goes beyond Einsteinian physics, and presents itself as "a comprehensive theory of both matter-energy and space-time." That a search for the philosophical basis of this theory might be found in Hegel's speculative geometry is suggested in this citation from the Princeton physicist, David Gross:

> To build matter itself from geometry—that in a sense is what string theory does. It can be thought of that way, ... a theory ... which is inherently a theory of gravity in which the particles of matter as well as the other forces of nature emerge in the same way that gravity emerges from geometry.[44]

I would submit that this conception of matter emerging from geometry accords with Hegel's own logic of nature. However, to say that either Einstein's General Theory or the recent "superstring" theory can find justification in Hegel's speculative geometry must remain here only as a suggestion for a future project. In this regard, there is also the matter of how speculative geometry might help to resolve the conflict that exists between n-dimensional geometries and the other so-called "congruence" geometries. These latter geometries are limited to Euclidean, Spherical and Hyperbolic geometries. These geometries in principle hold that "all spatial forms are invariant under translation and rotations,"[45] and they follow the direction laid out by Felix Klein in his development of the implications of Euclid's

Fourth Postulate—the same one that had most interest for Hegel. On the other hand, n-dimensional geometries rest directly upon numerical analysis for their development, and have moved even further away from the possibility of sensuous intuition than "congruence" geometries. Needless to say, this short paper can only propose that these unreconciled areas of geometric theory might well profit by a reconsideration of Hegel's speculative theory.

I will conclude with another's conclusion. Julian Lowell Coolidge, in his well-regarded work, *A History of Geometrical Method*, ends his extensive study with an Epilogue which begins by asking the question, "Can we draw any general conclusions from the five-thousand year story we have now completed?"[46] His answer is that, although there has been progress in the generalization of theory, particular problems still remain—such as the "four-colour map problem." And then, in a surprizing ending, Coolidge, in his final sentences, brings up a thought and a name which hitherto did not earlier appear in his history of geometry:

> The tendency to generalize in geometry will continue but we shall never lose all interest in particular results. Perhaps the correct formula was given years ago by one of the last of the Hegelians, Edward Caird, who said, somewhat cryptically, that it was the task of philosophy "to combine the universal and the particular in a higher unity."

Well, although Caird was a good Hegelian, he wasn't the last, and that a geometrician should find, however "cryptic," a "correct formula" from a Hegelian reflects Hegel's own confidence that "a time will come when this science will require for its satisfaction the philosophical notion."

Notes

1. *Hegel's Philosophy of Nature. Being Part Two of the Encyclopedia of the Philosophical Sciences (1830)*, translated by A. V. Miller (Oxford: Clarendon Press, 1970), §270 Zus. Subsequent references to the *Philosophy of Nature* will be placed in the main body of the text after the relevant citation.

2. John D. Barrow, *The World Within the World* (Oxford: Oxford University Press, 1988), pp. 109-10.

3. Max Jammer, *Concepts of Space* (Cambridge: Cambridge University Press, 1970), pp. 129-30.

4. See Herbert Schnädelbach, *Philosophy in Germany, 1831-1933*, translated by Eric Matthews (Cambridge: Cambridge University Press, 1984), pp. 66ff; also the "Göttingen Tradition of Mathematical Physics" in Vladimir P. Vizgin, "The Geometrical Unified Field Theory Program" in *Einstein and the History of General Relativity*, edited by D. Howard and J. Stachel (Boston: Birkhäuser, 1986), pp. 303ff.

5. One of the few attempts to reconcile Kantian theory to the new physics is the work of Alfred C. Elsbach, *Kant und Einstein: Untersuchungen über das Verhältnis der modernen Erkenntnistheorie zur Relativitätstheorie* (Berlin: de Gruyter, 1924). After a lengthy and rather strained argument, Elsbach can only come to the weak conclusion that, although "[Kantianism] might be thought of as an obstacle to the development of physics" (p. 201), the two theories are "not incompatible" (p. 368).

6. Roberto Bonola, *Non-Euclidean Geometry*, translated by H. S. Carslaw (New York: Dover Publications, 1955), p. 121.

7. R. Carnap, *Philosophical Foundations of Physics: An Introduction to the Philosophy of Science* (New York: Basic Books, 1966), p. 180.

8. G.W.F. Hegel, *Lectures on the History of Philosophy*, translated by E.S. Haldane and Frances H. Simson, 3 Vols (London: Routledge & Kegan Paul, 1955), **3**: 436.

9. Cited from *The Leibniz-Clarke Correspondence: With Extracts from Newton's PRINCIPIA and OPTICKS*, edited by H. G. Alexander (Manchester: Manchester University Press, 1970), p. 152.

10. B. Russell, *The Principles of Mathematics* (London: Allen & Unwin, 1938).

11. Carnap, *Philosophical Foundations of Physics*, pp. 182-3

12. H. Poincaré, "Space and Geometry," in *The World of Physics*, edited by J.H. Weaver (New York: Simon and Schuster, 1987), p. 118.

13. Carnap, *Philosophical Foundations of Physics*, p. 183.

14. Carnap, *Philosophical Foundations of Physics*, pp. 181-2.

15. M. Born, *Einstein's Theory of Relativity* (New York: Dover Publications, 1965), p. 333.

16. Edna E. Kramer, *The Nature and Growth of Modern Mathematics* (Princeton: Princeton University Press, 1970), p. 42.

17. H. S. M. Coxeter, *Non-Euclidean Geometry* (Toronto: University of Toronto Press, 1978), p. 4.

18. Barrow, *The World within the World*, p. 255.

19. Barrow, *The World within the World*, p. 257.

20. Carnap, *Philosophical Foundations of Physics*, p. 288.

21. Hans Reichenbach, *Philosophic Foundations of Quantum Mechanics* (Berkeley: University of California Press, 1944).

22. *Dokumente zu Hegels Entwicklung*, edited by Johannes Hoffmeister (Stuttgart: Frommann-Holzboog, 1974), pp. 288-300.

23. Kramer, *The Nature and Growth of Modern Mathematics*, p. 406. Klein accepted the superimposition of geometric figures as a key for extending Euclidean geometry into a "study of the properties unchanged by the group of all rigid motions [i.e., fundamentally invariant in terms of distance and angle] ... that [assume] the effects of motion must leave size *invariant*." It is upon the basis of Klein's critique of the congruency postulate that the whole of his subsequent geometry developed.

24. G.W.F.Hegel, *Jenaer Systementwürfe II. Logik, Metaphysik, Naturphilosophie*, edited by R.-P. Horstmann (Hamburg: Felix Meiner, 1982), p. 18.

25. G.W.F. Hegel, *Science of Logic*, translated by A.V. Miller (Atlantic Highlands, NJ: Humanities Press International, 1989), pp. 809-10. (Hereafter cited as Miller, *Logic*, pp. 809-10.)

26. Miller, *Logic*, pp. 809-810.

27. Miller, *Logic*, p. 813.

28. See Vittorio Hösle, "Raum, Zeit, Bewegung," in *Hegel und die Naturwissenschaften*, edited by Michael J. Petry (Stuttgart: Frommann-Holzboog, 1986), pp. 258-60.

29. The congruency of the triads initiating *Logic* and *Nature* is also found in the *Phenomenology of Spirit*. Here, "sense-certainty"

is linked to the initiating categories of "*pure being*" and space: "*Pure being* remains, therefore, as the essence of this sense-certainty," (*Hegel's Phenomenology of Spirit*, translated by A.V. Miller [Oxford: Oxford University Press, 1977], §99). By introducing "sense-certainty" through a discussion of the "this" in the form of a "here" at the first level of consciousness, Hegel has linked sense-certainty to the first category of logic (being) as well as to the first category of nature (space). Hence, in the *Phenomenology* the initiating triad of sense-certainty, perception, and understanding can be superimposed upon the initiating triads of the *Logic* (Being-Nothing-Becoming), and *Nature* (Space-Time-Motion).

30. "It is in motion that Space and Time first acquire actuality," *Hegel's Philosophy of Nature*, §261 Zus.

31. An illuminating survey of various failed attempts to provide a rationale for tri-dimensionality can be found in G. J. Witrow, "Why Physical Space has Three Dimensions," *The British Journal for the Philosophy of Science* 6 (1956): 13-31.

32. G.W.F. Hegel, *Elements of the Philosophy of Right*, translated by H.B. Nisbet, edited by A. Wood (Cambridge: Cambridge University Press, 1991), §34.

33. Richard Swineburne, *Space and Time* (New York: Macmillian, 1968), p. 150.

34. Swineburne, *Space and Time*, p. 150.

35. Herbert Menschkowski, *Noneuclidean Geometry*, translated by A. Shenitzer (New York: Academic Press, 1964), p. 8.

36. See Jammer, *Concepts of Space*, pp. 5-6. "Historically and psychologically, a discussion of space is preferable to that of time, since most probably the category of space preceded that of time as an object of consciousness."

37. Kramer, *The Nature and Growth of Modern Mathematics*, p. 418ff.

38. H. Minkowski, "Space and Time," in *Problems of Space and Time*, edited by J.J.C. Smart (New York: Macmillan, 1964), p. 297.

39. M. Schlick, "The Four-Dimensional World," in *Problems of Space and Time*, edited by J.J.C. Smart, p. 297. "The description of nature is solely a question of spatio-temporal coincidences. The meaning and scope of this proposition is most clearly demon-

strated—according to Minkowski's method—by a graphical representation in which time is introduced as the fourth co-ordinate in addition to the other three spatial co-ordinates."

40. On the relationship between "gyroscopic" motion and physical mass, see Dieter Wandschneider, "The Problem of Mass in Hegel," in *Hegel and Newtonianism*, edited by M.J. Petry (Dordrecht: Kluwer, 1993).

41. Carnap, *Philosophical Foundations of Physics*, p. 142.

42. See Michio Kaku, *Hyperspace: A Scientific Odyssey through Parallel Universes, Time Warps, and the 10th Dimension* (New York: Oxford University Press, 1994), pp. 36ff.

43. Kaku, p. 153.

44. Cited by Kaku, p. 157.

45. Edward R. Harrison, *Cosmology: The Science of the Universe* (Cambridge: Cambridge University Press, 1981), p. 148.

46. J. L. Coolidge, *A History of Geometrical Method* (New York: Dover, 1963), p. 423.

5

How to Save the Phenomena: Meaning and Reference in Hegel's Philosophy of Nature

Brigitte Falkenburg

1. Introduction

The relation between Hegel's philosophy of nature and the empirical sciences has remained unclear for a long time. Hegel's attitude towards physical theory, for example his sharp criticism of Newtonian science, has always provoked controversy. Some interpreters have taken it as a crude and ignorant misunderstanding of the science of the day;[1] others have considered it to foreshadow basic ideas in 20th century physics, e.g. relativity.[2] Such contrasting views of Hegel's philosophy of nature coincide, however, in so far as they disregard Hegel's own view of the very complex relationship between the tasks of a "speculative" philosophy of nature, the tasks of empirical science, and the structure of the phenomena which are the subject of these two disciplines.

An adequate view of Hegel's philosophy of nature can be achieved only on the basis of a careful investigation of the interrelations between Hegel's philosophy of nature, physical theory, and the phenomena. In a previous essay, I began such an investigation on a more specific level, with regard to Hegel's criticism of mechanistic models of light.[3] Here, I want to address the issue of these interrelations in a more general way. My central concerns, however, remain the same: How do the empirical sciences relate to the structures of natural phenomena, and how does Hegel's philosophy of nature relate to these structures? And how do his concepts relate to the structure and theoretical contents of empirical science? In the last analysis, these questions aim at understanding the most problematic (and most misunderstood) topic concerning his philosophy: how to identify and comprehend the *criteria* for the "self-determination of the Concept," and for establishing the relation of the Concept to the contents of empirical science. Hegel's philosophy of nature was quite often considered to be an *a priori* theory of nature.[4] The conclusion of my present investigation will differ from such a view: Hegel does not aim at an *a priori* theory of nature, either in a Kantian or in an empiricist sense.

Before giving a sketch of the structure of my paper, I would like to make some general remarks concerning Hegel and the empirical sciences. First, it should be kept in mind that the phenomena which are the subject of empirical science are not the empiricist's sense data. They are *regularized empirical observations*. The phenomena of empirical science are not "given" in a straightforward way, because they are theory-dependent; they are *structured* phenomena.[5] Hegel and the science of his day differed mainly on the question of *how* to structure the phenomena, or, to use an ancient topos, they differed on the question of *how to save the phenomena*, in the various levels and domains of theory-formation. A most important difference between them is that Newtonian science is directed towards establishing unified theories, whereas Hegel's philosophy conceives of nature as made up of phenomenal structures of increasing degrees of complexity, to which quite distinct conceptual structures apply.

Secondly, the subject under investigation, the interrelations between Hegel's philosophy, empirical science, and the phenomena, is expressed here in terms of *correspondence*. Our question is how theoretical concepts of two different types correspond to "the phenomena." The usual problems in understanding Hegel arise, in the last analysis, from an empiricist view of science and the related correspondence *criterion* of truth. It is well known that Hegel abandoned the correspondence criterion of truth in favor of an 'idealistic' *coherence* criterion. Yet, to what extent does he think that philosophical concepts nevertheless do correspond to the phenomena? In regard to natural philosophy, Hegel has a precursor in Kant. Although Kant adhered to the traditional correspondence view of truth, he attempted to comprehend the general structure of nature, or of the phenomena, in terms of *construction* rather than correspondence. Contrary to Hegel, Kant identified the general structure of nature with *a priori* laws which are supposed to guarantee that the axioms of Newtonian mechanics are necessary and universally valid.

Thirdly, Hegel's philosophy of nature was discredited due to its lack of accord with the structure of empirical science and its lack of accord with science's most successful developments during the nineteenth century. The development of nineteenth century science was dominated by two traditions. One of them entailed the elaboration of Newtonian science and the application of mechanical thought and explanation in new theoretical domains. In the end, this "mechanical" tradition led to Maxwell's and Boltzmann's attempts at grounding field theory on a mechanical model of the ether and grounding thermodynamics on kinetic theory or on atomism. The other development was the rise of empiricism within the empirical sciences, culminating in Mach's demand for a "phenomenological" physics dispensing with unobservable entities such as forces or atoms. Both traditions ran counter to Hegel's philosophy of nature as a speculative *metaphysics*, although they also ran counter to each other (as the Boltzmann-Mach controversy shows).[6] Nevertheless, one of these views of physical theory, namely the empiricist criticism of unobservables such as forces and atoms, was completely in the spirit of Hegel's own *phenomenological* attitude towards *physics* itself, and his sharp criticism of the Newtonian, ontological interpretation of atoms and forces.

The above observations suggest that we investigate how Hegel's way of saving the phenomena differs, on the one hand, from Newtonian science and, on the other, from Kant's way of *constructing* the phenomena in a Newtonian way (instead of *saving* them). Since two competing criteria of truth are involved in the opposition between Hegel's way and the Newtonian way of saving the phenomena, emphasis will be laid on the question of the *meaning* and *reference* of scientific concepts. This question is indeed crucial for correctly understanding Hegel's conceptualization of the phenomena and the rather different way in which Newtonian science conceives of them.

My main thesis is that Hegel's way of saving the phenomena is based on a shift from the usual *extensional view* of science to a *non-extensional* (or: *intensional*) view of scientific concepts. An extensional view of scientific concepts—in the modern, non-Leibnizian sense—is realized in Newton's concept of mass which relies on atomism, or in Kant's theory of pure intuition which supplies the concepts of pure understanding with a possible domain of application. Similarly, twentieth century philosophy of science is based on an extensional (set-theoretical) view of the mathematical structure of physical theory. Contrary to this, Hegel's view of the meaning and reference of philosophical concepts is *not* based on extensions which are given as classes of entities representing natural kinds (Newton), or provided by the schematism of pure understanding (Kant), or defined within set theory (modern logic). Hegel's concepts deal only with the conceptual content of concepts and of their relations. Their meaning is non-extensional and they refer to other concepts.

A good starting point for the explication and defense of this thesis is the famous, though obscure, §246 of the 1830 *Encyclopedia*:[7]

> What is now called *physics*, was formerly called *natural philosophy*. Physics is likewise theoretical, and indeed *thinking* consideration of nature. On the one hand, this consideration does not start from considerations which are external to nature, as those purposes are. [Hegel here refers to §245. –B.F.] On the other hand, its aim is cognition of that which is *universal* in nature, in such a way that it should be *determinate* in itself—the forces, laws, genera, which content additionally must not be a mere aggregate, but, put into orderings and classes, must exhibit an organized form. In that the philosophy of nature is *comprehending* consideration, its object is the same *universal*; it is however the universal *for itself*, which is considered in its *own immanent necessity*, according to the self-determination of the Concept.

The paragraph can be divided into two parts. First, Hegel sketches his view of Newtonian science, i.e. of "natural philosophy" in the earlier, traditional, sense. Secondly, he gives a characterization of his own philosophy of nature and its tasks. I shall analyze each part of §246 in two steps, one preparatory and one analytical. First, the aim of Newtonian science will be explained from a modern point of view (section 2). Then, Hegel's view of Newtonian science will be explained with reference to the first part of §246 (section 3). In the next step, I shall sketch Hegel's criticism of Kant's constructional view of nature (section 4). Finally, I will attempt to give an understanding of Hegel's view of the logic of nature, as it is revealed in the second part of §246; then I will return to the issue of the interrelations between Hegel's concepts, empirical science, and the phenomena (section 5).

2. How to Save the Phenomena in a Newtonian Way

In the beginning of §246, Hegel refers to "natural philosophy" as "physics," the usual meaning of the expression in Newton's day. Newton, Locke, and their contemporaries used "natural philosophy," "physics," or "experimental philosophy" synonymously. The experimental science now called physics was initiated by Galileo's investigations. It was a new science in Newton's day, based on Galileo's experimental method, and it was first put on an axiomatic basis in the *Philosophiae naturalis principia mathematica*. Newton's expression "natural philosophy" reminds us that physical theory, although relying on experiment rather than mere observation, is indebted to the cognitive goals of both ancient cosmology and modern astronomy as founded by Copernicus and Kepler. The aim of Newtonian science is *to save the phenomena*. This is an ancient expression which dates back to Eudoxus and which had been used in astronomy for a long time.[8] It indicates the unification of the most complex and apparently diverse phenomena by means of a unique theoretical description. Such a unification, however, is not only considered to be a device for achieving a most simple and economical description of the phenomena.

In Newtonian science as well as in astronomy, to save the phenomena means to unify them by explaining them, or, to put it another way, to explain on the basis of a coherent theory *why* the observed phenomena are as diverse and complicated as they are. We may say, therefore, that the meaning of the ancient astronomical expression, *to save the phenomena*, comes close to a view which identifies explanation and unification—a view of explanation which was advanced in recent philosophy of science by M. Friedman.[9]

In physical theory dating back to Newton's *Principia*, the unifying power and explanatory import of a unique description of diverse phenomena relies on the assumption of forces, which are axiomatized in the fundamental laws of a *dynamics*. The most significant achievement of the *Principia* was to explain Galileo's law of free fall and Kepler's laws from a common dynamics within a theory of universal gravitation. Newton's law of gravitation made it possible to unify terrestrial and celestial phenomena which were kept strictly apart by pre-Newtonian physics. Both kinds of phenomena were unified by an explanation from a common dynamic cause, the gravitational force. The unification was obtained by applying one and the same law under different boundary conditions. Such a unification, however, is essentially based on idealization and approximation, a price which Hegel refused to pay when attempting to re-establish an Aristotelian distinction between terrestrial (or finite) and celestial (or absolute) mechanics.[10]

The theoretical structures of physics, or of Newtonian science, describe the spatio-temporal features of the phenomena and their dynamic relations in the language of mathematics. From a formal point of view, a physical theory has two components: its *mathematics* and its physical *semantics*. According to modern (empiricist) philosophy of science, these components represent the distinction between a formal structure which *per se* has no meaning and reference, and an empirical interpretation which *fixes* the meaning and reference of the formal structure. From an empiricist point of view, it is desirable to axiomatize the formal structure of a theory in terms of set-theoretical structures, and to reconstruct the semantics in terms of empirical correspondence rules which are construed as maps from some part of the theory to some class of empirical phenomena. Obviously, according to such correspondence rules, the meaning of theoretical terms is given by their extensions.

Within "real" physics, however, the structure of a theory is not expressed in such a neat axiomatic way, nor is the semantics of a theory presented in terms of the well-determined extensions of theoretical concepts. The formal part of a theory is usually given as a mathematical structure which consists of differential (or integro-differential) equations, a manifold of solutions, and boundary conditions which pick out specific solutions from this manifold. The semantics of a theory, on the other hand, is given in terms of physical quantities and their dimensions and scales. Only the scale of a physical quantity is extensional, while the dimension is intensional. Different dimensions refer to distinct physical qualities of the phenomena: distinct properties such as length, weight, temperature, electrostatic or magnetic behavior of bodies, etc. There are two types of quantities: spatio-temporal quantities such as position, velocity, and acceleration; and dynamic quantities such as mass, momentum, charge, force, etc. When a theory is considered to be complete with regard to its formal structure, it is ripe for mathematical axiomatization. It turns out to be much more problematic to fix the empirical domains of a theory and its concepts. It is extremely difficult to reconstruct the meaning of physical quantities in terms of empirical extensions of given physical properties or of classes of phenomena of a given type which are independently fixed. One problem lies in the laws which relate the distinct quantities specified by a physical theory to each other. According to these laws, the extensions of theoretical terms cannot be given independently of each other. Another problem (which is closely related in physical theory) is the existence of co-extensive properties such as inertial and gravitational mass. Due to both, the meaning of physical quantities depends on theory.

Nevertheless, the semantics of the spatio-temporal quantities of physics has been considered unproblematic for a long time, at least as long as the theories of relativity were disregarded. In Newton's *Principia*, the meaning of the spatio-temporal quantities was simply presupposed. As Newton expressed it in the famous Scholium to the Definitions in the *Principia*, "I do not define time, space, place, and motion, as being well known to all."[11] At least with regard to the measurable (that is, non-absolute) spatio-temporal quantities, Newton's procedure could be taken as correct until the rise of relativity. The crucial part of the semantics of Newtonian science was the meaning and reference of the *dynamic* quantities, such as mass, force, charge, etc. Within empiricist attempts to reconstruct the structure of empirical theories, no agreement has been achieved about how to fix the dynamic interpretation of a physical theory uniquely in terms of correspondence rules. Within physics, the meaning of mass, charge etc. is given pragmatically in terms of operational instructions which are, however, only of restricted validity in the total scales of such quantities.

Newton attempted to fix the meaning of mass, momentum and force by *explicit definitions*. He defined mass as the product of density and volume, momentum as the product of mass and velocity, and (impressed) force as the external action which changes the state of rest or uniform rectilinear motion of a body. It is very important to notice that Newton's definitions were not circular, as Mach had objected later from an empiricist point of view. They were based on *referential* claims which were not made explicit within the definitions, since they were not subject to the mechanical laws and mathematical principles of the *Principia*. Newton's definition of mass becomes meaningless when split off from the hypothesis of *atomism*, according to which the mass of a body is in the last analysis reducible to the number of its atoms. Atomism was defended in the Queries in the *Opticks*, on the basis of analogical inferences which explain the structure of matter and its interaction with light in terms of mechanical models and analogies. For

Newton, the assumption of the existence of atoms was indeed much more than a mere hypothesis. He regarded it as correctly deduced (or inferred) from the phenomena in accordance with the four basic rules of reasoning given in the third book of the *Principia*, the methodological principles which restrict the admitted types of theoretical explanation.[12] With regard to atomism, the crucial principle is Rule III. It expresses the necessary and sufficient criteria for those qualities of matter which are primary, or which are the universal properties of all bodies:

> The qualities of bodies, which admit neither intensification nor remission of degrees, and which are found to belong to all the bodies within the reach of our experiments, are to be esteemed the universal qualities of all bodies whatsoever.[13]

All qualities fulfilling these criteria belong to the very concept of a body. They are the primary qualities of bodies in Galileo's, Descartes's, or Locke's sense. Newton lists "extension, hardness, impenetrability, mobility, and inertia,"[14] that is, what we now call the extensive quantities of macroscopic mechanical bodies. According to Rule III, they apply to all parts of such bodies. In the last analysis they apply to the atoms whose existence is assumed as part of the foundation of natural philosophy, or the foundation of any theoretical explanation of natural phenomena:

> and hence we conclude the least particles of all bodies to be also all extended, and hard and impenetrable, and movable, and endowed with their proper inertia. And this is the foundation of all philosophy.[15]

Obviously, Newton's own use of Rule III was to confirm that the explicit definition of mass refers to the number of atoms in a body of given matter and volume, and to "their proper inertia" as an irreducible quality of the atoms. In this regard, the meaning of mass is extensional in the *Principia*.

The mass of a body is simply the number of atomic masses in it.

Although the meaning of Newton's concept of impressed force is less clear, it is also based on a referential claim, providing it with an extensional meaning. The explicit definition of force relies on the existence of the (unknown) causes of the actions which change the state of motion of mechanical bodies. Although Newton had no quantitative theory about them, he was convinced that they should be identified with the effects of the ether, or of absolute space, on the atoms.

Newton's definitions of mass and force seem questionable from a modern point of view, because it has been known since the time of Hilbert's analysis of the axiomatic method that the terms or concepts in the axioms of a theory cannot be defined explicitly. According to that view, the explanation of mass in terms of atoms, and of gravitational force in terms of an unknown cause which was localized in the effects of an immaterial ether on matter, belong simply to another theory and not to mechanics. When restricted to a mechanics of macroscopic bodies, Newton's definition of mass is indeed as circular as Mach had claimed. It should be observed, however, that these explicit definitions cannot be replaced completely by implicit definitions based on the axioms of Newtonian mechanics. They have to be considered as irreducibly *extensional* in two quite different regards, since they are based on two kinds of *correspondence rule*. First, the concepts of mass and force correspond to *empirical observations* such as the weight of a body,[16] and to the non-uniform and non-rectilinear movements of terrestrial and celestial bodies. In this regard, these concepts have a referential meaning which is established by empirical correspondence and which may be expressed purely in terms of spatio-temporal quantities and their dimensionless ratios. Secondly, they correspond to the *unobservable causes* of such phenomena, that is, to atoms, and to their interactions with each other which (in Newton's view) are mediated by the ether. Newton considered the assumption of such causes to be legitimated by the application of his rules of reasoning, especially Rule I (the famous principle of the true causes which are sufficient to explain the appearances) and Rule IV (the principle of the exclusion of contrary hypotheses). In this regard, Newton's definitions have to be spelled out in terms of reference to unobservable entities. His concepts of mass and force have their referential meaning established by correspondence to atoms and their primary qualities (and their interactions with an immaterial substance, the ether or absolute space). This second kind of correspondence is fundamental in Newton's view.

So it has to be concluded that the meaning of the concepts of mass and force in the *Principia* is *extensional*. From Newton's point of view, the meaning of these terms is reducible to classes of particular bodies and their atomic constituents, or to the entities which carry physical properties and which constitute the domain of the application of the concepts of mass and force. From an empiricist point of view, the extension of mass and force is reducible to macroscopic, observable bodies and their accelerations. From both points of view, the intra-theoretical meaning of dynamic quantities such as mass and force is based on extensions, on the classes of bodies and their accelerated motions. For Newton, the class of bodies of a given mass is ultimately defined by a given number of atoms constituting a body. The extension of the mass *scale* is then given by the class of all bodies made up of any arbitrary (finite) number of atoms. Each mass *value* corresponds to a subclass. The class may be considered as made up of *individuals* in a logical sense, which are the members of a set in which the laws of mechanics are valid. It may be considered also to be made up of *substances* in a traditional (Lockean) sense, that is, of carriers of the properties, relations, etc. which were attributed to matter in natural philosophy. Newton conceived of properties subject to the application of Rule III as the primary qualities of all bodies, and he identified the carriers of them with the atoms.

It should be noted that Newtonian science, as based on the *Principia*, is associated with several *completeness claims* which provoked Hegel's criticism, and which turned out to be problematic also from the point of view of physics, as the twentieth-century development of physical theory has shown. Rule III, the principle from which Newton's atomism derives, supports analogical inferences which are simply invalid from a modern point of view. The rule proposes that the structure of macroscopic phenomena recurs in any physical realm, or that the spatio-temporal and dynamic quantities of mechanics can be attributed to all bodies of all sizes and in any part of the universe. So, first, two distinct *spatio-temporal* completeness claims derive from this principle, namely the claim concerning the universal validity of Newtonian mechanics for all length scales of matter, and the claim concerning its universal validity for all regions of space. Second, it is well-known that Newtonian mechanics gives a complete spatio-temporal and dynamical description of motions. Thus it implies a *dynamic* completeness, i.e. a completeness of the dynamic description of the state of a physical system, which today is restricted to a non-quantum domain. Third, Newtonian science purports to achieve a *systematic* completeness regarding the boundary conditions of different types of motion. The planetary movements are described by one type of conic section, according to Kepler's laws, whereas the free fall of a body represents another type, according to Galileo's law. Only the systematic completeness of Newton's theory of gravitation, a theory which may be specified in a systematic way for several types of application, made it possible to put together in one theory such diverse phenomena as those described by Galileo's and by Kepler's laws. The systematicity of Newtonian science and the related completeness claims especially impressed Kant. However, all Newtonian completeness claims, spatio-temporal, dynamic, and systematic, were challenged by Hegel.

3. Hegel's View of Newtonian Science

Hegel's account of Newtonian science differs substantially from the characterization given above. The first part of §246 presents physics and its cognitive goals in a way which differs in several regards from Newton's own view of "natural philosophy." According to Hegel, no analogical inferences which argue from the observable phenomena back to unobservable causes are admitted. In the Remark to §246, Hegel criticizes any use which is made of analogies to demonstrate that the objects of our knowledge correspond to the empirical appearances.[17] What is more, any causal explanation of the phenomena seems questionable to him. It should be noted that he speaks of "forces" and "laws" in the same way that he speaks of "genera" in §246; for him, forces and laws denote natural kinds, just as the genera and species of organic nature do. They count as phenomenological, not causal, concepts of science.

Another crucial point of difference between Hegel's and Newton's views of physics is the role of the dynamic quantities. Contrary to Newton, Hegel takes basically the same methodological approach to both the dynamic and the spatio-temporal quantities of physics. He would not favor giving Newton's dynamic concepts an exceptional status in an empirical theory of nature. In his view, all concepts of physics share the common feature of being abstractions which do not deal with the concrete properties of the phenomena. They should all be introduced one after another, and related to each other in a systematic conceptual structure which compensates for such abstractions. For Hegel, a conceptual structure is better if it is more complete regarding the *differentia specifica* of the natural phenomena. In his view, it is methodologically arbitrary to give definitions for abstract dynamic quantities such as mass or force without making any attempt at defining the more abstract (and, from a physical point of view, more basic) quantities of space and time. According to Hegel, the very concept of a measurable physical quantity requires that physics should start by developing the spatio-temporal concepts first, and derive a concept of matter later, when considering the semantical deficiencies of the conceptual starting point.

The most substantial difference, however, is that between the Hegelian and Newtonian views of the *law-like structures* of the phenomena, or, in Hegel's terminology, of the "universal in nature." For Hegel, the theoretical concepts which are used to conceptualize law-like structures have an *intensional* meaning which is tied to their *structure*. In his view, the term 'universal' neither means empirical generality, nor denotes the completeness of a class of entities, nor refers to the extension of a concept under consideration. For him, the term 'universal' comes close to meaning 'particular type of law-like structure'. Since it is not obvious exactly what that means, I will come back to Hegel's intensional view of the "universal in nature" later (in section 5).

These striking differences suggest that Hegel has at least a partially *non-Newtonian* view of Newtonian science or physics. An analysis of the first part of §246 sheds more light on his view of physics. Hegel characterizes physics as "theoretical, and indeed, *thinking* consideration of nature." He recognizes two types of "theoretical consideration" of nature: physics (which was "formerly called natural philosophy") and natural philosophy proper (that is, a speculative philosophy of nature). The latter is "comprehending consideration" of nature, as opposed to the former which is "thinking consideration." Both have in common that they are *theoretical* disciplines, in the ancient sense of *theoria* which was represented by Aristotelian cosmology. In this regard, both are opposed to the *teleological* consideration of nature which is the subject of the preceding paragraph of the *Encyclopedia*, §245. They do not start from "determinations, which are external to nature, as those purposes are." That is, they do not start from external, or teleological, considerations which are expressed in terms of means and ends. Both disciplines are closely related in their cognitive content, that is, they are "thinking" and "comprehending" consideration of the universal structures of the phenomena.

The aim of physics is the "cognition of that which is *universal* in nature." We may reformulate this cognitive goal in terms of the Newtonian aim, *to save the phenomena*, which was discussed in section 2. In doing so, we should recall Hegel's criticism of causal explanations and note that for him, *to save the phenomena* has no explanatory import at all, contrary to Newton's rules of reasoning and the related search for the *true causes* of the phenomena. For Hegel, the phenomena are saved when their *structural* necessity is shown, or when the line is drawn between their contingent diversity and their necessary, or structural, features which are subject to theoretical concepts.

The structure of the phenomena, or the "universal in nature," is the subject of physics "in such a way that it should be determinate in itself," not in an abstract and general way, but as based on the *differentia specifica* of the phenomena. The cognitive goal of physics is the determination of the natural kinds, or specific phenomenological properties, of the appearances. It is "cognition of the forces, laws, genera" (*Kräfte*, *Gesetze*, *Arten*), where forces, laws, and genera are taken together in the same list of most abstract, or general, natural kinds. Physics is an *abstract* science which disregards the *most* specific properties of the phenomena, although it does also deal with the specific forces and laws of nature. The most specific properties of the phenomena are known from empirical observation and measurement. They are considered as contingent from a physical point of view. Such contingencies include the number of planets and the initial conditions of the planetary movements within the solar system, or the conditions of approximation which specify the general law of gravitation either into Kepler's laws or into Galileo's law, that is, the given ratios of the mass and distance of two gravitating bodies.

Hegel emphasizes in addition that physics has a *systematic* structure. The cognitive content of physics, that is, the forces, laws, and genera which are the subject of physics, "must not be a mere aggregate, but, put into orderings and classes, must exhibit an organized form." This is non-Newtonian again, but in a very special sense. The "organized form" of Newton's *Principia* is the formal structure of an axiomatic system modelled after Euclid's *Elements*. Newton's theory is not expressed in terms of the concepts, judgments, and syllogisms of traditional (Leibnizian) logic. It deals with axioms and theorems and with the phenomena and unobservable entities to which they apply. Hegel's view of empirical science, however, is very much influenced by Kant's or Leibniz's view of a theory, which is expressed in terms of concepts, judgments, and syllogisms. According to Leibnizian logic, the extension of a concept is the class of the *concepts* falling under it. Leibnizian logic deals with classes of *species* rather than classes of individuals. According to Leibniz, an individual is sufficiently individuated by its complete notion, a concept which results from an infinite conjunction of predicates. It is not an individual entity in space and time but an individual species. Kant's logical account of the extension of a concept is exactly the same when we disregard his theory of intuition and look only at his logic lectures—and we *should* disregard intuition in physics as well as in natural philosophy, according to Hegel. For Hegel, the content of physics which has to be put into classes and orderings is made up of neither the particular phenomena, nor any individual entities, nor any empirical content of intuition *à la* Kant, but rather of the *properties* of the phenomena. These properties are put into an organized form within a conceptual system which is based on the *classification* of the intensions and reciprocal extensions of concepts in a Leibnizian sense. Such a conceptual system is generated by means of the logical operations of conjunction and disjunction, which operate on predicates, and the subsumption of predicates under concepts. According to a traditional, Leibnizian view of the extension of concepts, the *extensional* aspect of physics does not lie in the *individual entities* which make up the domain of a physical theory and which are to be identified either with the empirical appearances or with their unobservable causes. It lies rather in the specific *properties* or *qualities* of the phenomena, which are combined and classified in a system of natural kinds. Hegel's view of Newtonian science is thus indebted to the criteria of conceptual systematicity on which Kant's view of science is based and to the structure of traditional (Leibnizian) logic.

An analysis of the first part of §246 thus shows that Hegel's non-Newtonian characterization of Newtonian science is only *partially* directed against a Newtonian view of physics. It is *not* anti-Newtonian, in several very important regards. First, it does not differ from a Newtonian view as much as it does, for example, from an *empiricist* view of science. According to Hume, or Mach, or van Fraassen, *there are no laws of nature*. According to Hume, our theoretical principles such as causality are based on habit, whereas the phenomena *per se* have no necessity at all. According to Mach, the laws of physics are only theoretical tools which are constructed to bring forth a most simple and convenient organization of the phenomena. According to van Fraassen, science aims at empirical adequacy, and not at truth. Hegel, on the other hand, is not an empiricist, even though, in agreement with empiricism, he criticizes causal explanations, analogical ways of reasoning, and mechanical models of non-mechanical phenomena. He believes that there *are* laws of nature which represent a necessary and universal structure of the phenomena. He is as convinced as any Newtonian that science aims at truth and not only at empirical adequacy. But he has a view of the epistemic features of truth which differs substantially from the Newtonian's. For Hegel, our criteria of truth, and of universal validity, have to be spelled out in terms of *coherence* rather than correspondence. For him, the correspondence of scientific concepts to the empirical appearances is neither a necessary nor a sufficient criterion of truth. His only criterion of truth is the coherence of our concepts and of their content (which is expressed conceptually as well). The correspondence between our theoretical concepts within science and our empirical concepts pertaining to the phenomena is simply part of the required general conceptual coherence which also comprises the conceptual contents of our experience.

Secondly, Hegel's and Newton's views of science both rely on the general conviction that the aim of physics is *to save the phenomena*. Physics, for Hegel, is supposed to capture the *structure* of the appearances, the necessary relations between the particular phenomena which appear in a contingent diversity. But, in his view, the structure of the phenomena is *not* based on the *extensions* of the concepts in the modern logical sense of the individuals which make up their domain, nor in a traditional (Lockean) sense of the substances which carry a few primary properties and which are unobservable causes of the appearances. For Hegel, the structure of the phenomena captured by physics is based on classes of natural kinds which form extensions of concepts in a quite different, Leibnizian sense of the more specific concepts which fall under more general concepts. In considering Hegel's account of scientific concepts to be *non-extensional* from a modern (Fregean) logical point of view, we should thus consider his account of scientific concepts to be *extensional* from a traditional (Leibnizian) logical point of view. In addition, Hegel's view of concepts (in particular, of philosophical concepts) also exhibits a central *intensional* aspect in Leibniz's sense. This is perhaps the most problematic and most interesting feature of Hegel's logic of science, a feature to which I will come back in section 5.

Thirdly, in Hegel's view Newtonian science aims at *completeness* as it should, but does so *in the wrong way*. The spatio-temporal, dynamic, and systematic completeness claims of Newtonian science are subject to Hegel's most substantial criticism of the Newtonian world-view. According to Hegel, physics should *not* aim at the construction of universally valid theories, either with respect to spatio-temporal completeness or with respect to dynamic completeness; and the systematic completeness of physics should exhibit a *non-reductionist* structure which reflects the structural diversity of the phenomena, or the qualitative distinctions of different degrees of complexity of organization within nature. Physics should thus aim at systematic completeness in capturing: (1) the natural kinds of forces and laws; (2) the different types of boundary conditions which are needed to derive phenomenological laws from the most abstract assumptions of a general theory, e.g. to obtain Kepler's and Galileo's laws from Newton's law of gravitation; (3) the distinct kinds of physical system to which such phenomenological laws apply, e.g. the bodies of "finite" or of "absolute" mechanics which Hegel distinguishes in the Mechanics section of the *Encyclopedia*; and (4) the dimensions of the physical quantities in terms of which such phenomenological laws are expressed—these represent a very important structural aspect of the laws of nature, in Hegel's view.[18]

For Hegel, the structure of Newtonian science or physics—even when it operates within the limits which he sets for it—represents a *preliminary* stage in an adequate view of nature. According to him, the unavoidable methodological restrictions of Newtonian science demand a *philosophical*, or speculative, view of nature which would indeed capture the structure of the phenomena. He is convinced that physics has to be complemented, criticized and completed by a proper natural philosophy which is based on an "immanent" logical clarification of the theoretical contents of empirical science and of their relation to the structure of the phenomena. An attempt at such a conceptual clarification of the content of physics was already made with Kant's *Metaphysical Foundations of Natural Science (MAdN)*. In Hegel's view, however, it was not sufficiently thorough and systematic, and it did not really succeed.

4. Against Kant's Construction of Nature

Hegel's attitude towards empiricism sheds light on his view of Kant's theory of nature and *vice versa*. According to the Introduction to the 1830 *Encyclopedia*, both rely on related epistemologies. Here, Hegel subsumes the epistemological positions of empiricism and Kant's transcendental philosophy under the same Second Position of Thought with Respect to Objectivity. But Hegel does not think at all that both philosophies deserve the same degree of attention. After summarizing briefly the virtues and deficiencies of empiricism (§§37-9), he deals extensively with Kant's critical philosophy (§§40-60). The lengthy passages on Kant start by working out the features which empiricism and critical philosophy have in common, and those which distinguish them (§40 and Remark):

> Critical Philosophy has in common with Empiricism that it accepts experience as the *only* basis of our cognitions; but it will not count them as truths, but only as cognitions of appearances. ... Critical Philosophy *holds on to the factum* that *universality* and *necessity*, being also essential determinations, are found to be present in what is called experience.[19]

> The Humean scepticism does not deny the fact that the determinations of universality and necessity are found in cognition. But in the Kantian philosophy, too, this is nothing but a presupposed fact; in the ordinary languages of the sciences, we can say that this philosophy has only advanced another *explanation* of the fact.[20]

According to these passages, critical philosophy on the one hand and empiricism on the other are two related ways of considering the universal and necessary relations which are "found to be present" in experience. Recall that for Hume the principles of experience, such as causality, are based on habit. For Kant, however, they rest on the *a priori* elements of cognition. Hegel emphasizes that Kant's concepts of pure understanding belong to the "spontaneity of *thinking*" (§40), and that for Kant thinking is a "merely subjective activity" (§41). We may say that according to Hegel what most distinguishes Kant's general theory of nature from empiricism is the *constructivist* aspect, the fact that according to Kant the universality and necessity of the laws of nature are due to the faculties, or active powers, of human cognition. They are not due to external *objects* of cognition, or to the ideas of sensation or impressions which the human mind receives passively from them.

Kant's way of saving the phenomena is to *construct* them by means of the *a priori* concepts of the understanding, the categories, and the pure forms of intuition, space and time, and, as we learn in the *MAdN*, the empirical concept of "matter as the moveable in space." From an empiricist point of view, Kant's theory of nature gives rise to the question of how to save those phenomena which are *not* due to construction, that is, the empirical forces, laws, and genera, which are *contingent* and which are classified into an empirical system of natural kinds. The tasks and limits of reason in establishing an empirical system of natural kinds, and the regulative principles of reason according to which they are put into a systematic ordering, are expounded in the Supplement to the Transcendental Dialectic of the *Critique of Pure Reason*. In the Introduction to the *Critique of Judgement*, the problems involved in conceiving of nature as a system of natural kinds and of establishing an empirical system of knowledge are taken up again. As is well known, Kant was dealing with major systematic problems regarding the epistemological demands of establishing such a system of empirical knowledge. Hegel's criticism of Kant's general theory of nature was initiated by the problems which arise from the projected systematic unity of nature. One of the main targets of Hegel's criticism was the limitation of pure reason (outside the pure domain of mathematics) to an empirical domain, to the objects of possible experience. For Kant, the domain of empirical knowledge is identical with the domain of objective knowledge. For him, objective knowledge is identical with knowledge of the objects of possible experience. The domain of objective knowledge is *finite* in so far as it is *given* by sensibility, as an empirical content of intuition, and it is at most *potentially (but not actually) infinite* in so far as it *can be* given by sensibility. In Hegel's view, Kant's impressive epistemological triumph over pre-critical metaphysics is accompanied by a crucial defeat in establishing the systematicity of objective knowledge, and the defeat is due to a wrong use of the principles of empiricism, or of Humean skepticism.

To shed more light on this criticism, let me sketch Kant's account of the meaning and reference of scientific concepts. The general theory of nature is based on a penetrating criticism of basic referential claims of traditional metaphysics and of Newtonian science. The basic principles of Kant's epistemology concern the limitations of objective knowledge, limitations which are strengthened substantially by the doctrine of the Antinomies. According to these principles, unobservables which are in no way tied to the conditions of possible experience do not belong to the domain of concepts with objective reality. Hence all the "ultimate" entities which were postulated in traditional metaphysics (or "deduced" from the phenomena on the basis of Newton's Rules of Reasoning) are no longer considered to be true objects of cognition. Absolute space, absolute time, the atoms, and their interactions with an unobservable ether (which is supposedly identical with absolute space) on the one hand, and immaterial substances such as Leibnizian monads on the other hand, do not belong to the domain of objective knowledge. Kant replaces the pre-critical metaphysical referential claims with the "transcendental" claims of his epistemology. These are based on a theory of pure intuition which provides the concepts of the understanding with a non-conceptual, sensible content, and which makes it possible to restrict the domain of human cognition to the objects of possible experience. In addition, only mathematical objects which can be constructed in pure intuition are admitted. The theory of intuition saves the *extensionality* (in a modern, set-theoretical, non-Leibnizian sense) of Kant's general theory of nature. Pure intuition supplies the concepts of the understanding with a *domain of application* which has the structure of a *manifold*. In Kant's theory of nature, the meaning and reference of theoretical concepts are established in two separate steps. The schematism of pure understanding establishes *formal* meaning and reference, that is, it brings forth the principles for supplying the categories of pure understanding with a formal (i.e. non-empirical) content of intuition. The schemata of the categories are principles to generate, or to construct, specific models or applications of the categories. In Kant's view, they are not sufficient for establishing a correspondence between the categories and a well-defined material content of pure intuition. A *concretization* of the formal general theory of nature is needed to prove that the general theory of nature is not empty, or that there are specific objects of knowledge for which it is indeed valid. This second step is made with the *MAdN*. Kant argues that the meaning and reference of the general theory of nature is not established sufficiently without such a second step. In the preface to the *MAdN*, he emphasizes that

> the understanding is taught only through *instances* from corporeal nature what the conditions are under which alone the concepts of the understanding can have objective reality, i.e. meaning and truth. And so a separate metaphysics of corporeal nature does excellent and indispensable service to general metaphysics, inasmuch as the former provides instances (cases in concreto) in which to realize the concepts and propositions of the latter (properly, transcendental philosophy), i.e. to give to a mere form of thought sense and meaning.[21]

To provide the general theory of nature with instances, Kant derives principles for constructing the possibility of matter from the principles of pure reason, based on the empirical condition of the actual existence of an object of outer sense to which the predicate of mobility applies. ("Mobility" is the primary predicate of matter, it distinguishes material bodies from objects in general.) Some of the principles yield the axioms of Newtonian mechanics. Some others yield a "dynamic" construction of continuous matter, based on internal attractive and repulsive forces which play the role of Leibnizian derivative forces. They give rise to a purely *relational* concept of matter and to a non-referential account of the unobservable entities of Newtonian science (or its opponent, Leibnizian metaphysics). Absolute space, for example, is needed for the construction of empirical motions, but it has only the regulative status of an idea of reason. Similarly, the internal forces of matter are not dynamic *entities* (Leibnizian monads, or "physical" monads such as those postulated by the pre-critical Kant in 1755/56), nor are they conceived as properties of ultimate, atomic constituents of matter. They are only phenomenological Newtonian causes of the change of a motion. The only referential claims of Kant's theory of matter are based on the *phenomena* which are actually there, given that external sense has indeed an empirical object. According to the chapter on the transcendental amphibolies in the first *Critique*, however, we should conceive of the phenomena only in terms of relations and not in terms of *entia per se*.

Kant's view of the meaning of physical quantities differs substantially from the Newtonian, referential account. He attempts to give *explicit definitions* of the concepts of mass, momentum, and force, as Newton did in the *Principia*. But in the *MAdN* they are no longer based on existential presuppositions concerning atoms and their interactions. Kant's concepts of the forces which act between two parts of matter derive from his principle of causation. They are defined in purely phenomenological terms, or, to be more precise, in transcendental terms which apply to appearances and constitute their law-like structure. Kant's concepts of mass and of momentum are slightly different: they are supplied with *operational instructions* which are based on the laws of mechanics (momentum conservation).

Kant's criticism of the Newtonian referential view of the basic concepts of empirical science is closely related to a general criticism of the three kinds of Newtonian completeness claims which were mentioned at the end of section 2. The spatio-temporal, dynamic, and systematic completeness of empirical knowledge is not to be achieved. The quest for spatio-temporal or dynamic completeness in empirical knowledge gives rise to the cosmological antinomies. Nevertheless, all the completeness claims of Newtonian science are valid as regulative principles which are the guidelines for any expansion of our knowledge.

Hegel contends that Kant's account of meaning and reference is deficient in at least three regards. First, according to Kant's epistemology the *necessity* of all general and specific laws of nature depends in the last analysis on pure intuition, or on the human faculty of sensibility. That is, the objectivity or law-likeness of the laws of nature is supposed to rest on contingent and arbitrary grounds. Hence in Hegel's view, Kant's "transcendental" turn in epistemology is not at all sufficient to guarantee the required *logical* or *structural* necessity of the laws of nature. Hegel rejected Kant's theory of intuition and the related extensional view of the meaning and reference of the categories, since they were all based on a *concept of extension which is not logical*, and therefore were contaminated with elements which seemed arbitrary to him. (Would he have liked the set-theoretical approach to extensions in modern logic? And what would he have thought of the contradictions arising from Frege's logicism?)

Secondly, Hegel holds that Kant's relational theory of the phenomena is not sufficiently thorough or radical. In his view, it is at odds with the extensional aspects of Kant's own theory of intuition and the theory of matter based on it. These theories presuppose a domain of application which is non-empirical in the case of pure intuition and empirical in the case of matter. Pure intuition only gives rise to mathematical objects. However, the material objects which are subject to Kant's theory of matter can only be constructed from a concretization of the pure principles of reason, and of their domain. Kant needs *non-pure 'logical' individuals* which are the carriers of the primary property of matter ("mobility"), and which make up the domain of his concrete theory of nature.[22] They are the *relata* of the relations from which matter is constructed in the relational theory of matter which is expounded in the *MAdN*. They enter the *MAdN* in specifying the condition of the concrete (or specific) theory of nature: the empirical supposition that there is indeed an object of outer sense which is movable. In the last analysis, they are supposed to be empirical substances, or individuated parts of the *substantia phenomenon*, or the very object of the construction of the possibility of matter. In this regard, Kant's theory of matter is based on an existential presupposition. Recalling the above mentioned demand for a concretization of the general theory of nature, we see that this existential presupposition plays the role of providing Kant's theory of nature with non-trivial truth, that is, with validity in a non-empty domain. Hegel, however, interprets it in a different way. In the Remark to §262, he reproaches Kant for having presupposed exactly what he wanted to construct:

> It is among Kant's several merits that he, by attempting a so-called *construction* of matter, in his *Metaphysical Foundations of Natural Science*, made a start at establishing a *concept* of matter and, in so attempting, revived the concept of a *philosophy of nature*. In doing so, however, he assumed the reflexive determinations of *attractive forces* and *repulsive forces* as *fixed* against each other, and, moreover, in assuming that *matter* results from these forces, he presupposed matter as something *finished*. Thus it is already matter which is to be attracted and repelled.[23]

The objection is essentially the same as that which Kant had made against Lambert in the very Dynamics chapter of the *MAdN* which Hegel criticizes here. In the Remark to the demonstration of Proposition 1, Kant observes that the property of solidity should be constructed rather than presupposed in a satisfactory theory of matter, in order not "to prevent a return to the first principles of natural sciences."[24] Hegel's criticism reveals that in his view Kant did not succeed in constructing the possibility of matter from first principles. The concept of substance is *ambiguous* in the *MAdN*. On the one hand, Kant defends the purely relational concept of a phenomenal substance. On the other hand, in some regards he is still indebted to a traditional metaphysical concept of substance.[25] We should not disregard such residues of *pre-critical* metaphysics in Kant's critical theory of nature. In the given case, they are intimately related to a *logical concept of substance*, in the extensional (or set-theoretical) sense of the logical individuals which make up the domain of a theory. Kant needs them from a logical point of view, and Hegel's criticism of such an assumption is directed against what we now call extensional logic.

Thirdly, and most prominently, Hegel criticizes Kant's restrictions on the spatio-temporal, dynamic, and systematic *completeness claims* of empirical science in the doctrine of the Antinomies. According to Kant's resolution of the antinomies of pure reason, they only give rise to regulative principles. Hegel's criticism has three aspects which can only be discussed briefly here.

1. Hegel attacks Kant's presentation of the "mathematical" antinomies repeatedly. He objects that the proofs are both invalid and that the conclusions drawn from them are wrong. In his view, Kant's "extensional" interpretation of the cosmological antinomies, according to which they arise from using the categories beyond a restricted domain, should be replaced by taking them seriously as *conceptual* antinomies. He conceives of them as contradictions in the sense of traditional (Leibnizian) logic. He thinks that they arise from the traditional *praedicatum inest subiecto* doctrine. Therefore he is convinced that they cannot be resolved by epistemological reasoning.[26]

2. According to Hegel, the dynamic concepts of a theory of matter are not universally valid, in the usual (non-Hegelian, or extensional) sense of universality. To suppose that the abstract concepts of Newtonian mechanics (for example, the concept of inertial mass) apply to *any* spatio-temporal phenomenon within nature, is to disregard the *systematic* organization of nature. §249 of the 1830 *Encyclopedia* emphasizes that nature is organized in distinct levels of different degrees of complexity. Against the dynamic completeness claims of Newtonian science, Hegel emphasizes that the neglect of the systematic structure of natural phenomena is based on abstraction. A most prominent example of this view is his criticism of a Newtonian use of the law of inertia. Hegel holds that the strict validity of the law of inertia is simply not compatible with the universality of gravitation (in the Remark to §269). Both are only reconciled pragmatically by means of approximation. It cannot be denied that this criticism was legitimate from a logical point of view. Hegel favors an anti-reductionist view of nature, according to which the domain of any physical theory is restricted to a certain type of phenomenon of given structure. Here, quite another kind of constraint for the application of physical concepts is set than the extensional restriction met in Kant's resolution of the antinomies. It is *intensional* rather than extensional, that is, it is tied to the type of structure of a phenomenon, or to its qualities and

properties, rather than to the extension of the corresponding class of entities.

3. Hegel's view of *systematic completeness* leads to another criticism which can only be mentioned here. For Hegel, the systematic structure of Kant's transcendental logic and theory of nature is not complete, but completely *arbitrary*. This criticism is associated with the question whether Kant's systems of categories and judgments are complete, a question which is still discussed today. Hegel objected that the systematic principles according to which Kant's categories are related to each other remain obscure. In his view, the systematic relations between concepts have to be developed from an analysis of the logical structures of the concepts, and not from the (subjective, hence contingent) structure of the human faculty of cognition. His criticism of Kant's systematic philosophy culminated in the quest for *new criteria of the systematicity, completeness, and adequacy of concepts*. In his view, such criteria had to rely *only on logic*—on a non-extensional logic developed by means of a new scientific method which Hegel called *dialectic* in remembrance of Plato.

5. Logic and the Structure of the Phenomena

Now some preliminary answers may be given to the question of what Hegel's non-extensional logic of nature *could* be. In Hegel's day, dispensing with Kant's theory of intuition was a step back to a *Leibnizian* view of the intension and extension of concepts. According to such a view, *intensions* are the contents of concepts, i.e. the predicates making them up in a logical conjunction, and *extensions* are those concepts which fall under a given concept, i.e. the logical disjunctions of such combinations of predicates which agree in at least one predicate. At that time, there were no abstract theories of sets or classes. Nor do we know whether Hegel would have liked them and taken them seriously as useful abstract tools to spell out the logical relations of abstract concepts such as Being, Nothing, Becoming, Something, One, Many, Attraction, Repulsion, Pure Quantity, Measure, Existence, and so on. Leibniz's view of logic, on the other hand, was based on a metaphysical theory of substances, and on the *praedicatum inest subiecto* doctrine, both of which in Hegel's view were no better than Kant's theory of pure intuition and its marriage with conceptual structures. Most probably, even the abstract logical individuals of modern set theory would have been suspicious in Hegel's view, not on account of their abstractness, but because he would have considered them to be a logical residue of a most problematic Leibnizian concept of substance.

At the present stage of research, Hegel's logic has remained obscure in many regards. We need more solid logical and semantical investigations of it, such as those initiated by Michael Wolff.[27] I can give only a brief sketch here of what kind of theory Hegel's logic represents in my view.

Most evidently, it is a *non-referential* theory, and that is why Hegel is not a traditional-style metaphysician, and indeed not an ontologist at all. The meaning of the concepts of Hegel's *Logic* can not be expressed in the terms of any domain of entities. Meaning cannot be reduced to reference; for Hegel, it is the other way around. He explains the meaning of concepts in terms of pure logical relations which are only denominated by the expressions of traditional ontology but which no longer have the traditional ontological significance. The domain of *relata* on which these relations operate, or better, the concept of such a domain, is generated in the abstract terms of *other relations*. The relations are defined neither in sets nor in classes, and the relata are not logical individuals in a modern sense. The most striking (and, from a Quinean logical point of view, most horrible) feature of Hegel's logic is that, due to abstractness, a structural and semantical underdetermination of concepts is the starting point of a logical procedure—which reminds us of Münchhausen's way of pulling himself out of the morass by his own hair. In the beginning, a relation and the set of relata on which it should operate are conceptually "collapsed"; subsequently, their logical distinctness is "derived" by an analysis of the contradictions to which their missing distinction leads. The whole logical theory is then made up by intimately related concepts which form a systematic conceptual structure called the *Concept* in one regard, or the *Absolute Idea* in another regard. The whole structure is logically complete, in Hegel's view. Its kind of completeness differs substantially from the kind of completeness implied by the Newtonian and Kantian extensional, dynamic, and systematic completeness claims. Obviously, the theory also differs substantially from a theory in the sense of modern, Fregean extensional logic. It is a system of concepts and their relations, related to, as well as distinct from, both Leibniz's intensional logic of predicates and Kant's transcendental logic. It seems to be a semantic theory which deals with the most abstract *types* of structure, rather than with extensional structures defined as sets or classes of objects. The *intension* of a concept *à la* Hegel, I suggest, *may* be compared to a *structure type* in the sense of Bourbaki, *if* it can be put in precise terms at all from a modern, formal point of view.[28]

On the basis of such a view of Hegel's logic, it is now possible to analyze the second part of §246 of the *1830 Encyclopedia*. Natural philosophy proper in Hegel's sense, that is, the "*comprehending* consideration of nature" which is contrasted with the "*thinking* consideration" in physics, attempts to capture the structure of the phenomena in terms of what from the modern point of view is a non-extensional logic dealing with abstract types of structure rather than abstract classes of entities. Its "object," that is, "the same *universal*" which also comprises the forces, laws, and genera of empirical science, is given in non-extensional terms as well. It is a system of natural kinds, such as the systems of forces, laws, and genera which were discussed by Kant in his chapter on regulative principles at the end of the Transcendental Dialectic of the first *Critique*. It is a non-extensional, or intensional, object since we deal with a system of *properties*, or of *qualities of natural phenomena*, which cannot be comprehended in purely quantitative terms. In contrast to Newtonian physics, natural philosophy proper attempts to comprehend their systematic structure as "the universal for *itself*," that is, not in the arbitrary terms which are due to the structure of the science of the day, nor in the terms of an epistemology such as empiricism or Kant's theory of knowledge. According to Newtonian physics or to these epistemologies, the "universal of nature" is considered in terms of extensions: either in terms of atoms, absolute space, and so on (Newton), or in terms of the particular phenomena which appear to exhibit regularities (Hume), or in terms of the schemata of categories which give rise to the law-like structures of the phenomena (Kant). In all cases, the "universal"—or the regularities or law-like structure(s) of the phenomena—is not considered "for itself" but in some empirical representation, or spatio-temporal model, or transcendental representational scheme. Hegel's natural philosophy, on the other hand, proposes to regard the law-like structure(s) of the phenomena while *dis*regarding such models or representational schemes. It claims to consider it (or them) "in its *own immanent necessity*," which is the necessity of logical relations, and which is developed "according to the self-determination of the Concept" revealed by Hegel's dialectical method in the *Logic*. The contrast between these two ways of considering the "universal in nature" is based on a distinction between two kinds of necessity. The law-like structures which are the content of physics have an *epistemic necessity*. They are necessary only "for us," that is, relative to our best empirical theories. The law-like structure of "the Concept," on the other hand, which is the only adequate structure to comprehend nature in Hegel's view, has *logical necessity* in Hegel's sense. It is necessary not only "for us" but "for itself," that is, in an absolute sense which he assumes to have guaranteed in his *Logic*.

The interpretation of the second part of §246 should be complemented by some remarks concerning Hegel's view of the spatio-temporal character of nature and of the specific empirical structures of the phenomena. Hegel does not *altogether* disregard the extensionality of the phenomena and their diverse contingent structures. According to the above distinction of two kinds of necessity, the phenomena found in nature may be contingent in two regards, that is, epistemically contingent relative to an empirical theory, or *logically contingent* in an *absolute* sense. It is not at all easy to distinguish them in a particular case. What is more, in finding out their concrete distinguishing marks we are bound to the very structure of Hegel's *Logic,* since he failed, or refused, to provide any external criteria for our use. But it is logically necessary, in his view, that *there are* logically contingent phenomena within nature, and this is indeed the mark by which Hegel believes the sphere of nature is distinguished from the sphere of logic itself. Therefore, *some* notion of extensionality is a basic feature of his concept of nature. In §247, nature is explained as the "Idea in the form of otherness," and *"externality"* is given as the primary mark of nature. Therefore, we may suggest that Hegel considers nature as a spatio-temporal model of the systematic conceptual structure which is revealed in his *Logic*. *If* we want to explain Hegel's natural philosophy in such terms, however, we must take into account that we are not dealing at all with a faithful representation of a logical structure, that is, a true interpretation or a model in the strict, model-theoretical sense. Nature considered as an extensional representation of the "Concept," or of the "Absolute Idea," is a *defective* interpretation of it *by definition*. It is an *incomplete realization* of the conceptual structure presented in the *Logic*. Logical contingency, in whatever particular aspects of the phenomena it may be met, is essential to nature. So we have to conclude that according to Hegel, contrary the view of Newtonian science, and in *some* relation to Kant's doctrine of the antinomies, *the phenomena cannot be saved completely, for logical reasons*.

Hegel's concept of nature as the "externality" or "form of otherness" of the conceptual structure of the *Logic* is based on a very special notion of extensionality. What is extensional in nature? Once more, Hegel does not mean that the particular phenomena, or the *individual entities*, of nature should be considered as extensional in any regard. He means that the *distinct structure types* which make up the total conceptual structure of the "Concept" recur in nature as *coexistent*. They are realized in the *particular types of structure* of the phenomena, in the *distinct coexisting levels of nature* of different degrees of complexity, or of organization. They are found in the phenomenological forces, laws, and genera, which in his view should be put into the ordering of a system of natural kinds by empirical science. No part of the conceptual system of natural kinds, and of the corresponding logical types of structure, is universally valid. Every concept of physics, and of natural philosophy, saves only some structurally specified part of the phenomena. In this regard, Hegel's view of "good physics" comes close to the empiricists' quest for a phenomenological science. Both of these critical attitudes towards any "fundamental" theory claiming universal validity, however, have grown from completely different philosophical grounds.

Finally, Hegel's view of the mutual relations between empirical science, natural philosophy proper, and the phenomena may be summarized in the following way. The concepts of Hegel's *Logic* are abstract variants of corresponding types of structure which occur in nature, although the correspondence is not perfect, since the phenomena also bear logically contingent features. In contrast to an empiricist view of science, or to any fully extensional account of nature, the concepts of natural philosophy proper do not correspond to the particular phenomena, or to individual entities, but to the *empirical or phenomenological concepts* of physics which should be organized into a phenomenological *system of natural kinds*. In this sense, we may say that the concepts of Hegel's natural philosophy refer to the *intensions* of the concepts of empirical science (or to the "extensions" of scientific concepts in the Leibnizian, rather than a Fregean or a set-theoretical sense). Hegel emphasizes that we must not expect *all* specific properties to belong to the logically necessary, law-like structures of nature. The relation between logical structures and the specific properties of natural kinds does not involve a one-to-one map; the phenomena necessarily bear some irreducible contingency. According to Hegel, the phenomena cannot be saved completely; some of them *sind nicht zu retten*. Physics, on the other hand, is bound to an *epistemic* distinction between the necessary and the contingent features of nature. In the last analysis, natural philosophy proper is to eliminate such an epistemic distinction in favor of *logical* necessity and contingency. Physics is only a preliminary stage of a true comprehension of nature, and of its organization into natural kinds which correspond to logical structure types of varying degrees of complexity.

To explain Hegel's view of natural philosophy in this way also sheds light on his philosophical *methodology*. If physics is a preliminary stage of the true science of nature, and if both deal with natural kinds of phenomena rather than with observable or unobservable individuals in nature, then the starting point of natural philosophy should be the concepts of physics. The philosophical task is to help physics in organizing its concepts into an adequate phenomenological system of natural kinds. In doing so, natural philosophy is committed to *criticizing* physics whenever the preliminary concepts of that science do not denote natural kinds but unobservables, such as atoms, and whenever physics disregards the organization of concepts into an adequate structure in which no concept is universally valid. The systematic order of organizing the concepts of physics into a system of natural kinds is prescribed by the systematic order of conceptual types of structure as expounded in the *Logic*, starting from the most abstract (or structurally poor) concepts and ending up at the most complex (or structurally complete) concepts. Natural philosophy has therefore to *begin* with the most *abstract concepts of physics*, that is, space, time, motion, material bodies, mass, and so on. For each concept, the corresponding *logical* structure has to be picked up, and identified as the adequate correlate. I can not go in any methodological detail here, but it is evident that if Hegel were to proceed the other way around (i.e. if he were to start with the concepts of his *Logic* rather than with those of physics), then the tasks of natural philosophy as sketched above could not be realized at all. In any case, Hegel never expects to obtain a *complete* correspondence between his concepts and the contents of empirical science. Therefore, with regard to the *methodology* which is suggested by Hegel's view of natural philosophy and its relations to physics and to the phenomena, we have to conclude that his philosophy of nature is *not a priori*. It is clearly not *a priori* in a Kantian sense, since Hegel dispenses completely with Kant's transcendental idealism and the related epistemology. Nor is it *a priori* in an empiricist sense, since physics is based on empirical investigations of the phenomena, and natural philosophy presupposes the concepts of phenomenological natural kinds which are suggested by physics. I conclude by quoting a passage from the Remark to §9 of the 1830 *Encyclopedia* which both substantiates and summarizes my view of Hegel's methodology:

> Hence the relationship of speculative science to the other sciences is simply the following: speculative science does not leave the empirical content of the other sciences aside, but recognises and uses it, and in the same way recognises and employs what is universal in science, i.e. the laws, classifications [*Gattungen*, i.e. 'genera', –B.F.] etc., for its own content; but it also introduces other categories into these universals and gives them currency.[29]

Notes

* I would like to thank the Hegel Society of America and the School of Philosophy at the Catholic University of America for their kind invitation to the conference *Hegel and the Philosophy of Nature*, Michael Baur and Stephen Houlgate for their careful and most patient support in preparing the final version of the text, Michael Hallett for improving the English of my translations of the quotations from *EN* (1830), §246 and the Remark to §262, and Ken Westphal for helpful comments.

1. It is mainly the historians of science who are inclined to do so, since Hegel's attitude towards the science of his day looks rather strange when split off from its philosophical background. See, e.g. the recent criticism of Hegel's view of Kepler's and Newton's theories in W.R. Shea, "Hegel's Celestial Mechanics," or in F.H. van Lunteren, "Hegel and Gravitation," both in *Hegels Philosophie der Natur: Beziehungen zwischen empirischer und spekulativer*

Naturerkenntnis, edited by R.-P. Horstmann and M.J. Petry (Stuttgart: Klett-Cotta, 1986), pp. 30ff. and pp. 45ff.

2. See, e.g., S. Sambursky, "Hegel's Philosophy of Nature," in *The Interaction Between Science and Philosophy*, edited by Y. Elkana (Atlantic Highlands, N.J: Humanities Press, 1974), pp. 143ff.

3. B. Falkenburg, "Hegel on Mechanistic Models of Light," in *Hegel and Newtonianism*, edited by M.J. Petry (Dordrecht: Kluwer, 1993), pp. 531ff. My view of Hegel's criticism of modeling light after mechanical analogies is similar to Buchdahl's. See G. Buchdahl, "Conceptual Analysis and Scientific Theory in Hegel's Philosophy of Nature," in *Hegel and the Sciences*, edited by R.S. Cohen and M.W. Wartofsky (Dordrecht: Reidel 1984). I agree completely with Buchdahl's analysis regarding the phenomenological tendencies in Hegel's philosophy of science, and regarding Hegel's criticism of Kant's "construction of matter."

4. I also considered it in such a way in my book on Kant and Hegel. Cf. B. Falkenburg, *Die Form der Materie* (Frankfurt am Main: Athenäum, 1987).

5. Cf. I. Hacking, *Representing and Intervening* (Cambridge: Cambridge University Press, 1983), pp. 220ff., on the conceptual history of what are the phenomena of empirical science. The word 'phenomenon' is an ancient expression; the related word 'phenomenology' as a name for the science of the phenomena dates back to Lambert. —The theory on which the data confirming a theory are based, and the theory which is confirmed by the data, are, however, to be strictly distinguished.

6. Cf. Mach's attack on atomism, in E. Mach, *Die Mechanik in ihrer Entwicklung*, 9th edition (1933; reprint, Darmstadt: Wissenschaftliche Buchgesellschaft, 1988), pp. 466-7; and Boltzmann's cautious defense of atomism as a mere hypothesis in his popular writings, in L. Boltzmann, *Populäre Schriften* (1905; reprint, Braunschweig: Vieweg, 1979). See also S.G. Brush, "Ludwig Boltzmann and the Foundations of Natural Science," in *Principien der Naturfilosofi. Lectures on Natural Philosophy 1903-1906*, edited by I.M. Fasol-Boltzmann (Berlin: Springer Verlag, 1990), pp. 43ff.

7. G.W.F. Hegel, *Enzyklopädie der philosophischen Wissenschaften im Grundrisse (1830). Zweiter Teil: Die Naturphilosophie mit den mündlichen Zusätzen*, edited by E. Moldenhauer and K.M. Michel, *Werke in zwanzig Bänden*, Vol. 9 (Frankfurt am

Main: Suhrkamp Verlag, 1970), §246 (p. 15), my translation. (Hereafter cited as *EN* [1830], §246; *Werke*, **9**: 15.) Petry's translation is not precise enough in regard to Hegel's characterization of the *differentia specifica* of physics and philosophy. My translation is based on Petry's in the unproblematic parts; see *Hegel's Philosophy of Nature*, edited and translated by M.J. Petry, 3 Vols (London: Allen and Unwin, 1970). I follow Geraets, *et al.* in translating '*Begriff*' as 'Concept' and '*Erkenntnis*' as 'cognition'. See *The Encyclopaedia Logic (with the Zusätze)*, translated by T.F. Geraets, W.A. Suchting and H.S. Harris (Indianapolis: Hackett, 1991).

8. Cf. P. Duhem, *To Save the Phenomena* (Chicago: University of Chicago Press, 1969); J. Mittelstraß, *Die Rettung der Phänomene* (Berlin: de Gruyter, 1962). See also I. Hacking, *Representing and Intervening*, p. 222.

9. M. Friedman, "Explanation and Scientific Understanding," *Journal of Philosophy* 71 (1974): 5-19. B.C. van Fraassen, *The Scientific Image* (Oxford: Clarendon Press, 1980), ch. 2 (entitled "To save the phenomena") dispenses with the explanatory claims of unification by giving the expression a strictly empiricist reading. For him, 'to save the phenomena' means simply to embed the empirical models of data in a unique theoretical structure.

10. Cf. K.-N. Ihmig, *Hegels Deutung der Gravitation* (Frankfurt am Main: Athenäum, 1989).

11. I. Newton, *Philosophiae Naturalis Principia Mathematica*, translated by A. Motte, revised by F. Cajori (Berkeley: University of California Press, 1934), p. 6.

12. See, e.g., B.L. Horan, "Inference to the Unobservable: Newton's Experimental Philosophy," in *Scientific Methods: Conceptual and Historical Problems*, edited by P. Achinstein and L.J. Snyder (Malabar, Florida: Krieger Publishing Company, 1994), pp. 1ff.

13. I. Newton, *Principia*, p. 398.

14. I. Newton, *Principia*, p. 399. The relational property of weight is not included in the list since it is variable. Therefore gravity is not an essential, or primary, quality of matter, in Newton's view.

15. I. Newton, *Principia*, p. 399.

16. Newton distinguished inertial and gravitational mass as two related dynamic quantities. He took their proportionality as an

empirical fact which is proven by experiment; cf. *Principia*, p. 1, in the explanation following Definition 1.

17. The criticism of analogies in *EN* (1830), §246 Anm., however, is made in a different context. It is part of a polemic against Schelling, and not directed towards a Newtonian use of Rule III. It attacks a natural philosophy which relies on *Anschauung* (intuition), in "a procedure of imagination and fantasy (also of fantastic ideas), according to *analogies* which may be more contingent or more substantial and which impress determinations and schemata only *externally* onto the objects," *EN* (1830), §246 Anm.;*Werke*, **9**: 15 f., my translation.

18. Cf. *EN* (1830), §§267, 270 where Hegel discusses the dimensions of the quantities in Galileo's and Kepler's laws of motion. See also G. Buchdahl, "Conceptual Analysis and Scientific Theory in Hegel's Philosophy of Nature," pp. 13 ff.; pp. 22-3 of Buchdahl's article deal with Hegel's "dimensional argument" in *EN* (1830), §267.

19. G.W.F. Hegel, *Enzyklopädie der philosophischen Wissenschaften im Grundrisse (1830). Erster Teil: Die Wissenschaft der Logik mit den mündlichen Zusätzen*, edited by E. Moldenhauer and K.M. Michel, *Werke in zwanzig Bänden*, Vol. 8 (Frankfurt am Main: Suhrkamp Verlag, 1970), §40 (p. 112) (hereafter *EL* [1830]); Geraets, *et al.*, p. 80.

20. *EL* (1830), §40 Anm.; *Werke*, **8**: 113; Geraets, *et al.*, p. 81.

21. I. Kant, *Metaphysische Anfangsgründe der Naturwissenschaft. Kants Gesammelte Schriften*, Vol. 4 (Königlich Preußische [now Deutsche] Akademie der Wissenschaften, Berlin: G. Reimer [now de Gruyter], 1902–), (hereafter *MAdN* [*GS*, **4**]), p. 478; Kant, *Philosophy of Material Nature*, translated by J. Ellington (Indianapolis and New York: Bobbs-Merril Company, 1970), p. 16.

22. Cf. K. Cramer, *Nicht-reine synthetische Urteile a priori* (Heidelberg: Carl Winter, 1985). Cramer shows that Kant distinguishes between pure and non-pure synthetic judgments *a priori*. In a non-pure judgment *a priori*, the logical subject is an empirical concept but the attribution of the predicate is *a priori*. In the *MAdN*, the empirical concept of matter which is related to the primary predicate of mobility gives rise to such non-pure synthetic judgments *a priori*.

23. *EN* (1830), §262; *Werke*, **9**: 61; my translation.

24. *MAdN* (*GS*, **4**), p. 498; Ellington, p. 43.

25. This is indicated, for example, by the beginning of the Remark to Definition 5 in the *Dynamics* part of the *MAdN*: "The concept of substance signifies the ultimate subject of existence, i.e. that which does not in turn belong merely as a predicate to the existence of another," *MAdN* (*GS*, **4**), p. 503; Ellington, p. 48. Here, a partially Aristotelian and partially Cartesian concept of substance is used.

26. Hegel's criticism of Kant's antinomies is found in several places: in the *Science of Logic*, in the *Encyclopedia*, and in the lectures on the history of philosophy. See, e.g., *EL* (1830), §48 and Remark; *Werke*, **8**: 126; Geraets, *et al.*, p. 91: "In reason's attempt to be cognizant of the unconditioned [aspect] of ... *the world*, it gets involved in *antinomies*, i.e. in the assertion of two *opposed* propositions about the *same* ob-ject; and it finds, moreover, that each of the propositions must be affirmed with equal necessity. ... What is made explicit here is that it is the content itself, namely, the categories on their own account, that bring about the contradiction."

27. M. Wolff, in *Der Begriff des Widerspruchs: eine Studie zur Dialektik Kants und Hegels* (Königstein/Ts.: Hain, 1981) investigates the relation of Hegel's concept of contradiction to Kant's concepts of logical, real, and dialectical opposition. A recent attempt to analyze Hegel's *Logic* from a modern semantical point of view is P. Stekeler-Weithofer's, *Hegels Analytische Philosophie* (Paderborn, München, Wien, Zürich: Ferdinand Schöningh, 1992).

28. N. Bourbaki is the pseudonym of the group of French mathematicians who gave mathematics a new foundation based on a general concept of structure, making use only of the concepts of set and relation. Any mathematical object can be described in such a way. The structure type of a mathematical object is obtained from the power sets of some basic sets and from relations defined with respect to their Cartesian products. Bourbaki's most abstract way of defining mathematical objects exhibits *some* similarity to Hegel's abstract way of giving non-extensional explanations of concepts. The Bourbaki approach, however, is obviously extensional (since it is based on set theory), in contrast to Hegel's view of concepts.

29. *EL* (1830), §9 Anm.;*Werke*, **8**: 52; Geraets, *et al.*, p. 33.

6

On Hegel's Early Critique of Kant's *Metaphysical Foundations of Natural Science*

Kenneth R. Westphal

1. Introduction

Hegel claims that a proper criticism of a philosophy must be sufficiently immanent, detailed, and systematic to show that, and how, a more adequate view is introduced and justified by a thorough comprehension of the merits and deficiencies of another view.[1] However, Hegel's explicit criticisms of Kant can hardly be said to meet this exacting standard. As Karl Ameriks and Paul Guyer have argued, Hegel's criticisms of Kant are too often external, and thus admit easy Kantian rejoinders.[2] Hegel's lectures on Kant are only an overview. Hegel makes some detailed criticisms of Kant in the conceptual preliminaries of the *Encyclopedia Logic* and in a number of remarks in the *Science of Logic*, but these criticisms appear isolated. Hegel often criticizes Kant in his early writings, but those objections are embedded in his still embryonic philosophy, and as such do not constitute a thorough and mature Hegelian critique. There is, however, a criticism Hegel makes in the 1801 *Differenzschrift* of Kant's philosophy of nature which has been overlooked by Hegel's expositors and critics alike. I shall argue that this criticism is immanent and far more significant than it first appears.[3]

2. Kant's Transcendental Ground for the Metaphysics of Science

One major point of Kant's Critical system is to articulate the *a priori* and rational grounds of common sense and scientific judgments about natural forces and their causal laws.[4] Officially, Kant's "general metaphysics," set out in the first *Critique*, grounds the "special metaphysics" of moving bodies, set out in his *Metaphysical Foundations of Natural Science* (*MAdN*). "Special metaphysics," in turn, provides the rational part of physics, which in turn grounds the empirical part of physical science.

More specifically, Kant's transcendental *Critique* of empirical knowledge only considers understanding and reason themselves within a system of all concepts and principles which relate to objects in general, while abstracting from given objects[5] or events and their specific causes, and indeed even from the cause of change in general.[6] Its main aim is to analyze how synthetic cognitions *a priori* are possible.[7] Transcendental knowledge is not concerned with objects, but instead with our way of knowing objects (*Erkenntnisart*) in general, in so far as this is possible *a priori*.[8] This restriction does not rule out considering specific examples in the Analogies, because the form of the alterations considered there—the successive states of affairs illustrated by Kant's examples—can be explicated *a priori* according to the law of causality and the conditions of time.[9]

Among much else, the first *Critique* sets out the sources and conditions for the possibility of the metaphysics of nature.[10] The *MAdN* applies the transcendental principles of the "general metaphysics"[11] developed in the first *Critique* to a specific range of given objects: nature as a realm of extended things.[12] In this way, the *MAdN* serves to give sense and meaning to pure *a priori* concepts and principles set out in the first *Critique*:

> And so a separate metaphysics of corporeal nature does excellent and indispensable service to *general* metaphysics, in as much as the former provides instances (cases *in concreto*) in which to realize the concepts and propositions of the latter (properly, transcendental philosophy), i.e. to give to a mere form of thought sense and meaning.[13]

As Eckart Förster has noted,[14] this language is virtually identical to the language Kant uses in describing the role and significance of the Schematism in the first *Critique*:

> This significance [*sc*. relation to an object] is acquired by the categories from sensibility, which realizes the understanding in so far as it also restricts it.[15]

In giving "sense and meaning" to the categories, the *MAdN* provides the rational part of physics, which makes physics as an empirical science possible. Notice, for example, that after writing the *MAdN* (1786), Kant claims in the second edition Preface (1787) to the first *Critique*, that his transcendental idealist account of time explains the possibility of the synthetic *a priori* cognitions involved in the universal theory of motion.[16] This is a direct reference to his purported *a priori* proofs of the conservation of matter, the law of inertia, and the equality of action and reaction (Propositions 2-4 of *MAdN*, ch. 3, Mechanics); these are Kant's *a priori* foundations for Newtonian physics.

3. Hegel's Early Critique of Kant's *MAdN*

In 1801 Hegel makes a brief but, I will argue, incisive criticism of Kant's *MAdN*. The kernel is this:

> For Kant, ... forces are not merely superfluous; they are either purely ideal, in which case they are not forces, or else they are transcendent. The only construction of phenomena that he can allow is mathematical, not dynamical.[17]

Surprisingly, the year before, Kant privately reached the same conclusion:

> The transition to physics cannot lie in the metaphysical foundations [i.e. the *MAdN*] (attraction and repulsion, etc.). For these furnish no specifically determined, empirical properties, and one can imagine no specific [forces], of which one could know whether they exist in nature, or whether their existence be demonstrable; rather, they can only be feigned to explain phenomena empirically or hypothetically, in a certain respect.[18]

Kant also recognised that the only tenable part of the *MAdN* was the first chapter, Phoronomy, and subsequently he described the *MAdN* in terms only suitable to Phoronomy.[19] Now Phoronomy is the quasi-mathematical, and explicitly *non*-dynamical, treatment of individual bodies in motion and of mathematical combinations of motions in a single body. To say that this is the only sound part of the *MAdN* is to admit that Kant's dynamic construction of matter out of forces, begun in *MAdN*, chapter 2, Dynamics, was a failure; and it is to admit, as Hegel charged, that Kant's constructions could only be "mathematical" and not "dynamical." Significantly, Kant came to see that rectifying that failure required excising even Phoronomy—and indeed the very mathematical model on which it is based—from the metaphysical foundations of physics.[20] This is to admit that phoronomic constructions, grounded and justified by the first *Critique*, could not come to grips with dynamic phenomena; that is to say, they do not provide a sufficient basis for analyzing forces.[21]

4. The Internal Problems with Kant's *MAdN*

Neither Hegel nor Kant elaborates this criticism of the *MAdN*, but close examination of Kant's *MAdN* and its role in the Critical system shows that they are right. The whole account of why this is so is intricate; here I can only sketch the main points. Briefly, they are these: Kant came to recognize that his account of matter in *MAdN*, first, begs the question and, second, is circular. For these reasons, Kant's basic forces are "merely ideal." Third, Kant's proof of the law of inertia is fallacious. Therefore, real forces transcend Kant's Critical analysis. After discussing each of these points, I elaborate their significance for Kant's Critical system, and then indicate some of Kant's main responses to them in his *Opus Postumum*. Finally, I draw some conclusions from them about Hegel's post-Kantian philosophical reorientation.

4.1. Kant's Defective Proof of Matter's Basic Forces

Kant's proof in the *MAdN* that matter is constituted by forces begs the question in the following way.[22] At the beginning of the second chapter of *MAdN*, Dynamics, Kant appeals to the main principle of the first chapter, Phoronomy (kinematics), but gives it an interpretation that cannot be sustained by that first part. In Phoronomy Kant demonstrates several principles concerning the mathematical description and combination of motions—in explicit and necessary abstraction from any dynamic interpretation of those motions or their causes.[23] Phoronomy concerns movements pure and simple, not their causes or forces. The first Proposition of Dynamics is the main principle of Kant's dynamic theory of matter. It states that "matter fills a space, not by its mere existence, but by a special moving force."[24] In the proof of this Proposition, Kant claims that "nothing can be combined with any motion *as lessening or destroying* it but another motion of the same movable thing in the opposite direction (phoronomic proposition)."[25] "Lessening or destroying" are not pure mathematical concepts! They are dynamic concepts that make no sense except by reference to forces. Consequently, these concepts do not belong in any proposition of Phoronomy, and they are not justified by any proposition of Phoronomy. Kant's crucial proof of his first principle of dynamics thus begs the question. This problem was pointed out by one of the first reviewers of the *MAdN*, and Kant transcribed this objection on to the first sheet of what became the *Opus Postumum*.[26] This explains Kant's reduction of the *MAdN* to phoronomy. Because phoronomy is modeled as closely as possible on mathematics (though it includes motion and thus time), this objection establishes Hegel's point that Kant's constructions of forces are only "mathematical" and not dynamical.

4.2. Kant's Circular Account of Matter's Quantity

Before the anonymous review brought this question-begging to Kant's attention, he came to see that his proof that matter and its quantity can be defined in terms of a balance of attractive and repulsive forces is circular.[27] On Kant's dynamic theory of matter, any bit of matter is constituted by equipoised attractive and repulsive forces radiating from a common center. The quantity of matter in any such spatial sphere occupied by two such forces—that is, the density of that matter—should be directly proportional to the combined absolute value of the intensities of the two fundamental forces that counterbalance each other in that matter. The basic attractive force is supposed to be identical to gravitational force. However, to preserve the Newtonian principle that gravitational attraction is proportional to mass, Kant must distinguish between gravitational attraction and the original power of attraction that, on his theory, combines with the original repulsive power to determine the basic quantity of matter. This is because, to retain the Newtonian equation, gravitational attraction is a (mathematical) function of density and volume, while density and volume must be (on Kant's theory) functions (both mathematically and constitutively) of the absolute values of *both* the original attractive and the repulsive force. Therefore, gravitational attraction cannot be identified with the original attractive force that constitutes any quantity of matter, simply because the original attractive force is only one of the two forces of which gravitational attraction is a (constitutive, metaphysical) function. Therefore, there must be at least two kinds of attractive force: Kant's "original" attractive force and gravity.

This further entails that gravity cannot be a *basic* force, because it is a (constitutive) function of the two basic forces that constitute any bit of matter. Once gravity is demoted to a derivative force, then the relation between it and the alleged basic forces of attraction and repulsion that supposedly constitute matter is entirely a matter of speculation, and can afford only feigned explanations of gravitational attraction—just as Kant concluded in the passage quoted above from his *Opus Postumum*.[28] Just as Hegel charged, Kant's basic forces are "merely ideal"; they are merely *Gedankendinge*, and so are not real forces.

4.3. Why Forces Transcend Kant's Critical Analysis

Hegel's further claim, that real forces transcend Kant's metaphysical analysis, is borne out by critical examination of one of Kant's main principles of Mechanics. Kant's proof of Proposition 3 of Mechanics is fallacious.[29] Proposition 3 is Kant's "Second Law" of Mechanics, that all physical causation is external. There are two defects in Kant's third Proposition. First, Kant's proof of the Newtonian Law of Inertia begs the question. Second, Kant's purportedly metaphysical proof of the externality of physical causation rests on an illicit and unsupported empirical premise.

4.3.1. Kant's Failure to Prove Newton's Law of Inertia

Kant states his Second Law as follows:

> Second law of mechanics: Every change of matter has an external cause. (Every body remains in its state of rest or motion in the same direction and with the same speed unless it is compelled by an external cause to forsake this state.)[30]

Notice that Kant's law speaks of the causally unaffected state of a body as either rest or "motion in the same direction." What does "same direction" mean? According to Newton, "same direction" meant rectilinear motion, as he explicitly states in his First Law.[31] The closely parallel wording of Kant's and Newton's laws strongly suggests that Kant's phrase "motion in the same direction" means "rectilinear motion." This suggestion is reinforced by Kant's claim in Phoronomy that he cannot treat non-linear motions in that chapter because Phoronomy must abstract from all forces, and such motions presuppose forces.[32] This may seem to pick nits, but everything turns on how one understands "motion in the same direction." Newton defined it in terms of rectilinear motion. Aristotle would have defined "motion in the same direction" in terms of something moving towards its natural place. Understood in this way, Aristotle could accept most of Kant's Second Law (aside from Kant's claim about the constancy of velocity). In another case—planetary motion—Aristotle and other Greek cosmologists understood "motion in the same direction" as motion in the same *circular* direction, and, in this case, speed was thought to be constant, and motion ceaseless, too. The point is this: Kant's Second Law claims that "every change of matter has an external cause." However, this principle cannot justify the claim that all "changes" in the motion of material bodies are deviations from rest or *rectilinear* motion, without *presupposing* what needs to be proven, namely, that rest or rectilinear motion is the natural state of motion of bodies.[33] Kant's proof of Newton's First Law begs the question.

4.3.2. Kant's Failure to Disprove Hylozoism

Showing the inadequacy of Kant's proof that all physical causality is external is more intricate; here I can only state the most basic points. Kant's argument for his second law of mechanics, that every change of matter has an external cause, rests entirely on matter consisting solely of external spatial relations. His proof assumes the transcendental causal thesis (defended in the first *Critique*) that every event has a cause. He then argues as follows:

> Matter as mere object of the external senses has no other determinations than those of external relations in space and hence undergoes no changes except by motion. With regard to such change, in so far as it is an exchange of one motion with another, or of motion with rest, and vice versa, a cause of such change must be found (according to the principle of [general] metaphysics [i.e. the first *Critique*]). But this cause cannot be internal, for matter has no

> absolutely internal determinations and grounds of determination. Hence all change is based upon an external cause (i.e. a body remains etc.).[34]

Kant claims that this is the law of inertia, and then remarks:

> The inertia of matter is and signifies nothing but its *lifelessness*, as matter in itself. *Life* means the capacity of a *substance* to determine itself to act from an *internal principle*, of a *finite substance* to determine itself to change, and of a *material substance* to determine itself to motion or rest as change of its state. Now, we know of no other internal principle of a substance to change its state but desire and no other activity whatever but thought, along with what depends upon such desire, namely feeling of pleasure or displeasure, and appetite or will. But these determining grounds and actions do not at all belong to the representations of the external senses and hence also not to the determinations of matter as matter. Therefore all matter as such is lifeless.[35]

Kant goes on to remark on how the entirety of physics as a science depends on the lifelessness of matter, and that the opposite view, hylozoism, would be "the death of all natural philosophy"—i.e. of physics.[36]

Kant's argument here is not inconsistent with biology as a science. Organic beings are subject both to physical laws and to further biological laws. Physics focuses only on some characteristics of matter, and hence only on some characteristics of material beings, including those material beings that happen to be organic. While it is an empirical question whether any of the beings we observe consist solely of matter, or if some (or even all) are composites of matter plus animate substance,[37] that is irrelevant to the issue of whether the material aspects of these beings are subject to the laws of physics.

However, I do not think that Kant has an adequate argument against hylozoism, and I think the inadequacies in his argument show that the lifelessness of matter is an empirical fact, not a metaphysical necessity. If that is correct, then Kant has no adequate proof of the externality of physical causation. The question cannot be whether the organic beings we experience are immaterial. Kant holds that, by the bare fact that organic beings are observed to be extended occupants of space, the metaphysical concept of matter as "the movable in space" applies to those beings.[38] The applicability of that concept to organic beings provides purchase for Kant's metaphysical arguments (such as they are) to show that, since those beings are material, they must be subject to physical laws, including the law of inertia.

The basic issue can be put two ways. One way is to ask, *given* Kant's transcendental and metaphysical principles and arguments, whether spatially extended bodies invested with living forces could *violate* the laws of physics. Another way is to ask whether a physics of "dead" matter is possible *simply* because matter is something extended and movable in space. That is Kant's contention, but his arguments are unconvincing. I shall argue that on Kant's grounds, it is a distinct logical, transcendental, metaphysical, and empirical possibility that matter be animate, or that material bodies violate the laws of physics.

Consider a counter-example. What would Kant do if he were called to witness and analyze a recalcitrant billiard ball that rolled at random times in unpredictable directions? Suppose we had something close to the theories and equipment available at "the end of science" and scientists gave us full assurance that no detectable external forces were influencing that peculiar billiard ball, and that thorough non-destructive analysis of the ball revealed nothing unusual about its internal structure. The "externality" of the ball's spatial relations would not suffice to demonstrate the externality of the causal principles responsible for the ball's unusual behavior. Nothing about the ball's behavior makes it an impossible object of experience; we can see it and we can record its wanderings in exact detail. But nothing these ultimate scientists can detect shows that the causes of its behavior are external. The "externality" of the spatial relations involved in the ball's occupying space does not entail—not logically, not transcendentally, not metaphysically—that the ball's behavior can only be governed by external causes.

Kant's argument for the intrinsic lifelessness of matter rests on two crucial premises. One is that "[m]atter as a mere object of the external senses has no other determinations than those of external relations in space."[39] It is one thing to infer that matter has external relations because it is spatially extended; it is quite another to infer that matter consists *only* of external relations because it is spatially extended. Kant's argument requires this stronger conclusion. Is it plausible to suppose that matter necessarily consists only of relations? This is what Kant *says*. Kant treats matter as if it were just "thick space," so to speak; otherwise it is a *non sequitur* to infer that what occupies space as such can *only* have "external" relations. The fact that billiard balls can be governed by external causes, and so are subject to the laws of physics, if and so long as that is a fact, is an empirical fact. Kant's metaphysical analysis may provide grounds for showing how the judgments involved in developing and applying our physical theories are possible, but they do not show that those judgments concern the *only* possible features of the objects of our theories. It is a piece of contingent luck that treating matter as dead, extended, massy stuff is an adequate basis for a successful physics. For all Kant has shown, the lifelessness of matter as such is an empirical fact, not a metaphysical necessity.

The second crucial premise is Kant's claim that

> we know of no other internal principle of a substance to change its state but desire and no other activity whatever but thought, along with what depends upon such desire, namely the feeling of pleasure or displeasure, and appetite or will.[40]

Unlike what Kant says about life, which he defines as "the capacity of a substance to determine itself to act from an internal principle,"[41] this claim is not a definition; it is a claim about what we know. Unfortunately, Kant gives no reasons to think that this claim to knowledge is transcendental or metaphysical, rather than empirical. The same problem infects Kant's argument in the Amphiboly against the existence of monads within the phenomenal realm.[42] The only empirical element which is supposed to enter Kant's metaphysical analysis in the *MAdN* is the empirical *concept* (not proposition) of matter as the movable in space.[43] Consequently, Kant cannot rest a metaphysical argument on such empirical propositions. The fact that he does shows that his *MAdN* cannot provide a "construction" of matter out of dynamic forces. Therefore, real forces transcend Kant's Critical analysis, just as Hegel charged.[44]

5. The Ramifications of these Problems for Kant's First *Critique*

These problems not only mark a failure in Kant's application of metaphysical principles to natural science. Because of the fundamental role of the *MAdN* in Kant's system, they mark a decisive failure of Kant's *Critique* of empirical and scientific knowledge as a whole. Two reasons for this may be indicated briefly.

5.1. Kant's Table of Categories as a Groundplan for Rational Physics

Burkhard Tuschling explains the importance of the *MAdN* for Kant's first *Critique* in terms of the Table of Categories laying the groundplan for theoretical science, in particular, the groundplan for the metaphysical foundations of physics. Publishing the *MAdN* thus fulfilled Kant's aim, left unfulfilled in the twenty years since Kant accepted Lambert's offer to collaborate, an aim which led Kant in the interim to write the first *Critique* to establish the parameters for the *MAdN*.[45] In this connection, Tuschling cites an important remark Kant added to the second edition of the *Critique*, subsequent to publishing the *MAdN*:

> For that this table [of categories] is extremely useful in the theoretical part of philosophy, and indeed is indispensable for outlining completely the plan of a whole of a science, so far as it rests on concepts *a priori*, and for dividing it systematically according to determinate principles, is self-evident from [the fact] that the table contains all the elementary concepts of the understanding in their completeness, indeed [it] even contains the form of a system of them in the human understanding, and consequently indicates all the moments of a projected speculative science, indeed even their order; as I accordingly have essayed (*Probe gegeben*) elsewhere.[46]

Kant refers in a footnote to the *MAdN* as the intended locus of this test (*Probe*). Tuschling then points out that a systematic failure of the *MAdN* thus reflects directly back on to the soundness of the first *Critique*.

5.2. External Causation and Kant's Analogies of Experience

I think Tuschling's point is correct, but is only part of the story. I have argued elsewhere that the causal principle defended in the Analogies of Experience is not the principle stated in the text of the *Critique* (in either edition), that every event has a cause.[47] The Analogies aim to defend causal interaction between distinct physical substances. This is explicit in the third Analogy, and implicit in the other two. This is because the principles in the Analogies form an integrated, mutually supporting set of principles; no one of them can be applied without joint use of the other two.[48] Because they aim to justify causal interaction between physical substances, the Analogies require the principle that every physical event has an external cause. Kant formulates and defends this principle only in the *MAdN*.[49] Consequently, this principle is required, not only for physical science, but also for common sense judgments about ordinary physical objects; it is necessary for applying the category of causality to objects of possible experience. If Kant's defense of this specific, metaphysical causal thesis in the *MAdN* fails, then the Principles of the Analogies of Experience—the very core of Kant's transcendental justification of the validity of causal judgments about objects of possible experience—are left unsupported.[50]

6. Kant's Reconsiderations in the *Opus Postumum*

As noted above, Kant's errors in Dynamics and Mechanics entail that the only tenable part of the *MAdN* is its quasi-mathematical analysis of motions, Phoronomy. In the *Opus Postumum* Kant resolved the circularity and the question-begging involved in his proof of the first proposition of dynamics, by recognizing that dynamical principles and the concepts of force they employ simply cannot be constructed on a purely mathematical basis.[51] Eckart Förster has shown that Kant came to see that the mathematical expression of forces presupposes those forces as fundamental, because those forces are necessary for the means of measurement through which alone their mathematical relations can be determined. Quantities of force and matter can only be determined by measurement. Yet the very existence and functioning of instruments of measure, such as balance scales, presuppose dynamic forces, such as cohesion, in order that those instruments (and their parts) have a form and function at all.[52] Forces are basic. This leads Kant to develop, at one stage of his reflections, what Burkhard Tuschling called a "transcendental dynamics," which involves a transcendental argument for realism—for the reality of forces and their fields. The existence of a continuous dynamic field of physical forces is conditionally necessary for the possibility of self-conscious experience, but its reality is no longer merely "empirical reality."[53]

Eckart Förster has also shown that along with Kant's transcendental dynamics comes (ca. August 1799—April 1800) a new doctrine of "self-positing," according to which we can only identify perceptible objects in space if we first identify ourselves as physiological beings who are centers of active force. We perceive ourselves and objects through our dynamic interaction.[54]

Burkhard Tuschling has argued that in his last stage Kant retracts the "transcendental dynamics" that undergirds the *Selbstsetzungslehre* reconstructed by Förster.[55] Nervous about ceding to transcendental realism, Kant soon (1800 and after) develops transcendental idealism into an unqualified idealism. Kant's late theory of self-positing combines nature and freedom, theoretical and practical reason, and transcendental philosophy and theology, through a system of transcendental ideas (not categories). Kant's last theory of self-positing holds that we posit ourselves and the objects we experience within the space and time by which we intuit them. Because these objects and their relations are only appearances which we posit, synthetic judgments *a priori* are possible. These are a few of the main points of Kant's late theoretical philosophy, but they suffice for present purposes.

7. Hegel's Post-Kantian Reorientation

The problems with the *MAdN*, which Kant himself saw, vindicate Hegel's criticism of the *MAdN* in the *Differenzschrift*, and they do much to justify Hegel's shift away from Kant's transcendental idealism towards his own holistic naturalism. Five aspects of this shift may be briefly indicated; they concern the idea of system, the nature of necessity, the relation between philosophy and physics, the emptiness of Kant's categories, and the metaphysics of transcendental arguments.

7.1. The Idea of System

According to Christian Wolff, the principles of scientific reasoning are the same across scientific disciplines, and a rational system can be constructed only by carefully ordering a fully determinate and complete set of rational and empirical data. According to Kant, empirical systems can only be coordinated aggregates of data, while rational systems contain a synthetic unity of subordinated differentia. The synthetic unity of a system stems from its idea of the whole of its domain, where that idea has priority over the subordinate parts, and the idea stems from the rational purposes of the discipline in question.[56] While Kant admits that the founder of a discipline may not always have an adequate idea of that new science,[57] what we see in Kant's efforts to work out his Critical philosophy is the fundamental way in which the leading idea of a discipline cannot have the kind of priority over its parts on which Kant insisted.[58] The leading idea of a discipline must be revised on the basis of its adequacy to the parts or components of its domain. This insight does not require a return to Wolff. Instead it rests on recognizing that one must work out concurrently both the leading idea and the systematic interpretation of the components of a domain. This insight is fundamental to Hegel's view of dialectical argument and development.[59] We also see that, at least on this occasion, the history of the philosophy of system itself follows a dialectical development from Wolff to Kant to Hegel.

7.2. The Status of Necessity

Coupled with Hegel's reconception of the idea of system goes a reconception of the nature and status of necessity. Kant's late *Selbstsetzungslehre* involves some extraordinary claims about what is known *a priori*, e.g. that we consist of systems of moving natural forces. Why would Kant come so close to naturalism and yet insist on such theses being *a priori*? One basic reason, Hegel notes, is that Kant's point of departure is Hume's critique of inductive and causal reasoning.[60] Necessity and universality cannot be established *a posteriori*.[61] Kant read Newton's *Principia* and saw unqualifiedly universal synthetic statements apparently expressing necessity. Misled by this surface grammar, he took Newton's laws as synthetic *a priori* propositions, and tried to provide an epistemological account of them in those terms.[62] Aware of the problems in Kant's theory, Hegel rejects any ultimate distinction between analytic and synthetic, and between *a priori* and *a posteriori*,[63] and he makes explicit what others have found implicit in Kant's philosophy of science, namely an account of necessity as grounded in systematic coherence.[64]

7.3. The Relation between Philosophy and Physics

Adopting a dialectical idea of system involves giving up the neat order of philosophical priority that undergirds Kant's original conception of Critical philosophy, namely, that transcendental philosophy grounds metaphysics, which in turn grounds the rational part of physics, which in turn provides the basis for physics as an empirical science. Hegel made bold and rejected Kant's rationalist view of the foundational relation between philosophy and empirical knowledge.[65] Hegel insists that philosophy is rooted in the empirical sciences:

> Philosophy must not only accord with the experience of nature; indeed, the *genesis* and *formation* of philosophic science has empirical physics as its presupposition and condition.[66]

Though he made this remark late in his career (in 1827), the basis of Hegel's enormous post-Kantian philosophical re-orientation is already set in the *Differenzschrift* of 1801, at the beginning of his reflections on Newtonian physics.[67] Hegel recognized from the start that physics does not have the sort of "metaphysical foundation" Kant proposed in the *MAdN*.

7.4. The Emptiness of Kant's Categories

A related reason for Hegel's philosophical re-orientation also stems from his criticism of Kant's *MAdN*. I noted above that Kant describes the importance of the *MAdN* in terms directly linked to the Schematism, namely, the *MAdN* provides cases *in concreto* which give the otherwise empty forms of thought, the categories, sense and meaning.[68] If the *MAdN* fail, as

Kant and Hegel recognized and as I have argued in detail elsewhere, then Kant's architectonic hierarchy shifts to a syllogism *modus tollens*: the categories are "mere forms of thought," just as Hegel charged in 1802.[69]

7.5. The Metaphysics of Transcendental Arguments

Finally, Kant's interim "transcendental dynamics" involves putative transcendental arguments for realism, for the reality of forces as natural phenomena, including those natural forces that constitute subjects as centers of experience. Why subjects as centers of experience? Because matter can only affect our senses through its moving forces,[70] but for them to affect us, we must ourselves be centers of moving forces.[71] If such an argument, or argument strategy, is an immanent, legitimate development out of Kant's own Transcendental Deduction, then this has profound implications for Hegel's emphasis on "the" transcendental deduction.[72] Hegel had, I believe, profound insight into just what Kant's deduction involves: regressive, "transcendental" arguments can be made independently of transcendental idealism, and can be made on behalf of realism and naturalism. This is the strategy Hegel developed in the *Phenomenology*.[73]

Notes

1. G.W.F. Hegel, *Wissenschaft der Logik*, edited by F. Hogemann and W. Jaeschke, *Gesammelte Werke*, Vol. 12 (Hamburg: Felix Meiner, 1981), pp. 14 (l. 27)-15 (l. 1); *Science of Logic*, translated by A.V. Miller (Atlantic Highlands, NJ: Humanities Press International, 1989), pp. 580-1. (Hegel's *Gesammelte Werke* hereafter abbreviated as *GW*. His *Wissenschaft der Logik* hereafter abbreviated as *Logik* [*GW*, **11**, **12**, **21**]; Miller, *Logic*. In references to works by Hegel and Kant below, line numbers follow page numbers in parentheses where needed.) I have analyzed and reconstructed Hegel's phenomenological method, with this issue in mind, in *Hegel's Epistemological Realism* (Dordrecht: Kluwer, 1989).

2. Karl Ameriks, "Hegel's Critique of Kant's Theoretical Philosophy," *Philosophy and Phenomenological Research* 46, 1

(1985): 1-35; Paul Guyer, "Thought and Being: Hegel's Critique of Kant," in *The Cambridge Companion to Hegel*, edited by F.C. Beiser (Cambridge: Cambridge University Press, 1993), pp. 171-210.

3. This paper sketches one main theme of my current research, which will be presented in full in Part 1 of my next book, "Kant, Hegel, and the Objective Deduction of Categorial Concepts." Some of this research has appeared in independent papers, which are cited below. Those interested in a fuller treatment of the problems with Kant's views, which I can only sketch here, should please refer to those papers.

4. This section is drawn from my article, "Does Kant's *Metaphysical Foundations of Natural Science* Fill a Gap in the *Critique of Pure Reason*?" *Synthese* 103, 1 (1995): 43-86.

5. I. Kant, *Kritik der reinen Vernunft. Kants Gesammelte Schriften*, Vols. 3, 4 (Königlich Preußische [now Deutsche] Akademie der Wissenschaften, Berlin: G. Reimer [now de Gruyter], 1902–), A845/B873, A65-6/B90-1, A55-7/B79-82; *GS*, **3**: 546 (ll. 16-23), 83 (l. 33)-84 (l. 7), 77-8. Citations from Kant's first *Critique* refer hereafter to the usual 'A' and 'B' designations of its two editions, along with volume, page and line numbers (in parentheses) from the *Gesammelte Schriften* (abbreviated as *GS*). The pagination of *GS* appears in all recent translations of Kant's writings.

6. A171/B213, A206-7/B252; *GS*, **3**: 155, 178.

7. B19; *GS*, **3**: 39; I. Kant, *Prolegomena zu einer jeden künftigen Metaphysik, die als Wissenschaft wird auftreten können* (hereafter *Prol.*), §5 (*GS*, **4**), p. 279.

8. B25; *GS*, **3**: 43; cf. A11-12; *GS*, **4**: 23.

9. A207/B252; *GS*, **3**: 178. I have recalled only those points that are most important for my subsequent analysis. For more thorough discussion of Kant's transcendental level of analysis, see Eckart Förster, "Kant's Notion of Philosophy," *The Monist* 72, 2 (1989): 285-304, esp. 290-2.

10. Axxi; *GS*, **4**: 13-14; A845-8/B873-6; *GS*, **3**: 546-8; *Prol.* §5 (*GS*, **4**), p. 279.

11. I. Kant, *Metaphysische Anfangsgründe der Naturwissenschaft* (hereafter *MAdN* [*GS*, **4**]), pp. 469-70.

12. A845/B873; *GS*, **3**: 546; cf. "Welches sind die wirklichen Fortschritte, die die Metaphysik seit Leibnizens und Wolffs Zeiten in Deutschland gemacht hat?" Erster Entwurf, zweite Abteilung (*GS*, **20**), p. 285 (ll. 31-7).

13. *MAdN* (*GS*, **4**), p. 478 (ll. 15-20). Translation by J. Ellington in I. Kant, *Philosophy of Material Nature* (Indianapolis: Hackett, 1985).

14. Eckart Förster, "Is There 'A Gap' in Kant's Critical System?" *Journal of the History of Philosophy* 25, 4 (1987): 542. Michael Friedman takes up this point, too, and treats the *MAdN* as if it *is* the schematism of the categories, *Kant and the Exact Sciences* (Cambridge, MA: Harvard University Press, 1992), pp. 136-7, 159, 163-4, 171, 185, 202-3, 234, 255, 259. Friedman has greatly overstated the case. I criticize Friedman's interpretation in detail in "Kant's Dynamic Constructions," *Journal of Philosophical Research* 20 (1995): 33-81 (§X).

15. A147/B187; *GS*, **3**: 139 (ll. 36-7), my translation.

16. B49; *GS*, **3**: 59 (ll. 14-16). The official relations between the first *Critique* and the *MAdN* are complex, and have been subject to controversy. For a very good discussion of the topic, see Daniel Dahlstrom, "Kant's Metaphysics of Nature," in *Nature and Scientific Method*, edited by Daniel Dahlstrom (Washington, D.C.: Catholic University of America Press, 1991), pp. 271-90.

17. G.W.F. Hegel, *The Difference Between Fichte's and Schelling's System of Philosophy*, translated by H.S. Harris and W. Cerf (Albany: SUNY Press, 1977), p. 164; *GW*, **4**: 69 (l. 36)-70 (l. 4).

18. Xth Fascicle (August 1799-April 1800); *GS*, **22**: 282 (ll. 12-18); *Opus postumum*, translated by E. Förster and M. Rosen (Cambridge: Cambridge University Press, 1993), p. 100.

19. *GS*, **21**: 402 (ll. 11-24); cf. *GS*, **21**: 524 (ll. 10-16), 483 (ll. 14-18); Förster and Rosen, pp. 14-15, 36, 44. The first of these passages is quoted in part by Burkhard Tuschling in *Metaphysische und transzendentale Dynamik in Kants opus postumum* (Berlin: de Gruyter, 1971) (hereafter *Met. & tr. Dynamik*), pp. 62-3. I am indebted throughout to his, and to Eckart Förster's, work on Kant's *Opus postumum*.

20. Cf. *GS*, **21**: 482 (ll. 4-18); *GS*, **22**: 487 (l. 27)-490 (l. 27), 511 (l. 17)-517 (l. 2); Förster and Rosen, pp. 43, 138-9, 151-3.

21. In this regard, Kant's and Hegel's criticism of the *MAdN* parallels Aristotle's criticism of Pythagorean physics. The Pythagoreans, according to Aristotle, "do not tell us at all, however, how there can be movement if limit and unlimited and odd and even are the only things assumed, or how without movement and change there can be generation and destruction, or the bodies that move through the heavens can do what they do," *Metaphysics* 990a8-12; translation by W.D. Ross in *Aristotle's Metaphysics* (Clarendon Press: Oxford, 1924). I thank Daniel Dahlstrom for bringing this passage to my attention.

22. This and the next section are abridged from my "Kant's Dynamic Constructions," *Journal of Philosophical Research* (1995).

23. *MAdN* (*GS*, **4**), p. 494 (ll. 28-38).

24. *MAdN* (*GS*, **4**), p. 497 (ll. 15-16); translation by J. Ellington in Kant, *Philosophy of Material Nature*.

25. *MAdN* (*GS*, **4**), p. 497 (ll. 21-4), emphasis added; translation by J. Ellington in Kant, *Philosophy of Material Nature*.

26. Anonymous review in *Göttingische Anzeigen von gelehrten Sachen* 191 (December 2, 1786): 1914-18, pp. 1915-16; reprinted in *Rezensionen zur Kantischen Philosophie 1781-87*, edited by A. Landau (Bebra: Albert Landau Verlag, 1991), **1**: 479-81, p. 480. Gerhard Lehman quotes the relevant paragraph of the review (*GS*, **22**: 809). Kant's transcription is likely to have been made shortly after the review would have appeared, no later than 1787.

27. *GS*, **21**: (1st ed.) 348, (2nd ed.) 361 (l. 30)-362 (l. 2); letter to J.S. Beck, 16 Oct. 1792; *GS*, **21**: (1st ed.) 362, (2nd ed.) 376 (l. 35)-377 (l. 4). I wish to make a brief note of one piece of literature on Kant's *MAdN* which appeared after my "Kant's Dynamic Constructions" went to press. The circularity I sketch here is distinct from those referred to and addressed by Alfred E. and Maria G. Miller in their "Translator's Introduction and Commentary" to Peter Plaass, *Kant's Theory of Natural Science*, Boston Studies in the Philosophy of Science, Vol. 159 (Dordrecht: Kluwer, 1994). I do not believe that their means for resolving some other apparent circularities can be extended to the two I develop in "Kant's Dynamic Constructions," nor do I believe their means are sound. They import Kant's regressive, transcendental method of proof in the first *Critique* directly into the *MAdN*. In the first *Critique*, a Principle does serve as its own "ground of proof"

because it makes experience possible (A737/B765; Miller and Miller, p. 59). However, precisely because the transcendental principles of the first *Critique* are (purportedly) established prior to the *MAdN* (Miller and Miller, p. 60), Kant cannot offer transcendental arguments for the principles defended in the *MAdN*. The Millers' way of contrasting unthematic and thematic aspects of Kant's analysis (Miller and Miller, p. 59), and their way of emphasizing the internal consistency and mutual interdependence of the components of Kant's analysis of the metaphysical foundations of physics (Miller and Miller, p. 61), are not precise enough to distinguish transcendental, metaphysical, bootstrap, and viciously circular argument. However, their interpretation deserves more attention than I can give it here. I shall do so in my forthcoming book.

28. Xth Fascicle (August 1799-April 1800); *GS*, **22**: 282 (ll. 12-18), quoted above, p. 139. While I have not found exactly this objection to Kant's construction of matter from attractive and repulsive forces in Hegel, Hegel did severely, and effectively, criticize Kant's construction to much the same effect in the *Science of Logic*; see *GW*, **21**: 166-208; *GW*, **11**: 102-7; Miller, *Logic*, pp. 178-84.

29. This section is drawn from my "Kant's Proof of the Law of Inertia," in *Proceedings of the Eighth International Kant Congress*, edited by H. Robinson, 2 Vols (Milwaukee: Marquette University Press, 1995), **2.1**: 413-24.

30. *MAdN* (*GS*, **4**), p. 543; translation by J. Ellington in Kant, *Philosophy of Material Nature*.

31. "Every body continues in its state of rest, or of uniform motion in a right line, unless it is compelled to change that state by forces impressed upon it," I. Newton, *Mathematical Principles of Natural Philosophy*, translated by A. Motte, revised by F. Cajori (Chicago: Encyclopedia Britannica, 1952).

32. *MAdN* (*GS*, **4**), pp. 480 (ll. 15-18), 495 (ll. 5-12). At one point Kant recognizes that progressive movements might be curved (*MAdN* [*GS*, **4**], p. 483 [ll. 8-16]). However, two pages later he claims that curved motions involve a continuous change of direction, and thus presuppose forces (*MAdN* [*GS*, **4**], p. 495 [ll. 5-12]). This passage, I believe, clinches the point that by his phrase in his Second Law, "motion in the same direction," Kant intends rectilinear motions.

33. Kant indeed does assume this important point right at the beginning of Phoronomy. See previous note.

34. *MAdN* (*GS*, **4**), p. 543; translation by J. Ellington in Kant, *Philosophy of Material Nature*.

35. *MAdN* (*GS*, **4**), p. 544; translation by J. Ellington in Kant, *Philosophy of Material Nature*.

36. *MAdN* (*GS*, **4**), p. 544 (ll. 25-6).

37. Kant explains life expressly in dualist terms at *MAdN* (*GS*, **4**), p. 544 (ll. 7-19).

38. *MAdN* (*GS*, **4**), pp. 480-2.

39. *MAdN* (*GS*, **4**), p. 543 (ll. 25-6); translation by J. Ellington in Kant, *Philosophy of Material Nature*.

40. *MAdN* (*GS*, **4**), p. 544; translation by J. Ellington in Kant, *Philosophy of Material Nature*.

41. *MAdN* (*GS*, **4**), p. 544; translation by J. Ellington in Kant, *Philosophy of Material Nature*.

42. A285/B341; *GS*, **3**: 229 (ll. 10-12). For discussion, see James Van Cleve, "Inner States and Outer Relations: Kant and the Case for Monadism," in *Doing Philosophy Historically*, edited by P. Hare (Buffalo: Prometheus, 1988), pp. 231-47, esp. p. 244.

43. *MAdN* (*GS*, **4**), pp. 470 (ll. 1-12), 472 (ll. 4-6).

44. I would like to make two brief comments on my analysis of Kant's proof (in "Kant's Proof of the Law of Inertia," *Proceedings of the Eighth International Kant Congress*), in response to concerns raised at the Congress by William Harper and Stephen Palmquist. First, I claimed that Kant's statement of the Law of Inertia is not equivalent to Newton's. Kant's statement of Newton's law includes the term "speed" (*Geschwindigkeit*), which Kant may have understood in Newtonian, proto-vectorial terms. If so, his statement of Newton's law is correct. However, that would make Kant's statement redundant, since he states beforehand sameness of direction ("*Richtung*"). Translating Kant's term "*Geschwindigkeit*" by "velocity," as I followed Ellington in doing, may read too much Newton into Kant's actual formulation. Most importantly, though, my main objection still holds, that Newton's law does not follow from Kant's second law of mechanics ("Kant's Proof of the Law of Inertia," pp. 413-14). Second, in so far as my examples show that the errant billiard balls I describe are alive,

where life, according to Kant, "is the capacity of a substance to determine itself to change" (*MAdN* [*GS*, **4**], p. 544 [ll. 7-10]), my examples show that billiard balls could be alive even though they consist solely of external spatial relations and utterly lack any psychic states. This highlights the crucial way in which Kant's key premise, that "we know of no other internal principle of a substance to change its state but desire ... " (*MAdN* [*GS*, **4**], p. 544 [ll. 10-14]), concerns empirical ignorance. Moreover, my examples of non-Newtonian collisions do not require that billiard balls be alive, only that they respond to collisions in ways that violate Newton's Second Law, say, by spiraling away. In this regard, my examples underscore the crucial way in which Newton's law is based on an empirical, physical postulate concerning inertia, rather than on any metaphysical principle of the sort Kant seeks to justify. In these regards, my objections may require more careful and thorough presentation, but I submit that they are basically sound.

45. Tuschling, *Met. & tr. Dynamik*, pp. 37-9.

46. B109-10; *GS*, **3**: 95 (ll. 14-23), my translation.

47. In my "Does Kant's *Metaphysical Foundations of Natural Science* Fill a Gap in the *Critique of Pure Reason*?" *Synthese* (1995).

48. See Paul Guyer, *Kant and the Claims of Knowledge* (Cambridge: Cambridge University Press, 1987), pp. 168, 212-14, 224-5, 228, 239, 246, 274-5.

49. MAdN (*GS*, **4**), p. 543; cf. *Kritik der Urteilskraft* (*GS*, **5**), Einleitung, p. 181 (ll. 15-31) [hereafter *KdU*].

50. This marks the downfall of the whole of Kant's Critical analysis of the transcendental and metaphysical conditions of empirical knowledge because the other potential domain of application, psychology, is already foreclosed by Kant's arguments in the Paralogisms which entail that none of the Principles of the Analogies can be applied to the objects of inner sense ("psychology," as Kant understood it). This is because we cannot identify substances within the form of inner intuition, time, and identifying substances is necessary for applying each of the Principles of the Analogies. For discussion, see my paper, "Kant's Critique of Determinism in Empirical Psychology," in *Proceedings of the Eighth International Kant Congress*, **2.1**: 357-70.

51. *GS*, **22**: 282 (August-September 1798), quoted above, p. 139.

52. *GS*, **21**: 294 (ll. 29ff.), 299 (l. 10); cf. Loses Blatt Leipzig 1, in *Übergang. Untersuchungen zum Spätwerk Immanuel Kants*, edited by the Forum für Philosophie Bad Homburg (Frankfurt am Main: Vittorio Klostermann, 1991), p. 152 [hereafter cited as *Übergang*]. These passages are quoted and discussed by Eckart Förster in "Die Idee des Überganges. Überlegungen zum Elementarsystem der bewegenden Kräfte," *Übergang*, pp. 28-48, p. 36. Förster summarizes some of these points in §11 of "Kant's Third Critique and the *Opus Postumum*," *Graduate Faculty Philosophy Journal* 16, 2 (1993): 345-58. The interpretation of Hegel's critique of Kant's philosophy of science offered here was first sketched in my review of *Übergang* in *The Owl of Minerva* 24, 2 (Spring 1993): 235-42.

53. For the origins of this argument in the first *Critique*, see B. Jeffrey Edwards, "Der Ätherbeweis des *Opus Postumum* und Kants 3. Analogie der Erfahrung," *Übergang*, pp. 77-104.

54. E. Förster, "Kant's *Selbstsetzungslehre*," in *Kant's Transcendental Deductions*, edited by E. Förster (Stanford: Stanford University Press, 1989), pp. 217-38; cf. Förster, "Kant's Notion of Philosophy," *The Monist* (1989): 298-302.

55. B. Tuschling, "Die Idee des transzendentalen Idealismus im späten *Opus postumum*," in *Übergang*, pp. 105-45.

56. This summary is based on the fine analysis by Norbert Hinske, "Die Wissenschaften und ihre Zwecke: Kants Neuformulierung der Systemidee," in *Akten des 7. internationalen Kant-Kongresses*, edited by G. Funke, 2 Vols (Bonn: Bouvier, 1991), **1**: 157-77.

57. A834/B862;*GS*, **3**: 539 (l. 28)-540 (l. 6).

58. Kant continued to insist on this priority even in the *Opus postumum*. Cf. Loses Blatt 3/4; *GS*, **21**: 478 (ll. 11-16); Förster and Rosen, p. 42.

59. For a brief characterization of Hegel's dialectic, see my entry, "Dialectic (Hegel)," in *A Companion to Epistemology*, edited by E. Sosa and J. Dancy (Oxford: Blackwell, 1992), pp. 98-9. For full detail, see my *Hegel's Epistemological Realism*.

60. G.W.F. Hegel, *Vorlesungen über die Geschichte der Philosophie III*, edited by E. Moldenhauer and K.M. Michel, *Werke in zwanzig Bänden*, Vol. 20 (Frankfurt am Main: Suhrkamp Verlag, 1971), pp. 333, 335-6; *Lectures on the History of Philosophy*, translated by E.S. Haldane and F.H. Simson, 3 Vols (New

York: Humanities, 1955), **3**: 427-8; *Lectures on the History of Philosophy*, translated by R.F. Brown, 3 Vols (Berkeley: University of California Press, 1990), **3**: 217-18, 219-20.

Another reason for Kant's rejection of naturalism, of course, was to defend freedom, in part by foreclosing on the possibility of any materialist theory of mind (A383; *GS*, **4**: 240 [ll. 1-3]; B419-20, 421; *GS*, **3**: 274 [ll. 9-15], 274 [l. 36]-75 [l. 3]; *KdU* §89 (*GS*, **5**), p. 460 [ll. 20-32]). (For discussion, see my paper, "Kant's Critique of Determinism in Empirical Psychology," *Proceedings of the Eighth International Kant Congress*.) Hegel, too, sought to defend freedom, and he realized that freedom had to be defended very differently once one accepts naturalism. I have detailed one main set of Hegel's objections to Kant's account of freedom in "Hegel's Critique of Kant's Moral World View," *Philosophical Topics* 19, 2 (1991): 133-76. Also see "How 'Full' is Kant's Categorical Imperative?", *Jahrbuch für Recht und Ethik / Annual Review of Law and Ethics* 3 (1995): 465-509. I have outlined his main strategy for analyzing and establishing freedom in "The Basic Context and Structure of Hegel's *Philosophy of Right*," in *The Cambridge Companion to Hegel*, pp. 234-69, and in "Hegel on Political Representation: Laborers, Corporations and the Monarch," *The Owl of Minerva* 25, 1 (Fall 1993): 111-16.

61. B4, B13, B17, A2, A91/B124ff., A112, A114; *Prol.* (*GS*, **4**), p. 258. Cf. *MAdN* (*GS*, **4**), pp. 468-9.

62. Bx, B17-20; *GS*, **3**: 9, 38-40.

63. Hegel is explicit about this in *Glauben und Wissen* (*GW*, **4**: 335 [ll. 2-6]; translated by H.S. Harris and W. Cerf in *Faith and Knowledge* [Albany: SUNY Press, 1977]), where he links this directly to his sense of "speculative" knowledge.

64. On this aspect of Kant's philosophy of science, see Philip Kitcher, "Projecting the Order of Nature," in *Kant's Philosophy of Physical Science*, edited by R. Butts (Dordrecht: Reidel, 1986), pp. 201-38; Thomas Wartenberg, "Reason and the Practice of Science," in *The Cambridge Companion to Kant*, edited by Paul Guyer (Cambridge: Cambridge University Press, 1992), pp. 228-48; and Gerd Buchdahl, *Kant and the Dynamics of Reason* (Oxford: Blackwell, 1992), chaps. 8-13. (The problem with Buchdahl's interpretation of Kant is that he tries to make these elements out to be the whole of Kant's view.) On the relation between Kant's views and Quine's, see Philip Kitcher, "How Kant Almost Wrote *Two Dogmas of Empiricism* (and Why He Didn't)," in *Essays on Kant's*

Critique of Pure Reason, edited by J.N. Mohanty and R. Shahan (Norman: University of Oklahoma Press, 1982), pp. 185-215. On Hegel's anticipation of Quine, see B. Tuschling, "Sind die Urteile der Logik vielleicht 'insgesamt synthetisch'?" *Kant-Studien* 72, 3 (1981): 304-35. On Hegel's view of the role of systematic considerations, see Buchdahl , "Hegel's Philosophy of Nature and the Structure of Science," in *Hegel*, edited by M. Inwood (Oxford: Oxford University Press, 1985), pp. 110-36, and "Conceptual Analysis and Scientific Theory in Hegel's Philosophy of Nature (with Special reference to Hegel's Optics)," in *Hegel and the Sciences*, edited by R.S. Cohen and M. Wartofsky (Dordrecht: Reidel, 1984), pp. 13-36.

65. Eckart Förster has shown that Kant ultimately did give up his original distinction between transcendental and metaphysical philosophy ("Kant's Notion of Philosophy," *The Monist* [1989]). However, his late recoil from naturalism (documented by Burkhard Tuschling) shows that he refused to take this last step.

66. G.W.F. Hegel, *Enzyklopädie der philosophischen Wissenschaften im Grundrisse (1830). Zweiter Teil: Die Naturphilosophie mit den mündlichen Zusätzen*, edited by E. Moldenhauer and K.M. Michel, *Werke in zwanzig Bänden*, Vol. 9 (Frankfurt am Main: Suhrkamp Verlag, 1970), §246 Anm., my translation; cf. §246 Zus. (also from the Berlin period). [The *Enzyklopädie* is hereafter cited as *EL* or *EN*.] To say that philosophical science presupposes and is conditioned by empirical physics is not to say, as Hegel goes on explicitly to deny, that philosophical science is itself (only) empirically justified.

67. In the second edition of the *Enzyklopädie* (1827) Hegel had also added the following statement to his discussion of Kepler and Newton: "I shall not appeal to the fact that, moreover, an interest in these subjects has occupied me for twenty five years," (§270 Anm.; *GW*, **19**: 209 [ll. 11-13]). (A.V. Miller's translation of the *Philosophy of Nature* [Oxford: Clarendon Press, 1970] preserves this statement in a footnote. It is omitted from M.J. Petry's translation [*Hegel's Philosophy of Nature*, 3 Vols (London: Allen and Unwin, 1970)] and from *Werke in zwanzig Bänden*, Vol. 9, both of which follow the third edition [1830].) Twenty five years puts the beginning of these reflections at 1802, but in this context this figure is likely to be a round number. There are extensive reflections on Newton in Hegel's Jena *Systementwürfe*, but I have not found any specific discussion of Newton's three laws, much

less the first law, as such, nor of Kant's proof thereof. Hegel's interest was primarily directed towards Newton's theory of planetary motion, a selective focus that aided his re-validation of Kepler. Hegel does discuss inertia as a fundamental characteristic of matter (*EN* [1830], §§263ff.), and he relates it to the externality of physical causation (*EN* [1830], §264 Anm.), but he doesn't there discuss Newton's First Law or Kant's proof thereof. However, Hegel's careful study of Newton goes back to his Frankfurt period, from which an apparently detailed set of notes is now lost. Hegel's much maligned *Dissertatio philosophica de orbitis planetarum* (Jena: Prager, 1801) in fact offered some acute criticisms of Newton's proof of Kepler's second law and of the Titius-Bode law. See Cinzia Ferrini, "On Newton's Demonstration of Kepler's Second Law in Hegel's *De orbitis planetarum* (1801)," *Philosophia naturalis* 31, 1 (1994): 150-70, and Mauro Nasti De Vincentis, "Hegel's Worm in Newton's Apple" (in this volume). Also see Bernard Beaumont, "Hegel and the Seven Planets," *Mind* 62 (1954): 246-48.

68. See above p. 138.

69. I take this phrase from Kant's own statements in the first *Critique* and *MAdN*, quoted above, pp. 138-9. Hegel doesn't formulate his early critique of Kant's theoretical philosophy in terms of Kant's categories being mere empty forms of thought; instead he formulates it in terms of Kant's categories being merely formal identities (e.g. *Glauben und Wissen* [*GW*, **4**], pp. 328, 343, 383; Harris and Cerf, pp. 70-1, 92-3, 148). However, the point comes to the same; formal identities are contentless forms, whether in practical or theoretical philosophy (cf. *EL* [1830], §54).

Kant's architectonic has strong affiliations with syllogisms, both in terms of subsuming intuitions under concepts, and in terms of subsuming sensibility under understanding, and understanding under reason: "Der Verstand macht für die Vernunft eben so einen Gegenstand aus, als die Sinnlichkeit für den Verstand" (A665-6/B693-4; *GS*, **3**: 439 [ll. 29-30]). This underscores both the importance of the possibility of supplying cases *in concreto* for the categorial forms of thought (understanding), and the possibility of Hegel's argument *modus tollens* against the soundness of Kant's Critical theory of empirical knowledge as a whole, in view of Kant's ultimate failure to justify *a priori* the Principles of the Analogies.

70. A19-20/B34, A494/B522; *Prol.* Anm. II (*GS*, **4**), p. 289; *MAdN* (*GS*, **4**), p. 476; cf. *MAdN* (*GS*, **4**), p. 508. I defend the legitimacy of a causal interpretation of Kant's locutions about sensory affection in "Noumenal Causality Reconsidered" (*Canadian Journal of Philosophy* 27, 2 [1997]: 209-46).

71. *GS*, **21**: 490 (ll. 24-30), 213 (ll. 10-16); *GS*, **22**: 326 (l. 30)-327 (l. 3), 364 (ll. 24-5); Förster and Rosen, pp. 66, 110; quoted and discussed by Förster, "Kant's *Selbstsetzungslehre*," in *Kant's Transcendental Deductions*, p. 230ff.

72. Cf. Hegel, *Logik* (*GW*, **12**), pp. 17 (l. 28)-19 (l. 2); Miller, *Logic*, pp. 584-5.

73. Or so I have argued in *Hegel's Epistemological Realism*. The interpretation of Hegel's critique of Kant's *MAdN* developed here provides an independent ground to support the naturalistic, realist interpretation of Hegel I developed there. Also see my essay, "Kant, Hegel, and the Transcendental Material Conditions of Possible Experience," *Bulletin of the Hegel Society of Great Britain* 33 (1996): 23-41. In "Affinity, Idealism, and Naturalism: The Stability of Cinnabar and the Possibility of Experience" (*Kant-Studien* 88 [1997]: 139-89), I show that this strategy is employed by Kant himself in the first *Critique*. In "Transcendental Reflections on Pragmatic Realism" (in K.R. Westphal, ed. *Pragmatism, Reason, and Norms* [New York: Fordham University Press, 1997], pp. 17-59) I develop Hegel's transcendental argument for realism independently of Hegel's text. Hegel presents this argument in "Self-Consciousness" and "Reason" in the *Phenomenology*; see *Hegel's Epistemological Realism*, pp. 160-71.

Robert Pippin takes Hegel in a Fichtean, transcendental idealist direction in *Hegel's Idealism* (Cambridge: Cambridge University Press, 1989). Our differences were presented as plainly as possible at a symposium on his book, published in *International Philosophical Quarterly* 33, 3 (1993), which includes both my critique, "Hegel, Idealism, and Robert Pippin," (pp. 263-72) and Pippin's reply, "Hegel's Original Insight" (pp. 285-95). Henry Harris endorsed my realist view of Hegel in his review of my book (*Philosophy of the Social Sciences* 22, 4 [1992]: 512-34), and develops a realist interpretation of Hegel in his commentary on Hegel's *Phenomenology*, *Hegel's Ladder*, 2 Vols (Indianapolis: Hackett, 1997). (We agree about Hegel's realism; we don't agree about the structure of Hegel's argument in the *Phenomenology*. Some of our disagreements are presented in Harris's paper,

"Hegel's Correspondence Theory of Truth," and my comment on it, "Harris, Hegel, and the Truth about Truth," both in *Hegel's Phenomenology: A Reappraisal*, edited by G. Browning [Dordrecht: Kluwer, 1997], pp. 11-30.) For detailed discussion, see my "Harris, Hegel, and the Spirit of the *Phenomenology*" (*Clio*, 1998), with Harris's reply.

This is a revised version of a paper first presented at the Fifth Annual University of New Hampshire Philosophy Symposium, "Kant and Hegel: New Studies, New Considerations" (October 1993). I am grateful to my commentator on that occasion, Derek Perebom, for his helpful remarks. This version benefited from discussion at the Hegel Society of America meeting in Washington, D.C. at which it was presented, and particularly from suggestions from Daniel Dahlstrom and Cinzia Ferrini.

7

Hegel's Appropriation of Kant's Account of Teleology in Nature

Daniel O. Dahlstrom

"One of Kant's great services to philosophy," Hegel observes in the chapter on Teleology in the *Science of Logic*, "consists in the distinction which he sets up between relative or *external* and *internal* purposiveness; in the latter he opened up the concept of *life*, the *Idea*."[1] Kant's account of natural purposes, based upon the notion of internal purposiveness, gives expression, Hegel continues, to nothing less than "the *concrete universal*," incorporating both particularity and externality.[2] At the same time, however, Hegel finds Kant's elaboration of this teleological principle essentially "unsatisfactory" and he lambasts Kant for not simply "confusing," but even "ruining," this "highest idea."[3] Moreover, as is demonstrated in greater detail below, this censure of Kant's ultimate treatment of teleological judgments remains as constant in Hegel's writings as his praise for the idea of inner purposiveness.

The immediate aim of the following paper is to examine Hegel's ontological and critical appropriation of Kant's account of teleology in nature. There are at least two purposes that are served by pursuing this aim and that, accordingly, form the background and interpretive horizon for the examination. First, the examination demonstrates just how significantly Hegel's reading of Kant's *Critique of Judgment* figures in the development of his speculative metaphysics. As Klaus Düsing notes, of all the doctrines elaborated in Kant's three critiques, none stand closer in Hegel's eyes to his own position than those formulated in the Critique of Teleological Judgment.[4] Second, for all the differences exhibited by what each construes to be an adequate account of organic nature as well as the possibilities of such an account, Kant's and Hegel's philosophies of organic nature rest on certain shared assumptions. Some of these assumptions are compatible, others incompatible, with the neo-Darwinian synthesis dominating twentieth century biology.[5] Remarkably, these theoretical incompatibilities are resurfacing in recent challenges to the neo-Darwinian synthesis, a development briefly addressed in the final segment of the following paper. Precisely because such challenges to the regnant paradigm can be given a Kantian or Hegelian interpretation, the examination of the nature and validity of Hegel's critical appropriation of Kant's conception of natural purposes takes on added significance.

Purposiveness and Intuitive Understanding in Kant's Critique of Teleological Judgment

A scientist investigating some specific natural phenomenon is on the lookout for a rule under which it may be subsumed, that is to say, a general principle in terms of which that particular phenomenon may be explained. In other words, the scientist assumes the possibility of understanding that phenomenon, a possibility entailing the idea that there is an underlying unity to that phenomenon. In effect, the researcher investigates nature as though it in some way accords with, or is suited to, his or her abilities to understand it, as if it were there for him or her.[6]

"Purposiveness" is Kant's term for the principle at work here. Purposiveness in a broad sense signifies the sort of causality involved when a concept or, analogously, a future possibility of an object, at which the object is aimed or for which it is designed, is regarded as the object's cause.[7] Paradigmatically, purposiveness is the causal principle involved in human action, for example, in art or manufacture where the entertaining of some effect (such as going over the plans for a building) contributes to the production of that effect. Analogously, the working scientist regards the possible unity to specific natural phenomena (which otherwise present themselves merely as contingent) as the cause or explanation for the reality at hand, as though nature in all its particular manifestations followed some plan or concept, allowing scientists to grasp it as a system. In this way Kant argues in the *Critique of Judgment* that the transcendental principle of the purposiveness of nature serves as the necessary basis for the scientific researcher's attempt to grasp the myriad particular forms and laws of natural phenomena.[8]

An analogous use of the same principle, he contends, makes it possible to grasp the distinctive character of organic behavior which remains inexplicable on mechanical grounds alone.[9] Specifically, the reproduction of the species from one distinct individual to the next, the individual organism's development through assimilation of material lying outside it, and finally, the reciprocal renewal and maintenance by various organs within an entire organic being, all seem possible to Kant only on the basis of some central steering principle or "natural purpose."[10] An organism, he observes, has a kind of "*formative* force."[11] In each case, something that is merely possible—for example, the next generation or the growth, maintenance, and repair of the individual organism as a whole—is regarded as the cause of the processes which bring it about. More specifically, in order for something to be so regarded as a "natural purpose," the parts of the entity must be possible only through their relation to the whole entity and the parts must combine into the unity of the whole entity "by virtue of the fact that they are, in regard to one another, reciprocally cause and effect of the form of the unity."[12]

When Kant speaks of an "inner purposiveness," he has in mind precisely such an "*organized and self-organizing entity*."[13] Apart from any connection with other things, it has to be considered as a purposeful whole. Everything within it is at once reciprocally and, for the sake of the whole, necessarily means and end. Thus, in air-breathing vertebrates, for example, certain muscular movements, namely, a rhythmical expansion and contraction of the walls of the chest rush oxygen into the lungs where it is absorbed into the blood stream at the alveoli; the oxygenated blood is then conveyed to the left ventricle of the heart via the pulmonary veins and pumped by the heart to the medulla oblongata which in turn controls those muscular movements that induce air into the lungs. Such inner purposiveness stands in direct contrast to relative or external purposiveness, for example, the beneficial character of a particular environment, its supply of foodstuffs or the protection it affords.[14] Accordingly, Kant defines "the principle for the evaluation of inner purposiveness in organized entities" as follows: "*An organized product of nature is that in which everything is purpose and reciprocally also means.*"[15]

As mentioned earlier, Kant emphasizes that there is only an analogy, indeed a "distant analogy," between this organic sort of final causality and that characteristic of human action.[16] The similarity lies in the fact that in each case a future possibility is construed as the cause of what is actual. At the same time, however, this possibility is not a concept or plan entertained by the organism. The end or purpose lies in the organism itself and not, as in art, in the mind of a human agent.

Due in part to this distant analogy, Kant regards inner, materially objective purposiveness as merely a regulative principle of reflective judgment, not a constitutive principle.[17] The meaning of this regulative character becomes clear in Kant's treatment of the antinomy of teleological judgment. The proposition "Every production of material things is possible according to mechanical laws alone" and its opposite (where what is not engendered mechanically can only be produced teleologically) together yield a contradiction. These propositions yield a contradiction because together they both affirm and deny the same thing about every natural object. No such contradiction, however, is involved in maxims that are not judgments about objects, but rather subjective principles that guide research and reflection about objects. There is, in other words, nothing contradictory about attempting to explain specific natural phenomena "according to mechanical laws alone," in so far as that can be done, and at the same time allowing for the possibility that for some combinations of things in nature "a causality distinct from mechanism, namely, an (intelligent) cause of the world acting according to purposes" must be entertained.[18]

As this last qualification indicates, the teleological maxim entails the idea of a divine intellect (as does, in fact, the transcendental principle of nature's purposiveness).[19] Kant determines this idea by first reviewing its counterpart, the finite, discursive human intellect. A finite mind must proceed from a concept as an "analytic-universal" (a representation of a feature common to many objects) in order to understand, however imperfectly, the particular and then the individual.[20] To the extent that a finite mind is able to understand any particular thing, it must "run through" all the concepts applicable to that thing; in other words, it can understand the whole thing only by synthesizing all its parts or features.[21] A finite mind is further marked by the fact that particular things are given to it via contingent, empirical intuitions and, hence, whether those things can be adequately conceived (subsumed under suitable universals or rules) is an equally contingent affair.[22]

By contrast, a divine intellect, which is nothing but a "negative"[23] counterpart to the discursive, finite intellect of human beings, enjoys a spontaneous, intellectual intuition. This intellect has no need of concepts since it intuits (produces) the whole as such, grasping the particular thing in a so-called "synthetic-universal."[24] Rather than proceed from parts or, more exactly, from concepts as partial representations (*Teilvorstellungen*) as does the finite mind, the divine intellect grasps the whole in which all the parts are contained.[25]

A divine, intuitive intellect is a mere idea entailed, as already emphasized, by the principle of an intrinsic purposiveness or a natural purpose. Both that idea and this principle are drafted in order to make organic wholes understandable, given the discursive character of human understanding. Thus, the student of nature encounters organic wholes that seem to underlie their respective parts and the connection among those parts. In analogy with an intuitive intellect, a finite, discursive mind can entertain the idea of the possibility of the whole—in effect, the purpose—as the basis for the composition and combination of parts through which the whole is actualized.

Given this account, however, there can be no presumption that the assignment of purposes is objective or ontological or that the causal character of organic wholes has been adequately understood. The concept of purpose cannot, in Kant's words, be accorded "objective reality" for the familiar reason that purposes in nature are not observed, "not *given* to us by the object."[26] Moreover, for all Kant's emphasis on the necessity of regarding an organic entity as something designed,[27] he allows for the possibility of a mechanistic explanation of that apparent design:

> But then it would be presumptuous of us to have judged that in nature, if we could penetrate to the principle of it in the specification of its general laws which we know, a sufficient ground of the possibility of organized entities could not at all lie hidden without supposing an intention to their generation (thus in the mechanism alone of them); for how do we intend to come to know that?[28]

That Kant thus leaves the door open for a mechanistic explanation is not surprising given the primacy he repeatedly accords such an explanation. Only on the basis of nature's mechanism, he maintains, are we able to have any insight into the nature of things at all and without that mechanism there can be no natural science.[29]

Hegel's Ontological and Critical Appropriation

As his correspondence with Hölderlin and Schelling attests, Hegel was preoccupied with Kant's doctrine of natural teleology as early as January 1795.[30] However, the first clear indication of the eventual direction of his critical appropriation of the doctrine can be found in the *Difference* essay of 1801. There Hegel notes with approval both Kant's account of natural purposes inasmuch as it presents nature as a "subject-object," identifying "concept and being," and his notion of an intuitive understanding which establishes the possibility, as Hegel puts it, that "natural mechanism and natural purposiveness coincide."[31] Yet he also takes Kant to task for maintaining that "this view of nature obtains ... only as a maxim of our limited, discursively thinking, human intellect."[32]

Hegel expands on this same basic theme a year later in his first extended treatment of Kant's philosophy as he addresses in *Faith and Knowledge* "the most interesting point of the Kantian system," namely, the critique of judgment.[33] He lauds Kant's account of organic nature within the critique of teleological judgment for its clear articulation of the necessity of countenancing an identity to both the universal and the particular, the actual and the possible, and subject and object.[34] Influenced as he was at this time by a certain reading of Spinoza, Hegel regards the idea of this identity as at least equivalent to the idea of an intuitive understanding.[35] Thus, in contrast to Kant's own presentation, Hegel does not keep the concept of a natural purpose or inner purposiveness distinct from the idea of an intuitive understanding. Instead, he maintains that Kant's reflection on organic nature—labeled by Hegel here "the unconscious intuition of the reality of reason"—expresses the idea of an intuitive understanding, that is to say, an understanding "whose spontaneity is at once intuiting."[36] Accordingly, he characterizes the organism itself as "real reason" and "the supreme principle of nature and identity of the universal and the particular."[37]

None of these transformations of Kant's doctrine accompanying its exposition in *Faith and Knowledge* alter Hegel's basic criticism of that doctrine. There is no warrant, Hegel maintains, especially in the wake of Kant's acknowledgment of the inevitability of the idea, for insisting that the idea of natural purpose does not yield genuinely objective knowledge of organic nature. At the same time, in *Faith and Knowledge* Hegel makes no pretense of explaining Kant's insistence. Instead, he presents Kant's position as the result of a choice on Kant's part to remain with "appearances" by affirming the absolute finitude and discursiveness of the human intellect.[38]

In Hegel's maturer formulations of his philosophy[39] the historical and systematic context shifts, but he continues the critical appropriation of Kant's account of teleology in nature. Hegel's renewed reading of Aristotle (and no longer Spinoza) now looms over his interpretation of Kant's account which he uses as a springboard for the elaboration of his own speculative conception of life as "the Idea in its immediacy."[40] Thus, in the *Encyclopedia* he maintains that Kant, with the concept of inner purposiveness, "has re-awakened the Idea in general and the idea of life in particular," originally elaborated by Aristotle.[41] Similarly, in the *Lectures on the History of Philosophy* he notes with approval Kant's account of a natural purpose as an "intrinsically organized product of nature," such that "its end or purpose is not outside it; and its inner purposiveness is such that in it something is end and means. It is the Aristotelian concept ... the Idea."[42] Accordingly, Hegel maintains, in organic products of nature one observes "the immediate unity of concept and reality as something objective," where purpose is precisely the "in-dwelling concept" that in an organic being is also real.[43]

As can be gathered from the array of texts just cited, Kant's account of inner purposiveness in nature is in Hegel's mind nothing short of a disclosure of what Hegel understands as the "Idea." Hegel calls the unity of concept and reality the "Idea" and their immediate unity or the Idea in its immediacy, "life." Thus, in practically a paraphrase of Kant's definition of the principle of inner purposiveness, cited earlier,[44] Hegel characterizes life or the Idea in its immediacy as "the concept ... that pervades its objectivity and as an end unto itself has in that objectivity its means and posits that objectivity as its means, but is immanent in this means and in that objectivity is the realized end, identical with itself."[45] The contention that Kant's principle of inner purposiveness revives the Aristotelian conception of life betrays just how radically Hegel is re-interpreting that account even as he appropriates it. For Hegel life or the Idea in its immediacy is an ontological category, characterizing the status of organic entities in themselves, quite apart from their relation to a potential observer or researcher. For Kant, however, inner purposiveness is nothing more than a principle for reflective judgment, that is to say, a maxim for the working scientist who is searching for some rule to explain a given natural phenomenon or object, namely, organic entities, when no mechanical explanation succeeds. Use of this principle does not, Kant contends, result in knowledge of the ontological status of organic entities or in an adequate grasp of the causality involved.

Hegel's argument for rejecting Kant's contention, while only implicit in *Faith and Knowledge*, is spelled out in the *Encyclopedia*. The principle of inner purposiveness, Hegel observes, supersedes oppositions that define the discursive intellect, notably, the opposition between the universal and the particular and between subjectivity and objectivity. Hence, Hegel charges, Kant cannot legitimately identify the principle of inner purposiveness as something only subjective, as merely a way for a discursive intellect to entertain certain things.[46]

Kant grounds the principle of inner purposiveness, it must be remembered, in the discursive, finite character of the human intellect and its inability otherwise to make sense of the distinctive behavior of organic entities. By contrast, Hegel adopts Kant's idea of an intuitive understanding as a description of the very way we observe and comprehend organic entities.[47] In other words, for Hegel an intuitive understanding is not a mere thought, a corollary to the use of the principle of inner purposiveness, but the very way we know natural purposes. In this regard he chides Kant for not appreciating the fact that, contained in the idea of an intuitive intellect, is "the thought of another relation of the *universal* of the intellect to the *particular* of intuition" than obtains in theoretical or practical reason.[48] That other relation is not one of subsumption, but of an unfolding, necessary concretization, as elaborated in Hegel's own philosophy of nature. Moreover, as Hegel himself insists, that philosophical elaboration, far from being a departure from the observable order of things, "must be in conformity with the experience of nature."[49] Hegel's philosophy of nature is, to be sure, in no way an empirical science. Yet he insists that empirical, natural sciences must be presupposed by a philosophy of nature bent on contemplating nature "in its *own, immanent necessity*."[50]

Not surprisingly, Hegel criticizes Kant's treatment of the antinomy of teleological judgment. According to Kant, as noted above, the antinomy disappears as soon as it is recognized that mechanism and teleology are principles of reflective judgment, subjectively valid maxims and not propositions about the objective constitution of things. In the *Science of Logic* Hegel objects that this recourse to maxims leaves the fundamental contradiction in place. Rather than resolve the basic antinomy or, what is Hegel's own alternative, recognize this opposition both in the world and in the mind, Kant attributes the opposition to the mind alone (namely, the mind of the researcher or scientist alone). In effect, Hegel claims, Kant forces the student of nature to shelve the question of the truth and objective determination of things and he does so precisely by refusing to confront the opposition between mechanism and teleology in the world itself. Kant betrays, Hegel mockingly observes, far "too great a sensitivity to the world."[51]

Thus, for Hegel the contrast between mechanism and teleology is not simply about ways of understanding organic entities, but about the ontology of those entities themselves. However honestly intended, the refuge Kant takes in maxims of reflective judgment dodges this fundamental issue. As noted earlier, Kant construes the principle of inner purposiveness as a maxim because, among other reasons, of an attachment to the primacy of mechanical explanations and a failure to give such explanations of organic entities. And, indeed, Hegel can concur with Kant's declaration that "it is absurd ... to hope that another Newton could sometime emerge who would make even the mere generation of a blade of grass understandable according to laws of nature which no intention has ordered."[52] Precisely from this concurrence, however, Hegel draws the inference that it is incumbent on anyone who would understand organic entities to identify their purposes or ordering principles. For Hegel, in other words, no mechanist principles, even such as are presently hidden, can provide an adequate explanation of organic entities. The only adequate explanation is a teleological one and it can be given—without recourse to some occult or unobservable property—by "thoughtfully observing" the processes of formation of the individual organism ("the living individual") as a whole.[53]

Contemporary Biology and the Teleological Difference

In order for Kant's and Hegel's views on teleology in nature to be related even superficially to the philosophy of biology today, certain obvious caveats are in order. Kant's and Hegel's accounts of organic nature are limited by their knowledge and appreciation of the biological sciences in their respective times. Kant was clearly not as sympathetic to, and Hegel not as informed about, developments among their contemporaries in biology as one might have wished.[54] In addition, Kant and Hegel respectively embed their conceptions of natural purposes in systematic philosophical accounts (a critical or transcendental philosophy, on the one hand, and a science of logic and philosophy of nature, on the other). By contrast, contemporary philosophy of biology is largely motivated by and articulated in terms of developments in biology itself. Indeed, there is still something novel about philosophy of biology in the late twentieth century as it tries to assert itself in the context of a philosophy of science dominated by the paradigms of physics. Above all, however, contemporary biological thought is shaped by several achievements in evolutionary and molecular research, the earliest of which occurred almost thirty years after Hegel's death, namely, Darwin's publication of *The Origin of Species* in 1859, the rediscovery of Mendel and Weismann's account of germ plasma at the turn of the century, population genetics, and the discovery of the structure of deoxyribonucleic acid in 1953.

With these caveats in mind, it remains instructive, both from an historical and a systematic point of view, to consider the similarities and dissimilarities in Kant's and Hegel's approaches to the study of organic entities against the backdrop of contemporary biological thinking. For all their fundamental differences, Kant's and Hegel's approaches exhibit some basic similarities. Four similarities stand out in particular.

First, both thinkers in their own respective times endorse the thesis, forcefully advanced in the twentieth century by F. J. Ayala and Ernst Mayr, of the irreducibility of the principles, theory, or explanation of organic processes to those of physico-chemical processes; in contemporary terms, the thesis of biology's autonomy with respect to physics.[55] Indeed, while Kant may be seen as hedging his endorsement at times, Hegel's conception of nature as "a living whole" and the organic as its "*ideal* unity" anticipates calls for considering biology the unifying center of all natural sciences.[56]

Second, while the autonomy both thinkers accord biology is due to the purposiveness that they ascribe to organic behavior, neither Kant nor Hegel construes purposiveness in such a way that some nonexistent future is regarded as the cause of present. This typical criticism of traditional teleologists simply cannot be applied to Kant or Hegel.[57] Thus, according to Kant an organic entity possesses within itself from the outset "a self-reproducing, formative power" (*sich fortpflanzende bildende Kraft*).[58] Similarly, Hegel characterizes "needs" and "urges" as the nearest at hand examples of purpose.[59]

Third, in order to understand organic nature both Kant and Hegel make use of what might be considered anthropomorphisms, but in a way that is self-conscious and controlled.[60] Thus, just as Mayr argues that biologists can use terms like "purposive" or "goal-directed" without implying a transfer of human qualities, so Kant emphasizes that, as a guide to research, the concept of a thing as a natural purpose can be entertained "according to a distant analogy with our causality in terms of purposes."[61] In a comparable way, Hegel depicts the form of the plant organism as "not yet liberated from individuality to subjectivity," while the animal organism is the subjectivity whose concept, however, is "*in itself*, but not"—like that of a human being—"*for itself*."[62]

While these first three similarities are, as noted, echoed in much reflection on biology today, a fourth similarity puts

Kant and Hegel in stark contrast to contemporary thought. Not surprisingly, perhaps, this fourth similarity concerns their views on evolution. Both thinkers reject evolutionary theories of their respective eras, at least in so far as they were aware of them.[63]

As early as 1775, Kant dismisses—without explanation—both the idea that new species emerge and the notion that chance or "general mechanical laws" could produce the adaptations observable among organic entities. From this dismissal he then infers that such adaptations must be regarded as prefigured (*vorgebildet*).[64] A decade later, Kant reiterates his rejection of the thesis of species mutation, this time with the explanation that the thesis disables any attempt to determine what is "original" in nature and transgresses "the limits of reason," since it cannot be established by experiment, but only by "snatching up occasional perceptions."[65] In the *Critique of Judgment* Kant justifies his rejection with the observation that, as far as our experiential acquaintance with nature is concerned, such a *generatio heteronyma* is nowhere to be found.[66]

Hegel, it bears noting, seems to have been much more sanguine than Kant about the possibility in the manner that Darwin would later present it. Hegel's conception of how a biologist might plausibly understand evolution stems apparently from Voigt's *Lehrbuch der Botanik*. According to Voigt there is an evolution, but it is not the presupposition but rather the result of a basic organization of nature.[67] To what extent Hegel endorses Voigt's views is unclear, but in any event his quarrel is not with the reality of species mutation, but with the claim that the history of this mutation provides an explanation. Nature, Hegel argues, "is to be regarded as a system of stages, such that one proceeds *necessarily* from the others," but not such that the higher stage "was naturally born or produced" from the lower stages.[68]

Thus, in the end, again much like Kant, Hegel's difficulties with an evolutionary theory turn on its legitimacy as a scientific explanation. However, while Kant disputed its legitimacy on the basis of a lack of evidence and possibilities of experimentation, Hegel rejects evolutionary theory because it is not a science, but a history or narrative, telling us, to be sure, how something happened but not why. This last remark makes plain once more that, as basic as the four similarities between Kant's and Hegel's accounts of natural purposes are, Hegel appropriates Kant's account into an ontology profoundly alien to the originally transcendental framework of that account and into an epistemology (or theory of explanation) that does not construe observation in the restrictive sense that Kant does. For Hegel the purposes in nature are observable, even though they are not the sort of properties that, like a color, may be read off the object or, like a length, measured by juxtaposition with another object.

Contemporary biology is dominated by evolutionary and molecular theories profoundly different from the conceptions of organic nature in the writings of Kant and Hegel. Yet, the neo-Darwinian synthesis is by no means monolithic and, while natural selection and genetic code are not disputed, their interpretation is hardly settled. In this last respect Hegel's critical appropriation of Kant's thinking about organic entities and their determination remains instructive.

In order to appreciate this instructiveness, it will be helpful to review Ernst Mayr's sketch of some basic features of the regnant paradigm in biology. As part of an attempt to clarify the use of purposive language in biology while distinguishing it from its pre-Darwinian ancestry, Mayr invokes a distinction between teleonomy and teleology. The distinction roughly parallels the difference between Kant's notions of inner purposiveness and an intuitive intellect.[69] 'Teleonomic' refers to organisms' goal-directed processes which are based upon the operation of some program which is itself in part or entirely the product of natural selection.[70] By contrast 'teleology' typically refers to cosmic teleology, namely, the belief that there is a force immanent in the world leading it to "ultimate perfection of whatever telos the Creator had in mind."[71] While Mayr argues that teleonomic behavior must be countenanced, he is convinced that the accomplishments of evolutionary biology eliminate any need for cosmic teleology.[72] The source of teleonomic behavior is not divine design, but rather a natural selection that is fully mechanistic though in a probabilistic, not deterministic sense.

This last qualification is based in large part upon the belief that chance or spontaneous changes in a cell's genetic code (DNA) account for mutations and that, in Mayr's words, "the pathway from nucleic acids to proteins is a one-way street."[73] As Bernd-Olaf Küppers puts it: "The 'direction' of evolutionary processes depends decisively upon the micro-physical mutation events, which on their part are completely indeterminate."[74] Mutation is essentially a change in the DNA sequence and this change is ultimately based, Küppers maintains, "upon quantum-mechanical uncertainty."[75]

In recent years, however, this view has been challenged on the basis of certain experiments by John Cairns and others with a strain of Escherichia coli (the bacteria in the human stomach) which suggest that the cell's experience has an effect on its DNA. Unlike normal E. coli, the code of this strain is such that it is incapable of feeding on lactose. However, experiments show that, within two days, this strain of bacteria starts to feed on lactose, apparently "choosing" the appropriate mutation and thus "repairing" its defective gene.[76] Other experiments by the evolutionary biologist Barry G. Hall point to similar surprising conclusions about the adaptability of cells. Yet these conclusions are at odds with the established view that all mutation is random or, in other words, that a cell's experience cannot have any effect upon the sequence of bases in its DNA. Thus, while affirming that "nobody anymore doubts this stuff is real," Hall notes: "But nobody has a good explanation for it either."[77]

While these experiments and their theoretical context are vastly different from the considerations surrounding Hegel's critical appropriation of Kant's natural teleology, they obviously intersect in a fundamental way. The experiments by Cairns, Hall, and others suggest that the mixture of chance and mechanistic necessity posited by the contemporary synthesis of molecular and evolutionary biology, namely, random mutation, is in some cases an unlikely explanation for a cell's behavior. Is there any good reason not to entertain the hypothesis that this behavior is teleological (and not merely teleonomic)? To be sure, the development of this hypothesis would require the sort of synthesis of metaphysics and natural science given in Hegel's philosophy of nature, building upon the undeniable achievements of contemporary molecular and evolutionary biology that were unavailable to Hegel. What would be required, in other words, is a willingness to consider the possibility that some organic behaviors and, indeed, some mutations are based upon the purposive nature of the cell and not solely a matter of chance.

Notes

1. G.W.F. Hegel, *Wissenschaft der Logik. Zweiter Band: Die Subjektive Logik (1816)*, edited by F. Hogemann and W. Jaeschke, *Gesammelte Werke*, Vol. 12 (Hamburg: Felix Meiner, 1981), p. 157. (Hereafter cited as *Logik* [*GW*, **12**].) I am grateful to Michael Baur and Richard Hassing for the helpful advice they provided me in preparing this paper.

2. *Logik* (*GW*, **12**), p. 159.

3. *Logik* (*GW*, **12**), p. 159; G.W.F. Hegel, *Glauben und Wissen, Jenaer kritische Schriften*, edited by H. Buchner and O. Pöggeler (Hamburg: Felix Meiner, 1968), *Gesammelte Werke*, Vol. 4. p. 343 (hereafter *GW*, **4**).

4. Klaus Düsing, "Naturteleologie und Metaphysik bei Kant und Hegel," in *Hegel und die 'Kritik der Urteilskraft,'* edited by Hans-Friedrich Fulda and Rolf-Peter Horstmann (Stuttgart: Klett-Cotta, 1990), p. 149.

5. For useful outlines of the "Neo-Darwinian Synthesis," see Ernst Mayr, *Toward a New Philosophy of Biology: Observations of an Evolutionist* (Cambridge, Massachusetts: Harvard University Press, 1988), pp. 185-95 and Stuart A. Kauffman, *The Origins of Order: Self-Organization and Selection in Evolution* (Oxford: Oxford University Press, 1993), pp. 3-26.

6. For Kant's "deduction" of this transcendental principle of nature's purposiveness, see Immanuel Kant, *Kritik der Urteilskraft*, 2nd ed. (Berlin, 1793), *Kants Gesammelte Schriften*, Vol. 5 (Königlich Preußische [now Deutsche] Akademie der Wissen-

schaften, Berlin: G. Reimer [now de Gruyter], 1902–), pp. xxxi-xxxvi. (Hereafter cited as *KdU*. Page numbers follow pagination of text of *KdU*, not pagination of *GS*, **5** as a whole.) For a helpful discussion of the relation of this principle to the transcendental laws of nature and the three principles of homogeneity, specification, and continuity, elaborated in the *Kritik der reinen Vernunft*, see Klaus Düsing, *Die Teleologie in Kants Weltbegriff*, 2nd ed. (Bonn: Grundmann, 1986), pp. 51-65.

7. See *KdU*, p. 32.

8. The principle is transcendental and not metaphysical because it does not suppose any empirical content of objects and merely concerns the way they can be experientially known (*KdU*, p. xxx).

9. Thus, Kant distinguishes the subjective purposiveness of nature (such that human judgment is capable of grasping it in its empirical manifestations as a system) from the objective purposiveness of nature where "the laws of causality in terms of the mere mechanism of nature do not suffice" to explain specific objects; see *KdU*, pp. 267-9, 285. On how the subjective or, more precisely, the transcendental principle of nature's purposiveness prepares us for the principle of its objective purposiveness, see Düsing, *Die Teleologie in Kants Weltbegriff*, pp. 88-9. For the further distinction into formally and materially objective purposiveness, see *KdU*, pp. 271-9.

10. *KdU*, pp. 286-8.

11. *KdU*, pp. 378-9; see J. F. Blumenbach, *Über den Bildungstrieb* (Göttingen: Johann Christian Dieterich, 1781, 1789).

12. *KdU*, pp. 290-1.

13. *KdU*, p. 292.

14. *KdU*, pp. 280-4; 298-9.

15. *KdU*, pp. 295-6.

16. *KdU*, p. 295.

17. *KdU*, pp. 269-70; 300-1.

18. *KdU*, pp. 314-18.

19. *KdU*, p. 348.

20. *KdU*, p. 347; Immanuel Kant, *Logic*, *Kants Gesammelte Schriften*, Vol. 9, p. 91.

21. Kant, *Logic*, pp. 63-4; Düsing, *Die Teleologie in Kants Weltbegriff*, pp. 90-1.

22. *KdU*, pp. 347-8.

23. *KdU*, p. 347.

24. *KdU*, p. 349.

25. *KdU*, p. 352; *Kants Gesammelte Schriften*, Vol. 18, p. 478, Reflexion Nr. 6174: "God's knowledge determines each part in the whole; human beings' knowledge the whole through the parts."

26. *KdU*, p. 336.

27. *KdU*, p. 334: "Wir haben nämlich unentbehrlich nöthig, der Natur den Begriff einer Absicht unterzulegen, wenn wir ihr auch nur in ihren organisirten Producten durch fortgesetzte Beobachtung nachforschen wollen."

28. *KdU*, p. 338; cf. Düsing, "Naturteleologie und Metaphysik bei Kant und Hegel," p. 150.

29. *KdU*, pp. 315, 354, 363, 368; see John H. Zammito, *The Genesis of Kant's Critique of Judgment* (Chicago: University of Chicago Press, 1992), p. 223.

30. *Briefe von und an Hegel*, edited by J. Hoffmeister, 4 Vols (Hamburg: Felix Meiner, 1952-60), **1**: 17, 20.

31. *GW*, **4**: 69.

32. *GW*, **4**: 69.

33. *GW*, **4**: 338.

34. *GW*, **4**: 341.

35. Hegel traces Kant's ultimate failure to accept the objectivity of teleological judgments to his erroneous identification of "the spinozistic unity" with an "abstract unity of the understanding" rather than "the organic unity" of an intuitive understanding; see *GW*, **4**: 342.

36. *GW*, **4**: 340-1.

37. *GW*, **4**: 342.

38. *GW*, **4**: 341.

39. See Düsing, "Naturteleologie und Metaphysik bei Kant und Hegel," p. 148 for references to Hegel's discussion of teleology in

the Jena writings, the *Phänomenologie des Geistes*, and the Nürnberg Propaedeutic.

40. See Hegel's comments to this effect in the *Wissenschaft der Logik*, cited at the outset of the present essay.

41. G.W.F. Hegel, *Enzyklopädie der philosophischen Wissenschaften im Grundrisse (1830)*, edited by F. Nicolin and O. Pöggeler (Hamburg: Felix Meiner, 1969), §204 Zus., pp. 177-8; see also §360 Zus., pp. 298-9.

42. G.W.F. Hegel, *Vorlesungen über die Geschichte der Philosophie III*, edited by E. Moldenhauer and K.M. Michel, *Werke in zwanzig Bänden*, Vol. 20 (Frankfurt am Main: Suhrkamp Verlag, 1971), pp. 378-9.

43. *Vorlesungen über die Geschichte der Philosophie III*, pp. 378, 381.

44. See note 15 above.

45. *Logik* (*GW*, **12**): 177.

46. *Enzyklopädie* (1830), § 58, p. 82.

47. *Vorlesungen über die Geschichte der Philosophie III*, p. 381: "Wir betrachten es nach der Weise eines intuitiven Verstandes." This endorsement of an intuitive understanding cannot mean, after 1803 or so, that Hegel is positing an intellectual intuition. Given his criticism of this notion in Fichte and Schelling, it would seem more appropriate to interpret his claim that we regard organic nature "according to the manner of an intuitive intellect" as an attempt to use Kant's language against him, as part of an effort to demonstrate that, contra Kant, the intellect of human beings is not restricted by its discursivity. However, according to the mature Hegel, the human mind moves beyond the limitations of discursivity, not by means of an intellectual intuition, but rather by means of dialectical reasoning.

48. *Enzyklopädie* (1830), §56, p. 81 and §58 Zus., p. 82.

49. *Enzyklopädie* (1830), §246 Zus., p. 200.

50. *Enzyklopädie* (1830), §246, p. 200.

51. G.W.F. Hegel, *Wissenschaft der Logik, Erster Teil: Die Objektive Logik, Erster Band: Die Lehre vom Sein (1832)*, edited by F. Hogemann and W. Jaeschke (Hamburg: Felix Meiner, 1985), *Gesammelte Werke*, Vol. 21, p. 232; *Enzyklopädie* (1830), §48 Zus.,

pp. 72-3; Düsing, "Naturteleologie und Metaphysik bei Kant und Hegel," pp. 151-2.

52. *KdU*, pp. 338-9.

53. *Enzyklopädie* (1830), §249, p. 202; §343-9, pp. 287-291.

54. Kant does not consider the chemistry of his day, let alone the biology (or psychology), to be a legitimate "science"; see *Metaphysische Anfangsgründe der Naturwissenschaften* (1786), *Kants Gesammelte Schriften*, Vol. 4, p. 471. For a useful survey of Kant's well-read, but unsympathetic views of biology, see Zammito, *The Genesis of Kant's Critique of Judgment*, pp. 189-213. For comparable information on the sometimes limited sources of Hegel's understanding of biology, see the extensive notes by M. J. Petry in his translation, *Hegel's Philosophy of Nature*, 3 Vols (New York: Humanities Press; London: G. Allen and Unwin, 1970) (hereafter Petry, *PN*).

55. Ernst Mayr, *Toward a New Philosophy of Biology*, p. 18: "The conceptual framework of biology is entirely different from that of the physical sciences and cannot be reduced to it. The role that such biological processes as meiosis, gastrulation, and predation play in the life of an organism cannot be described by reference only to physical laws or chemical reactions, even though physicochemical principles are operant. The broader processes that these biological concepts describe simply do not exist outside the domain of the living world." See also Mayr, *Toward a New Philosophy of Biology*, pp. 10-11; F. J. Ayala, "Biology as an Autonomous Science," *American Scientist* 56 (1968): 207-21; and Michael Ruse, *Philosophy of Biology Today* (Albany, New York: SUNY Press, 1988), pp. 7-8.

56. *Enzyklopädie* (1830), §§251-2; see G. G. Simpson, *This View of Life* (New York: Harcourt, Brace and World, 1964), p. 107: "Biology, then, is the science that stands at the center of all science, and it is here, in the field where all the principles of all the sciences are embodied, that science can truly become unified."

57. For the view that teleology implies the future determining the past, see Michael Ruse, *Philosophy of Biology Today*, p. 44; for the contrary view, compatible with Kant's and Hegel's positions, see Larry Wright, *Teleological Explanations: An Etiological Analysis of Goals and Functions* (Berkeley, California: University of California Press, 1976), p. 10: "There is nothing in any of the ordinary ascriptions of goals or functions or motives or purposes or

aims or drives or needs or intentions which requires us to reverse the normal cause-before-effect sequence."

58. *KdU*, pp. 292-3.

59. *Enzyklopädie* (1830), §204 Zus., pp. 177-8.

60. Wright has defended such expressions as useful and appropriate metaphors, specifically "dead anthropomorphic metaphors"; see *Teleological Explanations*, pp. 14-21.

61. *KdU*, p. 294; Mayr, *Toward a New Philosophy of Biology*, pp. 40-1.

62. *Enzyklopädie* (1830), §345, p. 288 and §§374-6, pp. 308-9; see also *Enzyklopädie* (1830), §248 Zus., pp. 201-2.

63. Petry, *PN*, **3**: 229-31.

64. *Kants Gesammelte Schriften*, Vol. 2, pp. 434-5.

65. *Kants Gesammelte Schriften*, Vol. 8, pp. 96-7.

66. *KdU*, p. 370n.

67. Olaf Breidbach, "Hegels Evolutionskritik," in *Hegel-Studien* 22 (1987): 165-72. According to Breidbach, F. S. Voigt's *Lehrbuch der Botanik* appeared in Jena in 1808.

68. *Enzyklopädie* (1830), §249, p. 202.

69. Mayr, *Toward a New Philosophy of Biology*, pp. 38-60; Mayr urges that the analysis of putatively teleological phenomena begin with the attempt to reclassify them into one of four divisions: teleomatic processes, teleonomic processes, adaptive systems, and cosmic teleology.

70. The term 'teleonomic' was coined by Pittendrigh in 1958; see C. S. Pittendrigh, "Adaptation, Natural Selection and Behavior" in *Behavior and Evolution*, edited by A. Roe and G.G. Simpson (New Haven: Yale University Press, 1958) pp. 390-416. The sorts of program that Mayr has in mind in regard to teleonomic behavior are all antecedent material conditions of that behavior. "The programs which control teleonomic processes in organisms are either entirely laid down in the DNA of the genotype (closed programs) or are constituted in such a way that they can incorporate additional information (open programs) (Mayr 1964), acquired through learning, conditioning, or other experiences. Most behavior, particularly in higher organisms, is controlled by such open programs," Mayr, *Toward a New Philosophy of Biology*,

p. 49; see also Ernst Mayr, "The Evolution of Living Systems," *Proceedings of the National Academy of Sciences* 51 (1964): 934-41. Thus, for example, an animal's tendency to escape predators is acquired through natural selection while the knowledge of which animals in its environs actually prey on it is learned.

71. Mayr, *Toward a New Philosophy of Biology*, pp. 58-9, 234, 244-54, 264.

72. Mayr, *Toward a New Philosophy of Biology*, p. 193: "All the phenomena that previously had been ascribed to design or to finalistic causes Darwin was able to explain in terms of natural selection"; *KdU*, p. 335: " ... daß also die Teleologie keine Vollendung des Aufschlusses für ihre Nachforschungen, als in einer Theologie findet."

73. Mayr, *Toward a New Philosophy of Biology*, p. 538; see also p. 33: "The occurrence of a given mutation is in no way related to the evolutionary needs of the particular organism or of the population to which it belongs."

74. Bernd-Olaf Küppers, *Information and the Origin of Life* (Cambridge, Massachusetts: MIT Press, 1990), p. 164.

75. Küppers, *Information*, p. 167.

76. John Cairns, Julie Overbaugh, and Stephan Miller, "The origin of mutants," *Nature* 335 (September 8, 1988): 142: "As the result of studies of bacterial variation, it is now widely believed that mutations arise continuously and without any consideration for their utility. In this paper we briefly review the source of this idea and then describe some experiments suggesting that cells may have mechanisms for choosing which mutations will occur." See also Boyce Rensberger, "Choosing the Right Mutation?" *Washington Post* April 20, 1992.

77. Cited in Rensberger, "Choosing the Right Mutation?"

8

How Final Is Hegel's Rejection of Evolution?

Errol E. Harris

Evolution and Dialectic

> Had the Darwinian and later data been available, he would almost certainly have acknowledged the historical trends in Nature that he admits in the realm of Spirit: if any philosopher is a philosopher of evolution, that philosopher is Hegel.

So says John Findlay in his book, *Hegel: A Re-examination*, and I have in the past made similar submissions.[1] There can be little doubt that Findlay's contention is justified, although, had Hegel known about Darwin's theory, it is likely that he would have rejected its underlying assumption that species originate solely as a result of an accumulation of chance variations giving selective advantage.

If the term "evolution" is to have any distinctive meaning, it must connote more than a mere succession of changes. The prior stages of the process must harbor a potentiality to produce the later results and the later stages must involve their predecessors as the necessary condition of their emergence. There must be some specific kind of reciprocal implicative relation between earlier and later phases.

Other than Hegel, no philosopher has ever given a satisfactorily intelligible account of evolution properly conceived. Herbert Spencer pronounced a principle of increasing complexity, defining evolution as the passage from the homogeneous to the heterogeneous, its effects being concomitantly differentiation and integration. These ideas were descriptively useful but they explained nothing. Bergson postulated a life-force, the nature of which as well as its operation remained totally obscure. Lloyd-Morgan, J.C. Smuts, and Samuel Alexander maintained that configurations of entities on one level gave rise to emergent qualities at a higher level.

This was a new and welcome insight, but how and why emergence occurred they confessedly could not explain: Alexander recommended merely that the brute fact be accepted "with natural piety."

Hegel's dialectic, on the other hand, provides a principle, as he himself says, "of all movement, all life and all activity in the actual world." The dialectical process is the self-differentiation of a concrete, systematic whole, which unless it is differentiated is not justifiably conceivable as a whole. It must be a whole of interrelated parts such that their mutual relations are internal to their character and make them what they are. This is what is meant by describing the whole as systematic: that is, internally organized so that its structure is governed by a universal principle of order. The dialectical process then issues from the finite nature of the parts, each of which is what it is only in virtue of its place in the whole. Any one such part, therefore, taken in isolation, can maintain itself only by eliciting its supplementary other in the whole, and by uniting with it to constitute a more adequate exemplification of the ordering principle. The dialectical process is thus one of progressive advance from one finite form (or phase) to its negated opposite, and thence to their synthesis—from a less to a more adequate expression of the structural principle, in which the superseded moment is preserved, transformed at a higher level of integrity. Such a process, driven by a nisus to the whole, has determinable direction. Its earlier phases, because the principle of organization is immanent in them, are potentially (or implicitly) what they develop into, and the subsequent outcome sublates its precursors and is derived from them. The nature of the progression is thus evolutionary in the required sense, and the dialectic is necessarily a principle of development.

Rightly understood, this principle enables Hegel to develop a coherent theory both of nature and of mind, which requires, while it properly explains, an evolutionary process in nature. That Hegel was a philosopher of process and not of static substance is clear from his explicit statements. In the *Logic* the first concrete and most fundamental category, which provides the principle of the entire movement of the dialectic, is becoming; and Hegel declares that "the Idea is essentially process, in so far as it is absolute negativity and therefore dialectical."[2] It is eternal restlessness. The entire philosophical system is set out by Hegel as an evolutionary series of continuous levels of wholeness dialectically related.

What Hegel Denied

My immediate purpose is not to expatiate on the nature of the dialectic, but to explain why Hegel must be seen as providing a cogent theory of evolution. The thesis I am advancing seems prima facie to be contradicted by Hegel's emphatic rejection in the *Philosophy of Nature* of the belief that living species have been generated one from the other. But careful scrutiny of the passages in which this denial occurs will, I believe, show that they are not in fact incompatible with what I wish to maintain, but rather support it.

There can be no question that what Hegel denied was the gradual, or stepwise, modification of what we now call the phenotype to produce progressive changes in the genotype. But in his day, although this form of evolutionary process had already been adumbrated by such writers as Buffon and envisaged by others like Erasmus Darwin (Charles' grandfather), Oken, and Lamarck, no firm evidence had as yet been discovered to support the idea, and no clear theory of the nature of the process had been suggested or had gained any empirical support. Scientifically the notion was scouted. Sir William Dampier, in his *History of Science*, remarks that:

> the naturalists would have none of it. Even the botanist Godron, who collected much evidence about variation, rejected the idea of evolution as lately as 1859, the year of publication of Darwin's work. ... The naturalists were exercising true scientific restraint in not taking, even as a working hypothesis, a speculation for which there was as yet available no convincing evidence, and no satisfactory suggestion of a mode of operation.[3]

Hegel was fully aware of the views recently proposed by Buffon, Lamarck and others. He writes:

> The idea has long haunted the philosophy of nature and still prevails that the land animal arises out of the amphibian and the bird out of the land animal, further that mankind proceeds from the animal by wholly natural generation.[4]

He was, however, scrupulous in his respect for what had in his day been scientifically established; and, contrary to the accusations often ignorantly made against him, he conscientiously refrained from dictating to scientists what doctrines they ought to adopt in their own field. The biologists of the day, Linnaeus, Haller, Bonnet and Cuvier, were all insistent in their belief that species were not transformed one from another, but were fixed as originally created. Like the naturalists of his time, therefore, Hegel was exercising true scientific restraint in his rejection of the idea of progressive evolution of species. Nevertheless, what is significant is his emphasis on continuous development in the Concept and in the individual organism; and it must not be forgotten that, for him, nature is the Idea in the form of "otherbeing" (externality), and that the Earth is an organic whole (a notion to which I shall return).

The passages in which Hegel abjures the doctrine of historical evolution in the biological realm are well known: *Encyclopedia* (1830), §249, Zusatz, and §339, Zusatz 2. But of course, what Hegel is criticizing here are the contemporary notions of evolution, and at the time when he wrote the word had a special meaning, different from what it assumed after Darwin. So if we want to understand just what it is that Hegel is denying, we must consider what the theories of his time were asserting.

As Hegel says in the Zusatz to §249 of the *Encyclopedia*, the two current forms in which the progression of natural structures was conceived in his day were *evolution* and *emanation*, of which the first proceeded from the lowest and least formed to the highest and most elaborate, the second from the most complete and perfect by successive steps to the most crass and evil. Both of these forms he says are one-sided and each is therefore unsatisfactory, although he favors the second because it sets the most complete and perfect as the standard to which we must look for explanation of the lower kinds. This conforms more nearly to the principle of the dialectic, the driving force of which is the immanence of the whole (or Concept) in the part that is a moment within it. On the other hand, in Hegel's view, evolution committed the genetic fallacy by seeking in past occurrences the explanation of what now exists.

The essential point that Hegel is making, however, is that neither of these two methods of approach towards the diversity of nature is adequate because they do no more than list the various stages in a stipulated order without revealing the necessary relationship between them. Mere chronological difference, he says, has no interest for thought (conceptual apprehension). If it is no more than a matter of enumerating the series of natural species, preferable as that may be to mixing them together unsystematically, whether we proceed from the bottom up or from the top down,

> it must not be imagined that such a dry series is made dynamic or philosophical, or more intelligible, or whatever you like to say, by representing the terms as producing each other.[5]

In effect, then, what is wrong with the notion of progressive "evolution" or "emanation" is that neither is really evolutionary in the proper sense. They simply list the differences in order of complication, either from the least to the most or in reverse, and do not make them any more intelligible. In contrast,

> it is the necessity of the Idea which causes each sphere to complete itself by passing into a higher one, and the variety of forms must be considered as necessary and determinate.[6]

This is much the same criticism as I have suggested above of Spencer and later philosophers of evolution, that neither by describing it as a progressive increase in complexity nor as a mysterious emergence of new forms out of different configurations on a lower level, do they make the progressive process intelligible. The necessity of the progression has to be understood in terms of the Concept, of the Idea—that is, dialectically.

The very connotation of the word "evolution," however, was different for Hegel from what it is for us. There were two rival conceptions of biological development at the turn of the eighteenth century. One was *preformation*, the belief that a miniature version of the mature creature was encapsulated in the original germ, which in the course of time unfolded and grew in size to become the mature organism. The other was *epigenesis*, the idea that the germplasm was simple protoplasm which gradually multiplied and differentiated itself into the embryo and then grew larger to attain adult form. Some, like Lamarck, maintained that the development of species ran along similar lines to that of the individual, and that phylogenesis paralleled ontogenesis. The preformationists best known to Hegel would have been Bonnet and Robinet, the epigeneticists, Buffon and Lamarck. At the time it was primarily preformation that was understood as "evolution."

Now it is clear that preformation would be quite unacceptable to Hegel, for it involves a simple unfolding of what is already complete from the start, and this unfolding is in no sense what Hegel understood as development. That, for him, is the process (*Fortgehen*) of the Concept, in which all the distinguished moments are forthwith identified both with one another and with the whole.[7] The prior phases are recognized as being what they are only as moments of a systematic whole and as thereby mutually implicated. What emerges at the end of the process is what has been implicit (*an sich*), and only implicit, in the earlier phases—not, as Hegel tells us, as already existent, but only as ideally present. Now what is ideally present in Hegel's view is the whole (immanent in the part or phase). It is not present *realiter*, but only by implication. In the relevant passage in the *Encyclopedia Logic* (§161 Zus.) he explicitly rejects the preformation hypothesis:

> In the world of nature it is organic life that corresponds to the grade of the notion. Thus e.g. the plant is developed from its germ. The germ virtually involves the whole plant, but does so only ideally or in thought: and it would therefore be a mistake to regard the development of the root, stem, leaves and other different parts of the plant, as meaning that they were *realiter* present, but in very minute form, in the germ. That is the so-called "box-within-box" hypothesis; a theory which commits the mistake of supposing an actual existence of what is at first found only as a postulate of the completed thought [what is first found only in ideal form] (Wallace, *EL*, p. 224).

At the same time, and in the same passage, Hegel asserts that organic life, in the realm of nature, is what corresponds to the phases of the Concept, the process of which is asserted to be development. It should therefore be clear that what he rejects (and what he would have understood as evolution) is not *development* as such (not what we conceive as evolutionary) but only an inept and faulty theory of development: preformation.

Although he makes no mention of it, epigenesis would seem to be nearer to what Hegel required; but only superficially so, for the epigeneticist envisages transformation of the original germ continuously into the mature organism, but does not explain how this happens. The difference between the rudiment and what develops from it is one which Hegel would have regarded as merely quantitative, and, as he says in the Zusatz to §249 of the *Encyclopedia*, almost as if he had epigenesis in mind:

> This gradual alteration is called an explanation and understanding; it is a conception which comes from the Philosophy of Nature, and it still flourishes. But though this quantitative difference is of all theories the easiest to

> understand, it does not really explain anything at all (Miller, *PN*, p. 21).

Hegel was more sympathetic to the idea of metamorphosis as it had been expounded by Goethe. Here, he says, a single idea is basic, which persists in the diverse genera, or organs, so that they are all only variations (or manifestations) of one and the same form or type. What he means is that the conception of metamorphosis requires a whole (or concept) which differentiates itself into subspecies, or, in the case of the individual organism, limbs and organs. In the latter case, he admits, the process of development takes place in time, but he denies that this occurs with the genus, because the Concept posits all its internal differentiations qualitatively and coordinately, whereas the idea of evolution he is criticizing envisages a series of additions, all similarly determined and always with the same relation between them. This, incidentally, is precisely how modern Neo-Darwinism regards the successive results of random mutations. In this fashion the principle of generation is not revealed, and to arrange species in a serial order on this basis, Hegel contends, and to try to derive from it some sort of law of generation, is a futile undertaking.

The Primacy of the Whole

What Hegel constantly seeks to establish is the primacy of the whole. This is what his repeated reference to the Concept is meant to stress. For him nature is a whole—the Idea, even if in the form here of externality. The whole, moreover, is of necessity differentiated,[8] and the differentiations are generated by the persistent assertion, within the part, of the implicit whole which it represents. The result is the dialectical succession, the necessity of which is the governance of the process throughout by the whole that is in becoming. This kind of progression is obvious in the generation of individual organisms, but no sufficient empirical evidence was available when Hegel wrote that it could account for the diversity of species.

Nevertheless, Hegel expounds his philosophy of nature as a dialectical series, and in the sphere of organics concedes that its manner of progression in the growth of the individual is development. An acceptable theory of evolution which could satisfactorily explain the origin of species would have fitted well with his dialectical method; but no such theory was available to him. (It may well be questioned whether even now, as some modern biologists understand evolution, the accepted theory could be considered satisfactory.) For this reason, Hegel would not countenance the idea of evolution when he wrote. Nevertheless, he provides a dialectical structure that does accommodate an evolutionary world-picture, and which in many important ways anticipates biological concepts of the present day.

The Earth as Organism

In the *Philosophy of Nature*, the moments of the whole which is nature are Mechanics, Physics (Chemism), and Organics; but the first two are more aspects of, or ways of understanding, the nature of the whole than phases in a temporal progression. The world is not first a mechanical whole, and then a chemical one, which subsequently becomes organic. Mechanism and chemism are only moments of a whole which, for Hegel as it was for Schelling, is essentially and throughout organic.

The self-external totality is in the first instance material body; but its unity is merely implicit and ideal—only for us (as Hegel says in other contexts) but not for itself. To become explicit for itself the ideality has to be fulfilled as and in conscious subjectivity. Only as cognized is unity in difference fully realized. The nisus to the whole immanent in each and every moment, therefore, and incident at every stage, impels the bodily complex into which the whole is differentiated back to that from which it originated and which implicitly it is—back to the Idea. So Hegel writes in the *Encyclopedia*, §337:

> The real totality of body is the infinite process in which individuality determines itself to particularity or finitude, and equally negates this and returns into itself, re-establishing itself at the end of the process as its beginning, is thus an elevation into the first ideality of Nature, but an ideality which is fulfilled (*erfüllt*), and as self-related negative unity, has essentially developed the nature of self and become subjective. This accomplished, the Idea has entered into existence, at first an immediate existence, Life (Miller, *PN*, p. 273).

As we have learned from the *Logic*, the existent Idea is life, subjectively actualized in an existing body, a living organism. In nature, however, life is as yet only implicitly the Concept: it is only the first realization of ideality, its immediate actualization.

The development of organism in the *Philosophy of Nature* is (as usual) tripartite: geological, vegetable, and animal. To us it seems strange to classify the geological as organic, but it is here that Hegel's insight is, perhaps, most impressive. The geological organism, he says, is the general image or configuration of life, its universal embodiment—he calls it the "corpse" of the life-process. *Leichnam* is rather an unfortunate choice of a word, where what is meant is what Schelling (and Hegel also at times) calls *Einbildung*. The point he is making is that at this level all we have is the dead, still inorganic, basis for the emergence of life, the structure, so to speak, of its necessary material conditions. Hegel's submission is that the earth, geological nature, in which he includes water and air (Cf. *Encyclopedia*, §338 Zus.), is an organic whole. He says in the Zusatz to §337 that it is "*der Grund und Boden*" of life. *Der Boden* is the estate or soil—what life grows out of and what nourishes it.

Twentieth century scientists have come to a very similar conclusion. They draw attention to what has been called "the fitness of the environment." The earth is unique among known planets in the extraordinary and improbable combination of conditions it provides favorable to the emergence of life: the near circularity of its orbit around the sun keeping its overall temperature stable; the appropriateness of its distance from the sun maintaining the necessary levels of heat and cold, and the speed of its revolution on its axis, preventing extremes of temperature and climate; the buffering effect of its atmosphere mitigating heat in summer and cold in winter, and the protective ozone layer shielding living things from lethal cosmic radiation. Further, the presence in unusual abundance of water (probably the element in which life originated and the prevailing habitat of most living species, while also the major constituent of living matter), together with its unique versatility as a solvent and its peculiar properties dependent on the hydrogen bond, are all requisite for life. Similarly, the peculiar properties of carbon and oxygen, both indispensable constituents of protoplasm and essential ingredients of its ambient medium, and the fact that carbon dioxide (so important to the existence of life) is gaseous at the prevailing temperatures, whereas its cognate compounds are solid: all this and much more make the planet special in its adaptation for the existence of life.[9] The earth has indeed been discovered to be the soil and estate of life, as if it had been deliberately designed to produce it. "The Earth is the most excellent of all the planets," Hegel writes, "the mean, the individual: this its existence it owes solely to this permanent togetherness (*Zusammenhang*) of its moments; if one of these were lacking, the earth would cease to be what it is."[10]

What leads Hegel to this conception of the earth as organic and as the site and basis of all life is his inveterate holism and his perception that the proper nature and expression of the whole is only to be found in the last resort in organism and mind. The inorganic substratum, therefore, must be seen as the universal body of life as such, the precursor of self-conscious mind. In this again, as further instances presently to be offered will confirm, he prophetically anticipates the scientific conclusions of our own day.

Hegel contrasts geological nature with the living organism as a whole of parts in frozen externality with a whole in which the parts are mutually ends and means, are imbued with the nature of the whole that makes them its own in sensible unity. At the same time, he describes the geological system as pregnant and permeated with life, and he is constantly and acutely aware of the indissoluble continuity and interdependence of organism and environment. The meteorological changes and movements of the atmosphere and the circulation of ocean currents he identifies as the living process of geological nature:

> The life of the Earth is the process of atmosphere and sea in which it generates these Elements, each of which is an independent life for itself while all of them constitute only this process.[11]

Sea and earth, he tells us further, "erupt at every point into punctiform, transient life," which they sustain by their fecundity and fertility. So Hegel accounts for the phosphorescent life-forms in the sea, for infusoria, and for indeterminate living encrustations like lichens. Everything is seen and described as interdependent with everything else. Earth, sea, and air interpenetrate and interchange. The atmosphere is said to vivify the earth, and life grows out of, and draws its sustenance from, the elements. In short, the transition from inorganic to organic is continuous and the frontier between the two is blurred and shadowy.

Although Hegel has little or nothing to say about symbiosis and the interdependence of different species within a single eco-system, his recognition of the close interplay of organism and environment to some extent anticipates more modern doctrines, as set out, for instance, by J.S. Haldane in his Terry Lectures.[12] But especially Hegel seems to have had some premonition of the very recent Gaia Hypothesis advocated by James Lovelock, which shows reason to consider the earth as a single, highly complex, living being. Hegel actually describes the earth as a living body in the Zusatz to §341 of the *Encyclopedia*, scornfully rejecting the suggestion that springs can be mechanically explained as the mere percolation of water through the layers of earth and rock:

> just as springs are the lungs and secretory glands for the Earth's process of evaporation (*für die Ausdünstung der Erde*), so are volcanoes the Earth's liver, in that they represent the Earth's spontaneous generation of heat within itself. Everywhere we see tracts, especially sandstone beds, which are always giving off moisture (Miller, *PN*, p. 296).

Fanciful as this may be, it is not an idea altogether foreign to twentieth century writers. Lewis Thomas speaks of the earth in similar terms:

> Viewed from the distance of the moon, the astonishing thing about the earth, catching the breath, is that it is alive. The photographs show the dry, pounded surface of the moon in the foreground, dead as an old bone. Aloft, floating free beneath the moist gleaming membrane of bright blue sky, is the rising earth, the only exuberant thing in this part of the cosmos. If you could look long enough you would see ... the continents themselves in motion, drifting apart on their crustal plates, held afloat by the fire beneath. It has the organized self-conscious look of a live creature, full of information, marvelously skilled in handling the sun. ... When the earth came alive it began constructing its own membrane, for the purpose of editing the sun. ... The earth breathes in a certain sense ...

and so on.[13]

Evolution and Organism

The essence and fulfillment of organism, for Hegel is subjectivity, that phase of integration of the whole at which it becomes aware of itself as the Concept (the truth), and is actualized as and in a self-conscious subject. At the level of nature this goal takes the form of sentience, the transition stage to spirit proper. The self-external framework of organism is laid out in geological nature, which, as we have seen, burgeons forth into myriad points of life (as he says) "like Minerva fully armed from the head of Jupiter." But these, according to Hegel, are merely transitory. Ocean and earth subsequently generate plant and animal life, which present two phases of organism at different levels of integration, but in all cases the living being is an integral unified whole of parts tending in different degrees towards subjectivity.

The essential character of wholeness is unity in and through differences, so the living being is both one and many, a self-differentiating individual. At the vegetable level, we are told, the individuality does not separate itself from the actual particulars, but remains submerged in them, so that the plant is not yet for itself (*für sich seiend*) subjectivity. Its parts are by and large equipotential and semi-self-dependent, even when they together form a coherent differentiated whole.[14] In animal life, on the other hand, organic individuality exists as subjectivity in so far as the externality proper to embodiment (*Gestalt*) is idealized, converting parts into members instant with the life of the whole, mutually ends and means, which are what they are only as organs and instruments of the living system. They are all felt as one, as self, and the self feels itself in all of them. This unity is soul, the Concept which actualizes itself in the body in so far as it is the process of idealization.[15]

What I wish to emphasize is Hegel's unswerving and consistent perception of the wholeness and systematic integration of the bodily organism. Echoing Aristotle, who underlined the fact that a severed hand was, in its separation from the organic whole, no longer a hand, Hegel declares, "Cut off a finger, and it is no more a finger, but proceeds to decompose as a chemical process." He writes:

> The animal is the existent Idea in so far as its members are purely and simply moments of the form, perpetually negating their independence and bringing themselves back into their unity, which is the reality of the Notion and is for the Notion.[16]

The unity of the organism is the reality of the "Notion" or Concept—the Concept in actual observable existence—and this is so because the Concept is the whole become aware of itself as subject.

In its self-feeling the animal organism registers all the impingements upon its body of the external environment and so epitomizes the entire external world, which, we have already seen, is itself a unified whole organic in essence. Thus it has become the existing Idea. The Idea is the truth, which is the whole (as we were assured in the Preface to the *Phenomenology of Spirit*), and it exists in the bodily organism in so far as it feels itself as subject and is becoming self-conscious Spirit.

Now the truth which is the whole, we are told in the same context, is in its true form only as developed system (self-differentiated unity). It is the outcome (*Resultat*) of the entire process of the dialectic, which is nothing more nor less than the development of that whole by virtue of the immanence of its unifying principle (the Concept) in every partial element or representation. This is how and why the Idea is essentially process, is infinite restlessness, perpetual self-differentiation, without which it could not be a whole. Consequently, it is *evolutionary* throughout, and this does not cease to be the case, in principle, when the Idea is externalized as Nature. What is essential to the dialectical development is a conception of evolution implicit in the wholeness of the organism, and the science of Hegel's day could not provide any theory consonant with such a conception that was sufficiently supported by empirical evidence. Can the science of today do better?

Current Views of Evolution

The presuppositions of present-day Neo-Darwinism are that mutations occur by chance, that every gene determines a particular characteristic, and that mutation produces, in consequence, a small and more or less independent change, which, if advantageous in the existing environment, is naturally selected and becomes prevalent among the population, or, if not, prevents the plant or animal from surviving and is bred out. As mutations accumulate, they result in a gradual, stepwise, alteration of the phenotype, so as to produce a new variety, and ultimately a new species. There is a measure of truth in all this, but there are also weighty considerations that lead to the conclusion that it is not sufficient to explain the obvious facts.

When the entire biosphere is seen as a single organic whole and the systematic unity of the living organism is fully and adequately recognized, the conception of evolution has to be considerably modified from that entertained by the more radical Neo-Darwinians. Mere accumulation of random mutations is quite insufficient to explain organized progress towards the incredibly complex elaboration of an animal capable, as are human beings, of intelligent self-reflection, the patent observable result of evolution. Natural selection can do no more than eliminate what in any case will not survive, and what will not survive is what fails to be adequately systematic and organically integrated. What has survival value is the better adapted: that is, what is better integrated into the eco-system, what maintains the wholeness at once of the living thing and the ecological totality. Nowadays, even if not every biologist is prepared to adopt Lovelock's Gaia Hypothesis, the entire biosphere is admitted to be a single eco-system with organisms and environment mutually organically interrelated;[17] and the organism itself is recognized as an indivisible self-maintaining whole. The conception of evolution is thus bound to become something much more than merely additive, and something beyond mere random mutation and natural selection must be sought to explain it.

This is a contention I made some thirty years ago and have repeated ever since.[18] There is today copious evidence that phenotypical change is not simply dependent on random mutation, and even some ground for believing that not all mutation is purely random; rather that some may be induced by organismic pressures to maintain the integrity of the living thing in its surroundings. That the chromosome is not just a collection of genes like a string of beads, but operates as a whole, as does the entire genome, is now well established. The gene has been found to occur, not just as a single blob, but divided into pieces separated by intermittent strands of apparently redundant DNA, the parts acting in concert not only with one another but with the other elements of the chromosome. It is now known that single genes do not affect single characters independently. There seems clearly to be an overriding principle of organization at work governing the systematic coherence of the organism within itself and with its environment, buffering the effects of disrupting mutations and holding others in abeyance as recessive until such time as conditions enable them, when they become dominant, to survive or even perhaps to give reproductive advantage.[19]

That the doctrine of chance mutation and natural selection has to be supplemented and modified to include a principle of self-organization has been strongly maintained by Stuart Kauffman in his recent book, *The Origins of Order*, with powerful arguments, some of them corroborating those I had earlier put forward, and marshalling persuasive evidence mathematically supported, the general outcome of which gives massive support to my case. "Many properties of organisms," he writes,

> may be probable emergent collective properties of their constituents. The evolutionary origins of such properties, then, find their explanation in principles of self-organization rather than sufficiency of time. ... The task [of the biologist] must be to include self-organizing properties in a broadened framework, asking what the effects of selection and drift will be when operating on systems which have their own rich and robust self-ordered properties. For in such cases, it seems preeminently likely that what we observe reflects the interactions of selected processes and the underlying properties of the systems acted upon.[20]

The doctrine of mutation and selection, therefore, must be supplemented to give it an organismic turn, admitting some principle of self-organization. Nor can the individual be considered in isolation from the eco-system in which its symbiotic life is integral. What evolves has to be seen, not simply as the particular organism, or even the particular species, but as the entire biocoenosis—in the last resort, the biosphere as a whole.

This change of outlook promises a theory of evolution based on the nature of, and nisus toward, the whole: a process bound to be dialectical in essence. Had such a theory, with sound scientific credentials, been at Hegel's disposal in the early nineteenth century there can be little doubt that he would have embraced it with alacrity.

What I have striven to show is that, despite his firm and explicit rejection of a notion of evolution incompatible with his general principles and one that scientifically has since fallen into disrepute, Hegel in the *Philosophy of Nature* presents what is essentially an evolutionary doctrine. Nature, he tells us, is the Idea only implicitly; but what is implicit must through the dialectical process become explicit:

> Nature is, however, only implicitly the Idea, and Schelling therefore called her a petrified intelligence, others even frozen intelligence; but God does not remain petrified and dead; the very stones cry out and raise themselves to Spirit.[21]

Notes

1. Cf. J.N. Findlay, *Hegel: A Re-examination* (London: G. Allen and Unwin, 1958), p. 272; E.E. Harris, *Nature, Mind and Modern Science* (London: G. Allen and Unwin, 1954, 1968) p. 245, and *The Spirit of Hegel* (Atlantic Highlands, NJ: Humanities Press, 1993), pp. 136ff.

2. G.W.F. Hegel, *Enzyklopädie der philosophischen Wissenschaften im Grundrisse (1830). Erster Teil: Die Wissenschaft der Logik mit den mündlichen Zusätzen*, edited by E. Moldenhauer and K.M. Michel, *Werke in zwanzig Bänden*, Vol. 8 (Frankfurt am Main: Suhrkamp Verlag, 1970), §215; *Hegel's Logic. Being Part One of the Encyclopaedia of the Philosophical Sciences (1830),*

translated by W. Wallace (Oxford: Clarendon Press, 1975), p. 278. (Hereafter cited as *EL* [1830], §215; Wallace, *EL*, p. 278.)

3. Sir William Dampier, *A History of Science* (Cambridge: Cambridge University Press; New York: Macmillan, 1946), p. 293.

4. G.W.F. Hegel, *Philosophie der Natur*, K.G.J. Griesheims Nachschrift; Vorlesung des Wintersemesters 1823/24 (Staatsbibliothek Preußischer Kulturbesitz, Berlin. Ms. Germ. 4°), pp. 542-3. Cf. Wolfgang Bonsiepen, "Hegels Kritische Auseinandersetzung mit der Zeitgenössischen Evolutionstheorie," in *Hegels Philosophie der Natur: Beziehungen zwischen empirischer und spekulativer Naturerkenntnis*, edited by R.-P. Horstmann and M. J. Petry (Stuttgart: Klett-Cotta, 1986).

5. G.W.F. Hegel, *Enzyklopädie der philosophischen Wissenschaften im Grundrisse (1830). Zweiter Teil: Die Naturphilosophie mit den mündlichen Zusätzen*, edited by E. Moldenhauer and K.M. Michel, *Werke in zwanzig Bänden*, Vol. 9 (Frankfurt am Main: Suhrkamp Verlag, 1970), §249 Zus; *Hegel's Philosophy of Nature. Being Part Two of the Encyclopaedia of the Philosophical Sciences (1830)*, translated by A.V. Miller (Oxford: Clarendon Press, 1970), p. 21. (Hereafter cited as *EN* [1830]; Miller, *PN*.)

6. *EN* (1830), §249 Zus.; Miller, *PN*, p. 21.

7. Cf. *EL* (1830), §161; Wallace, *EL*, p. 224.

8. Cf. *EN* (1830), §249 Zus.; Miller, *PN*, p. 22: "It is important to hold fast to identity; but to hold fast to difference is no less important."

9. Cf. L.J. Henderson, *The Fitness of the Environmen*t (New York: Macmillan, 1913); J.D. Barrow and F.J. Tipler, *The Anthropic Cosmological Principle* (Oxford: Oxford University Press, 1986), Ch. 5; Errol E. Harris, *Cosmos and Anthropos* (Atlantic Highlands, NJ: Humanities Press, 1991), Ch. 4.

10. *EN* (1830), §339 Zus. 1; Miller, *PN*, p. 279.

11. *EN* (1830), §341 Zus.; Miller, *PN*, p. 294.

12. Cf. J. S. Haldane, *Organism and Environment* (New Haven: Yale University Press, 1917).

13. Cf. Lewis Thomas, *The Lives of a Cell* (1974; reprint, Harmondsworth: Penguin Books, 1987), pp. 145-7.

14. *EN* (1830), §§344-5, Miller, *PN*, pp. 305-21.

15. *EN* (1830), §350 and Zusatz; Miller, *PN*, pp. 351-2.

16. *EN* (1830), §350 Zus.; Miller, *PN*, p. 352.

17. Cf. Marston Bates, *The Forest and the Sea* (1963; reprint, New York: Viking Press, 1965), p. 31.

18. Cf. my *The Foundations of Metaphysics in Science* (London: G. Allen and Unwin, 1965), Ch. 12; *The Reality of Time* (Albany, NY: SUNY Press, 1988), Ch. 4; *Cosmos and Anthropos*, Ch. 6.

19. See my *The Foundations of Metaphysics in Science*, Ch. 12 (4) and the references given there.

20. Stuart A. Kauffman, *The Origins of Order: Self-Organization and Selection in Evolution* (Oxford: Oxford University Press, 1993), pp. 22ff.

21. *EN* (1830), §247 Zus.; Miller, *PN*, pp. 14-15.

9

Hegel's Nature

Donald Phillip Verene

In the *Phenomenology of Spirit* of 1807, Hegel identifies himself in the middle of the title page as "Dr. and Professor of Philosophy at Jena, assessor in the Ducal Mineralogical Society and member of other learned societies."[1] Such a declaration of credentials was not uncommon in academic works of the day, and can even be found in some such works today. Yet Hegel's declaration of his professional status seems especially fitting for a work in Germany, a country afflicted by hierarchy, authority, and uniforms. The reader is surprised to learn that the book on *Geist* he is about to read is by an author claiming to be both philosopher and mineralogist. Among the "other learned societies" of the title page Hegel would apparently intend the Westphalian Society for Natural Research, to which he had been elected on August 1, 1804.[2] In addition to whatever professional and political value it may have had to be a member of such authorized societies, Hegel's claim to them has placed in the reader's mind the thought that the "science of the experience of consciousness" may have some kind of association with geological science.

Perhaps it is an enormous joke, the first of Hegel's many careful ironies, placed in the first book of his career, expected by him to be overlooked, as indeed it has been. Ignored by his commentators and translators, it remains a quiet oddity of the work. It is noticed only by the reader who thinks to begin with the first page. Hegel, the first phenomenologist, is also the practicing mineralogist. Having become an "assessor" of the Jena Mineralogical Society in January 1804, Hegel was issued a pass in May by the University for a field trip to Göttingen and the Harz Mountains for geological study.[3] Hegel, the rock hound.

Hegel's interest in mineralogical and geological science plays no specific role in the *Phenomenology of Spirit*, where he speaks of inorganic nature in only general terms; but his knowledge of these subjects becomes part of his philosophy of nature in its earlier forms (1801-6) and later forms (1817, 1827, 1830). In his sections on "geological nature" in the *Encyclopedia* (§§338-42), Hegel declares himself to be neither a *vulcanist* (one who holds that the Earth's shape and stratifications are of igneous origin), nor a *neptunist* (one who holds that all is the result of an aqueous process). In his presentation of the "terrestrial organism" both of these conceptions of geological history are declared equally one-sided. Hegel says, "in the crystalline form of the Earth, in volcanoes, springs and in the mineralogical process in general, fire is just as operative as water."[4]

On the title page of his first published book, Hegel has identified himself as a combination of spirit and nature, as a professor of the love of wisdom and an assessor (one who sits by another as next in dignity, i.e., a qualified assistant) of a science of the earth—the spiritual and the terrestrial in one. Do I see too much significance in a simple convention? Rosenkranz speaks of Hegel, when he lectured in Jena, as having an "odd smile" behind which was benevolence; yet there was something "sharp" and "ironic" about it.[5] We must be careful with Hegel; like a poet and an ironist, he never lets anything go to waste.

In his thirty-seventh year, with his career in a certain sense well underway but in a precarious position at the moment, due to Napoleon's arrival in Jena in October 1806, Hegel introduced himself to the world as both philosopher and natural scientist. Although Hegel was a remarkable mind, the most comprehensive since Aristotle, it was not as remarkable as it seems today for him to lay claim to both the sciences of the soul and the sciences of nature. As John Findlay points out:

> the *élan* of scientific thought had not yet lost itself in a wilderness of detail, nor been paralysed by difficulties beyond its effective mastery. It was a time when a world-mind like Goethe could write easily and deeply on plant-

morphology and the theory of colour in a manner impossible to the poets of our own day.[6]

In fact, in Jena in the summer of 1806, a topic of common discussion between Goethe and Hegel was natural science, including geology and mineralogy.

For generations, for most of this century, Hegel's philosophy of nature has been the ignored or ridiculed part of his system. It was ignored by the British Idealists (Collingwood's *Idea of Nature* being an exception). For logical positivists and philosophers of science (whenever they knew it existed) it was the subject of immediate ridicule. Karl Popper, in his attack on Hegel in *The Open Society and its Enemies*, calls Hegel's discussion of the relation between sound and heat "gibberish." He calls Hegelian dialectics "the mystery method" that is supposed to replace "barren formal logic."[7] Analytic philosophers have discovered they can read Kant, a movement that began with the commentaries of Weldon and Strawson, and now much of Kant's epistemology and ethics are freely discussed and used in analytic philosophy. After all, Kant is all distinctions, one after another, something analytic philosophers have turned into a profession. But Hegel makes them mad; once Hegel speaks of the Idea, it does not take long until he shows a world that was not made for doing business. Hegel surmounts the Understanding with speculative Reason, with the dialectics of the "speculative sentence" (*spekulativer Satz*) and the literal-minded philosophers either laugh or leave the room.

It cannot be said too often that Hegel's philosophy of nature is not fanciful. The natural science of Hegel's day is outmoded and irrelevant, but, as Findlay says, "The scientific views of Hegel's day are as deserving of respect as the transitory opinions of our own. ... Hegel's grasp of contemporary science, was, moreover, informed and accurate. ... Hegel *gives* one the science of his own day."[8] Indeed, Hegel's *Philosophy of Nature* should be regarded as the great sourcebook of late eighteenth- and nineteenth-century science, in all fields. Petry's three-volume translation and commentary on it has certainly shown the truth of Findlay's claim.

No Hegelian today would remain uninformed of Hegel's achievement in this area. But the suspicion still remains, even among friendly readers of Hegel, that Hegelian philosophy cannot truly illuminate the process of the actual scientific investigation of nature, despite the demonstrations to the contrary that stretch from Errol Harris's eloquent tour de force, *Nature, Mind and Modern Science* (1954)[9] and his other works, to Petry's essay on "Scientific Method" and others in the 1986 volume of the Internationale Hegel-Vereinigung on the *Philosophy of Nature*,[10] to the essays in this collection. It is widely thought that the philosophy of the Idea cannot produce an account of what is truly there in experience as nature. There will always be something subjective, *a priori*, and arbitrary about the account, no matter how the account is begun, even if begun from the side of the object. Once the world of the Idea is entered, there is no exit back to what is there before and outside the Idea. Nature will always in the end fail in maintaining its independent reality and will remain a function of the Idea, no matter how cleverly the dialectics of its reality are explained.

It is this "idea-ization" of nature that concerns me as a devotee of the Sage of Jena. I wish to understand one sentence in Hegel's corpus. It is a sentence that has bothered me since I first read it thirty-four years ago. It is Hegel's claim in the last moments of the *Science of Logic* that

> The passing over [of the Idea into nature] is thus to be grasped here in this way, that the Idea *freely releases* itself in its absolute confidence and calm.
>
> Das Übergehen ist also hier vielmehr so zu fassen, daß die Idee sich selbst *frei entläßt*, ihrer absolut sicher und in sich ruhend.[11]

Or, as he puts it in the *Encyclopedia Logic*, the Idea resolves

> freely to *release out of itself* ... the *immediate Idea* as its reflection, or itself as nature.

> die *unmittelbare Idee* als ihren Widerschein, sich als *Natur* frei *aus sich zu entlassen*.[12]

The Idea freely goes forth as nature.

I have not spoken out freely on this before, and have on only a few occasions discussed it at length privately with students and with one or two colleagues. Now I wish to say frankly how I chose to understand it. It is something thrust upon me, for, as you know, the philosophy of nature is not my subject in Hegel. I am an amateur in this area and must speak as an amateur. What I wish to suggest concerning these words of Hegel, and the other words that surround them, follows from what I have said about Hegel in my book on the *Phenomenology—Hegel's Recollection*.[13] In my epilogue to this book I have outlined my views of the structure of Hegel's system. Few will agree with me once what I say is heard, but why should anyone expect otherwise, when one has spoken one's mind? If light can be thrown on how the Idea becomes nature, the whole of the system will be illuminated. It will be like putting the keystone in an arch: once placed, the whole arch will stand. How are we to understand these sentences, which commentators all pass over or say a few things about as they proceed into Hegel's account of space and time? Before we construct nature from space and time, let us make nature as a truth.

At this point you may expect me to enter the cave of hermeneutics. I must say something of this art that I would call "continental analytics" or "conalytics," for I cannot in good conscience follow it. What is needed is not a hermeneutics of the text, but an erotics of the text. I would liken hermeneutics to the art of embalming. Embalming was originally presented as an advance in hygiene. It guarantees with efficiency that the blood has stopped flowing in all cells and that the body is fully at rest. All twitching is removed. Hermeneutics has the power to quiet the text completely, to render it manageable—all paradox identified, all motion stilled to the level of complete interpretation.

It is a short step from the embalmer's art to the "memory image" of the funeral director—the grooming and rouging of the corpse to leave a good impression on the friends and family at the viewing. The funeral director's task is complete when he overhears: "Doesn't he (or she) look like himself (or herself)?" The team of hermeneuticists hovering about the text finishes its work and withdraws comfortably, knowing now the real meaning has been laid out—another successful product of critical reflection. No hermeneuticist or friend of hermeneutics will agree, but hermeneutics stills eros. Eros becomes Hegel's skeleton with tickets stuck all over it. Hermeneutics is *ängstlich* in the face of eros. Eros loves life and has its own ideas about form.

The villain that would stand in our way to understand Hegel is not continental hermeneutics or Anglo-American analytics as such. They are only philosophical movements that will pass, in their time, like others before them. The villain is literal-mindedness in philosophy; what Hegel calls *unsere Buchstabenphilosophen*, "our literal-minded philosophers."[14] These are the ones who do not know how to stand on their heads and hence only have upright vision. They are trapped in the Cyclops, the one-eyed vision of critical reflection, and cannot engage in the two-eyed vision of the speculative act of world inversion that is the key to seeing the whole. Who thinks abstractly? The literal-minded do—the philosophers of the part.

Eros was most certainly present on the nine nights that Mnemosyne, whom Hegel calls the "absolute Muse,"[15] had Jove locked in her moist embrace. She gave birth to her nine daughters of humanity—the Muses—one for each of the letters in her name. Hermes was not there, not even as an onlooker; he read the reports. Hegel was a man of eros, personally and philosophically. Mnemosyne, the absolute Muse, not Hermes, is our guide to the humanity of his text. She is our guide to the erotics by which Hegel gives birth to the greatest system of the modern world—in the process training philosophy to speak German, a great fringe benefit for the language.

How am I, perhaps we, to understand the last claim of the *Logic*, that the Idea freely goes forth as nature, freely releases itself? The reports on the dialectical reasoning are over; the commentators have done that. No amount of section-by-section commentary will solve it. Such can do no more than repeat in various ways what Hegel's claim is. Enough of this has been done, at least to convince me that the answer will not lie in this direction. In saying this, be it known that I am neither misogrammatist nor misologist; I am not an enemy of commentary and learning, nor of argument in philosophy. What is needed, I think, in answer to my quandary of the Idea freely going forth as nature, is the ancient *techne* of a "likely story." I shall tell it as a tale because in the tale "the true is the whole."

The tale requires us to be led by Memory back to the *Phenomenology*, where, Hegel tells us in the *Science of Logic*, logic itself is born. In my *Hegel's Recollection*, I concluded that the dialectic of the experience of consciousness was a two-step, not a three-step. Hegel's dance was a simple two-step, not the Lambada. His dialectic is closer to the ancient dialectic of "this" and "that" than to the Kantian triplicity which he complains about and calls a *geistloses Schema*. I understood Hegel's dialectic in the *Phenomenology* by what I called the "double *Ansich*," Hegel's double helix that is expressed in the phrase "*An und für sich sein*." The *Für sich* is another *An sich*, but one that cannot be collapsed back into the original *Ansich* from which it is generated as a response.

I will not remake my whole case here. Most of Hegel's direct explanation of his method is in the pages that open the *Phenomenology* proper—the Introduction. I wish to call attention to only two statements. Hegel says that something is *for* consciousness—namely, the *in itself*—and that the knowing (*Wissen*), or the being (*Sein*), of the object for consciousness, is itself *for consciousness* another moment. Hegel concludes that "upon this distinction, which is present as a fact, the examination rests" (*Auf dieser Unterscheidung, welche vorhanden ist, beruht die Prüfung*). In the following paragraph he says that this dialectical movement that consciousness exercises on itself in its knowing (*Wissen*) and on its object (*Gegenstand*) is precisely called experience (*Erfahrung*). Consciousness knows something as such and it is also something for consciousness. He says this is where the ambiguity of this truth enters: "*damit tritt die Zweideutigkeit dieses Wahren ein.*" He then says:

> We see that consciousness now has two objects: one is the first in-itself, the second is the being-for-consciousness of this in-itself.
>
> Wir sehen, daß das Bewußtsein jetzt zwei Gegenstände hat, den einen das erste Ansich, den zweiten, das Für-es-sein dieses Ansich.[16]

Consciousness lives within the ambiguity (*die Zweideutigkeit*) of two objects: one that is there, but that it does not own, and one that is its own. This is the nature of its experience, of experience as such. These are mutually required moments. We cannot conceive of one without the other which opposes it. There is no *transition* between the one and the other; that is, there is no specifiable relationship or principle that can be used to describe the passage from one moment to the other. There is an absolute gap between them. There are simply *two* objects. There is a movement from one to the other: what is "that" becomes what is "this," so to speak.

The bond between these two objects is as close as we can come to necessity as a phenomenon. One cannot actually be without the other. There is no literal truth that can be uttered equally of both of their beings. We are forced to speak always of the one *and* the other. We can speak of both, but to speak of both is just to note their "twoness." To speak the truth about them would be to find a way to speak of them as a whole, but this does not require that they be grasped as a unity. The object for consciousness, the object with being-for-itself, is just as ambiguous because its being is immediately transposed into a new in-itself. A third thing, a moment that would truly hold all together, is always just out of reach. Consciousness lives in ambiguity, without a way to stop its motion and find its wholeness that would be its final truth. Experience, for Hegel, always means "doubling up."

From this standpoint, each stage in Hegel's *Phenomenology* is predicated on the illusion that the ambiguity of the double *Ansich* can be resolved, i.e., that "sense-certainty" can still the movement between the two moments, or that "perception" can, or that "force and understanding" can, etc. The consciousness undergoing the process of the stages of the phenomenology struggles for wholeness, blindly at first and then more deliberately later. It hopes to seize upon some feature of appearance that will promise the truth of the whole and still the life of the double. The "we," the second perspective of the phenomenology, recollects these struggles as a theatre of memory in which each phenomenon of defective wholeness is brought upon the stage of experience to observe its performance. The "we" that attempts to see the role of each is from time to time caught up in the fascination of the play itself. At these times it realizes its own doubleness with the consciousness it recollects.[17]

Each stage in the phenomenology is an illusion, a failure to produce the whole, and the terms of its failure are the two moments that at first seem reached and then are seen only to generate a further ambiguity. The opening of each stage is a scene of hope and the end is a scene of despair—the "highway of despair" of which Hegel speaks. Hegel frequently reminds us that consciousness forgets the path it has come along and must begin again. Consciousness repeats its error of mistaking reductionism (i.e., one-sidedness) for wholeness and replays the drama in different terms on each stage. The illusion of wholeness builds up as the phenomenology progresses. The terms of the illusion become more elaborate: instead of the simple certainty of the senses, there is the context of selfhood, of reasoning about the world, of forms of social and ethical life. The last grand illusion is religion, in which wholeness is attempted in the most elaborate guises possible, only to find the ambiguity of the *Ansich* equal to the task.

Then comes wisdom, absolute knowing. Absolute knowing, if it is to be truly absolute, must differ, so to speak, in kind, not just degree, from each stage that has preceded it. Each stage has fallen apart through its own kind of illusion. To move from religion to absolute knowing is a real breakthrough. The achievement of absolute knowing is the realization that all stages up to it have refused to accept the ambiguity of experience. Each stage has believed that it could find a way to rewrite the formula of *An und für sich Sein* as *An-für sich Sein*, thus eliminating the "and," the *An und*. Each has believed it could accomplish the final equation, thereby turning the quest for wholeness into a quest for certainty. Absolute knowing is the genuine acceptance that the conjunction remains and no particular meaning can be assigned to it to produce an explicit realization of wholeness.

The Absolute is just the two-in-the-one, and the one is just the necessary mutuality of the twoness. But it is easy to backslide. That is why we keep reading the *Phenomenology* over and over: to see if there is not some way to have more than this "andness." It is why we become caught up in various stages in our general philosophizing, forgetting what the *Phenomenology* has already taught us about the one-sidedness of such and such a position. Although we have read the *Phenomenology*, we keep being caught up in stages that it has taught us are unwise. Its lessons must be relearned over and over, because to accept the absoluteness of the gap between the two moments of experience is to accept a true and severe story. It is an ironic and melancholic wisdom; it is philosophical wisdom. It is no longer a highway of despair. It is an acceptance of the "*what is*" in the world we inhabit as knowers. Wisdom is to see the conjunctions without illusions.

The passage from the *Phenomenology* to the *Logic* from this standpoint is one in which consciousness freely goes forth as thought. Having failed to produce as a phenomenon within experience what is needed to overcome the doubleness of experience, we step outside of it into thought. Hegel says: "*Logic is pure science*."[18] The *Logic* is a total discourse on the "and." Free of illusions, in the state of absolute knowing we can freely and deliberately think through the dialectical possibilities of overcoming the "and" through the power of the Idea. To do this, we must begin with being. Can the "and," if not overcome on the level of phenomena, be grasped in thought such that the doubleness, the ambiguity that is present in experience, is surmounted? Both sides of the *Ansich* surely *are*, so the first thought is being. But, as the reader of the *Logic* quickly learns, being in its concourse with nothing gives way to becoming, then to quality and to the total world of categories that, as Hegel says, are originally present in language. Hegel says that his system is a "circle of circles" (*ein Kreis von Kreisen*), and now the reader is in the circle of the *Logic*—a world in which the philosopher can feel quite at home. The *Logic* is an asylum from experience, a divine place where the philosopher can retreat and just think through thought. But there is still nature to worry about, another circle in Hegel's circle, a link in his chain (*Kette*).[19]

To my mind, the best commentator on the *Logic* is Bertolt Brecht, in a curious little work, *Flüchtlingsgespräche* (*Refugee Dialogues*). Here, in a conversation that breaks out between two refugees, Ziffel and Kalle, Brecht says:

> Concerning humor I always think of the philosopher Hegel. ... He had the stuff of one of the greatest humorists among philosophers; Socrates is the only other one who had a similar method. ... I once read his book, the "Larger Logic". ... It is one of the most humorous works in world literature. It deals with the life of concepts, their slippery, unstable, irresponsible existence, how they revile each other and do battle with knives and then sit themselves down together at dinner as if nothing had happened.

Brecht continues:

> They appear, so to speak, in pairs; each is married to its opposite and they settle their affairs in pairs, that is, they sign contracts in pairs, enter in legal actions in pairs, contrive raids and burglaries in pairs, write books and give affidavits in pairs, and do so as pairs whose members are completely at odds with each other. What order affirms,

> disorder, its inseparable partner, opposes at once, in one breath where possible. They can neither live without one another nor with one another.

And Brecht concludes: "I have never met a person without a sense of humor who has understood Hegel's dialectic."[20]

The *Science of Logic* is where Hegel takes himself least seriously, where we find that "odd smile" of Jena extended into Heidelberg. But I agree with Findlay about the final moment of the *Logic*, that "there is nothing but the utmost intellectual sobriety in Hegel's transition from the Idea to Nature."[21] I also agree with Findlay that the movement from Idea to nature and on to spirit is a process of divine creation, in which what is universal determines and finds itself in the otherness of the externality of nature and the internality of spirit. Hegel is clear that the movement from Idea to nature is not "*a process of becoming*" (*ein Gewordensein*), nor is it properly a "transition" (*Übergang*) such as exists within the dialectic of the *Logic*, e.g., as when "*the subjective end becomes life*" (*der subjektive Zweck zum Leben wird*). The passage to nature is an absolute liberation (*absolute Befreiung*), a freedom (*Freiheit*) that the *Begriff* at this point commands. The "Idea *freely releases itself*" (*die Idee sich selbst frei entläßt*).[22]

As the circular link of the *Phenomenology* locks around the circular link of the *Logic* in Hegel's system-chain, so the link of the *Logic* locks around that of the *Philosophy of Nature*. Both are pictures of divine self-knowledge. Both are acts structured by unresolved twoness and the freedom that exists between two necessary moments of actuality. Recall Hegel's gloss on Schiller's *Die Freundschaft*, that he gives as his last words in the *Phenomenology*: "From the chalice of this realm of spirits/foams forth for Him his own infinitude" (*Aus dem Kelche dieses Geisterreiches / schäumt ihm seine Unendlichkeit*). In the full context of the poem, the *Weltenmeister* was friendless and so created the world of *Geister*, but still found in his creation no perfect counterpart. Yet he found himself bound to his creation, like one friend to another.[23]

There is no trinity in this image, just God and his foaming cup, "doubling all the time." The key to freedom is the metaphor of friendship, the constant doubling of one-to-one human relationships, one self freely going forth into another and another. What is needed to understand the end of the *Logic* has already been given at the end of the *Phenomenology*, and Hegel need not belabor it a second time. Within a circular link there can be "transitions," but between links hooked together there can be none. They are just linked one to the other. The "transitions" within the circle of the dialectic of opposites are a source of humor; the links of the chain are sober and divine.

As Brecht shows, the dialectic within the *Logic* is a drama of the "odd couple." But how does the Idea go forth freely as nature? Does it do so as earth, air, fire, and water? Are earthquakes, hurricanes, volcanoes, and floods the Idea going forth as nature? Are mud slides, droughts, forest fires, and blizzards also examples of such? They are all acts of God, acts by which culture is continually surprised, and which are excluded from coverage in most insurance policies. Just when the forms of spirit seem to be getting on so well, nature reminds us of its own free existence in its primal scene of space and time. Within the human animal itself is always the day of the locust, the "labor of the negative" come to dinner, always an unwelcome guest.

Collingwood says:

> Nature, for Hegel, is real; it is in no sense an illusion, or something which we think to exist when what really exists is something else; nor is it in any sense a mere appearance, something which only exists because we think it. It really exists, and exists independently of any mind whatever.[24]

The reality of nature on my account has been there from the beginning, as the double of spirit—the ever-present *Ansich* to spirit's reality "for us." Nature is not the "fellow-sufferer who understands"; nature is the independent and unpredictable companion whose otherness no act of friendship can fully bridge.

The passage Hegel gives us is not actually one from the Idea to nature, but from divine thinking, "metaphysical thinking," to "philosophy of" thinking. "Philosophy of" thinking is modern thinking, that is, it is unwise thinking. "Philosophy of" thinking gives up on the true as the whole in the sense of wisdom as a "knowledge of things human and divine," and concentrates only on things simply human. From the purely human perspective, the whole is the putting together of all the truths arrived at in the individual sciences of nature and spirit. There can be a philosophy of each science and then a systematic ordering of those sciences that tell us what nature is under a philosophy of nature. The same can be done for spirit. Here all is *architectonic*, and triplicity holds sway. We might say that it is here that Hegel becomes Kant, or at least neo-Kantian. There is no greater modern comprehension of theoretical knowledge than Hegel's two "philosophies of" nature and spirit. They are, as Hegel so clearly calls them, an "encyclopedia of philosophical science in outline." The outline is to make everything into threes. Dialectic in the *Encyclopedia* is just a method of arrangement, but dialectic in the *Phenomenology* and the *Science of Logic* is the expression of the actual inner life of consciousness and thought. The little logic gets the arrangement going and it becomes an *encyclopedia*—a special table of contents of knowledge. As a pedagogical document it is a complete curriculum that would fill any university's general education requirements.

Why have Hegel's comments at the end of the *Logic*, about the freedom of the Idea as nature, seemed so puzzling? I think it is because of the myth of *Aufhebung*. The initiate into the Hegelian system is taken aside, at some point, and told of the mysteries of *Aufhebung*, that the dialectic depends upon this otherwise ordinary German verb, *aufheben*, and its noun, and that only when it is mastered will the blinding light of the interior room of the Absolute be seen. We expect to find *aufheben* between stages of the *Phenomenology* and the thoughts of the *Logic*, and in the millwheeling triplicity of the *Encyclopedia*—and we usually do, though not always, and not as often as we would like. This is especially so in the

Phenomenology, where we find more juxtapositions than transitions.

But we expect that the grand examples of *Aufhebung* will be found in the great links of the system, and we find there instead the open denial of any form of "transition." We have taken *Aufhebung* too seriously. Truly what Hegel's dialectic depends upon is not this verb at all. It depends on what all dialectic depends on: that old humanist faculty of *ingenium*—the ability to perceive a resemblance between two things, which in science results in the formation of hypotheses, in the arts results in the formation of the metaphor, and in philosophy results in the formation of dialectic. Without this faculty, which is the basis of all wit, humor and irony, we could not understand Hegel, and Hegel, like Socrates, the founder of self-knowledge, is throughout his works constantly playing on and training this capacity of the ingenious grasp in the reader. Without the sense of the incongruous, Hegel has no science. His dialectic depends upon the presence of humor in the reader's own existence. *Ingenium* makes the incongruous congruous, without eliminating its ambiguity. What I have called "doubling" is no mystery to anyone who has developed the capacity of *ingenium*. But it is not a feature of literal-mindedness.

Finally, it is said that for the mass of students at Jena Hegel was only an "obscure oddity," but that others clung to him. It is also said that, although he was always striving in his thought, he was dogmatic in its expression. Hegel was, in other words, philosophical. Well, these are old charges, and I have heard them before.

Notes

1. G.W.F. Hegel, *Phänomenologie des Geistes*, edited by J. Hoffmeister (Hamburg: Felix Meiner, 1952), p. 3. (Hereafter cited as *Phän.*) On the title page of the *Wissenschaft der Logik* Hegel identifies himself as Professor and Rector of the Gymnasium in Nürnberg, and on the title page of the *Enzyklopädie* (1830) Hegel identifies himself as Professor of Philosophy at Berlin.

2. *Briefe von und an Hegel*, edited by J. Hoffmeister, 4 Vols (Hamburg: Felix Meiner, 1952-60), **4** (edited by R. Flechsig): 91.

3. *Briefe von und an Hegel*, **4**: 90.

4. *Hegel's Philosophy of Nature*, edited and translated by M.J. Petry, 3 Vols (London: Allen and Unwin; New York: Humanities Press, 1970), **3**: 17. See also T.H. Levere, "Hegel and the Earth Sciences," in *Hegels Philosophie der Natur: Beziehungen zwischen empirischer und spekulativer Naturerkenntnis*, edited by R.-P. Horstmann and M.J. Petry (Stuttgart: Klett-Cotta, 1986), pp. 103-20.

5. Karl Rosenkranz, *G.W.F. Hegel's Leben* (1844; reprint, Darmstadt: Wissenschaftliche Buchgesellschaft, 1963), p. 215.

6. J.N. Findlay, *Hegel: A Re-examination* (1958; reprint, New York: Oxford University Press, 1976), p. 267.

7. Karl R. Popper, *The Open Society and its Enemies*, 2 Vols (1945; reprint, New York: Harper Torchbooks, 1963), **2**: 28.

8. Findlay, pp. 267-8.

9. E.E. Harris, *Nature, Mind and Modern Science* (London: Allen and Unwin, 1954).

10. M.J. Petry, "Scientific Method: Francoeur, Hegel and Pohl," and esp. the papers in the third section, in *Hegels Philosophie der Natur: Beziehungen zwischen empirischer und spekulativer Naturerkenntnis*, pp. 11-29, 331-412.

11. G.W.F. Hegel, *Wissenschaft der Logik*, edited by G. Lasson, 2 Vols (Hamburg: Felix Meiner, 1971), **2**: 505, my translation; *Hegel's Science of Logic*, translated by A.V. Miller (Atlantic Highlands, NJ: Humanities Press International, 1989), p. 843. (Hereafter cited as *Logik* [Lasson]; Miller, *Logic*.)

12. G.W.F. Hegel, *Enzyklopädie der philosophischen Wissenschaften im Grundrisse* (1830), edited by F. Nicolin and O. Pöggeler (Hamburg: Felix Meiner, 1959), §244 (p. 197); *The Encyclopaedia Logic (with the Zusätze)*, translated by T.F. Geraets, W.A. Suchting and H.S. Harris (Indianapolis: Hackett, 1991), p. 307, translation emended.

13. D.P. Verene, *Hegel's Recollection: A Study of Images in the Phenomenology of Spirit* (Albany: SUNY Press, 1985).

14. G.W.F. Hegel, "Das älteste Systemprogramm des deutschen Idealismus," in Hegel, *Frühe Schriften*, edited by E. Moldenhauer and K.M. Michel, *Werke in zwanzig Bänden*, Vol. 1 (Frankfurt am Main: Suhrkamp Verlag, 1971), pp. 234-6.

15. G.W.F. Hegel, "Über Mythologie, Volksgeist und Kunst"; see my translation and discussion in *Hegel's Recollection*, pp. 36-7.

16. *Phän.*, pp. 72-3; see *Hegel's Phenomenology of Spirit*, translated by A.V. Miller (Oxford: Oxford University Press, 1977), p. 55.

17. David Parry, *Hegel's Phenomenology of the "We"* (New York: Peter Lang, 1988).

18. *Logik* (Lasson), **1**: 53; Miller, Logic, p. 69.

19. *Logik* (Lasson), **2**: 504; Miller, *Logic*, p. 842.

20. Bertolt Brecht, *Flüchtlingsgespräche* (Berlin and Frankfurt: Suhrkamp, 1961), pp. 108-11, my translation. Brecht's work was written in Finland in 1941 and published posthumously. See my *Hegel's Recollection*, pp. 119-20.

21. Findlay, p. 269.

22. *Logik* (Lasson), **2**: 505; Miller, *Logic*, p. 843.

23. *Hegel's Recollection*, pp. 6-7.

24. R.G. Collingwood, *The Idea of Nature* (1945; reprint, New York: Oxford University Press, 1960), p. 124.

10

Hegel's Worm in Newton's Apple

Mauro Nasti De Vincentis

Newton's generalized areal law is a cornerstone of his *Principia*, as well as a milestone in the overall development of theoretical mechanics. To understand why, it is worth recalling that, in many physical systems (even when the total mechanical energy is not conserved, as in the case of the so-called non-conservative fields of force), the forces are of a special kind, namely *central* forces acting only along the line connecting the body on which the force is acting with the body producing the field of force, and that Newton's areal law is a fundamental property of any physical system in which the force is central (in fact the areal law holds if *and only if* a plane motion is central).

As is well known, Newton's law of areas is concerned with the case in which the first body is an orbiting mass-point and the second one is also a mass-point which is fixed at the center of force (since the central mass is assumed to be much greater than the mass of the orbiting body and the center of mass of these bodies is assumed to be in a state of rest). The (straight) line which connects the two bodies is the so-called radius vector. As is easily proved, the center of force and the velocity of the orbiting body (as a localized vector whose initial point always coincides with the moving mass-point) will always stay on a fixed orbital plane; and Newton's generalized areal law states just that the areal velocity (defined as the area swept through per unit time) is constant, i.e. the radius vector describes equal areas in equal times on the orbital plane, hence these areas are proportional to the times. As remarked above, this theorem, because of its generality, plays a fundamental role in Newton's dynamics. Moreover, what is now known as Kepler's second law is clearly deducible as one of its many consequences. As far as the generality of Newton's areal law is concerned, even the special case in which the field of the central force is conservative—that is, when the magnitude f of the force acting on a unit mass (i.e. the acceleration of the moving mass-point) depends only on the length r of the radius vector (as opposed to the non-conservative case in which it also depends, say, on the variable magnitude of the velocity)—provides many instances of the validity of that law, only one of which involves gravitational force (namely when the function $f(r) = k/r^2$ where k is a certain constant). As is also well known, when any force function $f(r)$ is itself a constant (that is, when the magnitude of the force is constant over the whole orbit), the orbit of the moving mass-point is circular (since r is constant) and, besides the areal velocity, the speed (i.e. the magnitude of the linear velocity) of the moving point is also constant; hence not only the areas swept through by the radius vector, but also the orbital arcs described by the moving mass-point, are proportional to the times. (Of course, when, more generally, r is not a constant in the force-function $f(r) = k/r^2$, the orbit of the moving body becomes a non-circular conic section, the fixed mass-point being in a focal position.) As to the difference between Newton's areal law and Kepler's areal (i.e. second) law, in order to immediately understand the much greater generality and the higher theoretical import of the former, it now suffices to restate Kepler's law in its standard well-known form: "the areas described by radii drawn from the sun to a planet (and from a planet to a satellite as well) are proportional to the times of describing them," where clearly (and unlike Newton's law of areas) only the special case of planetary motion is concerned.

The overall import and significance of Kepler's laws, at the time of their discovery, were of course different from the standard account one can easily find now in any current textbook of physics or celestial mechanics. Moreover, the standard proof of Newton's generalized areal law is now different from Newton's original proof, the standard proof being much more simple and straightforward, at least if the reader is acquainted both with vectors and just a bit of dynamics in its current form. However, since Hegel's target was Newton's original proof, it is the text of *Principia*, Book I, Theor. I that now cries out for elucidation.

The basic idea of Newton's proof becomes clearer by taking a look at the Figure (see p. 230), which, albeit not coincident with its genuine counterpart (namely the one Hegel actually had under his own eyes), is not too misleading, notwithstanding the fact that, say, in our figure Dd is not parallel to SC as it should be.[1] The point S (which, in accordance with Kepler's first law, may well stand for the focal position of the sun) is the center of motion, the vertices of the polygonal arc ABCDEF standing for different positions of the moving point on its orbit around S. The times of passage from A to B, B to C, C to D, etc. are assumed to be equal to each other. But (and this is the very core of the proof) the discontinuous rectilinear "jumps" (i.e. the displacements AB, BC, CD, etc.) are substituted for the continuous motion of an orbiting body on its actual curvilinear path (which is an elliptical one, if the first of Kepler's laws holds).

According to Newton's geometrical construction, AB = Bc (on the straight line ABc), BC = Cd (on the straight line BCd), etc., cC being parallel to BS, dD to CS, etc.; hence, in a few steps of elementary geometry, the areas of the triangles SAB, SBC, SCD, etc. are provably equal to each other.[2]

Thus, since (see above), the times of passage from A to B, B to C, C to D, etc. are assumed to be equal to each other, the polygonal areas such as SADS, SAFS, etc. are proportional to the times in which the moving mass point traverses the polygonal arcs ABCD, ABCDEF, etc.

According to Newton's proof, all this is nothing but the geometrical representation of the following physical situation. AB is merely intended to define the direction of the initial force-free (inertial) motion at B (its length measuring the approximating displacement during the first interval of time). In accordance with the scheme of the parallelogram (of forces, velocities and displacements), BC is the resultant of two components: namely, 1) a displacement BV = cC produced by an impulsive centripetal force of finite magnitude (which—as in the case of instantaneous strokes

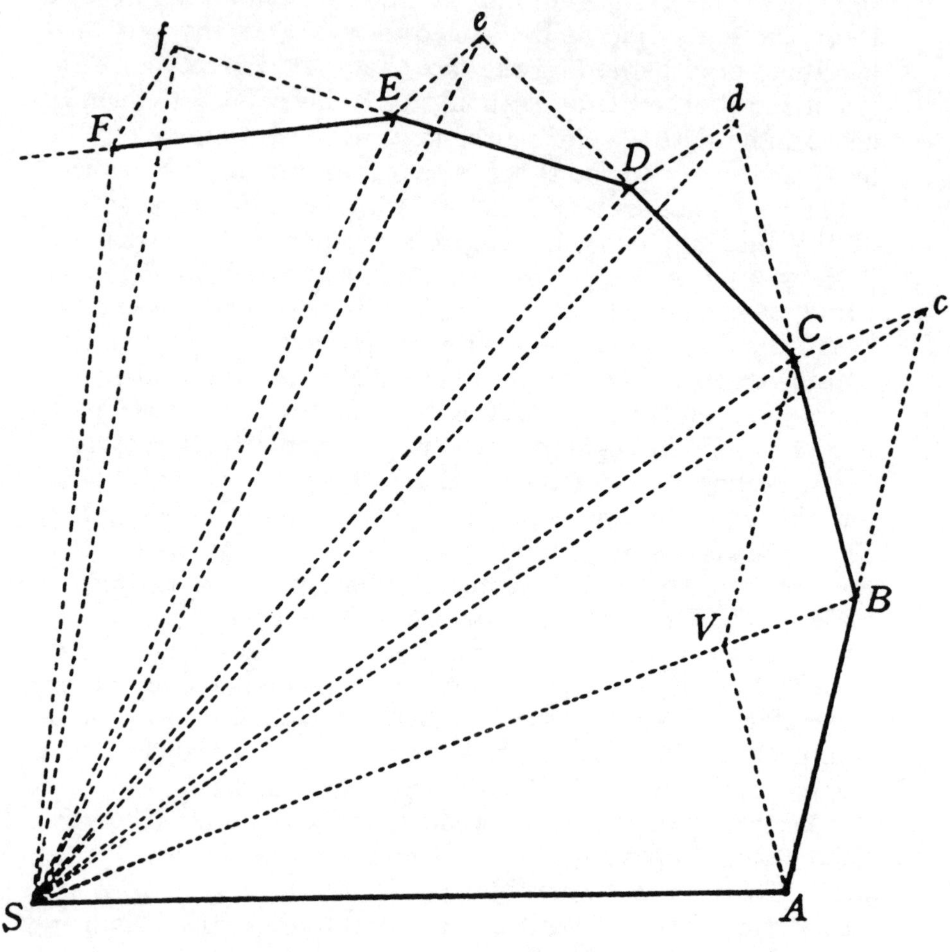

Newton's proof of the areal theorem (a simplified version of the Newtonian figure, *Principia*, Bk. I, Theor. I, drawn by M. Nasti De Vincentis).

or collisions—acts at B for a very short time only and is measured by the change of momentum it produces) and, 2) a purely inertial displacement, were the impulsive force not to act at all on the moving body during the second interval of time. Of course, the displacements CD, DE, etc. also result from the same scheme of composition. Hence the vector **CD** (its magnitude |**CD**| being the length of CD) is such that **CD** = **Cd** + **dD**, etc. (Unlike the localized displacements, CD, DE, etc., vectors in general are not localized; thus we may have a displacement of an assigned length in an assigned direction and sense but whose locality is not specified. In such a case, all equal and parallel lines in the same direction will represent the same vector).[3] Finally, Newton supposes that the triangles SBC, SCD, SDE, etc. become infinitely small and infinite in number (since, under almost the same forces, the intervals of time are made smaller and smaller, till they become vanishingly small). Thus, in the limit, the polygonal arcs coincide with the curvilinear arcs actually described by the orbiting body, the corresponding orbital sectors (focal sectors, if Kepler's first law holds) being always proportional to the times in which they are described by the radius vector. Therefore, the generalised areal law is proved: as Newton writes, "which was to be demonstrated," *Quod Erat Demonstrandum*.

As regards the *fortuna*, the future destiny—let alone a serious appraisal—of this crucial slice of Newton's apple, it is worth citing, to begin with, what D.T. Whiteside says in his unsurpassed edition of Newton's mathematical papers:

> it is only fair to add that none of his [i.e. Newton's] contemporaries and immediate successors—even Johann Bernoulli, his arch critic and an equal grand master of the infinitely small—saw fit to impugn the adequacy of Newton's demonstration.[4]

Although (as we shall see) "almost none" would be more apposite than "none" in Whiteside's passage, it is equally fair to add that Bernoulli's attitude seems to be widespread among *our* contemporaries as well, including (with a single exception, so far as I know, see below, endnote 14) the handful of scholars who are acquainted with Hegel's critical opinion regarding Newton's proof. Thus, De Gandt appears to be only the harbinger of a (more or less explicitly stated) received view when, as a comment on Hegel's opinion, he writes:

> Newton's proof ... is perfectly sound if taking the limit is admitted, since the polygonal arc becomes a curvilinear one when the number of sides is augmented up to infinity. Later on, Hegel will cast his doubts on this point of the argument (cf. *WdL*, I, 276).[5]

Here, as the reference to the passage in Hegel's *Science of Logic* also shows, what De Gandt is claiming is simply that the only plausible objections one could raise against Newton's proof do not really affect its specific mathematical validity, as they constitute an inherently philosophical attack, which could equally be delivered against any other limit-taking operation *à la* Newton just because these operations are performed "with the aid of the nebulous conception of the infinitely small."[6]

However, *pace* De Gandt, Newton's proof is by no means "perfectly sound," no matter whether any naive (Newton style) appeal to notions of the infinite is ruled out or not. In fact, even if modern style phrases are substituted for the original ones (such as *ultima perimeter* [ultimate perimeter], *augeatur* [let be augmented] ... *in infinitum* [up to infinity] and so on)[7] in Newton's own proof, a crucial flaw is still *not* ruled out. In his proof that an orbital arc is the curvilinear limit of a sequence of polygonal arcs, Newton says that the proposition to be proved holds because of the fourth corollary of the third lemma (Book I), according to which a curvilinear arc is adequately approximated, by means of a suitable limit-taking operation, through a sequence of polygonal arcs. Now, this corollary holds only under the assumption (explicitly made by Newton in his second lemma) that a (unique) limit, namely the curvilinear arc, actually exists. Therefore, in order to prove his generalized areal law,

Newton ought also to prove that, for *any* central force function *f*, there is an orbital arc of trajectory which is adequately approximated by taking the limit of the Newtonian sequence of polygonal arcs with an increasing number of decreasing sides. But this is just what Newton (wrongly) takes for granted and does *not* prove at all; hence he also takes for granted that any property which is intended by him, notably the validity of the areal law, is preserved by his limit-taking operations (see below, p. 240).[8] Newton soundly proves his areal law for *polygonal arcs* (no matter whether they are finite or infinitesimally small), but his proof, as it stands, does not soundly prove that what holds for finite polygonal arcs also holds for the corresponding finite *curvilinear orbital arcs*. Thus, as Whiteside rightly remarks,

> Newton's proof [...] is considerably less cogent than it may at first appear. [...] he ignores whether significant error is introduced in the total action by supposing at each stage that a continuous force instantaneously directed to the center *S* (and so varying infinitesimally in direction over the vanishingly small continuous arc in question) is adequately approximated by an equivalent impulse of force striking instantaneously at just one point; nor does he justify his assumption that the limit-polygonal arc *BCDE* ... *F* passes into a unique orbital arc *BF* as the number of bombarding force-impulses increases to infinity. Furthermore, he will in sequel at once suppose that the direction of the total "spatium superatum" (deviation from the initial rectilinear path *AB*) is also uniquely—and intuitively—given.[9]

Moreover,

> the necessary requirement for these unconsidered subtleties to be (in present context) negligible is, in fact, that the total orbital arc *BF* be itself infinitesimally small, in which case the general distance *Sp* of the orbiting body does not vary appreciably in magnitude, and therefore the

> central force, *f* say, acting over the whole arc *BF* may be considered to be constant.[10]

Here *p* stands for any position of the revolving mass point on its orbit, *f* being the magnitude of the central force. Actually, to deduce that *f* is constant from the constancy of $r = Sp$ one should also assume that the central force is conservative (as Whiteside implicitly does and we do, too, hereafter). The import of what Whiteside says is thus quite clear: the only way out for Newton's proof amounts to restricting its validity to central conservative[11] forces acting over an infinitely small orbital arc, namely to a (first-order) infinitesimal arc of orbit. In other words, Newton's generalized areal law becomes a *local* theorem and not a *global* one (i.e. valid also for any orbital arc of finite length). Yet, it should be a global one, since Kepler's second law is valid for orbital arcs of planetary size; moreover, as is easily shown, the standard way of deducing Kepler's third law from the second one is ruled out by a local theorem.

Whether Newton himself was aware of these heavy limitations is not clear—though the explicit mention, in his first lemma of Book I, of the finite intervals of time within which his limit-taking operations are assumed to be valid could be circumstantial evidence that he had in mind a global theorem. Be this as it may, if one does assume that Newton's proof is valid and that the orbital arc *BF* is rectifiable (i.e. has a *finite* length), then, by a well-known modern theorem (Scheeffer, 1884-85), an upper bound to the inscribed polygonal arcs must also exist (if the orbit is a continuous curve). But, by the very nature of Newton's proof, a proof that his limit-polygonal arc coincides with that upper bound ought also to be provided and this is just what Newton fails to do. Therefore, the assumptions that his proof is valid and that *BF* is not infinitesimal, are actually inconsistent with one another. Hence Whiteside's assessment is, of course, right: Newton's proof becomes valid if and only if the "unconsidered subtleties" he mentions are negligible. Newton's mountain has thus brought forth a (first-order infinitesimal) mouse.

Now, let us assume for the moment that the curvilinear arc *BF* does have a finite arbitrary length. This of course introduces an almost immediate inconsistency with the assumption that Newton's proof is valid. Nevertheless (owing to Whiteside's assessment), if Newton's proof is valid (i.e. in Whiteside's terms, when the unconsidered subtleties are negligible), then $Sp = r$ may be considered to be constant and the magnitude $f(r)$ of the central (conservative) force is constant, too. But the constancy of f plus the finite length of the arc *BF* yields (as we already know) a uniform motion of the mass-point on its (arbitrary finite portion of) circular orbit. This simply means that, under the (absurd) assumption that Newton's proof is a sound proof of a global theorem, i.e. that the proof holds also for any finite orbital arc (otherwise stated, that Kepler's second law is soundly deducible, via Newton's proof, from the generalized areal law), what is actually proved is that, for *any* central conservative force of magnitude $f(r)$, not only the areas swept through by the radius vector but also the orbital arcs described by the moving mass point are always proportional to the times of describing them. This is of course an absurd consequence since, say, if $f(r) = k/r^2$, then many non-circular orbits are obviously allowed (e. g. the orbit is a parabola when the square of the speed at any point is equal to $2k/r$).

What Newton's proof should properly deduce as its own conclusion is that, under the action of a central force, only the areas (and not at all the arcs) must be proportional to the times. But now we know that this is possible only if Newton's proof is restricted to the proof of a local theorem, namely only if its validity is restricted to first-order infinitesimal arcs of orbit. Of course, this is not to say that the converse holds, since the restriction of Newton's proof to the case of a first-order infinitesimal total orbital arc is necessary, but not sufficient by itself, to prove (by means of the Newtonian procedure) that the areal law holds and also that, in general, the orbital arcs are not proportional to the times during which they are covered. By itself, the *mere* restriction of Newton's proof to the case of an infinitesimal *BF* cannot account for the case in which *BC* and *EF* are infinitesimal but *CE* is finite. Yet, it is precisely in such a case that the *areas* covered in equal times are always exactly equal to one another, whereas (unless *CE* is an arc of a circle *ex hypothesi*) the corresponding *arcs* are *not* (since the "osculating" circles at *C* and *E* have different centers and different radii, and the orbital arcs are therefore neither exactly equal nor almost equal to one another). For Newton's proof to be wholly sufficient, therefore, it has to be implemented in a way that falls outside the scope of the present analysis.

In the present context, the worm in Newton's apple stands for the fact that his proof of the law of areas is not limited *explicitly* to the case of (conservative central forces acting over) first-order infinitesimal orbital arcs, as it should be, if the proof is to be unquestionably sound; and a painstaking journey towards the interior of the apple is nothing but the price to be paid in order to reach our goal, namely to assess the real import of what Hegel says about Newton's proof.

In his 1801 dissertation, *De orbitis planetarum (On the Orbits of the Planets*), Hegel writes:

> Moreover, the talent is not to be envied of the one who is willing to regard as a true demonstration the proof given by Newton of the proposition that "the areas, which orbiting bodies describe by radii drawn to an immovable center of force are proportional to the times." *For that demonstration proves that the arcs, as much as the areas, must be proportional to the times; but it had to be proved that the areas only, and not at all the arcs, must be proportional to the times* [my italics].[12]

Here, the resemblance between Hegel's key statements and the almost immediate consequence we have already drawn from Whiteside's assessment of Newton's proof is decidedly striking. Hegel's worm looks very like the real worm in Newton's apple, since what Hegel here says, far from being the outcome of a misreading of Newton's text (*pace* De Gandt, who says: "It seems that Hegel misread Newton's argument"),[13] does not significantly differ from the outcome of a sophisticated modern analysis of Newton's proof. Thus, far from being wrong, Hegel is in fact perfectly right: Hegel *ab hoc naevo vindicatus*, acquitted of this fault. Thus, in a half-serious vein, one could even say that "It seems that Hegel read Whiteside's argument in the right way."

Nevertheless (in a more serious vein) Hegel's passage still cries out for elucidation. First, he does not speak at all of the (first-order) infinitesimal orbital arcs; secondly, his training in mathematical physics, albeit good, was not a vocational one. Hence, we should at least raise the question whether his statement is flour from his own mill or not. Therefore, the main questions still to be answered concern the possible sources of his crucial statement. On this subject, Whiteside's remark is not encouraging since, according to him, Newton's proof was accepted without argument (at least by "his contemporaries and immediate successors," see above).[14] Thus, one still has (so to speak) the *onus inveniendi*, the burden of finding a source for Hegel's criticism.

Pace Whiteside, there is in fact at least one of Newton's contemporaries who saw fit to impugn the adequacy of Newton's demonstration and who is, most probably, Hegel's source: the French Jesuit Louis-Bertrand Castel.[15] In fact, the missing link between Newton's proof and Hegel's criticism is most probably to be found in the following lines of Castel's *Treatise of Physics*:

> For example, in that fundamental proposition, namely the first one of the *Sect. 2, Book 1 of Princ. Math.*, the sapient geometrician assumes that a body travels from A to B during the first moment of time; now, during the second moment, the same motion would bring the body from B to c, (Bc = AB), but the centripetal force, directed as cC, pushes the body up to C at the end of the second moment of time. Till now, all is consistent with the assumption of a uniform motion. According to Newton, during the third moment of time, the body would be travelling over the line Cd (equal to the line BC which has just been covered), but the centripetal force, directed as dD, pushes the body over

> CD, etc. I think that the uniform motion is annihilated just by assuming that Cd = BC, since, in order that this assumption may hold, *AB=BC=CD=DE, etc. should always hold, unlike the claim that the uniform motion is sometimes equal to AB, sometimes to BC, sometimes to CD; now, AB, BC, CD are equal to each other only in the case of a circle* [my italics], are always augmenting over a parabola, always diminishing over a hyperbola and sometimes augmenting, sometimes diminishing over an ellipse. Therefore, the constancy of the areas discovered by Kepler is not a thing so well demonstrated in this way as it could seem at first sight.[16]

The resemblance of the conclusion of Castel's argument with Hegel's criticism in *De orbitis* is, again, striking (whence my italics, of course). But Castel's argument is also very interesting on its own. Since the argument is quite clear (though a bit compressed), a few points about its real cogency can be quickly made. Whenever Cd and BC have a finite length, the geometrical construction, whose outcome is Cd = BC (B, C, d being on the same straight line BCd), can obviously always be performed according to Euclidean geometry. Therefore Castel's phrase "*afin qu'elle se soutint*" ("in order that it [i.e. this assumption, see above] may hold") is surely interchangeable with something like "were Cd = BC always true," i.e. true also in the limit, when Cd and BC become vanishingly small; and in his phrase "*il faudroit que toujours*" ("should always" [hold]), "*toujours*" amounts to saying "always, for any central orbit, hence also in the limit." Thus, if one assumes, as Castel does, that the straight lines ABc, BCd, CDe, etc. become, in the limit (i.e. when the sides AB, BC, CD, etc. of the polygonal approximating arcs become vanishingly small), tangent to the orbit, and if one also assumes, as Castel does, that, even in the limit, not only AB = Bc, but also BC = Cd, CD = De, etc. *exactly* hold (hence that they hold also for any *finite* orbital arc), then this simply means that the magnitude v of the (tangential) velocity of the orbiting body is constant over the orbit, hence also that the orbit is circular even when it should not be circular at all. In fact, to say that these equalities *exactly* hold also in the limit amounts to saying that even a (first order infinitesimal) variation dv of the speed v is such that dv = 0 over the whole orbit.

Now (if Newton's proof is sound), the first assumption (that the straight lines ABc, BCd, Cde, etc., become in the limit tangent to the orbit) is obviously right, whereas the second one (that uniform inertial motions over finite approximating paths yield, in the limit, a motion with the same speed over any orbital arc) is more problematic. When the sides of the polygonal arcs become very small, the very short time during which the impulsive force acts on the revolving body cannot be neglected; hence (as is easily shown to be an almost immediate consequence of Newton's second law) even the tangential motion becomes non-inertial, since the acceleration is finite, and by no means infinite, when the velocity abruptly changes. In fact, Newton's second law of motion ("force = mass x acceleration") requires that, whenever there is a non-zero tangential component of the centripetal force, a non-zero tangential (component of the centripetal) acceleration must also be present, the magnitude of which can be written (by means of the differential calculus) as dv/dt or, equivalently, d^2s/dt^2, i.e. as the (differential) quotient obtained as the ratio of a very small (actually a second-order infinitesimal) displacement of length d^2s to a very small time dt^2. Of course, if (and only if) the orbit is not a circle (i.e. the radius vector and the tangent are not perpendicular to one another), the tangential component of the centripetal force is not zero, and neither is the tangential acceleration. Thus, in more technical (and precise) terms, if f is the magnitude of the central force (acting on a unit mass, hence the magnitude d^2s/dt^2 of the acceleration of the moving body, see below), the magnitude of the tangential acceleration is $f \sin \gamma$, where γ is the (acute) angle between the radius vector and the (principal) normal to the orbit at any point, both oriented outwards. One could also say that, if dt is an infinitesimal interval of time, the (second-order) non-inertial tangential displacement has the magnitude $\partial \omega = f \sin \gamma \, dt^2$. Therefore (according also to the Newtonian orthodoxy) one can say that, in the limit, Castel's second assumption is not justified, since (as an almost immediate consequence of Newton's second law of motion) the magnitude of the differences Cd – BC, De – CD, etc. is, in the limit (i.e. at a second-order approximation), just equal to $\partial\,\omega$; hence it is equal to zero at any point of the orbit (when $f \neq 0$) if and only if $\sin\gamma = 0$, i. e. if, and only if, the orbit is circular.[17]

It should be noted that *both* Newton's proof and Castel's argument against it are clearly (albeit implicitly) based upon two different versions of the same (mistaken) assumption (let it be called M), namely that a limit-configuration must have all the *intended* properties (i.e. the properties one intends to be preserved even under the limit-taking operations) which are the limiting case of the corresponding properties of approximating configurations. In Newton's version M_n of M (notably in Newton's proof), the intended property is the areal law. In Castel's version M_c of M (notably in Castel's argument), the intended property—the constancy of the speed over the orbit—is the limiting case of the uniform motion over the rectilinear finite segments Bcd, Cde, etc., just because Newton actually assumes that the equalities Cd = BC, De = CD, etc., *exactly* hold in the approximating configuration.

Of course, the areal property does indeed hold for the approximating configuration and for the focal curvilinear sectors as well. However, this does not entail that M_n *must* be true *just because* it is a (Newtonian) version of M: as is well known, one could prove by means of (a suitable version of) M that any side of an equilateral triangle is twice itself in length.[18] As far as Castel's argument is concerned, we see that it is also based on a crucial step of Newton's proof, namely Cd = BC. Since Castel's argument (unlike Newton's proof) has an absurd conclusion, he deduces by reductio that this innocent Cd = BC must be denied. Castel thus remains unaware that what is actually culpable, and what actually needs to be denied, is M.[19] Nevertheless, thanks precisely to the joint action of M and Cd = BC, Castel does do the right thing, namely, cast heavy doubt on the soundness of

Newton's proof—even though he does so in a mistaken way (by discharging Cd = BC instead of M). In this way, Castel is also, to some extent, vindicated.

To restate Castel's argument in abridged form: "were Newton's proof sound, Cd and BC would be equal to each other also in the limit, hence [the tangential velocity would always be constant in magnitude (over a finite orbital arc), hence] AB = BC = CD = DE always [i.e. also in the limit], i.e. the orbits would be only circular. Since this is obviously false, Newton's proof of the areal law is unsound."[20] It is fair to add, and relevant to note, that most probably Castel was fully aware of the fact that, from a Newtonian point of view (and because of Newton's second law of motion [see above]), M_c—unlike M_n—does not in fact hold. Rather, according to what Castel writes (see here note 19), one might say that, in Castel's opinion, Newton *should* be committed to M_c in order to preserve the physical relevance of his own proof. On this assumption that Newton should be committed to M_c, Castel shows that Newton's proof leads to the absurd conclusion that all central orbits are circular. Now, it should be stressed that Castel's book does not include any explicit incorrect report of what Newton thinks about M_n and M_c. Nevertheless, in so far as Newton does *not* in fact assume M_c, one can say that Castel misrepresents Newton's position. However, it should be stressed that Castel does not *simply* misrepresent Newton's position: because he rightly points out (and Hegel follows him in this crucial claim) the absurd consequences of any application of the Newtonian proof to the *relevant physical* systems. After all, the planetary orbits (*unlike* the orbits that in this case—i.e. on a global scale—are the outcome of Newton's proof) are elliptical and not circular at all. As we have seen above, if the scientist is to save Newton's proof in its original form (which assumes M_n but *not* M_c) and to avoid the absurd conclusion that all central orbits must be circular, that proof must be restricted to being a merely local proof. Indeed, the scientist must recognize that Newton's proof is only sound at all *as* a local proof.

The very way in which Castel's passage has been opened up here shows that, if it is true that Newtonian studies may be helpful to Hegelian studies, the converse also holds. Furthermore, as we now shall see, the assessment of Castel's contention is also a good starting point for a better understanding of what Hegel says about Newton's proof in the second edition (1832) of his *Science of Logic*. There, apropos of what he calls the forms (*Bestimmungen*) and propositions (*Sätze*) of the analytical form (*Gestalt*) of mechanics, Hegel also says:

> But in the earlier, still naive period of the infinitesimal calculus, the aim was to assign to those forms and propositions represented in geometrical diagrams a real meaning of their own and to make that meaning plausible, and to apply the forms and propositions bearing such meaning in the proof of the main propositions concerned (see Newton's proof of his fundamental proposition of the theory of gravitation in *Princ. mathem. philosophiae naturalis*, lib. I, Sect. II, Prop. I, and *cf.* Schubert's *Astronomy*—Ist ed., vol. III. B, Section 20, where it is admitted that the position is not *exactly* as Newton assumes, i.e. at that point which is the nerve of the proof).[21]

The passage from Schubert which Hegel has in mind is this one:

> This [Areal] Law is proved by its first finder in the following way ... Nevertheless, according to a most exact judgment, it is not right to say that Bc = AB, their difference being just what above (§16) has been called $\partial \partial s - \partial \omega = \partial \omega$. But since this is a second-order infinitesimal, it can be neglected with respect to the first-order differentials AB, Bc.[22]

Again, regarding Schubert's passage, a few points can be quickly made. First of all, to say, as Schubert says here, that $\partial \partial s - \partial \omega = \partial \omega$, is wrong, since it amounts to saying that central circular orbits are *a priori* excluded. More precisely, and in more technical terms, Schubert is plainly wrong, since $\partial\,\partial\,s$ is nothing but his own notation for d^2s (i.e. the magnitude of the resultant [second-order] displacement $f\ dt^2$); hence, according to him, $\partial\,\omega = f\ dt^2/2$. Now, as we already know (see above), if $f \neq 0$, then $\partial\,\omega = 0$ at any point when the orbit is circular (a case Schubert by no means excludes), whereas $f\,dt^2/2$ is always different from zero (if $f \neq 0$).[23] Since Schubert, unlike Castel, obviously does not discriminate at all between AB = Bc and BC = Cd, one could also say that, according to him, any of these equalities fails to hold in the limit (i.e. as Schubert writes, see above, when AB, Bc are first-order differentials), owing to the second-order difference $\partial\,\omega \neq 0$ (which he wrongly evaluates). Of course, to say: "$\partial\,\omega$ is not equal to zero" is not to say: "Newton's proof is unsound just because $\partial\,\omega$ is not equal to zero" (and Schubert does not claim that Newton's proof is unsound). Think of, say, the property of being the meeting point of two rectilinear portions BC, CD of the path described by the moving mass-point under the action of a force-impulse. According to a Newtonian scientist, the fact that this property holds for the orbital point C when BC, CD have a finite length, whereas it fails to hold in the limit (i.e. on a curvilinear orbit), is just as irrelevant for the soundness of Newton's proof as is the fact that the equality Cd = BC is *exactly* true when Cd, BC have a finite length, whereas it is only *approximately* true in the limit (since both facts are unintended properties for a Newtonian scientist, see above). On the contrary, to say that a non-zero $\partial\,\omega$ (at any point of a non-circular orbit) entails the unsoundness of Newton's proof of the areal theorem, could only be the outcome of an anti-Newtonian point of view (actually, it is an almost immediate consequence of what Castel says). As a matter of fact, no criticism of Newtonian dynamics is anywhere to be found in Schubert's book. As to the passage cited here,[24] Schubert simply says that "nevertheless [or "but actually" (*freylich*)], according to a most exact judgment (*im strengsten Verstande*), it is not right [to say] that AB = Bc," since, as he also says, the (limit second-order) difference is $\partial\,\omega$. But, *pace* Hegel,[25] Schubert nowhere says that, immediately after his "*freylich*" (and in order to elucidate it), something like "contrary to what happens under the assumption that Newton's proof is sound" could be added (before "*es nicht im strengsten Verstande*"). Schubert says only that (in comparison with AB, Bc), $\partial \omega$ can be neglected whatever the case. Moreover, in spite of what Hegel says ("the position is not *exactly* as Newton assumes," see above), Newton did not think at all that $\partial \omega = 0$, since he perfectly well knew both that it is not equal to zero and that it can be neglected (up to a first-order approximation).[26] Actually, the correct elucidation of Schubert's "*freylich*" most probably is something like: "nevertheless, contrary to what actually happens under the assumption that AB, Bc have a finite length, it is not strictly correct to say that Bc = AB holds (no matter whether in the limit or not), since their second-order difference (*Unterschied*) is (on the contrary) $\partial \omega$." (It is fair to add that Schubert's statement, at least as it stands, may well be just a bit misleading, since in the Newtonian Figure Bc and AB are segments of finite length).

Thus, it can hardly be denied that Hegel's interpretation reads too much into Schubert's text. Since Hegel was usually an accurate, penetrating and bona fide reader, his misunderstanding of Schubert's passage needs to be explained. Now, if someone knows (and agrees on) the key point of Castel's passage (and correctly infers that, unlike Castel, Schubert thinks that Bc = AB and Cd = BC are freely interchangeable so far as their limit-values are concerned), then her/his (mis)reading *à la* Castel of Schubert's passage could be more easily explained. In fact, all becomes more clear if one remembers what Castel says about Newton's proof, notably that, were the proof sound, the speed of an orbiting body would always be constant over the orbit, hence also the difference between Cd and BC (whence equivalently, according to Schubert, also between Bc and AB) would always be zero, even in the limit. Now suppose one (mistakenly) assumes both that Castel is right and that Schubert rightly agrees with him on the main point: it is quite clear, under these assumptions and by a single step of Modus Tollendo Tollens, that Hegel's misreading of Schubert's passage becomes a fully authorized interpretation. In fact, under the tacit assumption that Schubert implicitly admits, as Castel explicitly does, something equivalent to the truth of the conditional (let be it called "Castel's major premiss"): "if Newton's proof is sound, then the difference between, say, Bc and AB (or Cd and BC, etc.) is zero also in the limit," one can also immediately deduce what Hegel says, namely that Schubert admits that Newton's proof is not sound, since Schubert actually says (as the minor premiss of a Modus Tollens, whose implicit major is of course Castel's major premiss) that, in the limit, that very difference is not equal to zero. Hegel thus misconstrued Schubert as a critic of Newton, not only because he did not realize that Newton would have acknowledged and discounted the point that Schubert makes (namely, that $\partial \omega$ is not *exactly* equal to zero), but also, importantly, because he shares Castel's view that M_C holds and that Newton should be committed to it (see above). Thus, Hegel's explicit reference to Schubert's *Astronomy* in the second edition of the *Science of Logic* may well provide further circumstantial evidence of an implicit reference in the *De orbitis* to Castel's *Traité*. Perhaps, in Hegel's phrase "*es ... sich nicht so verhalte, wie Newton annimmt*" (i.e. "the matter ... is not such as Newton assumes") there is still a flavor of Castel's phrase "*n'est pas une chose aussi demontrée par-là qu'on pourroit bien le croire*" (i.e. "is not a thing so well demonstrated in this way as it might seem at first sight," see above). In fact, Hegel's interpretation of Schubert's statement becomes now more clear. According to Hegel, Newton, in his proof—owing to his (mistaken) general notion of the infinitesimally small, and just because of what "is admitted" (*zugestanden wird*) in Schubert's statement, namely that $\partial \omega \neq 0$—fails to actually assign a real meaning (*Sinn*), which "had to be assigned" (*sollte ... angegeben ... Werden)* by means of a geometrical diagram, notably the construction of Cd = BC, etc., to the form (*Bestimmung*) of constant speed. But, again, what Hegel means here (notably via the phrase "*zugestanden wird*") most probably presupposes his acquaintance with Castel's argument against Newton's demonstration.

Hegel's claim against Newton's proof of the areal theorem takes up a bit more than eight lines of printed text in the original edition of the dissertation, *De orbitis planetarum*. Nonetheless, not only does a proper understanding of what Hegel means result in recognizing the correctness of his evaluation of a cornerstone of Newton's *Principia* (where, as Whiteside remarks, "the theorem is rightly given pride of place as Proposition I of Book I"),[27] but an elucidation of the real import of Hegel's criticism is also the starting point for a real understanding of Hegel's (alleged) blunder in his dissertation concerning the ascription of a tangential direction to the centrifugal force. One could show that, contrary to the received view, Hegel's alleged blunder (apart from one minor mistake) is actually not a blunder at all, since it is nothing but a sophisticated and penetrating analysis of some real shortcomings of Newton's model. Hegel's *Dissertatio*, is thus also, from the standpoint of the history of celestial mechanics, more relevant than it is commonly reputed to be. But this is a different story.[28]

Notes

1. See also *Isaac Newton's Philosophiae Naturalis Principia Mathematica*, edited by A. Koyré and I.B. Cohen (Cambridge: Cambridge University Press, 1972), p. 89 for a slightly different (but equally poor) version of the Figure.

2. SBC is equivalent to SCD, for example, because they are both equivalent to the same triangle SCd (SBC and SCd are equivalent, since BC = Cd by construction and the distance of S from the straight line BCd is also the height of both triangles above their bases BC, Cd; SCd and SCD are equivalent, since they have the same basis SC, the distances of d and D from SC being also equal because Dd is parallel to SC).

3. Incidentally, it is worth noting that this part of Newton's proof is not seriously affected by the fact that the centripetal displacements (such as dD) are produced by a genuine force, whereas the inertial ones (such as Cd) are the effect of a force-free motion (of a *vis insita* in Newton's terms), since, after all, the *vis insita* (or *vis inertiae*) is an old counterpart of momentum and, according to Newton's scheme, the centripetal force is here represented by force-impulses, hence also measured by sudden

changes in momentum. The centripetal component displacements (such as BV, etc.), which would be actual paths, were the moving body in a state of rest when about to be struck, are almost inertial, since the force-impulses are almost instantaneous, so that the velocities, albeit changing abruptly (in direction and possibly in magnitude) at B, C, D, etc., do not change in magnitude over almost all the points of any single centripetal displacement.

4. See *The Mathematical Papers of Isaac Newton*, edited by D.T. Whiteside, 8 Vols (Cambridge: Cambridge University Press, 1967-81), Vol. 6 (1684-1691) [published 1974], footnote 19, pp. 35-7; the passage quoted is to be found on p. 37.

5. See G.W.F. Hegel, *Les orbites des planètes*, traduction et notes par François De Gandt (Paris: Vrin, 1979), p. 134 (my translation of this passage and of all subsequent passages from De Gandt). De Gandt's abbreviated reference is actually to the Lasson edition of the *Science of Logic*, notably to the passage here discussed at length below (see pp. 242-6), where reference is made instead to the following edition and pages: G.W.F. Hegel, *Wissenschaft der Logik. Erster Teil: Die Objektive Logik, Erster Band: Die Lehre vom Sein (1832)*, edited by F. Hogemann and W. Jaeschke, *Gesammelte Werke*, Vol. 21 (Hamburg: Felix Meiner, 1985), pp. 271-2. (Hereafter cited as *Logik* [*GW*, **21**].)

6. *Logik* (*GW*, **21**), p. 272; translation by A.V. Miller, see *Hegel's Science of Logic* (Atlantic Highlands, NJ: Humanities Press International, 1989), p. 273.

7. See *Newton's Principia*, edited by Koyré & Cohen, p. 90.

8. As an aside, it is relevant to note that a case in which Newton's approximating procedure is hopelessly inadequate is when (even under the action of a central conservative force) the limit-polygonal arc almost coincides with an entire (portion of a) plane (think of, say, a path almost coincident with Peano's well-known curve). Unfortunately, and ironically enough, this is just what happens in the case of the planetary orbits, according to Einstein's theory of general relativity.

9. See Whiteside, *The Mathematical Papers of Isaac Newton*, **6**: 35-6.

10. See Whiteside, *The Mathematical Papers of Isaac Newton*, **6**: 37. See also D.T. Whiteside, *The Mathematical Principles Underlying Newton's "Principia Mathematica"* (Glasgow: University of Glasgow Press, 1970), pp. 12-13.

11. As is well known (and noted by H. Hertz exactly hundred years ago, in 1894), "conservative systems are exceptions, and even exceptions attained only more or less approximately; so that for any natural system taken at random the probability of its being conservative is infinitely small" (see H. Hertz, *The Principles of Mechanics* [New York: Dover, 1956], p. 251). Nonetheless, even in advanced textbooks, "central force" is sometimes defined as short for "central *conservative* force." But, of course, in this way, the vertical fall of a parachutist (an obviously central rectilinear motion, where the areal velocity is always equal to zero) would be the effect of a non-central total force, since the force in this case depends on the square of the speed; hence, it is not conservative.

12. See G.W.F. Hegel, *Dissertatio philosophica de orbitis planetarum* (Jena: Prager, 1801), p. 7, lines 13-22: "Qui autem illam, quam Newton propositionis: areas, quas corpora in gyros acta radiis ad immobile centrum virium ductis describunt, temporibus esse proportionales, demonstrationem dedit, pro vera demonstratione habere velit, ejus facilitati non invidendum est; *ea enim demonstratio arcus aeque ac areas temporibus esse proportionales efficit; verum neutiquam arcus sed areas tantum temporibus esse proportionales efficiendum erat* [my italics]." The English translation is here an emended version of Adler's translation in "Hegel, *Philosophical Dissertation on the Orbits of the Planets* (1801). Preceded by the 12 Theses Defended on August 27, 1801," edited and translated by P. Adler, *Graduate Faculty Philosophy Journal* 12, 1-2 (1987): 269-309, see p. 283. Besides De Gandt, *Les orbites des planètes*, other easily available editions/translations are: G.W.F. Hegel, *Le orbite dei pianeti*, edited and translated by A. Negri (Bari: Laterza, 1984) and G.W.F. Hegel, *Dissertatio philosophica de orbitis planetarum / Philosophische Erörterung über die Planetenbahnen*, translation, with introduction and commentary by W. Neuser (Weinheim: Acta Humaniora d. VCH, 1986).

13. See De Gandt, *Les orbites des planètes*, p. 134.

14. That is why (I think), in the only case in which (so far as I know) Hegel's *De orbitis* and Whiteside's *The Mathematical Papers of Isaac Newton*, Vol. 6 are both mentioned and properly collated, a devious (albeit possibly ingenious) interpretation of Hegel's criticism is also proposed: see M. Nasti De Vincentis, "Newton contra Keplerum apud Hegel: contradiction ou

incommensurabilité?" in *Atti del Congresso "Nuovi problemi della logica e della filosofia della scienza,"* edited by D. Costantini and M.C. Galavotti (Bologna: CLUEB, 1991), **1**: 261-8, esp. pp. 265-8. According to that interpretation, what really matters for Hegel (mainly because of his pitting Kepler against Newton in *De Orbitis*) is the explanation of the fact that the planetary orbits are actually (non-circular) ellipses. Thus, in my former opinion, Hegel's claim is that a new theorem should be substituted for Newton's areal one by adding suitable assumptions (e.g. regarding the initial velocity of the orbiting body) to the original ones in order to get a stronger conclusion: namely, that the law of areas holds, the (planetary) orbits being only non-circular ellipses. I will now show, by means of an elementary example, why I think that my former, and superseded, interpretation of Hegel's passage, despite its possible ingenuity, is, all in all, untenable. Let $c^2 = a^2 + b^2$ be the well-known (conclusion of) Pythagoras's theorem, from which one gets a new theorem (for isosceles right triangles), namely $c^2 = 2l^2$, by adding the further assumption $a = b = l$. Professor X, a philogynous bachelor, prefers the new theorem just because it is called "Bride's Theorem" in ancient Byzantine texts. But he would never say (as Hegel does in the case of Newton's original proof) that Euclid's proof of Pythagoras's theorem is not a "vera demonstratio," since this phrase, in any New Latin text, simply means "sound proof." It is only fair to add that Hegel's dissertation is actually concerned with the problem of deducing the necessity of non-circular elliptic planetary orbits (hence also of getting rid of any fictitious system with circular orbits; see just the few lines that immediately precede Hegel's criticism of Newton's proof of the areal theorem, and what I say on the subject in "Newton contra Keplerum," pp. 263-5; that is why, *inter alia*, my English rendering of Hegel's "autem" in Hegel's *De orbitis*, p. 7, line 13, is "moreover," see above, p. 236). M.J. Petry ("The Significance of Kepler's Laws," in *Hegel and Newtonianism*, edited by M.J. Petry [Dordrecht: Kluwer, 1993], pp. 439-513) cites—and quotes—both Hegel's criticism (in Hegel, *De orbitis*, p. 7; Neuser, *Dissertatio*, p. 88) and (as an indirect quotation of only its first part) Whiteside's assessment of Newton's proof (see Whiteside, *The Mathematical Papers of Isaac Newton*, **6**: notably pp. 35-6), but, surprisingly enough, without any mention of the fact that the former amounts to an almost immediate corollary of the latter (hence Petry in "The Significance of Kepler's Laws," has apparently also missed [p. 268, endnote 2 of] my "Newton contra

Keplerum"). Moreover, according to Petry, "The Significance of Kepler's Laws," p. 439 (but see also p. 497), "practically every point he [i.e. Hegel] makes in both the *Dissertation* and the *Encyclopedia*, is in complete accordance with Newton's own interpretation of Kepler's laws as expounded in the *Principia*." Of course, in the same vein one could also say that Russell is in complete accordance with Frege's *Grundgesetze* (since Russell's paradox is nothing but the exception that proves the rule). A more fruitful approach (as regards the concept of force) can be found in K.-N. Ihmig, "Hegel's Rejection of the Concept of Force," in *Hegel and Newtonianism*, edited by M.J. Petry, pp. 399-414, and especially (as regards the more general problems raised by Hegel's Physics) in B. Falkenburg, in "Hegel on Mechanistic Models of Light," in *Hegel and Newtonianism*, edited by M.J. Petry, pp. 531-46.

15. As to the way in which this source was disclosed, the story is more or less as follows. Dr. Cinzia Ferrini told me that she had found in the text of *De orbitis* several plain (albeit not explicitly acknowledged) references to J.-E. Montucla's work, *Histoire des mathématiques*, where (ever since its first publication in 1758, and precisely in a footnote to one of the passages Hegel tacitly made reference to) another book is mentioned, namely the second volume of L.-B. Castel's *Traité de physique sur la pesanteur universelle des corps* (published in Paris, 1724, see below). Castel was an anti-Newtonian scientist, and the passage of his book which is mentioned and discussed by Montucla is about an argument against the interplay of centripetal and centrifugal forces in the case of a non-circular elliptical orbit, which one can easily find, in an almost identical form, in Hegel's dissertation (and from the *Phenomenology* up to the *Encyclopedia* as well). Thus, pointing out Montucla's reference to Castel, I suggested to Dr. Ferrini that she examine carefully Castel's *Traité*, looking for an ancestor of Hegel's worm. She actually found there a key passage—extensive excerpta from Castel's book can be found in C. Ferrini, "On Newton's Demonstration of Kepler's Second Law in Hegel's *De orbitis planetarum* (1801)," *Philosophia Naturalis* 31, 1 (1994): 150-70, see p. 160 for the key passage—together with some circumstantial evidence that Hegel could have read the *Traité* in Geneva, about six years before the publication of his *De orbitis* (cf. C. Ferrini, "On Newton's Demonstration," pp. 157-8). I wish to acknowledge here my debt of gratitude to Dr. Ferrini, who also

made readily available to me Castel's and Schubert's rare texts, see below.

16. See L.-B. Castel, *Traité de physique sur la pesanteur universelle des corps*, Vol. 2 (Paris: Cailleau, 1724), pp. 533-4: "Par exemple, dans cette Proposition fondamentale, qui est la première de la *Sect. 2 du Liv. 1 des Princ. Math.* le sçavant Géomètre suppose un Corps porté de A en B, au premier instant; or dans le second instant le même mouvement le porteroit de B, en c, (Bc = AB) mais la force centripète c [sic; possibly a misprint for "cC," see below], fait qu'il arrive en C, à la fin de ce second instant; jusques-là il n'y a rien que de conforme à la supposition du mouvement uniforme. Dans le troisième instant le Corps, dit M. Newton, parcoureroit la ligne Cd = BC, qui vient d'être parcouruë; mais la force centripète dD [sic; here, "directed as dD," or something similar, should be substituted for "dD"; this kind of slight inaccuracy was widespread at the time] lui fait parcourir CD, etc. C'est dans cette nouvelle supposition de Cd = BC, que je trouve le mouvement uniforme anéanti. Car afin qu'elle se soutint, *il faudroit que toujours AB=BC=CD=DE, etc., et non pas que le mouvement uniforme fût égal tantôt à AB, tantôt à BC, tantôt à CD, lesquelles AB, BC, CD, ne sont égales que dans le Cercle* [my italics], vont toujours en augmentant ou en diminuant dans la Parabole, et l'Hyperbolc, et tantôt en augmentant, tantôt en diminuant dans l'Ellipse. De sorte que l'uniformité des Aires découverte par Kepler n'est pas une chose aussi démontrée par-là qu'on pourroit bien le croire." The English translation of the French passages here quoted is mine. In this one, I have only eliminated the most obvious misprints and five occurrences of the ampersand (as a paleotype for "et"). Castel's Figure is actually an extremely poor version of Newton's one (even the vertex E and the side DE are lacking, and this could explain one of the misprints, namely the occurrence of "De" instead of "DE" in the part of Castel's text I have italicised). Anyway, an improved version of Castel's original Figure has been redrawn (see Ferrini, "On Newton's Demonstration," p. 170, where the right-hand occurrence of [upper case] 'C' should actually be a lower case one).

17. Nevertheless, in the case of infinitesimally small orbital arcs, Castel is certainly right since, as we already know, these arcs are almost coincident with circular arcs. On the other hand, when the orbital arcs have a finite length (including the case of an entire ellipse, hyperbola or parabola mentioned by Castel), let n be an integer however great (let n = 1, 2, ...) for which the P_n-th

approximating polygonal arc is such that at least one of the differences Cd – BC, De – CD, etc. is different from zero. Of course, in this case, it would be impossible to prove the generalized areal law by means of Newton's geometrical construction (since every step of a sound proof must be sound and the step where the equivalence of all focal triangles is deduced becomes unsound). Therefore, if Newton's proof is sound (for finite arcs of orbit), then BC = Cd, CD = De, etc. even when the straight lines BCd, CDe, etc. almost coincide with the tangents to the orbit. This long "if ... then" assumption is certainly true (since, as we know, its antecedent and its consequent are both absurd) and should, of course, be substituted for Castel's original ones, in order to be able to deduce that the (tangential) velocity is almost constant in magnitude and that (for any orbit, under the sole assumption that the force is central and conservative) the orbits do not significantly differ from circular orbits (an equally absurd and slightly different version of Castel's original statement, both being only a crucial step to finally deduce the unsoundness of Newton's proof). The real problem is that the only case in which (by means of Newton's geometrical construction and approximating procedure as well) a limit-polygonal arc (of finite length, namely: lim P_n, when n tends to infinity) provably coincides with a (unique) curvilinear orbital arc, is the case in which it is also assumed *ab initio* that this latter is a (finite) arc of circle, i. e. when *f* is assumed to be constant over a finite orbital arc. Thus (according to the ancient 'method of exhaustion'), the sides of P_1 become the sides of a square inscribed in the circle (or rather of a regular octagon, if one does not like the initial centripetal displacement to be twice the radius vector in length), the sides of P_2 become the sides of a regular polygon of 16 sides, etc. But of course in this way Newton's proof is by no means the original one, just because an extra assumption has been added. Moreover, for *any* central motion, one must assume that the approximating force-impulses always yield in the limit a finite and continuous force function whose first derivatives are also finite and continuous.

It is relevant to note that, in his lecture dated March 13, 1964, which until recently was lost, the leading theoretical physicist R.P. Feynman restated in a crystal-clear, and to a large extent novel, way all of Newton's original proofs of Kepler's laws. As regards the Newtonian proof of the areal law, Feynman's restatement clearly points out where flaws are to be located, even though any detailed assessment of the proof *à la* Whiteside lies outside the scope of Feynman's lecture. Thus, although they are not mentioned, Hegel and Castel are to some extent vindicated by Feynman's restatement as well. (See D. L. Goodstein and J. R. Goodstein, *Feynman's Lost Lecture: The Motion of Planets Around the Sun* [New York and London: W.W. Norton and Company, 1996], esp. p. 156, but also pp. 85-8. Thanks are due to Prof. G. Trautteur for pointing out, and to Prof. A. De Laurentiis for sending me, this book.)

18. By means of this argument, one can (soundly) prove that, a) the limit-configuration coincides with a side of the equilateral triangle and, b) any approximating configuration is twice that side in length. Therefore, by means of b) and M, one can also (unsoundly) prove that the limit-configuration is twice that side in length and whence, by a), that any side of an equilateral triangle is twice itself in length. In Newton's original proof of the areal theorem, there is of course a sound proof of a step b') corresponding to b), but there is no proof at all of any step a') corresponding to a). In order to deduce Kepler's second law as a special case of Newton's areal theorem, a proof of a') should amount to proving that, under the action of any central force, Newton's limit-configuration coincides with the (plane) orbital arc *BF* (see above, p. 233) of finite length (having a tangent at any point). Thus, a more or less implicitly alleged a'), plus M, plus b'), yields the (true) conclusion of a plausible restatement of Newton's proof (as a plainly unsound proof of a global theorem). In Castel's argument, the proof of the step a")—corresponding to a') and a)—amounts to (soundly) proving that, were the arc *BF* the limit-configuration in a'), Castel's limit-configuration would be the tangent *t* at any point of the arc *BF*. Thus, a"), plus M, plus an obvious b") yields the constancy in magnitude of the velocity for any *t* (see below, note 19, as to Castel's b")). According to Castel (see Castel, *Traité*, Vol. 2, pp. 536-7, with an implicit reference also to Vol. 1, pp. 363-81), in any standard version of Descartes' theory of vortices only circular orbits are permitted in equilibrium conditions. (See also D.S. Schier, *Louis-Bertrand Castel, Anti-Newtonian Scientist* [Cedar Rapids, Iowa: The Torch Press, 1941], where only Vol. 1 of Castel's *Traité* is actually discussed. Schier has apparently missed also P. Brunet, *L'introduction des théories de Newton en France au XVIIIe siècle – Avant 1738* [Geneva: Slatkine Reprints, 1970], originally published in Paris, 1931, where one could also find the ancestors of Schubert's mistaken

proof, see below, endnote 23. Heartfelt thanks are due to Prof. A. De Laurentiis who made available to me a copy of Schier's book.)

19. His way of arguing against Cd = BC ("I think that the uniform motion is annihilated," see above, and also in Castel, *Traité*, Vol. 2, p. 536: "Mais voilà une belle uniformité qui ne dure qu'un instant infiniment petit, et qui se change à tous moments en une difformité ou variation continuelle"; "but here is a beautiful uniformity, during no more than an infinitesimally small moment of time and becoming at any moment a difference, notably a continuous variation") strongly recalls the way in which another Jesuit, Gerolamo Saccheri, argued against the new theorems of the hyperbolic non-Euclidean geometry he himself discovered by saying that "they are repugnant to the nature of the straight line." Thus, Castel could likewise say that Cd = BC is repugnant to the nature of uniform motion (unless AB = BC = CD = DE, etc. also holds). It is worth noting that a seemingly cogent justification of what Castel could say can actually be provided by means of a simple argument, all of whose steps are sound except one. To assume that Cd = BC, De = CD, etc. hold *and* that AB = BC = CD = DE, etc. does not hold (just as in the Newtonian figure, to say nothing of the fact that Ac is there not perpendicular to BS) amounts to saying that the speeds over BC and CD are different from one another if, say, BC = CD does not hold, but C belongs to both BC and CD, whence the speed at C is not uniquely defined. Thus, owing to a variant of M_C (the only unsound step of the whole argument), the speed at point C of the *limit* curvilinear orbit (which obviously is the *same* point C of any approximating configuration) is also not uniquely defined, i. e. the orbiting mass-point simultaneously has two different speeds at C. But this is absurd for obvious physical reasons; moreover, under, say, a gravitational force, the speed at C depends only on the length of the radius vector CS, which is of course uniquely determined. Therefore, if the variant of M_C is (wrongly) maintained, one must conclude (by reductio), as Castel actually does, that AB = BC = CD = DE, etc. is *entailed* by Cd = BC, etc., namely by the obvious (Castel's) b"), see above note 18.

20. The square-bracketed steps are not explicitly stated in Castel's text, their insertion being authorized by the scope of the phrases "*afin qu'elle se soutint*," "*il faudroit que toujours*" (see above, p. 238).

21. More literally, although in bad English: "it is admitted that the thing [is] not *just so*, i.e. at that point which is the nerve of the proof is not so as Newton assumes." See (the whole passage in) *Logik* (*GW*, **21**), pp. 271-2; Miller translation, pp. 272-3 (including footnote). In the footnote in Miller's translation, "vol. III. B, Section 20" (see above) obviously mistranslates Hegel's German text—which reads "III. B. [short for 'Band'] §. 20," i.e. "Vol. III, §20"—since the 'B' should be excised. Indeed, "Vol. III, §20" should actually be "Part III, § 20," since Schubert uses "Theil" and not "Band" (although in this case they actually coincide). Moreover, still in Miller's footnote, the first German title is wrong, and the second one, namely *Populäre Astronomie*, is not directly relevant, since the passage Hegel has in mind has been excised from this later version of Schubert's Treatise.

22. My translation. See F.T. Schubert, *Theoretische Astronomie*, Vol. 3 (Physische Astronomie) (St. Petersburg: Kayserliche Akademie der Wissenschaften, 1798), p. 25; see also *Logik* (*GW*, **21**), p. 435 (Anmerkung 272, 6), where 'δ' is uniformly substituted for Schubert's '∂': "Von dem ersten Erfinder ward dieses Gesetz auf folgende Art bewiesen ... [here follows (after a misprinted reference, in a footnote, to the relevant passage from the *Principia*) Newton's proof of the law of areas in an abridged form]. Freylich ist es nicht im strengsten Verstande richtig, daß Bc = AB ist, und der Unterschied [here, one of Schubert's technical terms or phrases (another being "zweyte Differenz") for a second-order difference; for a first-order one, he sometimes uses "Differenz" tout court or "erste Differenz," see e.g. Schubert, *Theoretische Astronomie*, p. 21] ist eben das, was oben (§. 16.) $\partial \partial s - \partial \omega = \partial \omega$ hies. Da dis aber ein unendlich Kleines der zweyten Ordnung ist, so verschwindet es gegen die Differenziale der ersten Ordnung AB, Bc."

23. Schubert also (wrongly) proves that $\partial \omega = f\,dt^2/2$ (see Schubert, *Theoretische Astronomie*, pp. 21-2). It would be interesting (although outside the scope of the present paper) to show how and why Schubert's proof is wrong, since Hegel himself read this proof. Hegel's at first sight rather sibylline statement—"in einer gleichförmig beschleunigten Bewegung ... immer hinzukomme" (see *Logik* [*GW*, **21**], p. 271, lines 21-4; Miller translation, p. 272, "in a uniformly accelerated motion ... constantly accrues [an increment from the force of gravity]")—is nothing but an implicit, albeit clear, reference to Schubert's proof. Actually, $f\,dt^2/2$ is the length of the deviation arc from the initial rectilinear path AB

when the orbital arc has a first-order infinitesimal length (see Whiteside, *The Mathematical Papers of Isaac Newton*, **6**: 37 for a sound proof). Nevertheless, Schubert's wrong equality can be easily corrected by substituting $f \sin \gamma \, dt^2$ for $f \, dt^2/2$ in its right member. Hence, as could be easily proved, Schubert's mistaken value is actually the (never reached) upper bound for half the maximum value of $\partial \omega$ over an elliptical orbit of ever increasing eccentricity, the length of the semimajor axis being $a = 1$.

24. And in *Logik* (*GW*, **21**), see above; see also Ferrini, "On Newton's Demonstration," p. 151.

25. And *pace* Ihmig, "Hegel's Rejection," p. 403. Moreover, Hegel's and Ihmig's misreadings most probably may not be explained in the same way, since, unlike Hegel, Ihmig was most probably unaware of Castel's argument against the Newtonian proof (notably of 'Castel's major premiss', see below).

26. As to the case of a non-circular ellipse, see e.g. *Newton's Principia*, edited by Koyré & Cohen, Book I, Prop. XI, notably p. 119, lines 15-20.

27. See Whiteside, *The Mathematical Papers of Isaac Newton*, **6**: 37.

28. To tell the story, a nearly word-by-word commentary on Hegel's *Dissertatio* was actually needed (see C. Ferrini, *Guida al "De orbitis planetarum" di Hegel ed alle sue edizioni e traduzioni*, in coll. con M. Nasti De Vincentis [Bern: Haupt, 1995]), in which a thorough vindication of Hegel's arguments against the Newtonian model can also be found as an Appendix (see M. Nasti De Vincentis, "Gli argomenti hegeliani contro il modello newtoniano," in C. Ferrini, *Guida al "De orbitis planetarum,"* pp. 203-40). As regards this model, one should also point out the unsound proof in which Newton rightly evaluates (in magnitude) the centrifugal force as far as the simple case of uniform circular motion is concerned (see *Newton's Principia*, edited by Koyré & Cohen. p. 101 [ll. 19-32]). Suffice it to say here that in his deduction, owing to the subtle interplay of *two* wrong steps, Newton is able to get to the right conclusion. Thus, one may say that, even in this case, the errors of a genius surely are peculiar errors.

11

The Ontological Foundations of Hegel's Dissertation of 1801

Olivier Depré

On 27 August 1801, in the presence of Schelling and his brother, Niethammer and a student from Bamberg, Hegel marked his thirty-first birthday by defending the twelve theses of his *Habilitation*, which was to qualify him to teach philosophy as a *Privatdozent* at the University of Jena. The oral defence of these theses, however, constituted only a part of the full requirements for the *Habilitation*. In addition, Hegel was required to give a public lecture and to publish an original dissertation, which he submitted on 18 October.[1] Thus, between 27 August and 18 October, Hegel revised and prepared for publication a Latin dissertation devoted to the physical problem concerning the calculation of the distances of the planets from the sun,[2] a topic of research, which, K. Rosenkranz has pointed out, "must have already been with him for some time."[3]

The question which I shall address in my paper concerns the place that Hegel's dissertation occupies in the corpus of his work. I shall endeavour to establish the following points:

(1) Firstly, that this text should not be viewed as a purely formal or academic exercise, but rather as a philosophical work in its own right—a document which reflects Hegel's philosophical convictions at that time.

(2) Secondly, the philosophical content of this dissertation must, on the one hand, be seen against the background of the development of Hegel's ideas in the period immediately preceding its writing, namely, the Frankfurt period, and, on the other hand, as prefiguring his First Jena Logic, the *Introductio in Philosophiam* of 1801-2. I would suggest, therefore, that we consider Hegel's dissertation as a text which marks a transition point in his thought between the founding of an ontology at Frankfurt and the first outlines of a systematic philosophy at Jena, and that Hegel's Jena

period should thus be understood to begin not with his *Differenzschrift*, which was completed in July 1801, but rather with his dissertation. There are two lines of thought which have led me to think thus.

(1) To begin with, we must ask ourselves how is it conceivable that, in the space of only seven months (from January to July 1801), Hegel was able to produce a dissertation which was not only first written in German and then reformulated in an abridged Latin version,[4] but which dealt with highly technical questions of physics—questions which were apparently new to Hegel in relation to his former texts. It is necessary, I think, to suppose that when Hegel left Frankfurt he already had with him a finished outline of this scholarly project—especially since completion of the dissertation was to be a condition of his taking up a teaching position at Jena.

(2) Furthermore, as is well-known, Hegel had a particular interest in the natural sciences of his day and in the nature of their progress. During his student days he produced a number of essays concerning mathematics and geometry, and, according to his sister Christiane, physics was at that time one of his passions. Later on Hegel would accumulate detailed reading notes on mechanics, Kantian astronomy, Newton and Kepler.[5] We are therefore justified in considering the *Geometrical Studies* of 1800[6] as the only *extant* testimony—among many texts that are now lost—to an extensive interest in mathematics and science on Hegel's part in the period immediately prior to his arrival at Jena.

T. Haering has already emphasised that "one cannot understand this writing without locating it in the context of previous works."[7] In order to show that Hegel's dissertation, *On the Orbits of the Planets*, fits perfectly into the context of the ontology which was slowly developed at Frankfurt, I should like to suggest, then, that at the heart of Hegel's critique of Newton formulated in this text, there is to be found his conception of nature as a living whole, together with the re-evaluation of a *qualitative* physics which this notion implies. If we take the conception of being and the problem of its knowability—the two fundamental problematics around which Hegel's philosophical preoccupation centred after his re-encounter with Hölderlin in Frankfurt—as the guiding threads of our interpretation of Hegel's texts, we discover that there exists, in fact, a stronger continuity between the thought of the Frankfurt period and that of the Jena period than one might have at first imagined. The dissertation provides us with an excellent illustration of the continuity between these two periods in Hegel's intellectual development.

As we know, Hegel's treatment of the problem concerning the distance between the planets in the final pages of his dissertation has not helped his reputation. Nevertheless, contrary to commentators such as F. De Gandt who have denounced Hegel's "ridiculous pretensions,"[8] I do not believe that it was ever Hegel's intention to put himself forward as a scientist, but rather to show philosophically that the ontological presuppositions of a strictly *quantitative* mechanistic science were unable to account for the order of the universe without recourse to the laws of reason. We must now turn to a closer analysis of this speculative project.

1. Hegel and the Law of Titius-Bode

1.1. The Law of the Planetary Distances. Brief Summary

As is well known, the problem of the law governing the distance of the planets from the sun goes back as far as Plato's *Timaeus*.[9] In 1766, J.D. Titius (1729-1796) had already proposed a rule of arithmetical progression corresponding to the distances of the planets, and in 1772 this rule was taken up by the German astronomer J.E. Bode (1747-1826)—hence the name of this law: the "Law of Titius-Bode." According to this law, the arithmetical sequence of these distances is established in the following way:

> One takes the sequence 0-3-6-12-24-48-96-192, one adds 4 to each term and divides by 10—this operation allows one easily to determine the distance of each planet to the sun,

> the units thus obtained being calculated in A.U. (astronomical units; 1 A.U. = 10^8 km).[10]

In more mathematical terms, if one posits the distance of Mercury (the closest planet to the sun) as a, where a = 4 and b = 3, then the distance of Venus = a+b, Earth = a+2b, Mars = a+4b, Jupiter = a+16b, Saturn = a+32b; each of these terms needs to be divided by ten to obtain the A.U. One observes, however, that the fifth element of the first series, 24, or a+8b in the second series, does not correspond to any planet, which should theoretically be situated between Mars (12 or a+4b) and Jupiter (48 or a+16b). This missing planet quickly led to the founding of an international association formed by 24 astronomers—a coincidence ... ?—who, following the Gotha congress of 1796, set themselves the task of tracing the recalcitrant star. Their research was given added encouragement by the fact that the recent discovery of Uranus by W. Herschel in 1781 seemed to confirm the hypothetical law: for this new planet was found precisely at the eighth place in the series, with a distance in relation to the sun corresponding to the number 192!

1.2. Hegel's Reaction to the Law of Titius-Bode

Aware of the inadequacies of this astronomical law, Hegel, for his part, believed that the problem had to be approached from an entirely different angle. It is customary to understand Hegel to hold that nature is governed by the laws of reason, and it is significant that, in the present case, he suspected the mathematical rule of being inexact, precisely because he regarded this rule as being simply *quantitative* and *non-rational* in nature. Consequently, Hegel sought to discover another mathematical sequence, one which could account for the gap between Mars and Jupiter. His implicit argument can be formulated in the following manner: numbed by a non-rational arithmetical sequence, the scientists have postulated a new planet in order to corroborate mathematical constructions resulting from nothing but the arbitrariness of their own faculty of understanding.

It is, in fact, this implicit argumentation which constitutes the principal focus of the last section of *De orbitis planetarum*. If the question concerning the distance of the planets seems, as Hegel writes, "to pertain only to experience, in reality the measure and number of nature cannot be foreign to reason."[11] Thus, what is important here is the fact that Hegel already clearly affirms that nature is the realization of the Idea or of reason and must, therefore, bear its seal. Indeed, it is upon this conviction that Hegel founds the legitimacy of the scientific project as such: "the study and knowledge of the laws of nature are based upon nothing other than this: we believe that nature has been formed by reason, and we are convinced that all the laws of nature are identical."[12] Moreover, Hegel emphasises that, through their very activity—and indeed through their experience of joy at the correspondence of natural phenomena to their laws—scientists betray their agreement with this conviction. Indeed, "if other phenomena are not equally in agreement with the law, it is the experiences that they [the scientists] put in doubt, and they endeavour to realize at all cost the harmony between the two,"[13] i.e. between the hypothesised law and the empirical observations—a clear allusion to the law of Titius-Bode.

1.3. The Priority of Reason over Understanding

As one can now see, Hegel's intention was in no way to interfere with a field beyond his own domain, but simply to challenge a scientific procedure which did not conform fully to reason. The arithmetical progression of Bode, Hegel claims, "follows in no way the *generation of numbers from themselves*, that is to say, the powers; hence it does not in any way concern philosophy."[14]

Hegel is being faithful here to the intuitions of his youth in denouncing the tyranny which makes itself felt in astronomy, that is, the tyranny exercised by the external power of mathematics—the tyranny of mere numbers as such over the life that is tangible in the "powers."

In accordance with this philosophical belief, Hegel then proposes a different numerical series inspired by Plato's *Timaeus* and by the Pythagorean school: 1-2-3-4-9-16-27. In order to arrive at the distance of the planets from the sun, Hegel claims to derive the cubic root of the fourth power of each of these terms. This operation yields, in Hegel's view, the following series: 1.4-2.56-4.37-6.34-18.75-40.34-81, a series whose terms do not have the value of the A.U. but rather the value of 10^8 "Parisian feet," where 1 Parisian foot = 0.3248 m.[15] (It should be noted that, with the exception of the cubic roots of 4^4 and 27^4, all the numbers given by Hegel are actually wrong—a somewhat surprising fact explained by W. Neuser as an "error of interpolation" due to a manual of mathematics which was part of Hegel's library and which he might well have used.[16] As far as the first number is concerned, Hegel arrives at it by calculating the cubic root of 3 "in order not to forget the unity," but he provides no further explanation for why he should proceed in this way.)[17]

Hegel's substitution of his series for the Bodean one has provoked considerable sarcasm. For Hegel simply replaced the number 8 of the actual Platonic series (1-2-3-4-9-8-27) with the number 16, without offering any concrete explanation: "It might be permitted," Hegel writes, "to replace the 8, which we read in the text, with 16."[18] M.J. Petry sees in this quotation a mark of "irony" on the part of Hegel.[19] Hegel's proposal for a new numerical sequence based upon Pythagorean and Platonic elements provoked the wrath of K. Fischer;[20] and closer to Hegel's own time, Baron F. von Zach registered a sharp protest against the aberrations of transcendental philosophy, illustrated, in his view, by Hegel's dissertation.[21]

Taking our distance from such scathing dismissals, let us return to Hegel's text to examine more closely the intention which underlies the proposal of this new numerical series. As we have already seen, the future *Privatdozent* criticizes the astronomy of his time for not "respecting the generation of numbers from themselves, that is to say, the powers." The Platonic series, by contrast, corresponds to an *exponential* sequence, not an *arithmetical* one: 1-2-3-4-9-8-27 can actually be written as $1\text{-}2\text{-}3\text{-}2^2\text{-}3^2\text{-}2^3\text{-}3^3$. The series which Hegel employed is therefore based upon a series in which the three first whole natural numbers are followed by the squares and cubes of 2 and 3 respectively. Hegel's intentions here seem reasonably clear (though it is not clear by what authority he grants himself the right arbitrarily to replace the 8 of the Platonic series by 16, without even the slightest justification). His new geometrical progression allows him to account for the absence of the planet between Mars and Jupiter, because, as he says, "it is clear that the fourth and the fifth rows are separated by a large space [4/9], and that in this place there is no planet missing."[22] In substituting a new law for that of Bode, Hegel thus believed he had saved the *appearances* and saved *reason*, which "forms" nature according to the law of planetary distances which Hegel thought to have discovered. The lesson is simple: in order to do science it is necessary to follow the laws of reason, rather than attempting to force nature to bow to a strictly mathematical interpretation.

However, one has to acknowledge that this safeguarding of the demands of reason is only achieved at the price of sacrificing the demands of the understanding! For no justification is offered for the substitution of 16 for 8. Therefore, two possibilities arise: either Hegel is being ironic, as M.J. Petry thinks. (Appearances notwithstanding, however, this is quite unlikely in a text which was not, after all, a pamphlet but rather an academic thesis in which much was at stake.) Or, it is possible that it was not in fact Hegel's intention to adhere strictly to the Platonic series, but only to produce an exponential sequence which would be rational and save the appearances, in which case *2^3 and 2^4 both serve the same function*. The most plausible explanation seems to be this second one. Thus, from each term of the series, Hegel deduces the cubic root of its double square in order to obtain, in "Parisian feet," the distance of the planets to the sun;[23] but, by substituting 16 for 8, he obtains the result 40.34×10^8 Parisian feet for Saturn, a result which he could obviously not obtain on the basis of 8![24]

However, when Hegel defended his thesis, scientific experience appeared to contradict him, since G. Piazzi had discovered in the sky over Palermo the asteroid, Ceres, whose orbit was interpreted as a confirmation of the astronomical hypothesis of Titius-Bode.

As is well known, Hegel's blunder provoked a heated controversy. At the time, Baron von Zach, who had been one of the initiators of the research concerning the missing planet in 1800 and was a fervent advocate of the law of Titius-Bode, expressed perhaps the greatest contempt for Hegel's position. However, the question remains open as to whether Hegel had in fact known about Piazzi's discovery when he maintained that there was no planet missing between Mars and Jupiter. It also remains an open question, therefore, whether or not Hegel neglected to observe the facts of experience. Indeed, this seems *not* to have been the case. Piazzi's letter of January 24, 1801 did not reach Bode until March 20. At that point in time, the Italian astronomer had only been able to follow the trajectory of the new celestial object to within 9° of the sun. Piazzi fell ill, and the celestial object entered a zone too close to the sun to be able to be followed. Gauß subsequently determined its orbit, but did not publish the result of his research before 1808. His discovery did come to be known in scientific circles long before its publication, however; and it was on January 1, 1802 that H. W. M. Olbers refound the lost object: Ceres, the biggest of the asteroids. Now, even if we assume that news travelled rapidly from Berlin to Jena, it must be acknowledged that the information which was available to Hegel at the time of writing and revising his dissertation must still have been too sketchy and hypothetical for him to have taken it into account as scientific truth. Indeed, the very title of F. von Zach's first publication on this topic in the *Monatliche Correspondenz* (1801) betrayed the uncertainty of the partisans of the law of Titius-Bode themselves: *Über einen zwischen Mars und Jupiter längst vermuteten, nun* wahrscheinlich *entdeckten neuen Hauptplaneten unseres Sonnen-Systems* (my emphasis).

To conclude, then: either Hegel was unaware of this new discovery, or he had heard of it, but looked upon it as being only *conjecture* still awaiting experimental confirmation. In my opinion, this latter hypothesis seems to be the most plausible one. First, because it is unlikely that Hegel should not have known of the *Monatliche Correspondenz*, one of the most prestigious scientific reviews of its time, which was published in Berlin and which Hegel is known to have read later on. Second, because the two last pages of the 1801 dissertation have the character of an appendix. Thus, one can very well imagine that, once he had learned about the ongoing attempt to corroborate the scientific validity of the law of Titius-Bode, Hegel suddenly added, in a somewhat extrinsic way, his mathematical considerations with the intention of refuting a theory *which he did not consider satisfactory* independently of the eventual discovery of the famous asteroids.

Hegel was, therefore, wrong to believe that there was no need to search for a celestial body between Mars and Jupiter; and he later acknowledged his mistake when, in the first edition of the *Encyclopedia*, he called his "initial attempt" insufficient.[25] This admission, which was undoubtedly painful, was never repeated. It should be noted, however, that, even though Hegel clearly committed a blunder,[26] he had actually been right not to trust the law of Titius-Bode—as the discovery of Neptune in 1846, which does not correspond to the law of Titius-Bode, would later demonstrate.

In my view, what is most important here is to investigate the philosophical intention underlying Hegel's position, rather than to take pleasure in petty arguments whose only goal is to play experimental science off against speculative philosophy. This philosophical intention will appear even more clearly in what follows. May it suffice to remember that Hegel took offence at a certain conception of science which he considered to be an *oppression of nature*, whilst he, for his part, was seeking to conceive of nature as the *free realization of reason*.

2. The Intention of *De orbitis planetarum*: a New Speculative Physics

K. Rosenkranz has characterised the project which Hegel was pursuing here in the following manner: "the dissertation aimed at developing *a priori* Kepler's laws of the form of planetary orbits and of the motion of the celestial bodies."[27] In his dissertation, Hegel himself actually declares his intention to explain "what true philosophy establishes concerning the organization of the solar system, and principally the planetary orbits."[28] In accordance with this intention, Hegel conceived of his work as an indictment of a conception of nature which subjects it to the exterior authority—"positive" authority to use the jargon of Frankfurt[29]—of mathematics, instead of viewing its laws as a natural expression of *reason*. Hegel sees this mechanistic conception of nature as being nowhere better illustrated than in Newtonian astronomy, which he denounces from the very beginning of his dissertation.

> When one gets to this part of physics [i.e., astronomy], one easily sees that one is dealing with a celestial mechanics rather than a physics, and that the laws expounded in this astronomical science originate in *another science*, namely, in mathematics, rather than having really been derived from nature itself; that is to say, constructed by reason.[30]

Thus, in the Newtonian account, according to Hegel, it is in fact *another science* than physics which gives its laws to nature. The fundamental intent of Hegel's philosophy of nature is encapsulated in this introductory sentence: to denounce the reduction of astronomy to mechanics, and hence to denounce the deduction of the laws of celestial movements by means of mathematics, rather than from nature herself. His goal is to overcome the scientific domination of nature by mere *understanding*—a domination already denounced in the Frankfurt formula "conceiving is dominating." At the same time, our quotation clearly shows the continuity of thought between this new idea, on the one hand, and the ontology of Frankfurt, on the other: the spirit of the times posits the reason of the whole as existing in the totality of the *quantitative measure of its parts*, rather than in the *whole itself* as the embodied law from which the parts are deduced. In reaction to this tyranny of the understanding, Hegel will attempt to prepare the ground for a physical astronomy—and then for a physics *tout court*—originating in reason. In this crusade against Newtonianism, Hegel would to the end of his life defend the position of Kepler, his Swabian compatriot who also attended the *Stift* at Tübingen: "Newton is supposed to have proven the same laws as Kepler according to principles which are not physical, but simply geometrical, and in doing so nevertheless to have incorporated astronomy into physics."[31]

The replacement of physics by geometry, of speculative reason by the calculating understanding—that is the gist of the accusation levelled by Hegel in this text against the cosmological physics of his time. In Newton's transformation of the laws of Kepler, Hegel sees the displacement of the forces of matter into an external principle, whereas "on the contrary, it is necessary to maintain that these forces ... actually belong to matter, that [in fact] they constitute the very nature of matter."[32] This philosophical explanation of the identity of nature and of the immanence of its forces is the objective of the project which Hegel identifies here as physics, and is what he already had in mind when he called for a new physics in *The Earliest System Program*.[33] This project, which seeks to rediscover the inherent structure of the life of the whole of nature, can be termed a rehabilitation of *qualitative* physics. In this context it is worth mentioning that Hegel's first critique of Newton centers on the latter's *quantitative* approach to nature: for, as we have seen, accord-ing to Hegel, the laws of Kepler are no longer deduced by Newton from physical reasons but rather from geometrical reasons. In conceiving his theory of gravitational force, Newton "has only compared the *quantity* pertaining to the gravitational force which experience shows to exist in the bodies belonging to earth, with the *quantity* of the celestial motions. As for the rest, he has carried out everything according to mathematical relations, by geometry and calculus." In short, Hegel protests against the confusion of "purely mathematical relations with physical relations."[34]

Nothing is known about the possible existence of a logic at the time Hegel left Frankfurt. Indeed, prior to the recent discovery of fragments of the lecture entitled *Introductio in philosophiam* of 1801-1802, there had only been the weak testimony of K. Rosenkranz concerning Hegel's first lectures at Jena. It is thus impossible to ascertain how far along Hegel's research on logic was when he composed his dissertation. All that we can know for sure is that when Hegel began to develop his system at Jena, he situated logic and metaphysics at the very foundation of the systematic development of the Idea—both in the philosophy of nature and the philosophy of spirit. Nevertheless, it is most likely that Hegel must have progressively conceptualised the relation between logic and metaphysics on the basis of his ideas concerning the relationship between Newtonian science and nature. Moreover, this conceptualisation must also have been influenced by the critique of positivity as an oppression of nature and of the living whole, which he had formulated in Frankfurt.

In fact, when Hegel attacks the *reduction* of physics to applied mathematics, which he believes must be criticised in Newton, this is because to his mind physics amounts to more than a merely quantitative grasp of natural reality—which of course it is as well! Comparable to the fate of positivity, the legalism of the quantitative finds its negative place *within* the living and rational comprehension of the whole. If it is necessary to distrust the confusion between geometric constructions and the true forces of nature, as Hegel maintains, one should not, on the other hand, "consider the mathematical totality as something which is purely ideal or formal, it is real and physical as well!"[35] The relations which exist between quantities and which are thematized by mathematics, are indeed real relations; as Hegel puts it, these relations are themselves "inherent to nature, and once they have been grasped (*si intelligantur*), they become laws of nature."[36] It is clear, then, that Hegel does not deny that mathematics expresses the real in establishing its laws;

though it is necessary that the real nature of mathematics be understood. *This suggests to us that it is in fact from his critique of Newtonian physics that Hegel's logic emerged.* To my mind this is confirmed by his lecture notes on logic and metaphysics which have been handed down to us by I.P.V. Troxler.[37] By thus insisting on the legitimacy of mathematics, Hegel means to suggest that it constitutes—if I may be permitted this metaphor taken from the relationship between the understanding and reason—the reflection of the *Ur-bild* which is nature.[38] In other words, if mathematics does indeed express the real, albeit under a limited form (namely, in *quantitative* terms), one is tempted to think that it *imitates* philosophy—to anticipate yet again Hegel's later position *vis-à-vis* the understanding and reason.[39]

Under these conditions, one could ask what mathematical physics lacks to be real physics. Also, what is the nature of the physics which Hegel calls for from the time of *The Earliest System Program*?

In order to respond to these questions, two points need to be made. First, as I have just suggested, mathematics proceeds by way of abstracting from the whole of nature, according to the paradigm of the understanding, with the consequence that the truths at which it arrives are *finite* truths. Second, the conviction that time and space constitute a unity which forms the cornerstone of Hegel's philosophy of nature—which is here in its embryonic state—is a conviction from which Hegel never departed. In effect, Hegel replies as follows:

> it is necessary to separate from this reason of the whole (*totius ratione*) the analysis and the explanation of the whole which abstracts from the totality of nature, because the relations in the knowledge of the formal totality are in fact separated from the effective relations of nature, in which space and time are inseparably linked: geometry, as a branch of mathematics, abstracts from time, while arithmetic abstracts from space; the first constructs the whole of geometry only upon the basis of the principle of space, whereas the second constructs the totality of arithmetic upon the basis of time.[40]

The analysis and explanation of the rational whole will later become the primary function of Hegel's first logic: "the object of a true logic will be ... [to] present the forms of finitude ..., such as they proceed from reason."[41] But contrary to this logic—that is, the finished logic which leads to the threshold of metaphysics or of the speculative knowledge of the Idea—mathematical understanding, which is at issue here, precisely does not present the forms of knowledge as they are produced by reason. Its relation to knowledge is separated from any relation to the whole of nature, because it remains at the level of abstracting from space and time. Logic, however, by way of showing the effort of the understanding to unify its determinations, will reach the point of eliminating the finitude of these determinations by means of reason, so as to permit access to speculation. Mathematics, then, abstracts as "finite knowledge, where reflection abstracts from the absolute identity of that which, in rational knowledge, is mutually related."[42]

Finally, we should attend closely to this central passage for another reason. For it contains another key notion of Hegel's philosophy which is already seminally present in the *System Fragment* of 1800, namely, the notion of the "bad infinite." In truth, Hegel concedes that the mathematicians have understood the necessity of reuniting space and time, which geometry and arithmetic dissociate: such is in fact the object of "higher geometry." But higher geometry "eliminates this separation only negatively through the notion of the infinite; it does not provide the genuine synthesis of the two terms, and in its treatment differs in no way from the formal method which is the distinctive feature of geometry and arithmetic."[43] The unification of space and time by means of "higher geometry" is thus of the same kind as the unification of opposites to which the Jewish religion applied itself according to the Frankfurt texts: namely, the fixing in the infinite of two heterogeneous terms without genuine unification. Later on in the same texts, Hegel reproaches mathematics and geometry for either "veiling under the name of infinite" the identity of incommensurable terms by passing from the line to the surface and from the surface to the body, or reducing the surface to the line and the line to the point, that is to say, to "infinite smallness."[44] In this *ad hoc* use of infinity by mathematics, Hegel once again denounces the abstraction from "the things themselves" (*rebus ipsis*) which occurs to the benefit of the mere comparison of "numbers" and "measures," but not to the benefit of the "things" which are incommensurable for mathematics, namely, space and time. One can show in a detailed way that the reduction of physics to mathematics is illustrated by the Newtonian theory of forces, which Hegel interprets as a theory of two elementary opposed forces whose unity is lacking.

In his critique of the Newtonian theory of forces, Hegel's theoretical error was to interpret the tangent in the Newtonian model as a *centrifugal force*. In fact, the tangent is not a force governing the planet at all, but is simply the inert trajectory which this planet would follow, according to the principle of inertia, if no other force were exerted on it. Hegel's second error was to interpret Newton's account of the motion of the planets according to this schema—a schema which could only be valid in the case of circular motion. In the case of the elliptical movement of the planets, the centrifugal force in no case corresponds to a tangential line.

But the first of these two errors by our philosopher is important—which is rarely pointed out by commentators—if one desires to understand the intention which underlies Hegel's project of a new physics. For in the course of (mistakenly) conceiving of Newton's tangent as an *exterior force* exerted on the planet, Hegel also expands on his denunciation of the reduction of physics to geometry by pointing out that "the [mere] geometrical necessity of a tangential line in no way entails the necessity of a tangential physical force."[45] Moreover, not only does Hegel take Newton to task in this way for using geometry to ground physical force, he goes on to criticize the idea that tangential force could suffice to explain all planetary movement. For he means to explain the *free* movement of the planets without recourse to the *exterior* forces that are exercised on the planets:

> the decomposition of simple phenomena, represented by a straight or curved line, into other lines is a mathematical postulate, which in mathematics fully justifies itself by its manifold utility, but whose principle depends upon another science.[46]

Hegel is mistaken to interpret the tangent in the Newtonian model as a centrifugal force, because in reality it is a mere geometrical representation of inertia. However, this mistake is highly revelatory of Hegel's method: for the problem is not just his confusion between centrifugal force and tangential inertia, but the fact that he wrongly attributes a physical reality to Newton's tangential component at all. In other words, had Hegel not mistakenly confused centrifugal force and tangential inertia, he would still have committed another mistake, namely, that of interpreting inertia in Newton's account as a *universal force* acting upon every celestial body and thus putting it into motion. (Inertia, of course, is in fact just the absence of force.) Now Hegel could not accept what he understood to be the Newtonian conception of inertia as an external force initiating motion, because following Kepler and Leibniz, he held that inertia is a tendency towards rest or, put negatively, is a *resistance* against the *natural* propensity of matter to move.[47] From this we see that, in Hegel's view, matter is actually defined by its own natural or *internal* force—as he will say explicitly in his *Philosophy of Nature* of 1803-4 and of 1804-05.[48] By contrast, Newton (according to Hegel's interpretation) has to invoke a *deus ex machina* which moves matter solely by means of *exterior* forces[49]—a view for which Hegel reproaches Newton towards the end of his dissertation.

Therefore, 1) the real scientific mistake committed by Hegel is to conceive of inertia as a tendency towards *rest*, rather than as a tendency towards indefinite movement. Hence, 2) he cannot understand Newton's tangent as a merely *geometrical* representation of inertia. For this reason, 3) he comes to see Newton's tangent as the representation of a *universal force* which constrains planetary movement from the outside and which does not suffice, in his view, to explain *free* planetary movement.

In the remaining part of my paper, I should like to focus upon Hegel's conception of the solar system in the context of a genuine physics.

3. The Solar System: A Living System

Against geometry and "the experimental philosophy, which ... the whole of England has always considered to be the best,"[50] Hegel sets philosophy *a priori*. This *a priori* philosophy attributes to matter two fundamental forces which Kant had analyzed in his *Metaphysical Foundations of Natural Science*, namely, the attractive force and the repulsive force; but, at the same time, it specifies "that gravity, that is to say, identity itself, constitutes the condition of these forces."[51] The contrary is the case for Newton, according to whom, as Hegel says, gravity is "identical to the centripetal or attractive force" itself.[52] According to Hegel, Newton thus sought to explain the motion of the planets by means of two heterogeneous and independent forces—autonomous forces, in the pejorative sense of the term established at Frankfurt[53]—namely, the centripetal or gravitational force, on the one hand, and the centrifugal force, on the other. In fact, since the centrifugal force which Hegel sees in Newton's "force" of inertia is not actually an exterior force at all, it is clear that Newton only makes use of a single universal force in his theory. Nevertheless, this correction does not seem to me necessarily to discredit Hegel's argument. Regardless of whether planetary movement is governed by *two independent* forces or whether it is governed by a *single universal* force, Newton's explanatory schema falls outside the ontological framework set up by Hegel: namely, the principle of a *self-differentiated unity*, which is the conceptual achievement of Frankfurt and is implied here in Hegel's criticism. For Hegel, neither a universal force (like the Judaic God of Frankfurt), nor two concurrent forces (such as law in opposition to forgiveness in the *Spirit of Christianity*), but two unified co-original forces in their absolute identity, must be thought in physics. However, in Newtonian physics, in Hegel's view, "there can be no principle of *relation* [*conjunctio*] [of these opposed forces]."[54] It would seem to me that this is the central point of Hegel's criticism in his dissertation—the point which we must try to understand, rather than simply ridiculing his scientific incompetence.

As is undoubtedly clear, Hegel criticised classical physics in the name of a living conception of nature: whereas experimental philosophy, on the one hand, begins from a principle "borrowed from the mechanics which imitates nature on the level of dead matter,"[55] "mechanical science," on the other hand, "remains foreign to the life of nature."[56] One should not therefore be surprised to see Hegel propose that the true scientific method is one which "posits the whole and deduces from it the relations of the parts, instead of composing the whole from opposed forces, that is to say, from the parts."[57]

The philosophy of nature which Hegel outlines here originates in a theory of *gravity as constitutive of matter*. "Matter is objective gravity,"[58] that is to say, it is the realization of gravity under an objective form, in the same way in which, in the first outline of his system, nature will be the *objective realization of the Idea*. After criticising the decomposition of forces, according to which the movement of a body is explained by means of a mechanical relation which is foreign to the living force that animates it, Hegel applies himself to showing the identity of the centrifugal and centripetal forces. For, the contradiction inherent in the Newtonian distinction (as Hegel understands it) between the centrifugal and the centripetal forces stems, as Hegel shows, from the fact that the first is represented by the tangent and the second by the versed sine, although the two forces are nevertheless said to be equal. If the two forces were actually opposed, as the theory stipulates, it would be necessary that "the one decreases as the second grows."[59] This, however, is not at all the case, because "the versed sine and the tangent augment or decrease simultaneously"[60]—though here again, this affirmation holds good only in the case of a circular motion. The total phenomenon, Hegel thinks, is thus described "by one or the other force, these two forces being dependent upon a third force, which is *their true principle and their identity*."[61]

Now Hegel continues, if "the distinction between the centripetal force and the centrifugal force is an empty one ... , one is wrong to attribute any augmentation or diminution to the force of gravity."[62] What Hegel obviously wants to safeguard here is the strict *qualitative* determination of gravity, in which "no quantity or quantitative relation of any description is involved."[63] This determination is a constant. Hence, such is Hegel's cosmological creed: the elliptical movement of the planets around the sun is explained by the absolute identity of a single force which governs the order of the solar system. In conformity with the principles of the Frankfurt ontology, this force is clearly the connection of two opposites, space and time: "in other words, one might say: space in rest and space created by movement in time."[64] Contrary to centrifugal force and centripetal force, these two elements augment and decrease in inverse relation to each other, whereas "their absolute identity"—gravity—remains invariable. In thus reducing the explanation of the movement of the planets to the sole force of gravity without having to break it up into two mathematical representations, Hegel believes that he can maintain that the forces "constitute the nature of matter, this latter being an internal and immanent principle of opposed forces."[65] By this move, Hegel gains "the principle of identity which posits difference within itself"[66] and no longer needs the "exterior or mechanical" God[67] which Newton depended upon in order to explain the origin of these forces. Thus, he founds physics upon the free self-determination of matter.

In conclusion, our study has authorized us to read *De orbitis planetarum* as an application to physics of the ontology of life, which Hegel developed in Frankfurt while reflecting upon the phenomenon of religion. What is more, we have seen that his critique of Newton and his analysis of the relation between mathematics and physics already anticipates the epistemology which he will develop in his 1801-2 lectures on logic and metaphysics. His 1801 dissertation represents, therefore, a conclusion as well a beginning, and in this way shows itself to be thoroughly Hegelian![68]

Notes

1. Cf. H. Kimmerle, "Dokumente zu Hegels Jenaer Dozententätigkeit," *Hegel-Studien* 4 (1967): 21-99.

2. *Dissertatio philosophica de orbitis planetarum* quam Rectore Academiae Magnificentissimo Serenissimo Principe ac Domino Carolo Augusto Duce Saxoniae Iuliaci Cliviae montium angariae et Guestphaliae rel. consentiente amplissimo philosophorum ordine pro licentia docendi rite obtinenda publico examini submittit Ge. Wilh. Frid. Hegel philosophiae Doctor, Ienae typis Prageri et Soc., MDCCCI.

3. K. Rosenkranz, *Hegels Leben* (1844; reprint, Darmstadt: Wissenschaftliche Buchgesellschaft, 1963), p. 151.

4. Cf. Rosenkranz, *Hegels Leben*, p. 152.

5. On this point, cf. Rosenkranz, *Hegels Leben*, p. 14, and the testimony of Hegel's sister, Christiane: "physics was his favourite science at school" (*Der junge Hegel in Stuttgart. Aufsätze und Tagebuchaufzeichnungen 1785-1788*, edited by F. Nicolin [Stuttgart/ Marbach am Neckar: Deutsches Literaturarchiv, 1970], p. 84).

6. Cf. *Dokumente zu Hegels Entwicklung*, edited by J. Hoffmeister (Stuttgart-Bad Cannstatt: Frommann-Holzboog, 1974), pp. 288-300.

7. T. Haering, *Hegel. Sein Wollen und sein Werk. Eine chronologische Entwicklungsgeschichte der Gedanken und der Sprache Hegels*, 2 Vols (1929; reprint, Aalen: Scientia Verlag, 1963), **1**: 699.

8. Fr. De Gandt, "Introduction" to G.W.F. Hegel, *Les orbites des planètes. (Dissertation de 1801)*. Traduction et notes par Fr. De Gandt, avec une introduction sur la critique de la mécanique newtonienne chez Hegel. Préface de D. Dubarle (Paris: Vrin, 1979), p. 51.

9. Cf. Plato, *Timaeus*, 35b-36b. For the following, see O. Closs, *Das Problem der Gravitation in Schellings und Hegels Jenaer Zeit* (Heidelberg: Carl Winter's Universitätsbuchhandlung, 1908); Fr. De Gandt, "Introduction" to G.W.F. Hegel, *Les orbites des planètes*, pp. 51-2 and "La formule de Bode et la découverte des

astéroïdes," in G.W.F. Hegel, *Les orbites des planètes*, pp. 188-90; W. Neuser, "Hegels Habilitation und Reaktionen auf seine Habilitationsschrift," in G.W.F. Hegel, *Dissertatio philosophica de orbitis planetarum. Philosophische Erörterung über die Planetenbahnen*, translation, with introduction and commentary by W. Neuser (Weinheim: Acta Humanoria VCH, 1986), pp. 50-60 (hereafter *DOP*); Th.G. Bucher, "Wissenschaftstheoretische Überlegungen zu Hegels Planetenschrift," *Hegel-Studien* 18 (1983): 65-137.

10. Fr. De Gandt, "La formule de Bode et la découverte des astéroïdes," in G.W.F. Hegel, *Les orbites des planètes*, p. 189.

11. Hegel, *DOP*, p. 136.

12. Hegel, *DOP*, p. 136.

13. Hegel, *DOP*, p. 136.

14. Hegel, *DOP*, pp. 136-8, my emphasis.

15. Cf. Neuser, "Hegels Habilitation," p. 54.

16. Cf. A. Vlacq, *Tabellen der sinuum, tangentium, secantium, logarithmi de sinuum, tangentium und Zahlen von 1-10, 000* (Frankfurt/Leipzig: Fleischer, 1767).

17. Hegel's text here is very problematic, because the philosopher seems to have no respect for mathematics: the first number of the series should be the cubic root of 1^4, i.e. 1, and even the cubic root of 3 is not 1.4! Cf. on this point Neuser, "Hegels Habilitation," p. 51, and T.G. Bucher, "Wissenschaftstheoretische Überlegungen zu Hegels Planetenschrift," p. 86.

18. Hegel, *DOP*, p. 138.

19. Cf. *Hegel's Philosophy of Nature*, edited and translated with an Introduction and explanatory Notes by M.J. Petry, 3 Vols (London: G. Allen & Unwin, 1970), **1**: 372.

20. Cf. K. Fischer, *Geschichte der neueren Philosophie*, Vol. 8, *Hegels Leben, Werke und Lehre, 1* (Heidelberg: Carl Winter's Universitätsbuchhandlung, 1901), pp. 322-3.

21. Cf. Fr. von Zach, "Notiz," *Monatliche Correspondenz zur Beförderung der Erd- und Himmelskunde* (April, 1802): 334, quoted by Neuser, "Hegels Habilitation," p. 1.

22. Hegel, *DOP*, p. 138.

23. Cf. Neuser, "Hegels Habilitation," p. 52.

24. From a merely theoretical point of view, the Hegelian series 2-4-16 is an exponential series (2^1-2^2-2^4) which, despite the absence of the third power, is a series of growing numbers, which is not the case in the Platonic series in which there is a decline after 9 (2-4-9-8). What is more, the irregularity in Hegel's exponential series makes it a finite series, and thus it does not become a "bad infinite." It is necessary to admit, however, that Hegel would not have been able to attribute a numerical value to Neptune which was discovered in 1846. In the discussion following my paper, Cinzia Ferrini drew my attention to the fact that Hegel's substitution of 16 for 8 makes an indefinite progression of the series impossible; cf. C. Ferrini, "Tra etica e filosofia della natura: il significato della *Metafisica* aristotelica per il problema delle grandezze del sistema solare nel primo Hegel," in *Hegel e Aristotele*, Atti del Convegno di Cagliari (11-15 Aprile 1994), ed. G. Movia (Cagliari: Edizioni AV, 1997), pp. 173-91. From all this I draw the conclusion that by a rational numerical series Hegel understands a series of numbers engendered by themselves, but that above all his intention is to save the phenomena of nature against the theoretical pretensions of the mathematicians. His approach is therefore largely characterized by the spirit of the Frankfurt texts—among others, of *The Earliest System Program of German Idealism*, in which he demanded that physics once more be given wings, and of *Moralität, Liebe, Religion*, in which he defines the divine as the unification of nature and freedom.

25. G.W.F. Hegel, *Enzyklopädie der philosophischen Wissenschaften im Grundrisse und andere Schriften aus der Heidelberger Zeit*, edited by H. Glockner, *Sämtliche Werke. Jubiläumsausgabe* (Stuttgart: Frommann-Holzboog, 1968), Vol. 6, §224.

26. Hegel would still maintain in his *Encyclopedia* of 1830 that the true law was yet to be discovered.

27. Rosenkranz, *Hegels Leben*, p. 152.

28. Hegel, *DOP*, p. 82.

29. In *Moralität, Liebe, Religion*, written in Frankfurt, Hegel maintains that a religion is positive when it "establishes the representations of something objective, which could not become subjective, as the principle of life and actions" (*Hegels Theologische Jugendschriften. Nach den Handschriften der Königlichen Bibliothek in Berlin*, edited by H. Nohl [Tübingen: J.C.B. Mohr, 1907], p. 374). In this way we understand why Hegel's

slogan at Frankfurt, which we find in this same text, was: "conceiving is dominating." C. Ferrini has shown that this text of the young Hegel provides a meeting point between Hegel's interest in religion at Frankfurt and his approach to the empirical sciences at the beginning of his Jena period. Cf. C. Ferrini, "Nuove fonti per la filosofia della natura del primo Hegel," in *Rivista di storia della filosofia* (1993): 719, n. 12.

30. Hegel, *DOP*, p. 82, my emphasis.

31. Hegel, *DOP*, p. 82.

32. Hegel, *DOP*, p. 118.

33. "I would like to give wings once more to our backward physics, that advances laboriously by experiments," *The Earliest System Program of German Idealism*, in H.S. Harris, *Hegel's Development. Toward the Sunlight, 1770-1801* (Oxford: Clarendon Press, 1972), p. 510.

34. Hegel, *DOP*, p. 82.

35. Hegel, *DOP*, p. 84.

36. Hegel, *DOP*, p. 84, my emphasis.

37. See *Schellings und Hegels erste absolute Metaphysik. Zusammenfassende Vorlesungsnachschriften von I.P.V. Troxler*, herausgegeben, eingeleitet und mit Interpretationen versehen von K. Düsing (Köln: Dinter, 1988).

38. Cf. *Daß die Philosophie...*, in G.W.F. Hegel, *Schriften und Entwürfe, 1799-1808*, unter Mitarbeit von T. Ebert, herausgegeben von M. Baum u. K.R. Meist, *Gesammelte Werke*, Vol. 5 (Hamburg: Felix Meiner [in preparation]), pp. 269-75. (Hereafter *GW*, **5**.)

39. Cf. Hegel, *GW*, **5**: 272: "the understanding in its finitude imitates reason." Hegel also explicitly speaks in these terms in his dissertation, when he says of mechanics that it "imitates nature." (Hegel, *DOP*, p. 96.)

40. Hegel, *DOP*, p. 84.

41. Hegel, *GW*, **5**: 272.

42. Hegel, *GW*, **5**: 271.

43. Hegel, *DOP*, p. 84.

44. Hegel, *DOP*, p. 130.

45. Hegel, *DOP*, p. 92. Hegel is right here, since, in the construction of the parallelogram of forces, no physical reality is attributed to the two directions upon which the force is projected: there is but one force—that which is broken down.

46. Hegel, *DOP*, p. 90.

47. On this point, see De Gandt, "Introduction" to G.W.F. Hegel, *Les orbites des planètes*, p. 71ff.

48. See Hegel, *Jenaer Systementwürfe I*, edited by K. Düsing and H. Kimmerle, *Gesammelte Werke*, Vol. 6 (Hamburg: Felix Meiner, 1975), p. 28: "Die himmlischen Körper sind keine bewegte; sie sind absolut selbständige Bewegungen, *unmittelbar* Eines mit der Selbständigkeit," and *Jenaer Systementwürfe II*, edited by R.-P. Horstmann and J.H. Trede, *Gesammelte Werke*, Vol. 7 (Hamburg: Felix Meiner, 1971), p. 204: "die Materie ist wesentlich Bewegung ... Sie ist wesentlich sich bewegend."

49. This conception of God is the Judaic conception of God according to Hegel's Frankfurt texts. See, for instance, Newton's conception of God in his *Principia*: "Hic [God] omnia regit, non ut anima mundi, sed ut universorum dominus. Et propter dominium suum, dominus deus Pantocrator dici solet. Nam deus est vox relativa et ad servos refertur: et deitas est dominatio dei, non in corpus proprium, uti sentiunt quibus deus est anima mundi, sed in servos" (*Philosophiae naturalis principia mathematica*, 3rd ed., edited by A. Koyré and I.B. Cohen [Cambridge, MA: Harvard University Press, 1972], p. 528).

50. Hegel, *DOP*, p. 94.

51. Hegel, *DOP*, p. 96.

52. Hegel, *DOP*, p. 82.

53. For Hegel in Frankfurt, to be "autonomous" means to be "separated." In his text on Love, Hegel writes: "the individual in his innermost nature is something opposed [to objectivity]; he is an *independent* unit for whom everything else is a world *external* to him," *Hegels Theologische Jugendschriften*, p. 303, my emphasis.

54. Hegel, *DOP*, p. 96.

55. Hegel, *DOP*, p. 96.

56. Hegel, *DOP*, p. 116.

57. Hegel, *DOP*, p. 98.

58. Hegel, *DOP*, p. 120.

59. Hegel, *DOP*, p. 102.

60. Hegel, *DOP*, p. 104.

61. Hegel, *DOP*, p. 104, my emphasis.

62. Hegel, *DOP*, pp. 112-14.

63. Hegel, *DOP*, p. 114.

64. Hegel, *DOP*, p. 114.

65. Hegel, *DOP*, p. 118.

66. Hegel, *DOP*, p. 120.

67. Hegel, *DOP*, p. 118.

68. This article had already gone to press when I learnt of Cinzia Ferrini's book, *Guida al "De orbitis planetarum" di Hegel ed alle sue edizioni e traduzioni. La* pars destruens: *confutazione dei fondamenti della mecanica celeste di Newton e dei suoi presupposti filosofici*, con la collaborazione di Mauro Nasti De Vincentis (Bern/Stuttgart/Wien: Haupt, 1995).

12

Framing Hypotheses: Numbers in Nature and the Logic of Measure in the Development of Hegel's System

Cinzia Ferrini

One of the most famous, and most criticized, aspects of Hegel's 1801 dissertation, *De orbitis planetarum* (*On the Orbits of the Planets*), is certainly its conclusion. In the last couple of pages, Hegel "demonstrates" (with reference to a famous example drawn from the Platonic-Pythagorean tradition)[1] how "true philosophy" can be used to determine the mathematical ratios of magnitudes which are actually existent in nature (in this case, the distances of the planets from the sun).[2]

Hegel's attempted demonstration takes issue with the Titius-Bode series,[3] according to which there ought to be a planet between Mars and Jupiter.[4] The epistemological issue at stake involves opposing speculative philosophy both to the pure formality of Bode's arithmetical sequence and to the methodology of doing all that is possible in order to make the phenomena fit with one's own abstract schemes.[5]

As is well known, Hegel took no account of the fact that in the meantime Bode's law had undergone a process of successful verification, starting with Piazzi's discovery of the asteroid, Ceres, in January 1801.[6] How did Hegel deal with the matter in his later writings, when he clearly showed that he had become acquainted with the advance in empirical observation?[7] As Henry S. Harris puts it: "Within a few years four asteroids were known, and Hegel duly takes account of them in his Berlin lectures on celestial physics." And in the footnote to this sentence he goes on to say: "Hegel explicitly acknowledged that his *Dissertation* was mistaken in the 1st edn. of the *Encyclopaedia* (1817, sect. 224)." Those remarks are used to support Harris's view that Hegel

> committed none of the sins of apriorism that have so often been credited to him. He admits that the discovery of

> planets and their distances is a matter of empirical inquiry. He only claims, as any scientific investigator must, that the empirical inquiry is carried on in the belief that natural phenomena conform to a rational pattern.[8]

It is worth noting, however, that the coherence of Harris's picture is obtained by overlooking a discontinuity in Hegel's attitude between the Heidelberg and Berlin versions of the *Philosophy of Nature*, which forms the second part of Hegel's *Encyclopedia*. For what happens to this line of argument, when we 'duly take account of' the fact that in the Berlin version of the same section Hegel gets rid of the acknowledgment that his *Dissertation* was mistaken by simply deleting the sentence which in 1817 contained his self-criticism? The general aim of this paper is to answer this question.

To summarize the main points: in §224 of the 1817 Heidelberg *Encyclopedia* (hereafter H),[9] as well as in the parallel §280 of the 1827 Berlin and 1830 Berlin editions (hereafter B1 and B2 respectively),[10] we are told that, as regards the series of the planets, astronomy "has not yet discovered any actual law" concerning the "*distance*" from the sun (in B2 Hegel changes this into: "their *distances*"). In H the general frame mentions the complete failure of the scientific quest for a rule governing these empirical quantities. Astronomy is said to have even been unable to discover "anything rational" in this respect (though the phrase "*vielweniger etwas Vernünftiges*" was deleted in 1830).

In H Hegel adds to this, parenthetically, a critical observation regarding his own early attempt to find such a law, saying that he can now no longer consider it to be satisfactory. There then begins a new sentence introduced by "*ebenso*" ("in the same manner"), which also appears in B1 and B2, in which Hegel mentions the attempts made by philosophers of nature to find a "rational" law for such empirical numbers. It is worth noting that the typesetting of this whole passage in H (the critical remark on the *Dissertation* is set between dashes and follows the assessment of the results of astronomy) indicates that Hegel seems to place his *De orbitis* on an equal footing with science, introducing a methodological distance between his own early work and the approach of the *Naturphilosophen* who make use of analogies "devoid of reason." This nuance is lost in B1 and B2, where the sentence beginning "*ebenso*" directly follows Hegel's comments on the failure of the astronomers, the remark on *De orbitis* having been completely deleted. In B1 and B2, moreover, Hegel is more direct in targeting specific philosophers of nature for criticism (explicit mention is now made of the tentative analogy drawn by Schelling and Steffens between the planetary series and the series of metals; see the B2 Addition, where the point is developed and clarified); and he is also much more disparaging about the methodology employed by these philosophers of nature. In H he confined himself to saying that the task facing such philosophers was "to demonstrate the rationality of the series within the physical quality of things" (*der physischen Beschaffenheit*), but that their attempts could be considered so far (*bisher*) to be only (*nur*) the beginning of the appropriate point of view. In B1 and B2, on the other hand, "*bisher nur*" is changed to "*kaum*" ("hardly"), so that the analogies put forward by philosophers of nature, such as Schelling and Steffens, now come to miss the point.

It is worth noting that in B1 and B2, Hegel avoids passing a similar judgment on *De orbitis* by simply keeping away altogether from calling his 1801 attempt into question: we do not have to deal with any further positive modification of the content. We can take this move in at least two ways. For instance, we can regard it as philosophically insignificant. The causes for it could be rooted in a personal wish to remove any self-criticism, given the growing importance of Hegelian philosophy in the Berlin period. But we could also *frame the hypothesis* that Hegel's second thoughts are indicative of a more complex conceptual change in dealing with the problem of the relationship between what is external (and only empirical) and what is rational in physical reality. This paper aims specifically at showing how far one can go by pursuing this second line of inquiry.

It is important to note from the outset that any interpretation of the textual variation under consideration cannot be justified merely by comparing the parallel versions of these few sentences in Hegel's *Philosophy of Nature*. For the most relevant differences appear here to be no more than a matter of emphasis: in B2 the polemical tone becomes less intense with regard to astronomy, whereas in B1 and B2 the polemical tone is raised against "the external application of some schema already in hand to objects,"[11] such as the use made by philosophers of nature of the series of metals—a formalism, one should note, with which Hegel had openly reproached Schelling, as well as the followers of the philosophy of nature, from the time of the 1807 *Phenomenology*.[12] According to our hypothesis, to understand fully why Hegel alters his text in the way he does, one needs to look beyond the rhetoric of the passages themselves for a major change in Hegel's *philosophical* conception of mathematics—a change which involves a fundamental reappraisal of the relation between philosophy and empirical numbers in nature.

It seems more fruitful to me to compare the layout of the Heidelberg *Philosophy of Nature* more generally with that of the later editions, for the most striking difference is to be found precisely in the systematic assessment of mathematics. According to the final Berlin version of the division of the science of the Idea in its being-other (B2 §252), the Idea, as nature, is "in the determination of externality" (*des Aussereinander*; i.e. Mechanics, divided into three further divisions: space, time, place and motion), "in the determination of particularity" (*Besonderheit*; i.e. Physics), and "in the determination of subjectivity" (*Subjektivität*; i.e. Organics). Looking back from B to H, one can see that a major change occurs right at the beginning of the Berlin *Philosophy of Nature*; for, in 1817, the first division of the *Philosophy of Nature* was not Mechanics but Mathematics, the paragraphs of which (§§197-203) dealt with the notions of space and time. Mechanics, the object of which was masses and bodies, constituted the first part of the second division, called The Physics of the Inorganic. When did Hegel start to rework this point, and what can be the significance of this change?

As a result of research carried out by Wolfgang Bonsiepen on the notes taken by auditors at Hegel's lectures on the philosophy of nature, we know that, generally speaking, the adoption of both the division and the terminology of the second edition of the *Encyclopedia* occurred as early as in 1821/22.[13] Evidence is provided as well that the process of rearrangement of the contents had begun soon after the first edition of the *Encyclopedia* was published. It is worth noting, however, that although there is a host of variations in the systematic layout and contents of the *Philosophy of Nature*, Hegel always maintains the correspondence between the *Logic* and the *Philosophy of Nature*. In the Berlin version, the Logic of Being appears to be the framework of Mechanics, which in B2 §254 begins with what is quantitative (*mit dem Quantitativen*; Petry: with quantity). Even though entitled Mathematics, the same conceptual assessment was made in H §197 (with which B1 coincides): "Space is, in general, pure quantity," and "therefore Nature does not begin with Quality, rather it begins with Quantity." The sphere of essence shows itself to be the framework of Physics in the Addition to B2 §274, which can be compared with H §210, where mention is made of gravity as something "at first already grasped in the sphere of reflection." In B1 §337, the Subjective Logic proves to be the framework of Organics, as is also pointed out more clearly in B2 (lines 14-15); but the same characterization of nature as essentially "*selbstisch*" and "*subjektiv*" was already stated in H §260. Bonsiepen also remarks that, in a surviving systematic prospect of the time, the first part of the *Philosophy of Nature*, regarding "matter in its generality, as heavy matter," appears to be related to the Logic of Being, and the second part ("matter particularizing itself in physical properties and in corporal individuality") to the Logic of Essence.[14] It seems therefore sound to assume that any significant reorganization in the *Philosophy of Nature* can be traced back to a conceptual change in the *Logic*, which seems to constitute the proper locus of our inquiry.

As a first step in this investigation, we turn to Bonsiepen's detailed comparison of the beginning of the sections on Mathematics and Mechanics in H and B1 respectively. It is interesting to note how he points to the conclusion of the Remark to H §202, which reads as follows:

> The truly philosophical science of mathematics as the doctrine of magnitudes (*Grössenlehre* [the text of B2 §259 coincides with this]) would be the science of measures, but this already presupposes the real particularity of things, which is first existing (*vorhanden*) in concrete nature.

The parallel B1 §259 adds: "But because of the *external* nature of magnitude (*der Grösse*), this would certainly be the most difficult science." According to Bonsiepen's reading, the addition reflects the fact that Hegel is becoming more aware of the difficulties met by his philosophical conception of mathematics, realizing also that the proper place to clarify this was the *Logic*, rather than the *Philosophy of Nature* (as is well known, in the 1832 Doctrine of Being two ample remarks were added on the point at issue).[15]

The new sentence seems to involve reference to a logical reappraisal of the relation between quanta and their conceptual determination; for, in the development of philosophical science, what must be emphasized is the notion of externality that defines quantity as a category. Therefore, it seems that the most promising approach to resolving our problem is to take into account Hegel's revised version of the category of measure in the second edition (1832) of the *Science of Logic*'s Doctrine of Being (hereafter L2. The first edition published in 1812 is referred to hereafter as L1). In this way, the hypothesis framed at the outset is going to suggest its own tests: the *logical* framework of the relation between the empirical quantities and the philosophical science of mathematics, which is set forth in H and which underlies the dismissal of the *Dissertation*, ought to be found in L1. Furthermore, any significant conceptual change in this respect, which may suffice to explain the new attitude in the Berlin *Philosophy of Nature*, ought to be found in L2. Later we shall have to try to make sense of this puzzling "relation-in-progress" between the "science of the Idea in and for itself" (logic) and the "science of the Idea in its being other" (philosophy of nature). But for now, we return to the fact that in B1 and B2 Hegel was shaping a different approach to concrete externality from the one he took in H.

To bring this point into sharper focus, I suggest that we raise the issue from the standpoint of the entirely new text of B1 and B2 §246 which has no parallel in H.[16] Including the Remark and Addition (only in B2), the main points made by Hegel appear to stress the notional aspect of the matter under consideration, and they are as follows:

i) Physics is the theoretical and thinking consideration of nature, directed toward the knowledge of the *universal* itself, such that the latter is, at the same time, determinate within itself (*in sich*), as forces, laws, and genera.

ii) That which is universal in real, specific nature has to be understood neither as a Kantian subjective and heuristic form of thought, nor as a Schellingian, purely intellectual identity (which, for example, uses electro-chemistry to unify magnetism and chemistry by leaving out the determinations). Rather, it has to be understood as an immanent (which sounds rather Aristotelian) Platonic Idea, a substantial genus that is existing in the singular thing and which is its truth, its objectivity and its actuality.

iii) The universal understood by physics in the empirical world is then handed over to the philosophy of nature. Philosophy translates this already treated material into the Concept, for philosophy shows how physics's universal issues from the Concept as a whole that is necessary in itself.

It is in this context that the following Remark is placed (we refer specifically to B2, where the conceptual aspect is brought into sharper focus than in B1):

> It is not only that philosophy must be in agreement with the experience of nature, but the genesis (*Entstehung*) and formation (*Bildung*) of the philosophical science have empirical physics as [their] presupposition and condition. But the course of the genesis and the preliminary works of a science are one thing, the science itself is another; in the science, those elements can no longer appear as the basis, that here has rather to be the necessity of the concept (*in dieser können jene nicht mehr als Grundlage erscheinen, welche hier vielmehr die Notwendigkeit des Begriffs sein soll*; Petry: for in this latter case it is no longer experience, but rather the necessity of the Notion, which must emerge

> as the foundation). - It has already been recalled that, in addition to the fact that the object is to be presented (*anzugeben*) according to its conceptual determination within the philosophical procedure, the empirical appearance, which corresponds to that determination, has still further to be identified, and it has to be demonstrated of the [empirical] appearance that it does in fact correspond to the conceptual determination. Doing this, however, since it is connected with the necessity of the content, is not an appeal to experience (*Dies ist jedoch in Beziehung auf die Notwendigkeit des Inhalts kein Berufen auf die Erfahrung*; Petry: This is not however an appeal to experience in regard to the necessity of the content).[17]

It has been noted that the need to demonstrate the correspondence between empirical appearance and conceptual determination (which involves reference to the problem of contingency) is of the highest importance for the Post-Kantian Idealists. Indeed, after the elimination of the *Ding-an-sich*, of the dualism between concept and sensuous intuition, and the irreducible otherness of the object, nothing could hinder a cognitive use of pure reason. As is well known, by positing the transcendental ego as the absolute principle, the Post-Kantian Idealists grounded the identity of subject and object in the identity of the philosophical subject and the absolute subject: the object results from an activity of the subject that the philosopher can know since it is inherent in human (not divine) spirit:[18] philosophy can then seek to deduce reality by constituting concrete universals through self-reflection. But how to be sure of the validity of the philosophical deduction? Schelling saw the most reliable proof of the soundness of it in the "coincidence" of the empirical product and its construction.[19] But it has been observed that in this way it is the reality of experience that justifies the whole construction, and it is on experience that reason in fact turns out to depend.[20]

It is worth noting that Hegel's approach to the problem here is exactly the reverse:

i) in the Remark from B2 quoted above, Hegel employs the verb "*übereinstimmen*" (to be in agreement with) once, and "*entsprechen*" (to be in conformity with) twice, as a way of identifying the relationship between empirical appearance, our experience of nature, and our conceptual determination of it, but always from the point of view of the necessity of the content, which does not rest upon experience.

ii) To show what is implied by this threefold relationship, is something that has not yet been accomplished by philosophy. That this task has yet to be carried out, is clearly emphasized by the use of "*noch weiter*." Notice as well the nuance provided by the preposition "*zu*," which joins the infinitive of the verbs "*angeben*" (to provide, to establish), "*aufzeigen*" (to demonstrate) and the clause "*namhaft machen*" (to identify).

iii) We are told that in the sphere of the philosophy of nature, the presuppositions of a particular science, such as physical astronomy or chemistry, cannot appear as what is basic. In other words, attention is focused on the foundation of the content of the *Philosophy of Nature*, a content that the empirical sciences have provided without demonstrating its necessity. In the last sentence of our quotation, it is made clear that this foundational role, according to which it has to be demonstrated that the empirical appearance actually accords with the conceptual determination (and not vice versa), falls neither to experience, with its endless variation and one-sidedness, nor to immediate intuition, with its lack of rigour. Indeed, the Remark goes on to criticize the "fanciful analogies" of the latter, in terms which recall those we noticed in our starting point, that is §280, with regard to Schelling's and Steffens's comparison of planets to metals.

The Addition (in which notes from different periods are merged) clarifies this point, for there Hegel speaks of the role played by the metaphysical nature of thinking in the empirical sciences as well as in the philosophy of nature. It goes without saying that in this context, "metaphysics" is not to be understood as a body of doctrines, but is taken to be "as it were the diamond-net into which we bring all the material (*allen Stoff*) and by means of which (*dadurch*) we first (*erst*, omitted in Petry) make it understandable." Otherwise stated, Hegel holds that any empirical material—such as, in the case of celestial mechanics, the magnitudes that we find in the solar system, the quantitative determinations of the motion of the planets, of their distance and so on—falls within, and is caught by, the rational net of a law. Hence, these immediate quanta of nature ascertained by the empirical observation are captured by the universal form of determinations of quantity by empirical science, and demonstrated in their necessity by philosophy.

Are both this grasping of the quantitative aspect of the empirical data through abstractions of the understanding, and its dynamic incorporation into a rational structure, consistent with the conceptual framework of the transition between space and time in the revised version of the *Philosophy of Nature*? Turning to that transition, the following points are worth noting:

Both in the Heidelberg Mathematics and Berlin Mechanics:

i) the nature of space and time is merely abstract and ideal (it goes without saying that here "ideal" is taken to be synonymous with "purely formal"). For instance, in H §197, as well as in its parallel B1 and B2 §254, space is always defined as "*das ganz ideelle Nebeneinander.*" H §201, where time is "*ein schlechthin abstractes, ideelles Seyn,*" has a parallel in B1 and B2 §258 ("*Die Zeit ist ... ein schlechthin Abstraktes, Ideelles*").

ii) the existing identical unity of space and time (the mutual transition of one into another being motion) is immediately matter, both in H §203 and in its parallel B1 and B2 §261. The issue at stake here is the intelligibility of the transition from space and time to matter, a passage that is asserted to be "beyond the comprehension" of the understanding both in H §203 Remark and in B1 and B2 §261, Remark. Attention is then focused on this problem, for the transition we have to deal with is the one "from ideality to reality, from abstraction to concrete determinate being."

iii) Hegel notes that the transition from ideality into reality also occurs in well-known phenomena of mechanics (such as the cases of the lever and velocity). He spells out the transition by saying that "ideality can take the place of reality (*die Stelle der Realität vertreten kann*) and vice versa (*umgekehrt*)."

This is the common content of H and B. However, in the Berlin version we find some slight linguistic changes, which in my opinion are important from a conceptual point of view. They are all concerned with the context in which we have to place the transition from space into time and vice versa.

It is worth noting that, *prima facie*, the common feature of the systematic moves indicated above *seems* to be, in both versions, a matter of simple interchangeability (Hegel uses the word "*Vertauschbarkeit*") in which one element passes into the other and then the second passes back into first, so that only at the end of these two distinct transitions does there issue, as their result, the inner identity of the two opposite terms. Now, it is true that in the Heidelberg *Philosophy of Nature*, the mutual transition of space and time that gives rise to motion (i.e. "place as spatial now or time") is defined in accordance with the simple notion of "*Übergang*," as the "*passing away*" (*Vergehen*) that involves the "*re-generation*" (*Wiedererzeugen*) of space in time and time in space. However, in the Berlin version, Hegel uses the reflective form "*Sich-wiedererzeugen*," *self-re-generation*, as a substitute for "*Wiedererzeugen*," to refer to what is now implied by the "transition." Furthermore, in §203 of the Heidelberg *Encyclopedia*, the *Übergang* that is at stake is "a" becoming that is also immediately "the *identical existing* unity" (*die identische daseyende Einheit*) of space and time; but, when, as noted above, in point ii), the same words return in the parallel B2 §261, the context in which they are placed is transformed by a new clause added to this "becoming," which is said to be "*in itself* the falling *together* of its contradictions" (my italics). What is more, according to the Heidelberg edition, the becoming is regarded as a synonym of "immediate externality" and "negativity," whereas, in the Berlin version, these terms have the same meaning as "the being-for-self of singularity," the reference to becoming having been deleted. It is also worth noting that a passage of §203 of the Heidelberg edition has its parallel not in B2 §261, but in the preceding one. In H, space is in itself the contradiction of indifferent juxtaposition and of continuity devoid of difference, the pure negativity of itself, and this characterization is left unchanged in the final version (§260). Nonetheless, in the Heidelberg *Encyclopedia* the final phrase reads: "and [space is] the transition into time" (*das Übergehen in die Zeit*); whereas in the Berlin version it is changed to: "and [space is] the transition in the first instance into time" (*das Übergehen zunächst in die Zeit*).

It seems to me that all these variations point to a transition in B2 that occurs *within* the interrelationship of space and time, and *on the basis* of their unity. As regards the notion of *Übergang* involved here, it seems to me that it can in no way be taken as a simple "passing away" of one into the other; rather, it implies that the moment of relation is both inherent and immanent in the two opposite terms taken together.

As has been pointed out by John Burbidge in his thorough reading of the *Science of Logic*:

> Since concepts are signs for the dynamic activity of intelligence, they signify both the abstractions of understanding and their dialectical implications. By becoming self-consciously aware of their setting within the functions of intelligence, however, thought transforms itself from understanding into speculative reason. It then recognizes that the relations are inherent in the terms.[21]

But the question must now arise, in the light of our earlier discussion, whether or not both the same reappraisal of the meaning of transition, and the same inherence of relation, is to be found in L2 vis-à-vis L1.

According to the standard view, the whole sphere of Being in the *Science of Logic* is characterized as thinking that simply passes from one concept or category over to another, so that at the end being would dissolve itself in essence. In my opinion such a reading would require constantly using the notions "transition" (*Übergang*) and "becoming" (*Werden*) in their immediate meaning of "vanishing" (*Verschwinden*), as found throughout the first edition of the Doctrine of Being, and in accordance with the rule governing the first of the three final syllogisms of the *Encyclopedia*, namely "the external form" (*die äusserliche Form*) of transition. An example of this simple use of the notions of *Übergang* and *Werden* can be seen, right at the outset, in the section called "the general division of Being," where in 1812 Hegel understands the outcome of the last category of Being, Measure: i) in accordance with the *external* relation between content and thought expressed by Kantian modality; ii) in the light of its mere dissolution (*Auflösung*) by means of the Measureless; iii) in conformity with the conceptual meaning Hegel ascribes to Spinoza's substance, which is taken to represent "the negative one in which everything is absorbed"—a general determination which, indeed, in 1812 characterizes the "absolute indifference" that constitutes the final moment of Measure, when being as a whole vanishes into Essence.[22]

Elsewhere I have pointed out that this is *not* how we have to take the general significance of the path of Being in the final version of the *Science of Logic* of 1832. The point is made clear by Hegel after his revision of "the general division of Being," where the "external" significance of not contributing to the determination of the content is ascribed exclusively to Kantian modality, and it is precisely this significance which is clearly separated off from the concept of "measure" as such.[23] What is more, with respect to "absolute indifference," Hegel now writes: "But when substance is conceived as indifference, it is tied up with the need for determining it and for taking this determining into consideration; it is not to remain Spinoza's substance."[24] We have, then, a new context, which in the first part of the Objective Logic brings the "need for determining," namely the dimension of the knowing subject, into sharper focus. Within this general reappraisal, we can gain further insight into Hegel's revision of the notion of transition by looking at the final version of The Ratio of Powers concerning the category of Measure that emerges as the unity of quality with its opposite or negation, that is quantity. At this point, Hegel introduces what he calls a "double" transition between Quality and Quantity, which occurs within their interrelationship and *on the basis* of their unity.

It is clear that within this frame, whatever transition may happen, no dissolution or vanishing can any longer be expected; the terms remain permanently related. In this way we have a mediated, posited totality; the "double" transition is governed by the *immanent* presence of the identity of the two opposites. It needs to be pointed out that this "double" transition thus *cannot* be regarded as matter of a simple interchange, as was the case in 1812: namely, Quality that passes into Quantity and then vice versa, so that only at the end of the process, by adding up these simple transitions, the identity of the opposites would immediately result.[25]

As is well known, according to Hegel, reflection "is the movement of becoming and passing over that remains within itself." In my view, the "double transition" meets this requirement. Thus the final version of the origin of Measure—as well as the revised account of the transition between space and time in the Berlin Mechanics—anticipates the modes of reflection within the immediacy of being. This implies an alternative to the standard reading of the sphere of Being which sees it as governed by simple transitions, namely by the model of becoming set out in the first syllogism.[26] Rather, the progressive determination of Being now seems to express the one-sidedness and then the self-superseding of the external and immediate way of knowing, in the abstract element of thought and by reason that knows itself (*die sich wissende Vernunft*), in accordance with the model of the self-judgment (*Sich-Urteilen*) of the Idea in the third of the final syllogisms.[27]

In L1 we find a completely different approach to this point, which has its counterpart in the assessment of the transition between space and time in the first part—Mathematics—of the Heidelberg *Philosophy of Nature*. This implies that the major change I have outlined in the conceptual significance of Measure in the *Science of Logic* lies behind the changes introduced to the Berlin *Philosophy of Nature*. Furthermore, I suggest that this reading may also be helpful to understand why, in B1 and B2, space and time are no longer considered in the sphere of Mathematics. As Hegel puts it, from the time of *De orbitis*, mathematics abstracts from time (as arithmetic) and space (as geometry), as well as from their unity, for the infinitesimal calculus does not go beyond formal ratios.[28] Mechanics (matter, motion), on the other hand, is the ground of the unity of space and time; so it must serve as the proper locus for their "double" transition.[29]

What is more, in this way we are also able to cast light on the sentence added to B1 and B2 §259, in which, speaking of his philosophical conception of mathematics, Hegel writes that it is just because of the external nature of magnitudes that the science of measure would be the most difficult science. Indeed, concrete externality played a less problematic role in the Heidelberg edition than in the Berlin version; for it is clear enough that as long as the relation between conceptual determination and empirical appearance is ruled by the model of *simple*, rather than *double*, transition (that is, by the model of becoming as mere 'vanishing'), what comes later always remains in *external* relation to what is earlier. On this view (clearly expressed by Hegel as early as the 1812/13 *Philosophical Encyclopedia*), the empirical numbers of nature, as immediate quantitative determinations of concrete magnitudes, are external and irreducible to the formal and essential structure of their physical law, and so cannot be captured by the "diamond-net." Therefore, in no way can they be deduced conceptually or have their necessity demonstrated; because of the ideal character of mathematics, which is only "applied" to the concrete relations of magnitude, the numbers are taken from experience, so that it may be just by chance that a "law" of nature is actually found.[30]

That is Hegel in L1, at the end of the first chapter (Specific Quantity) of Measure, part C: Ratio of Qualities (*Verhältniss von Qualitäten*).[31] The context is the familiar one of pitting Kepler against Newton. It is important in Hegel's view that the formulas, such as Galileo's law of falling bodies and Kepler's laws of the planetary motion, by measuring the qualities of space and time as ratios, have been able to discover a universal form for numbers of nature. Just before the beginning of part C we read the following sentence:

> It is a great service to ascertain the empirical numbers of nature, e.g. the distances of the planets from one another; but it is an infinitely greater service when the empirical quanta are made to disappear and they are raised into a universal form of determinations of quantity so that they become moments of a law or of a measure.

At this point L1 and L2 coincide.[32] However, in the L1 Ratio of Qualities, we find the following noteworthy passage:

> These qualities [i.e. space and time, in so far as they are moments of one measure] have the two sides as qualities which firstly are to be indifferent (*gleichgültig*) in respect to their relation of measure (*Maasbeziehung*) as well in respect to the quantitative side, and secondly [as qualities] which are to stand in this relation (*Beziehung*). ... But their indifference (*Gleichgültigkeit*) in respect to measure has also another side, namely, the direct meaning of their emerging (*Heraustreten*) out of measure. Indeed the qualities are only through measure itself, for in measure lies the moment of the immediacy that is determined in itself (*an sich*). But this moment, as immediacy (*als Unmittelbarkeit*), is the simple unmediated (*unvermittelt*) quotient of the measure, that is to say the superseded measure.[33]

We can conclude, then, that in L1, since the qualities are "outside of the measure" (*ausser dem Maasse*), the empirical numbers of a physical law appear to be nothing but the restoration (*Wiederherstellung*) of the immediate quantum.[34] Interpreters have emphasized the irreducibly empirical element here posited by Hegel within measure, which condemns to failure any attempt made by mathematical physics, as well as philosophy of nature, to be totally deductive and formalized.[35]

Since Hegel had taken this position in the 1812 *Science of Logic*, it seems reasonable to conclude that, when accounting for the failure of astronomy in discovering an actual physical law for the distances of the planets in his 1817 *Encyclopedia*, he could no longer regard his speculative attempt in *De orbitis* as satisfactory. In the conceptual framework of the first edition of the *Philosophy of Nature* any aprioristic approach of that kind was in fact logically wrong.

In the revised edition of the Doctrine of Being, part C has a different title: *Das Fürsichseyn im Maasse.* We are here told right at the outset that the matter under consideration—which is still the relation between quality, quantum and their specific ratio of measure—is no longer to be viewed as something that "emerges out" of this ratio, as "negated" or "superseded" measure, but rather belongs to the "being-for-self" of measure itself. Hegel writes:

> the immediate quality has also a merely *immediate quantum*. Therefore the specific measure has as well a side that in the first instance (*zunächst*) is of external alteration, the progression of which is merely arithmetical, unaffected by the specific measure, and in which falls the external, hence only empirical, determinateness of magnitude. Quality and quantum as thus also proceeding (*auftreten*) outside (*ausser*) the specific measure are at the same time within the relation (*in der Beziehung*) with it; immediacy is a moment of those [sides] which themselves belong to measure. ... The immediately determined quantum as such, although, as moment of measure, it is otherwise (*sonst*) inherently (*an sich*) grounded in a conceptual connectedness (*Begriffszusammenhang*), is, in the relation to the specific measure something externally given.[36]

It is clear that for Hegel the empirical numbers of nature are now "*an sich*" captured by the conceptual net, the "*Begriffszusammenhang*," which reveals something basic to them: namely, their qualitative aspect. How to give sense to this statement?

I suggest that Hegel is referring to all these elements (the kind of exponent or proportionality, the ratio of a progression, the constancy of a coefficient etc.) that constitute the *specific form* of a mathematical relation among physical magnitudes. What do we gain with this new perspective?

In the light of the contemporary epistemological debate, from my point of view Hegel would have denied the possibility of speaking of regularities in nature irrespective of our knowledge of them, and he would have given a negative answer to the following question: "Can philosophy provide an analysis of the form of laws of nature, while disregarding the importance of laws of science?" Moreover, he would have rejected the claim that "we can develop theories for laws of nature which may not hold for laws of science."[37]

As for the theoretical issue here involved, Hegel's statement in L2 implies that the immediately determined quanta are no longer to be thought of as "simple unmediated" quotients of measure that "emerge out" of the network of the universal determinations of thought. They do not constitute any longer the superseding and negation of the specific measure of a law. Rather they appear as *its* immediate moment, thus remaining inherently and immanently related to it, under the surface (so to speak) of their external, not further determinable, merely numerical variation. Scholars have interpreted this rather cryptic reference to a "partial externality" (as Doz puts it), by pointing out that the conceptual structure of a law requires the existence of such an empirical element without determining its value. According to the example provided by Doz, the empirical element translates the coefficient a in the formula $s = at^2$, so that, granted the essential form of the ratio, other numbers are possible. In this way, the magnitudes that are actually existent in nature turn out to be, at the same time, "immediate and dependent."[38] All this also implies a need to reappraise the relations connecting induction, the finding of a law and chance; for conformity to a rational pattern plays a constitutive role within the contingency (*Zufälligkeit*) of concrete externality, but it is not able to determine the numerical value of the specific measure of a law, as it was attempted in *De orbitis* for the distances of the planets.

To conclude, it is worth pointing out the specific difference between the two editions of the Doctrine of Being, to the extent that their diverse logical assessments of the relation between concrete externality and conceptual determination systematically affect the Heidelberg and Berlin versions of the *Philosophy of Nature*. Within the framework of L2, in the light of the recognition of immediacy as something that is the external, empirical side of a specific ratio of measure (the physical laws), and that is grounded in the "diamond-net" as well, it is unlikely that Hegel would be basically dissatisfied with his speculative attempt of 1801. Indeed, at the outset of his treatment of the distances of the planets in the *Dissertation*, we find stated that, although the ratio of the planetary distances might appear to be simply a matter of experience, "in truth the measure and number of nature cannot (*nequeunt*) be alien to reason."[39]

Simply put: in my view, returning to *De orbitis* in the light of the 1812 Doctrine of Being in the *Science of Logic*, the *Philosophical Encyclopedia* of 1812/13, and the Heidelberg *Encyclopedia*, Hegel would have deleted the clause "and number" in the sentence quoted above, denying the very possibility of replacing Bode's arithmetical series by providing a numerical progression that is of direct philosophical significance (i.e. involving powers, or the generations of the numbers out of themselves).

In the light of the Berlin *Philosophy of Nature* and of the revised 1832 Doctrine of Being, Hegel would still have had to leave to arithmetic what belongs to arithmetic, by recognizing that its dominion covers the side of the external, empirical determinations of the measurement within a physical law. However, in my opinion, he would have kept the clause "and number," adding "in itself" ("*in se*," "*an sich*") to it,[40] since the mathematical ratios among physical magnitudes have now been established as in themselves grounded in a conceptual network, at least as regards their qualitative aspect.

Little wonder that Hegel chose to avoid criticizing his early venture.[41]

Notes

1. For the actual significance of this reference and the philosophical context in which it should be placed, see: H.S. Harris, *Hegel's Development. Night Thoughts (Jena 1801-1806)* (Oxford: Clarendon Press, 1983), pp. 92-7; M. Baum, "Kosmologie und Dialektik bei Platon und Hegel," in *Hegel und die antike Dialektik*, edited by M. Riedel (Frankfurt am Main: Suhrkamp Verlag, 1990), p. 195 and pp. 199-200; C. Ferrini, "Features of Irony and Alleged Errors in Hegel's *De orbitis planetarum*," *Hegel-Jahrbuch* (1991): 467-9; C. Ferrini, *Scienze empiriche e filosofie della natura nel primo idealismo tedesco* (Milano: Guerini e Associati, 1996), pp. 81-90 and pp. 107-20.

2. Hegel's Latin text reads as follows: "quid vel in quantitatum determinandis rationibus mathematicis philosophia valeat, praeclaro ex antiqua philosophia petito exemplo demonstrem" (*Dissertatio philosophica de orbitis planetarum* [Jena: Prager, 1801], p. 4, [ll. 4-7]). On Hegel's example, see Harris, *Night Thoughts*, p. 93. It is also worth noting that attention had been focused on Timaeus Locrus by Bardili in a seminar, attended by Hegel, held at Tübingen in the Winter Semester 1789/90 (cf. R. Pozzo, *Hegel: "Introductio in philosophiam." Dagli studi ginnasiali alla prima logica* [Firenze: La Nuova Italia, 1989], pp. 86-9, in particular p. 86, note 102). The quotation from the *Timaeus* implies neither that Hegel's first philosophy of nature was influenced only by that tradition, nor that he was establishing once and for all the Pythagoreans' authority by finding an alleged empirical proof for it. For instance, elsewhere I have suggested that the way in which Hegel revises that ancient series may involve taking into account the charge levelled by Aristotle (*Metaphysics* 1090b24-27) against the abstract formalism of numbers which "contribute nothing to actuality," as well as: i) Aristotle's criticism of the doctrine according to which numbers would come before existing magnitudes (*Metaphysics* 1077a19); ii) his view that numbers are neither substance nor cause, for "the ratio (logos) is the substance" (*Metaphysics* 1092b16-17); and iii) his appraisal of the Academy's theories about the generation of numbers (*Metaphysics* 1083b-1084a7): cf. C. Ferrini, "Tra etica e filosofia della natura: il significato della *Metafisica* aristotelica per il problema delle grandezze del sistema solare nel primo Hegel," in *Hegel e Aristotele*, Atti del Convegno di Cagliari (11-15 Aprile 1994), ed. G. Movia (Cagliari: Edizioni AV, 1997), pp. 173-91.

3. On the Titius-Bode series, cf. M.M. Nieto, *The Titius-Bode Law of Planetary Distances: Its History and Theory* (New York: Pergamon Press, 1972), quoted in "Hegel, *Philosophical Dissertation on the Orbits of the Planets* (1801). Preceded by the 12 Theses Defended on August 27, 1801," translation, foreword and notes by P. Adler, *Graduate Faculty Philosophy Journal* 12, 1-2 (1987): 273, note 5.

4. For a thorough account of the matter see: T.G. Bucher, "Wissenschaftstheoretische Überlegungen zu Hegels Planetenschrift," *Hegel-Studien* 18 (1983): 65-138; W. Neuser, "Die Entdeckungsgeschichte der Asteroiden und Hegels Habilitationsschrift," in Hegel, *Dissertatio philosophica de orbitis planetarum. Philosophische Erörterung über die Planetenbahnen*, translation, with introduction and commentary by W. Neuser (Weinheim: Acta Humaniora VCH, 1986), pp. 50-60. Neuser's German translation of *De orbitis* includes a Latin parallel text which corresponds, in lines and pages, to the original 1801 text. The facsimile of the 1801 edition is now available, together with a critical apparatus, in C. Ferrini, *Guida al "De orbitis planetarum" di Hegel ed alle sue edizione e traduzione*, in coll. con M. Nasti De Vincentis (Bern: Haupt, 1995), pp. 11-50.

5. See *De orbitis*, p. 31 (ll. 26-32); Adler, p. 301: "When those who seek the laws on the basis of experience and induction chance upon (*forte*) the form (*species*) of a law, they acknowledge this identity between reason and nature by the joy they experience in the face of the discovered law; and if other phenomena do not sufficiently agree with the law, they acknowledge it by the way in which they doubt the experiments and aspire to bring the two into harmony (*et utriusque omni modo harmoniam constituere studeant*)." (In the last clause cited, Adler fails to translate "omni modo" [by all means].) That this passage may also involve reference to the philosophers of nature is later confirmed by Hegel's notes and fragments from the Jena period. As regards the work of followers of Schelling such as Görres and Wagner, Hegel remarks that it is just a matter of "the roughest empiricism together with the formalism of matters and poles, adorned by unreasonable analogies and elated flashes of thought" (see Hegel, *Notes et fragments. Iena 1803-1806*, Texte allemand, traduction et commentaire par C. Colliot-Thélène *et al.* [Paris: Aubier, 1991], Frag. 10, p. 38, and the commentary on it, pp. 113-14; see also on this point, J.-M. Lardic, "Hegel et Schelling: Critique du Formalisme et Prise en Charge de la Contingence," *Archives de*

Philosophie 57 [1994]: 683-91). It is also worth noting that *De orbitis*, p. 31 (ll. 26-32) shows stylistic analogies with Aristotle, *De Caelo*, 293a23-b21.

6. See Neuser, pp. 53-5 and p. 69, note 142. Neuser points out that either Hegel was not aware of the fact or he did not take the celestial body discovered by Piazzi to be a planet but a comet (as Herschel still believed in November, 1802). On the circumstances and meaning of Piazzi's discovery, see: Ferrini, "Features of Irony," p. 475, note 71; J.J. de La Lande, *Bibliographie Astronomique avec l'Histoire de l'Astronomie depuis 1781 jusqu'à 1802* (1803; reprint, Amsterdam: Gieben, 1970), p. 687; and R.H. Allen, *Star Names: Their Lore and Meaning* (1898; reprint, New York: Dover, 1963), pp. 415-16 [original title, *Star-Names and their Meanings*]. It is worth noting that, in the first instance, Piazzi did not himself intend to confirm Bode's law.

7. Cf. Hegel, *Phänomenologie des Geistes*, edited by W. Bonsiepen and R. Heede, *Gesammelte Werke*, Vol. 9 (Hamburg: Felix Meiner, 1980), p. 139 (ll. 29-33). For the English translation, see: *Hegel's Phenomenology of Spirit*, translated by A.V. Miller (New York: Oxford University Press, 1977), §245, p. 148: "to discover ... even a new planet which, although an individual, possesses the nature of a universal, can be the lot of only a lucky few." (Hereafter cited as *Phän.* [*GW*, **9**]; Miller, *Phen.*) In the same vein, see also: *Enzyklopädie der philosophischen Wissenschaften im Grundrisse (1830). Zweiter Teil: Die Naturphilosophie mit den mündlichen Zusätzen*, edited by E. Moldenhauer and K.M. Michel, *Werke in zwanzig Bänden*, Vol. 9 (Frankfurt am Main: Suhrkamp Verlag, 1970), §270 Zus. (pp. 105-6). For the English translation, see: *Hegel's Philosophy of Nature*, translated by M.J. Petry, 3 Vols (London: Allen & Unwin Ltd; New York: Humanities Press, 1970), **1**: 280 (l. 35)-281 (l. 15). I suggest that the fact that Hegel was always speaking in terms of "*Glück*" when acknowledging the discovery of new planets or asteroids, such as Ceres, Vesta, Pallas, etc., means that he did not ascribe to these empirical data the crucial value of raising Bode's merely arithmetical progression into the rational pattern of a physical law (i.e. one based on a ratio) that is able to predict its empirical quanta.

8. Harris, *Night Thoughts*, p. 96. On Hegel's retraction of his Jena attempt to determine the interplanetary distances, see Neuser pp. 48-9.

9. I refer to the following edition: Hegel, *Sämtliche Werke. Jubiläumsausgabe*, edited by H. Glockner, Vol. 6 (Stuttgart: Frommann-Holzboog, 1968).

10. I refer to the following editions: 1) *Enzyklopädie der philosophischen Wissenschaften im Grundrisse (1827)*, edited by W. Bonsiepen and H.-C. Lucas, *Gesammelte Werke*, Vol. 19 (Hamburg: Felix Meiner, 1989); 2) *Enzyklopädie der philosophischen Wissenschaften im Grundrisse (1830)*, edited by W. Bonsiepen and H.-C.Lucas, in co-operation with U. Rameil, *Gesammelte Werke*, Vol. 20 (Hamburg: Felix Meiner, 1992). Where the Additions (*Zusätze*)—translated in the Petry edition—are concerned, I refer to the German text of *Werke in zwanzig Bänden*, edited by Moldenhauer and Michel, Vol. 9.

11. See the argument in "The First *Encyclopedia* Article on Hegel (1824, 1827)," translated by C. Butler, *Clio* 13, 4 (1984): 371-2.

12. Cf. Hegel, *Phän.* (*GW*, **9**), pp. 36 (l. 17)-38 (l. 14); Miller, *Phen.*, §§50-51, pp. 29-31. The point was already made in Hegel, *Notes et fragments*, Frag. 71 and 82. See also: *Enzyklopädie* (1830), §231; for the English translation, see: *The Encyclopaedia Logic*, translated by T.F. Geraets, W.A. Suchting, H.S. Harris (Indianapolis: Hackett Publishing Company, 1991), p. 299: "The misuse of this [geometrical] method and its formalism, in philosophy and in the sciences, has been replaced in more recent years [with respect to Spinoza's and Wolff's times] by the misuse of what is called 'construction'." Moreover, it is worth looking at Verra's explanatory note to the notion of "construction" set forth in this paragraph: cf. *La scienza della logica*, a cura di V. Verra (Parte prima della *Enciclopedia*, con le *Aggiunte*) (Torino: UTET, 1981), pp. 452-3. On the parallel passage in the 1817 edition of the *Encyclopedia Logic* (§ 176), cf. Hegel, *Vorlesungen über Logik und Metaphysik. Heidelberg 1817*, transcribed by F.A. Good, edited by K. Gloy (Hamburg: Felix Meiner, 1992), pp. 187-8, Commentary, pp. 312 f.

13. See W. Bonsiepen, "Hegels Vorlesungen über Naturphilosophie," *Hegel-Studien*, 26 (1991): 48-51. In particular, it is worth considering that in the chapter that deals with the inner division of the first part of the *Philosophy of Nature* in the lecture of 1819/1820, we read: "*Mechanik, nicht bloss Mathematik*"; see Hegel, *Die Vorlesung von 1819/20*, edited by M. Gies with the cooperation of K.-H. Ilting, *Naturphilosophie*, Vol. 1 (Napoli: Istituto Italiano per gli Studi Filosofici, 1982), pp. 11-12. On the other

hand, from 1810/11 and 1812/13, that is, from the time of his lectures on "Philosophical *Encyclopedia*" at the Nuremberg Gymnasium, Hegel held the view that mathematics was the first of the "principal sciences in the philosophy of nature"; see "Hegels 'Philosophische Enzyklopädie' in Nürnberg. - Mit einer Nachschrift von 1812/13, herausgegeben von Udo Rameil," *Hegel-Studien* 30 (1995): 9-38.

14. Bonsiepen, "Hegels Vorlesungen," p. 50.

15. See W. Bonsiepen, "Hegels Raum-Zeit-Lehre. Dargestellt anhand zweier Vorlesungsnachschriften," *Hegel-Studien* 20 (1985): 23.

16. Indeed, the Heidelberg *Encyclopedia Logic* ends with §191, which has its parallel in the 1830 edition in §244; but if the 1st edition of the *Philosophy of Nature* consequently begins with §192, in the final version the corresponding paragraph is §247, and not §245.

17. I wish to thank Prof. Manfred Baum for his revision of the translation here suggested. For a different interpretation of the relation between Notional determination and empirical phenomena in §246 (Remark and Addition), see M. Drees, "The Logic of Hegel's Philosophy of Nature," in *Hegel and Newtonianism*, edited by M.J. Petry (Dordrecht: Kluwer, 1993), pp. 97 ff.

18. See J.-M. Lardic, "La Contingence chez Hegel," in *Hegel: Comment le sens commun comprend la philosophie*, translation, presentation, and with an essay by J.-M. Lardic (Vendôme: ed. Actes Sud, 1989), pp. 65-6.

19. Lardic ("La Contingence," p. 68) quotes two unmistakable passages by Schelling from the *Erster Entwurf* (*Schellings Werke*, edited by M. Schröter, 6 Vols and 6 Supplementary Vols [C.H. Beck: Munich, 1958], **2**: 20) and from the *Zeitschrift für spekulative Physik* 2, 1: 134.

20. See Lardic, "La Contingence," p. 69.

21. J. Burbidge, *On Hegel's Logic. Fragments of a Commentary* (Atlantic Highlands, NJ: Humanities Press, 1981), p. 56. See also his *Hegel on Logic and Religion* (Albany: SUNY Press, 1992), Chap. 3, "Transition or Reflection," pp. 19-27.

22. See C. Ferrini, "On the Relation Between 'Mode' and 'Measure' in Hegel's *Science of Logic*: Some Introductory Remarks," *The Owl of Minerva* 20, 1 (Fall 1988): 41-4.

23. See C. Ferrini, "Logica e filosofia della natura nella Dottrina dell'Essere hegeliana (I)," *Rivista di storia della filosofia* (1991): 724-8.

24. Hegel, *Wissenschaft der Logik. Erster Teil: Die Objektive Logik, Erster Band: Die Lehre vom Sein (1832)*, edited by F. Hogemann and W. Jaeschke, *Gesammelte Werke*, Vol. 21 (Hamburg: Felix Meiner, 1985), pp. 380 (l. 25)-381 (l. 2). (Hereafter *Logik* [*GW*, **21**].) For the English translation, see: *Hegel's Science of Logic*, translated by A.V. Miller (Atlantic Highlands, NJ: Humanities Press International,1989), pp. 382-3 (hereafter Miller, *Logic*).

25. For a comparison of the two meanings attached to "transition" in the 1st and the 2nd version of the origin of the category of Measure, see Ferrini, "Logica e filosofia della natura (I)," pp. 717-18. By seeing "the movement of becoming and passing over that remains within itself" in the "double" transition of Quality and Quantity which gives rise to Measure—that is, by seeing that the 1832 version anticipates the modes of reflection within the immediacy of being—my interpretation differs from Burbidge's (see his *Hegel on Logic and Religion*, p. 21 and pp. 22-3).

26. See G. Jarczyk, *Système et liberté dans la logique de Hegel* (Paris: Aubier Montaigne, 1980), p. 113 and p. 281; J. Biard et al., *Introduction à la lecture de la Science de la logique de Hegel*, Vol. 1, *L'Etre* (Paris: Aubier Montaigne, 1981), p. 21. In my view, this assessment gives a faithful account of the 1812 Doctrine of Being only.

27. This alternative reading is set forth, with different arguments, both in Ferrini, "Logica e Filosofia della Natura" (I) and (II), and in C. Ferrini, "La funzione del sillogismo nel sistema enciclopedico di Hegel," *Paradigmi* 34 (1994): 69-75.

28. Cf. *De orbitis*, p. 5 (ll. 6-22); Adler, p. 281.

29. This is to respond to a challenge by Prof. Verra, to whom I owe a debt of gratitude for having drawn my attention to this problem. For a different perspective see V. Hösle's account of the matter in his *Hegels System*, 2 Vols (Hamburg: Felix Meiner, 1987), **2**: "Philosophie der Natur und des Geistes"; cf. Chap. 5.1: "Zu Hegels Raum-Zeit-Lehre" and 5.1.1: "Der Ort der Mathematik in Hegels System," pp. 288-97. In his approach to Hegel's treatment of space, time and motion, Hösle follows D. Wandschneider's well-known interpretation of Hegel's most remarkable statements as a genuine

anticipation of certain crucial aspects of contemporary physics (see Hösle, *Hegels System*, pp. 285-7). The most recent challenge to this view is to be found in H.-H. von Borzeszkowski, "Hegel's Interpretation of Classical Mechanics," in *Hegel and Newtonianism*, pp. 62-73.

30. In this respect it is worth quoting the text of §28 of Hegel's Philosophical Encyclopedia, edited by U. Rameil: "Applied mathematics is not at all an immanent science, rather it is only the application of pure mathematics to the relations of magnitude which are existing in nature and which are gathered from experience" (*Die angewandte Mathematik ist keine immanente Wissenschaft, sondern nur die Anwendung der reinen Mathematik auf die Größenverhältnisse, die in der Natur vorhanden und aus der Erfahrung aufgenommen werden*), "Hegels 'Philosophische Enzyklopädie' in Nürnberg," p. 32, my translation.

31. I refer to the following edition of the 1812 German text: Hegel, *Wissenschaft der Logik. Erster Band: Die Objective Logik (1812/1813)*, edited by F. Hogemann and W. Jaeschke, *Gesammelte Werke*, Vol. 11 (Hamburg: Felix Meiner, 1978). (Hereafter *Logik* [*GW*, **11**].) "Verhältnis" can mean both "relationship" and "ratio." Given the context (the measure of a physical law), I prefer the latter rendering. English readers may find a comment on this terminological issue in the Introduction by H.S. Harris and T.F. Geraets to *The Encyclopaedia Logic*, p. xix.

32. The passage under consideration appears as such both in *Logik* (*GW*, **11**), p. 201 (ll. 7-11), and in *Logik* (*GW*, **21**), p. 340 (ll. 14-18); Miller, *Logic*, p. 343.

33. *Logik* (*GW*, **11**), pp. 201 (l. 35)-202 (l. 1) and p. 202 (ll. 3-8). The English translation is mine.

34. Cf. *Logik* (*GW*, **11**), p. 202 (ll. 9-13).

35. Cf. J. Biard et al., *Introduction*, pp. 249-52; see also Hegel, *Science de la logique*, I, *L'Etre*, Édition de 1812, edited by P.J. Labarrière and G. Jarczyk (Paris: Aubier Montaigne, 1972) pp. 311-12, notes 88, 90, 91.

36. *Logik* (*GW*, **21**), p. 342 (ll. 3-9 and 14-16). The English rendering is a revision of Miller's translation (see Miller, *Logic*, pp. 344-5).

37. I refer to F. Weinert, "Laws of Nature. A Structural Approach," *Philosophia naturalis* 2 (1993): 147-71. For another conclusion

regarding what kind of knowledge can be provided by Hegel's appraisal of the relation between logic and contingency, see Drees (who refers only to the *Encyclopedia*), "The Logic of Hegel's Philosophy of Nature," pp. 99-100. It goes without saying that philosophers of science could find much of interest in Hegel's positions, provided they take into account that he seems not to be aware that a scientific law such as Kepler's third law (on which, see Weinert, p. 150 and p. 159) only has approximate validity within the framework of Newtonian mechanics itself. Cf. on this point M. Nasti De Vincentis, "Newton contra Keplerum apud Hegel: contradiction ou incommensurabilité?" in *Atti del Congresso "Nuovi problemi della logica e della filosofia della scienza"* (Viareggio, 8-13 Gennaio 1990), edited by D. Costantini and M.C. Galvotti (Bologna: CLUEB, 1991), **1**: 262-3.

38. See Hegel, *La théorie de la mesure*, translation and commentary by A. Doz (Paris: PUF, 1970), pp. 141-2: "Hegel semble considérer ... que les physiciens, en attribuant le coefficient à la pesanteur, oublient qu'il n'a de sens qu'à l'intérieur de la formule et dissocient la pesanteur elle-même de son extériorisation, c'est-à-dire du rapport concret de l'espace et du temps" (p. 142). For placing this aspect into the more general perspective of the relation between the necessary, universal truths of reason and the accidental, the singular in Hegel's system, see Burbidge, *Hegel on Logic and Religion*, p. 4: "reason can overreach its opposite and discover there a necessity inherent in the contingency, an infinite network of relations that sets the context for the finite, explanatory disjunctions that situate singulars. ... The achievement of pure thought, then, is appropriately two-sided. Thought has become self-consciously partial; on its own it can know nothing about external contingencies. ... To do justice to them it must take account of how they are different and unique. Nevertheless, it has tools for thinking about the ways they are different and for discovering how those differences are themselves related as components of identities, how singulars are integrated into generals and how some contingencies relatively condition others."

39. *De orbitis*, p. 31 (ll. 21-2): "Verum mensura et numerus naturae a ratione alieni esse nequeunt." The Latin word "ratio" has the double meaning of "reason" and (quantitative) "ratio."

40. Since we know from Bonsiepen that the change in the ground of space and time, from mathematics to mechanics, occurs soon after the Heidelberg *Encyclopedia* was issued (a change that in

our reading indicates the use of a more complex notion of "transition"), it is worth considering Neuser's quotation of a manuscript note taken by G. Bernhardy from Hegel's 1819/20 lectures on the philosophy of nature, concerning the series of the planets: "the number is an immediate, merely qualitative [sic, but likely a misprint for quantitative] determination, the progression [that one can recognize in the series] is entirely formal, but a merely formal advance is not what is natural" (*die Zahl ist eine unmittelbare, bloss qualitative Bestimmung, die Progression ist ganz formal, ein bloss formeller Fortgang aber ist nicht das Natürliche*).

What is more, besides the reference to, and the evaluation of, Schelling's analogy between planets and metals and Kepler's *Harmonice Mundi* (i.e. Kepler's attempt is said to be "unsuccessful," but not his idea, which "is to be developed further"), mention of the *Dissertation* is also retained, albeit in descriptive, neutral terms (Neuser, p. 49).

41. The first draft of this paper was prepared under the careful supervision of Prof. Dr. A. Graeser (University of Bern), during the 1993-94 renewal of my exchange grant there. The final version has been discussed in detail with Prof. Dr. M. Baum (University of Wuppertal), my mentor for a 1994-95 Alexander von Humboldt-Stiftung research fellowship. Finally, I wish to thank: all those who, like Brigitte Falkenburg, participated in the discussion making every effort to make me thoughtful; H.S. Harris and J. Burbidge for their presence of mind; J. Burbidge and S. Houlgate for their kind and patient attempt at making sense of my English.

Bibliography

The bibliography includes all works referred to in this collection.

Works by Hegel

Gesammelte Werke, Rheinisch-Westfälische Akademie der Wissenschaften & Hegel-Archiv der Ruhr-Universität Bochum (Hamburg: Felix Meiner, 1968–).

Sämtliche Werke. Jubiläumsausgabe, edited by H. Glockner (Stuttgart: Frommann-Holzboog, 1968).

Werke in zwanzig Bänden, edited by E. Moldenhauer and K.M. Michel (Frankfurt am Main: Suhrkamp Verlag, 1969–).

Der junge Hegel in Stuttgart. Aufsätze und Tagebuchaufzeichnungen 1785-1788, edited by F. Nicolin (Stuttgart / Marbach am Neckar: Deutsches Literaturarchiv, 1970).

Frühe Schriften, edited by E. Moldenhauer and K.M. Michel, *Werke in zwanzig Bänden*, Vol. 1 (Frankfurt am Main: Suhrkamp Verlag, 1971).

Hegels Theologische Jugendschriften. Nach den Handschriften der Königlichen Bibliothek in Berlin, edited by H. Nohl (Tübingen: J.C.B. Mohr, 1907).

The Earliest System Program of German Idealism, translated by H.S. Harris in H.S. Harris, *Hegel's Development. Toward the Sunlight, 1770-1801* (Oxford: Clarendon Press, 1972).

Über Mythologie, Volksgeist und Kunst, translated by D.P. Verene in D.P. Verene, *Hegel's Recollection: A Study of*

Images in the Phenomenology of Spirit (Albany: SUNY Press, 1985).

Dissertatio philosophica de orbitis planetarum (Jena: Prager, 1801).

Dissertatio philosophica de orbitis planetarum in C. Ferrini, *Guida al "De orbitis planetarum" di Hegel ed alle sue edizioni e traduzioni*, in coll. con M. Nasti De Vincentis (Bern: Haupt, 1995).

Dissertatio philosophica de orbitis planetarum. Philosophische Erörterung über die Planetenbahnen, translation, with introduction and commentary by W. Neuser (Weinheim: Acta Humanoria VCH, 1986).

"Hegel, *Philosophical Dissertation on the Orbits of the Planets* (1801). Preceded by the 12 Theses Defended on August 27, 1801," edited and translated by P. Adler, *Graduate Faculty Philosophy Journal* 12, 1-2 (1987): 269-309.

Les orbites des planètes, translation and notes by François De Gandt (Paris: Vrin, 1979).

Le orbite dei pianeti, edited and translated by A. Negri (Bari: Laterza, 1984).

Jenaer Kritische Schriften, edited by H. Buchner and O. Pöggeler, *Gesammelte Werke*, Vol. 4 (Hamburg: Felix Meiner, 1968).

The Difference Between Fichte's and Schelling's System of Philosophy, translated by H.S. Harris and W. Cerf (Albany: SUNY Press, 1977).

Faith and Knowledge, translated by H.S. Harris and W. Cerf (Albany: SUNY Press, 1977).

Hegel: Comment le sens commun comprend la philosophie, translation, presentation, and with an essay by J.-M. Lardic (Vendôme: ed. Actes Sud, 1989).

Hegel: "Introductio in philosophiam." Dagli studi ginnasiali alla prima logica, edited by R. Pozzo (Firenze: La Nuova Italia, 1989).

Schellings und Hegels erste absolute Metaphysik. Zusammenfassende Vorlesungsnachschriften von I.P.V. Troxler, herausgegeben, eingeleitet und mit Interpretationen versehen von K. Düsing (Köln: Dinter, 1988).

Schriften und Entwürfe, 1799-1808, edited by M. Baum and K.R. Meist, with assistance from T. Ebert, *Gesammelte Werke*, Vol. 5 (Hamburg: Felix Meiner [in preparation]).

Jenaer Systementwürfe I, edited by K. Düsing and H. Kimmerle, *Gesammelte Werke*, Vol. 6 (Hamburg: Felix Meiner, 1975).

Jenaer Systementwürfe II, edited by R.-P. Horstmann and J.H. Trede, *Gesammelte Werke*, Vol. 7 (Hamburg: Felix Meiner, 1971).

Jenaer Systementwürfe II. Logik, Metaphysik, Naturphilosophie, edited by R.-P. Horstmann (Hamburg: Felix Meiner, 1982) [based on *Gesammelte Werke*, Vol. 7].

Notes et fragments. Iena 1803-1806, German text, translation and commentary by C. Colliot-Thélène et al. (Paris: Aubier, 1991).

Phänomenologie des Geistes, edited by J. Hoffmeister (Hamburg: Felix Meiner, 1952).

Phänomenologie des Geistes, edited by E. Moldenhauer and K. Michel, *Werke in zwanzig Bänden*, Vol. 3 (Frankfurt am Main: Suhrkamp Verlag, 1970).

Phänomenologie des Geistes, edited by W. Bonsiepen and R. Heede, *Gesammelte Werke*, Vol. 9 (Hamburg: Felix Meiner, 1980).

Hegel's Phenomenology of Spirit, translated by A.V. Miller (Oxford: Oxford University Press, 1977).

Wissenschaft der Logik I. Erster Teil: Die Objektive Logik, Erstes Buch, edited by E. Moldenhauer and K.M. Michel, *Werke in zwanzig Bänden*, Vol. 5 (Frankfurt am Main: Suhrkamp Verlag, 1970).

Wissenschaft der Logik II. Erster Teil: Die Objektive Logik, Zweites Buch. Zweiter Teil: Die Subjektive Logik, edited by E. Moldenhauer and K.M. Michel, *Werke in zwanzig Bänden*, Vol. 6 (Frankfurt am Main: Suhrkamp Verlag, 1970).

Wissenschaft der Logik, edited by G. Lasson, 2 Vols (Hamburg: Felix Meiner, 1971).

Wissenschaft der Logik. Erster Band: Die Objektive Logik (1812/1813), edited by F. Hogemann and W. Jaeschke, *Gesammelte Werke*, Vol. 11 (Hamburg: Felix Meiner, 1978).

Wissenschaft der Logik. Zweiter Band: Die Subjektive Logik (1816), edited by F. Hogemann and W. Jaeschke, *Gesammelte Werke*, Vol. 12 (Hamburg: Felix Meiner, 1981).

Wissenschaft der Logik. Erster Teil: Die Objektive Logik, Erster Band: Die Lehre vom Sein (1832), edited by F. Hogemann and W. Jaeschke, *Gesammelte Werke*, Vol. 21 (Hamburg: Felix Meiner, 1985).

Hegel's Science of Logic, translated by A.V. Miller (Atlantic Highlands, NJ: Humanities Press International, 1989).

La théorie de la mesure, translation and commentary by A. Doz (Paris: PUF, 1970).

Science de la logique, I, *L'Etre*, Édition de 1812, edited by P.J. Labarrière and G. Jarczyk (Paris: Aubier Montaigne, 1972).

Vorlesungen über Logik und Metaphysik. Heidelberg 1817, transcribed by F.A. Good, edited by K. Gloy (Hamburg: Felix Meiner, 1992).

"Hegels 'Philosophische Enzyklopädie' in Nürnberg. - Mit einer Nachschrift von 1812/13, herausgegeben von Udo Rameil," *Hegel-Studien* 30 (1995): 9-38.

Enzyklopädie der philosophischen Wissenschaften im Grundrisse und andere Schriften aus der Heidelberger Zeit, edited by H. Glockner, *Sämtliche Werke. Jubiläumsausgabe*, Vol. 6 (Stuttgart: Frommann-Holzboog, 1968).

Enzyklopädie der philosophischen Wissenschaften im Grundrisse (1827), edited by W. Bonsiepen and H.-C. Lucas, *Gesammelte Werke*, Vol. 19 (Hamburg: Felix Meiner, 1989).

Enzyklopädie der philosophischen Wissenschaften im Grundrisse (1830), edited by F. Nicolin and O. Pöggeler (1959; Hamburg: Felix Meiner, 1969).

Enzyklopädie der philosophischen Wissenschaften im Grundrisse (1830), edited by W. Bonsiepen and H.-C. Lucas, in co-operation with U. Rameil, *Gesammelte Werke*, Vol. 20 (Hamburg: Felix Meiner, 1992).

Enzyklopädie der philosophischen Wissenschaften im Grundrisse (1830). Erster Teil: Die Wissenschaft der Logik mit den mündlichen Zusätzen, edited by E. Moldenhauer and K.M. Michel, *Werke in zwanzig Bänden*, Vol. 8 (Frankfurt am Main: Suhrkamp Verlag, 1970).

Hegel's Logic: Being Part One of the Encyclopaedia of the Philosophical Sciences (1830), translated by William Wallace (Oxford: Clarendon Press, 1975).

The Encyclopaedia Logic (with the Zusätze), translated by T.F. Geraets, W.A. Suchting and H.S. Harris (Indianapolis: Hackett, 1991).

La scienza della logica, a cura di V. Verra (Parte prima della *Enciclopedia*, con le *Aggiunte*) (Torino: UTET, 1981).

Enzyklopädie der philosophischen Wissenschaften im Grundrisse (1830). Zweiter Teil: Die Naturphilosophie mit den mündlichen Zusätzen, edited by E. Moldenhauer and K.M. Michel, *Werke in zwanzig Bänden*, Vol. 9 (Frankfurt am Main: Suhrkamp Verlag, 1970).

Hegel's Philosophy of Nature: Being Part Two of the Encyclopaedia of the Philosophical Sciences (1830), translated by A.V. Miller (Oxford: Clarendon Press, 1970).

Philosophy of Nature, edited and translated by M.J. Petry, 3 Vols (London: George Allen and Unwin, 1970).

Die Vorlesung von 1819/20, edited by M. Gies with the cooperation of K.-H. Ilting, *Naturphilosophie*, Vol. 1 (Napoli: Istituto Italiano per gli Studi Filosofici, 1982).

Philosophie der Natur, K.G.J. Griesheims Nachschrift; Vorlesung des Wintersemesters 1823/24 (Staatsbibliothek Preußischer Kulturbesitz, Berlin. Ms. Germ. 4°).

Enzyklopädie der philosophischen Wissenschaften im Grundrisse (1830). Dritter Teil: Die Philosophie des Geistes mit den mündlichen Zusätzen, edited by E. Moldenhauer and K. Michel, *Werke in zwanzig Bänden*, Vol. 10 (Frankfurt am Main: Suhrkamp Verlag, 1969).

Hegel's Philosophy of Mind: Being Part Three of the Encyclopaedia of the Philosophical Sciences (1830), translated by William Wallace and A.V. Miller (Oxford: Clarendon Press, 1971).

Elements of the Philosophy of Right, translated by H.B. Nisbet, edited by A. Wood (Cambridge: Cambridge University Press, 1991).

Vorlesungen über die Geschichte der Philosophie, edited by E. Moldenhauer and K.M. Michel, *Werke in zwanzig Bänden*, Vols. 18, 19, 20 (Frankfurt am Main: Suhrkamp Verlag, 1971).

Lectures on the History of Philosophy, translated by E.S. Haldane and Frances H. Simson, 3 Vols (London: Routledge & Kegan Paul, 1955).

Lectures on the History of Philosophy, translated by R.F. Brown, 3 Vols (Berkeley: University of California Press, 1990).

Briefe von und an Hegel, edited by J. Hoffmeister, 4 Vols (Hamburg: Felix Meiner, 1952-60).

Dokumente zu Hegels Entwicklung, edited by J. Hoffmeister (Stuttgart: Frommann-Holzboog, 1974).

Works by Kant

Kants Gesammelte Schriften (Königlich Preußische [now Deutsche] Akademie der Wissenschaften, Berlin: G. Reimer [now De Gruyter], 1902–).

Kritik der reinen Vernunft, *Kants Gesammelte Schriften*, Vols. 3, 4 (Königlich Preußische [now Deutsche] Akademie der Wissenschaften, Berlin: G. Reimer [now De Gruyter], 1902–).

Critique of Pure Reason, translated by Norman Kemp Smith (New York: St. Martin's Press, 1965).

Prolegomena zu einer jeden künftigen Metaphysik, die als Wissenschaft wird auftreten können, *Kants Gesammelte Schriften*, Vol. 4 (Königlich Preußische [now Deutsche]

Akademie der Wissenschaften, Berlin: G. Reimer [now De Gruyter], 1902–).

Metaphysische Anfangsgründe der Naturwissenschaft, *Kants Gesammelte Schriften*, Vol. 4 (Königlich Preußische [now Deutsche] Akademie der Wissenschaften, Berlin: G. Reimer [now De Gruyter], 1902–).

Metaphysical Foundations of Natural Science, translated by James W. Ellington (1970), in Immanuel Kant, *Philosophy of Material Nature* (Indianapolis: Hackett, 1985).

Kritik der Urteilskraft, *Kants Gesammelte Schriften*, Vol. 5 (Königlich Preußische [now Deutsche] Akademie der Wissenschaften, Berlin: G. Reimer [now De Gruyter], 1902–).

Logik, *Kants Gesammelte Schriften*, Vol. 9 (Königlich Preußische [now Deutsche] Akademie der Wissenschaften, Berlin: G. Reimer [now De Gruyter], 1902–).

Reflexionen, *Kants Gesammelte Schriften*, Vol. 18 (Königlich Preußische [now Deutsche] Akademie der Wissenschaften, Berlin: G. Reimer [now De Gruyter], 1902–).

Welches sind die wirklichen Fortschritte, die die Metaphysik seit Leibnizens und Wolffs Zeiten in Deutschland gemacht hat?, *Kants Gesammelte Schriften*, Vol. 20 (Königlich Preußische [now Deutsche] Akademie der Wissenschaften, Berlin: G. Reimer [now De Gruyter], 1902–).

Opus postumum, *Kants Gesammelte Schriften*, Vol. 22 (Königlich Preußische [now Deutsche] Akademie der Wissenschaften, Berlin: G. Reimer [now De Gruyter], 1902–).

Opus postumum, translated by E. Förster and M. Rosen (Cambridge: Cambridge University Press, 1993).

Other Works

Achinstein, P. and Snyder, L.J., eds. *Scientific Methods: Conceptual and Historical Problems* (Malabar, Florida: Krieger Publishing Company, 1994).

Alexander, H.G., ed. *The Leibniz-Clarke Correspondence: With Extracts from Newton's PRINCIPIA and OPTICKS*, (Manchester: Manchester University Press, 1970).

Allen, R.H. *Star Names: Their Lore and Meaning* (1898; reprint, New York: Dover, 1963).

Ameriks, K. "Hegel's Critique of Kant's Theoretical Philosophy," *Philosophy and Phenomenological Research* 46, 1 (1985): 1-35.

Ameriks, K. "Recent Work on Hegel: The Rehabilitation of an Epistemologist," *Philosophy and Phenomenological Research* 52, 1 (March 1992): 177-202.

Aristotle, *The Complete Works of Aristotle*, edited by J. Barnes, 2 Vols (Princeton: Princeton University Press, 1984).

Aristotle's Metaphysics , translated by W.D. Ross (Clarendon Press: Oxford, 1924).

Augustine, Saint. *Confessions*, translated by R.S. Pine-Coffin (Harmondsworth: Penguin Books, 1979).

Ayala, F.J. "Biology as an Autonomous Science," *American Scientist* 56 (1968): 207-21.

Barrow, J.D. and Tipler, F.J. *The Anthropic Cosmological Principle* (Oxford: Oxford University Press, 1986).

Barrow, J.D. *The World Within the World* (Oxford: Oxford University Press, 1988).

Bates, M. *The Forest and the Sea* (1963; reprint, New York: Viking Press, 1965).

Baum, M. “Kosmologie und Dialektik bei Platon und Hegel,” in *Hegel und die antike Dialektik*, edited by M. Riedel (Frankfurt am Main: Suhrkamp Verlag, 1990).

Beaumont, B. “Hegel and the Seven Planets,” *Mind* 62 (1954): 246-48.

Beiser, F.C. ed. *The Cambridge Companion to Hegel* (Cambridge: Cambridge University Press, 1993).

Biard, J. et al., *Introduction à la lecture de la Science de la logique de Hegel*, Vol. 1, *L'Etre* (Paris: Aubier Montaigne, 1981).

Blumenbach, J.F. *Über den Bildungstrieb* (Göttingen: Johann Christian Dieterich, 1781, 1789).

Boltzmann, L. *Populäre Schriften* (1905; reprint, Braunschweig: Vieweg, 1979).

Bonola, R. *Non-Euclidean Geometry*, translated by H. S. Carslaw (New York: Dover Publications, 1955).

Bonsiepen, W. “Hegels Raum-Zeit-Lehre. Dargestellt anhand zweier Vorlesungsnachschriften,” *Hegel-Studien* 20 (1985): 9-78.

Bonsiepen, W. “Hegels Kritische Auseinandersetzung mit der Zeitgenössischen Evolutionstheorie,” in *Hegels Philosophie der Natur: Beziehungen zwischen empirischer und spekulativer Naturerkenntnis*, edited by R.-P. Horstmann and M. J. Petry (Stuttgart: Klett-Cotta, 1986).

Bonsiepen, W. “Hegels Vorlesungen über Naturphilosophie,” *Hegel-Studien*, 26 (1991): 40-54.

Born, M. *Einstein's Theory of Relativity* (New York: Dover Publications, 1965).

Borzeszkowski, H.-H. von “Hegel's Interpretation of Classical Mechanics,” in *Hegel and Newtonianism*, edited by M.J. Petry (Dordrecht: Kluwer, 1993).

Brann, E.T. *The World of The Imagination* (Savage, Maryland: Rowman and Littlefield, 1991).

Breidbach, O. "Hegels Evolutionskritik," *Hegel-Studien* 22 (1987): 165-72.

Brecht, B. *Flüchtlingsgespräche* (Berlin and Frankfurt: Suhrkamp, 1961).

Bronowski, J. *The Ascent of Man* (London: BBC, 1973).

Browning, G., ed. *Hegel's Phenomenology: A Reappraisal* (Dordrecht: Kluwer, 1997).

Brunet, P. *L'introduction des théories de Newton en France au XVIIIe siècle – Avant 1738* (Geneva: Slatkine Reprints, 1970).

Brush, S.G. "Ludwig Boltzmann and the Foundations of Natural Science," in *Principien der Naturfilosofi. Lectures on Natural Philosophy 1903-1906*, edited by I.M. Fasol-Boltzmann (Berlin: Springer Verlag, 1990).

Buchdahl, G. "Conceptual Analysis and Scientific Theory in Hegel's Philosophy of Nature," in *Hegel and the Sciences*, edited by R.S. Cohen and M.W. Wartofsky (Dordrecht: Reidel 1984).

Buchdahl , G. "Hegel's Philosophy of Nature and the Structure of Science," in *Hegel*, edited by M. Inwood (Oxford: Oxford University Press, 1985).

Buchdahl, G. *Kant and the Dynamics of Reason* (Oxford: Blackwell, 1992).

Bucher, Th.G. "Wissenschaftstheoretische Überlegungen zu Hegels Planetenschrift," *Hegel-Studien* 18 (1983): 65-137.

Burbidge, J. *On Hegel's Logic. Fragments of a Commentary* (Atlantic Highlands, NJ: Humanities Press, 1981).

Burbidge, J. *Hegel on Logic and Religion* (Albany: SUNY Press, 1992).

Butler, C., trans. "The First *Encyclopedia* Article on Hegel (1824, 1827)," *Clio* 13, 4 (1984): 371-2.

Butts, R., ed. *Kant's Philosophy of Physical Science* (Dordrecht: Reidel, 1986).

Cairns, J., Overbaugh, J. and Miller, S. "The origin of mutants," *Nature* 335 (September 8, 1988): 142-5.

Carnap, R. *Philosophical Foundations of Physics: An Introduction to the Philosophy of Science* (New York: Basic Books, 1966).

Cartwright, N. *How The Laws of Physics Lie* (Oxford: Oxford University Press, 1983).

Castel, L.-B. *Traité de physique sur la pesanteur universelle des corps* (Paris: Cailleau, 1724).

Closs, O. *Das Problem der Gravitation in Schellings und Hegels Jenaer Zeit* (Heidelberg: Carl Winter's Universitätsbuchhandlung, 1908).

Cohen, R.S. and Wartofsky, M.W., eds. *Hegel and the Sciences* (Dordrecht: Reidel 1984).

Collingwood, R.G. *The Idea of Nature* (London: Oxford University Press, 1945).

Coolidge, J.L. *A History of Geometrical Method* (New York: Dover, 1963).

Costantini, D. and Galavotti, M.C., eds. *Atti del Congresso "Nuovi problemi della logica e della filosofia della scienza"* (Bologna: CLUEB, 1991).

Coxeter, H.S.M. *Non-Euclidean Geometry* (Toronto: University of Toronto Press, 1978).

Cramer, K. *Nicht-reine synthetische Urteile a priori* (Heidelberg: Carl Winter, 1985).

Dahlstrom, D.O. "Kant's Metaphysics of Nature," in *Nature and Scientific Method*, edited by Daniel O. Dahlstrom (Washington, D.C.: Catholic University of America Press, 1991).

Dahlstrom, D.O., ed. *Nature and Scientific Method* (Washington, D.C.: Catholic University of America Press, 1991).

Dampier, W. *A History of Science* (Cambridge: Cambridge University Press; New York: Macmillan, 1946).

De Gandt, Fr. "Introduction" and "La formule de Bode et la découverte des astéroïdes," in G.W.F. Hegel, *Les orbites des planètes. (Dissertation de 1801)*. Traduction et notes par Fr. De Gandt. Préface de D. Dubarle (Paris: Vrin, 1979).

Descartes, R. *The Philosophical Writings of Descartes*, translated by J. Cottingham, R. Stoothoff, and D. Murdoch, 2 Vols (New York: Cambridge University Press, 1985).

Di Giovanni, G., ed. *Essays on Hegel's Logic* (Albany: SUNY Press, 1990).

Drees, M. "The Logic of Hegel's Philosophy of Nature," in *Hegel and Newtonianism*, edited by M.J. Petry (Dordrecht: Kluwer, 1993).

Duhem, P. *To Save the Phenomena* (Chicago: University of Chicago Press, 1969).

Düsing, K. *Die Teleologie in Kants Weltbegriff*, 2nd ed. (Bonn: Grundmann, 1986).

Düsing, K. "Naturteleologie und Metaphysik bei Kant und Hegel," in *Hegel und die 'Kritik der Urteilskraft'*, edited by H.-F. Fulda and R.-P. Horstmann (Stuttgart: Klett-Cotta, 1990).

Edwards, B.J. "Der Ätherbeweis des *Opus Postumum* und Kants 3. Analogie der Erfahrung," in *Übergang. Untersuchungen zum Spätwerk Immanuel Kants*, edited by the Forum für Philosophie Bad Homburg (Frankfurt am Main: Vittorio Klostermann, 1991).

Elkana, Y., ed. *The Interaction Between Science and Philosophy* (Atlantic Highlands, N.J: Humanities Press, 1974).

Elsbach, A.C. *Kant und Einstein: Untersuchungen über das Verhältnis der modernen Erkenntnistheorie zur Relativitätstheorie* (Berlin: de Gruyter, 1924).

Falkenburg,B. *Die Form der Materie* (Frankfurt am Main: Athenäum, 1987).

Falkenburg, B. "Hegel on Mechanistic Models of Light," in *Hegel and Newtonianism*, edited by M.J. Petry (Dordrecht: Kluwer, 1993).

Fasol-Boltzmann, I.M., ed. *Principien der Naturfilosofi. Lectures on Natural Philosophy 1903-1906* (Berlin: Springer Verlag, 1990).

Ferrini, C. "On the Relation Between 'Mode' and 'Measure' in Hegel's *Science of Logic*: Some Introductory Remarks," *The Owl of Minerva* 20, 1 (Fall 1988): 21-49.

Ferrini, C. "Features of Irony and Alleged Errors in Hegel's *De orbitis planetarum*," *Hegel-Jahrbuch* (1991): 459-77.

Ferrini, C. "Logica e filosofia della natura nella Dottrina dell'Essere hegeliana (I)," *Rivista di storia della filosofia* 4 (1991): 701-33.

Ferrini, C. "Logica e filosofia della natura nella Dottrina dell'Essere hegeliana (II)," *Rivista di storia della filosofia* 1 (1992): 103-24.

Ferrini, C. "Nuove fonti per la filosofia della natura del primo Hegel," in *Rivista di storia della filosofia* 4 (1993): 717-60.

Ferrini, C. "La funzione del sillogismo nel sistema enciclopedico di Hegel," *Paradigmi* 34 (1994): 53-75.

Ferrini, C. "On Newton's Demonstration of Kepler's Second Law in Hegel's *De orbitis planetarum* (1801)," *Philosophia naturalis* 31, 1 (1994): 150-70.

Ferrini, C. *Guida al "De orbitis planetarum" di Hegel ed alle sue edizioni e traduzioni*, in coll. con M. Nasti De Vincentis (Bern: Haupt, 1995).

Ferrini, C. *Scienze empiriche e filosofie della natura nel primo idealismo tedesco* (Milano: Guerini e Associati, 1996).

Ferrini, C. "Tra etica e filosofia della natura: il significato della *Metafisica* aristotelica per il problema delle grandezze del sistema solare nel primo Hegel," in *Hegel e Aristotele*, Atti del Convegno di Cagliari (11-15 Aprile 1994), edited by G. Movia (Cagliari: Edizioni AV, 1997), pp. 173-91.

Findlay, J.N. *Hegel: A Re-examination* (London: G. Allen and Unwin, 1958).

Fischer, K. *Geschichte der neueren Philosophie*, Vol. 8, *Hegels Leben, Werke und Lehre, 1* (Heidelberg: Carl Winter's Universitätsbuchhandlung, 1901).

Förster, E. "Is There 'A Gap' in Kant's Critical System?" *Journal of the History of Philosophy* 25, 4 (1987): 536-55.

Förster, E. "Kant's *Selbstsetzungslehre*," in *Kant's Transcendental Deductions*, edited by E. Förster (Stanford: Stanford University Press, 1989).

Förster, E., ed. *Kant's Transcendental Deductions* (Stanford: Stanford University Press, 1989).

Förster, E. "Kant's Notion of Philosophy," *The Monist* 72, 2 (1989): 285-304.

Förster, E. "Die Idee des Überganges. Überlegungen zum Elementarsystem der bewegenden Kräfte," in *Übergang. Untersuchungen zum Spätwerk Immanuel Kants*, edited by the Forum für Philosophie Bad Homburg (Frankfurt am Main: Vittorio Klostermann, 1991).

Förster, E. "Kant's Third Critique and the *Opus Postumum*," *Graduate Faculty Philosophy Journal* 16, 2 (1993): 345-58.

Forum für Philosophie Bad Homburg, ed. *Übergang. Untersuchungen zum Spätwerk Immanuel Kants* (Frankfurt am Main: Vittorio Klostermann, 1991).

Foster, M. "The Christian Doctrine of Creation and the Rise of Modern Science," *Mind* (1934): 446-68.

Friedman, M. "Explanation and Scientific Understanding," *Journal of Philosophy* 71 (1974): 5-19.

Friedman, M. *Kant and the Exact Sciences* (Cambridge, MA: Harvard University Press, 1992).

Fulda, H.-F. and Horstmann, R.-P., eds. *Hegel und die 'Kritik der Urteilskraft'* (Stuttgart: Klett-Cotta, 1990).

Funke, G., ed. *Akten des 7. internationalen Kant-Kongresses*, 2 Vols (Bonn: Bouvier, 1991).

Goodstein, D.L. and Goodstein, J.R. *Feynman's Lost Lecture: The Motion of Planets Around the Sun* (New York and London: W.W. Norton and Company, 1996).

Guyer, P. *Kant and the Claims of Knowledge* (Cambridge: Cambridge University Press, 1987).

Guyer, P. *The Cambridge Companion to Kant* (Cambridge: Cambridge University Press, 1992).

Guyer, P. "Thought and Being: Hegel's Critique of Kant," in *The Cambridge Companion to Hegel*, edited by F.C. Beiser (Cambridge: Cambridge University Press, 1993).

Hacking, I. *Representing and Intervening* (Cambridge: Cambridge University Press, 1983).

Haering, T. *Hegel. Sein Wollen und sein Werk. Eine chronologische Entwicklungsgeschichte der Gedanken und der Sprache Hegels*, 2 Vols (1929; reprint, Aalen: Scientia Verlag, 1963).

Haldane, J.S. *Organism and Environment* (New Haven: Yale University Press, 1917).

Halper, E. "Self-Relation in Hegel's *Science of Logic*," *Philosophy Research Archives* 7 (1981): 89-133.

Halper, E. "Hegel and the Problem of the Differentia," in *Essays on Hegel's Logic*, edited by George di Giovanni (Albany, New York: SUNY Press, 1989).

Hare, P., ed. *Doing Philosophy Historically* (Buffalo: Prometheus, 1988).

Harris, E.E. *Nature, Mind and Modern Science* (London: G. Allen and Unwin, 1954, 1968).

Harris, E.E. *The Foundations of Metaphysics in Science* (London: G. Allen and Unwin, 1965).

Harris, E.E. *The Reality of Time* (Albany: SUNY Press, 1988).

Harris, E.E. *Cosmos and Anthropos* (Atlantic Highlands, NJ: Humanities Press, 1991).

Harris, E.E. *The Spirit of Hegel*, (Atlantic Highlands, NJ: Humanities Press, 1993).

Harris, H.S. *Hegel's Development. Toward the Sunlight, 1770-1801* (Oxford: Clarendon Press, 1972).

Harris, H.S. *Hegel's Development. Night Thoughts (Jena 1801-1806)* (Oxford: Clarendon Press, 1983).

Harris, H.S. Review of *Hegel's Epistemological Realism* by K. Westphal, *Philosophy of the Social Sciences* 22, 4 (1992): 512-34.

Harris, H.S. "Hegel's Correspondence Theory of Truth," in *Hegel's Phenomenology: A Reappraisal*, edited by G. Browning (Dordrecht: Kluwer, 1996).

Harris, H.S. *Hegel's Ladder*, 2 Vols (Indianapolis: Hackett, 1997).

Harrison, E.R. *Cosmology: The Science of the Universe* (Cambridge: Cambridge University Press, 1981).

Hartmann, K. "Hegel: A Non-Metaphysical View," in *Hegel: A Collection of Critical Essays*, edited by Alasdair MacIntyre (New York: Doubleday, 1972).

Henderson, L.J. *The Fitness of the Environment* (New York: Macmillan, 1913).

Hertz, H. *The Principles of Mechanics* (New York: Dover, 1956).

Hinske, N. "Die Wissenschaften und ihre Zwecke: Kants Neuformulierung der Systemidee," in *Akten des 7. internationalen Kant-Kongresses*, edited by G. Funke, 2 Vols (Bonn: Bouvier, 1991), Vol. 1.

Horan, B.L. "Inference to the Unobservable: Newton's Experimental Philosophy," in *Scientific Methods: Conceptual and Historical Problems*, edited by P. Achinstein and L.J. Snyder (Malabar, Florida: Krieger Publishing Company, 1994).

Horstmann, R.-P. and Petry, M.J., eds. *Hegels Philosophie der Natur: Beziehungen zwischen empirischer und spekulativer Naturerkenntnis* (Stuttgart: Klett-Cotta, 1986).

Hösle, V. "Raum, Zeit, Bewegung," in *Hegel und die Naturwissenschaften*, edited by M. J. Petry (Stuttgart: Frommann-Holzboog, 1986).

Hösle, V. *Hegels System*, 2 Vols (Hamburg: Felix Meiner, 1987).

Howard, D. and Stachel, J., eds. *Einstein and the History of General Relativity*, (Boston: Birkhäuser, 1986).

Ihmig, K.-N. *Hegels Deutung der Gravitation* (Frankfurt am Main: Athenäum, 1989).

Ihmig, K.-N. "Hegel's Rejection of the Concept of Force," in *Hegel and Newtonianism*, edited by M.J. Petry (Dordrecht: Kluwer, 1993).

Inwood, M.J. *Hegel* (London: Routledge & Kegan Paul, 1983).

Inwood, M.J., ed. *Hegel* (Oxford: Oxford University Press, 1985).

Jammer, M. *Concepts of Space* (Cambridge: Cambridge University Press, 1970).

Jarczyk, G. *Système et liberté dans la logique de Hegel* (Paris: Aubier Montaigne, 1980).

Kaku, M. *Hyperspace: A Scientific Odyssey through Parallel Universes, Time Warps, and the 10th Dimension* (New York: Oxford University Press, 1994).

Kauffman, S.A. *The Origins of Order: Self-Organization and Selection in Evolution* (Oxford: Oxford University Press, 1993).

Kimmerle, H. "Dokumente zu Hegels Jenaer Dozententätigkeit," *Hegel-Studien* 4 (1967): 21-99.

Kitcher, P. "How Kant Almost Wrote *Two Dogmas of Empiricism* (and Why He Didn't)," in *Essays on Kant's Critique of Pure Reason*, edited by J.N. Mohanty and R. Shahan (Norman: University of Oklahoma Press, 1982).

Kitcher, P. "Projecting the Order of Nature," in *Kant's Philosophy of Physical Science*, edited by R. Butts (Dordrecht: Reidel, 1986).

Kramer, E.E. *The Nature and Growth of Modern Mathematics* (Princeton: Princeton University Press, 1970).

Küppers, B.-O. *Information and the Origin of Life* (Cambridge, Massachusetts: MIT Press, 1990).

La Lande, J.J. de *Bibliographie Astronomique avec l'Histoire de l'Astronomie depuis 1781 jusqu'à 1802* (1803; reprint, Amsterdam: Gieben, 1970).

Landau, A., ed. *Rezensionen zur Kantischen Philosophie 1781-87* (Bebra: Albert Landau Verlag, 1991).

Lardic, J.-M. "La Contingence chez Hegel," in *Hegel: Comment le sens commun comprend la philosophie*, translation, presentation, and with an essay by J.-M. Lardic (Vendôme: ed. Actes Sud, 1989).

Lardic, J.-M. "Hegel et Schelling: Critique du Formalisme et Prise en Charge de la Contingence," *Archives de Philosophie* 57 (1994): 683-91.

Levere, T.H. "Hegel and the Earth Sciences," in *Hegels Philosophie der Natur: Beziehungen zwischen empirischer und spekulativer Naturerkenntnis*, edited by R.-

P. Horstmann and M.J. Petry (Stuttgart: Klett-Cotta, 1986).

Mach, E. *Die Mechanik in ihrer Entwicklung*, 9th edition (1933; reprint, Darmstadt: Wissenschaftliche Buchgesellschaft, 1988)

MacIntyre, A., ed. *Hegel: A Collection of Critical Essays* (New York: Doubleday, 1972).

Maker, W. "Beginning," in *Essays on Hegel's Logic*, edited by George di Giovanni (Albany: SUNY Press, 1990), pp. 27-43.

Mayr, E. "The Evolution of Living Systems," *Proceedings of the National Academy of Sciences* 51 (1964): 934-41.

Mayr, E. *Toward a New Philosophy of Biology: Observations of an Evolutionist* (Cambridge, Massachusetts: Harvard University Press, 1988).

Menschkowski, H. *Noneuclidean Geometry*, translated by A. Shenitzer (New York: Academic Press, 1964).

Miller, A. E. and Miller, M.G. "Translator's Introduction and Commentary" to P. Plaass, *Kant's Theory of Natural Science*, Boston Studies in the Philosophy of Science, Vol. 159 (Dordrecht: Kluwer, 1994).

Minkowski, H. "Space and Time," in *Problems of Space and Time*, edited by J.J.C. Smart (New York: Macmillan, 1964).

Mittelstraß, J. *Die Rettung der Phänomene* (Berlin: de Gruyter, 1962).

Mohanty, J.N. and Shahan, R., eds. *Essays on Kant's Critique of Pure Reason* (Norman: University of Oklahoma Press, 1982).

Montucla, J.-E. *Histoire des mathématiques* (Paris: Jombert, 1758).

Movia, G., ed. *Hegel e Aristotele*, Atti del Convegno di Cagliari (11-15 Aprile 1994) (Cagliari: Edizioni AV, 1997).

Nasti De Vincentis, M. "Newton contra Keplerum apud Hegel: contradiction ou incommensurabilité?" in *Atti del Congresso "Nuovi problemi della logica e della filosofia della scienza,"* edited by D. Costantini and M.C. Galavotti (Bologna: CLUEB, 1991).

Nasti De Vincentis, M. "Gli argomenti hegeliani contro il modello newtoniano," in C. Ferrini, *Guida al "De orbitis planetarum" di Hegel ed alle sue edizioni e traduzioni*, in coll. con M. Nasti De Vincentis (Bern: Haupt, 1995), pp. 203-40.

Neuser, W. "Die Entdeckungsgeschichte der Asteroiden und Hegels Habilitationsschrift" and "Hegels Habilitation und Reaktionen auf seine Habilitationsschrift," in G.W.F. Hegel, *Dissertatio philosophica de orbitis planetarum. Philosophische Erörterung über die Planetenbahnen*, translation, with introduction and commentary by W. Neuser (Weinheim: Acta Humanoria VCH, 1986).

Newton, I. *Philosophiae Naturalis Principia Mathematica*, translated by A. Motte, revised by F. Cajori (Berkeley: University of California Press, 1934; Chicago: Encyclopedia Britannica, 1952).

Newton, I. *Isaac Newton's Philosophiae Naturalis Principia Mathematica*, edited by A. Koyré and I.B. Cohen (Cambridge: Cambridge University Press, 1972).

Newton, I. *The Mathematical Papers of Isaac Newton*, edited by D.T. Whiteside, 8 Vols (Cambridge: Cambridge University Press, 1967-81).

Nieto, M.M. *The Titius-Bode Law of Planetary Distances: Its History and Theory* (New York: Pergamon Press, 1972).

Parry, D. *Hegel's Phenomenology of the "We"* (New York: Peter Lang, 1988).

Petry, M.J. "Scientific Method: Francoeur, Hegel and Pohl," in *Hegels Philosophie der Natur: Beziehungen zwischen empirischer und spekulativer Naturerkenntnis*, edited by R.-P. Horstmann and M.J. Petry (Stuttgart: Klett-Cotta, 1986).

Petry, M.J., ed. *Hegel und die Naturwissenschaften* (Stuttgart: Frommann-Holzboog, 1986).

Petry, M.J., ed. *Hegel and Newtonianism* (Dordrecht: Kluwer, 1993).

Petry, M.J. "The Significance of Kepler's Laws," in *Hegel and Newtonianism*, edited by M.J. Petry (Dordrecht: Kluwer, 1993).

Pippin, R. *Hegel's Idealism* (Cambridge: Cambridge University Press, 1989).

Pippin, R. "Hegel's Original Insight," *International Philosophical Quarterly* 33, 3 (1993): 285-95.

Pittendrigh, C.S. "Adaptation, Natural Selection and Behavior" in *Behavior and Evolution*, edited by A. Roe and G.G. Simpson (New Haven: Yale University Press, 1958).

Plaass, P. *Kant's Theory of Natural Science*, translated by A.E. and M.G. Miller, Boston Studies in the Philosophy of Science, Vol. 159 (Dordrecht: Kluwer, 1994).

Plato, *The Collected Dialogues of Plato*, edited by E. Hamilton and H. Cairns (Princeton: Princeton University Press, 1961).

Plato, *Timaeus and Critias*, edited by D. Lee (Harmondsworth: Penguin Books, 1965).

Poincaré, H. "Space and Geometry," in *The World of Physics*, edited by J.H. Weaver (New York: Simon and Schuster, 1987).

Popper, K.R. *The Open Society and its Enemies*, 2 Vols (1945; reprint, New York: Harper Torchbooks, 1963).

Pozzo, R. *Hegel: "Introductio in philosophiam." Dagli studi ginnasiali alla prima logica* (Firenze: La Nuova Italia, 1989).

Reichenbach, H. *Philosophic Foundations of Quantum Mechanics* (Berkeley: University of California Press, 1944).

Rensberger, B. "Choosing the Right Mutation?" *Washington Post* April 20, 1992.

Riedel, M., ed. *Hegel und die antike Dialektik* (Frankfurt am Main: Suhrkamp Verlag, 1990).

Robinson, H., ed. *Proceedings of the Eighth International Kant Congress*, 2 Vols (Milwaukee: Marquette University Press, 1995).

Roe, A. and Simpson, G.G., eds. *Behavior and Evolution* (New Haven: Yale University Press, 1958).

Rosen, M. *Hegel's Dialectic and Its Criticism* (Cambridge: Cambridge University Press, 1982).

Rosenkranz, K. *G.W.F. Hegel's Leben* (1844; reprint, Darmstadt: Wissenschaftliche Buchgesellschaft, 1963).

Ruse, M. *Philosophy of Biology Today* (Albany, New York: SUNY Press, 1988).

Russell, B. *The Principles of Mathematics* (London: Allen & Unwin, 1938).

Sambursky, S. "Hegel's Philosophy of Nature," in *The Interaction Between Science and Philosophy*, edited by Y.

Elkana (Atlantic Highlands, N.J: Humanities Press, 1974).

Schellings Werke, edited by M. Schröter, 6 Vols and 6 Supplementary Vols (C.H. Beck: Munich, 1958).

Schelling. F.W. "Anhang zu dem Aufsatz des Herrn Eschenmayer betreffend den wahren Begriff der Naturphilosophie, und die richtige Art ihre Probleme aufzulösen," *Zeitschrift für spekulative Physik* 2, 1: 111-46.

Schier, D.S. *Louis-Bertrand Castel, Anti-Newtonian Scientist* (Cedar Rapids, Iowa: The Torch Press, 1941).

Schleiden, M.J. *Schelling's und Hegel's Verhältnis zur Naturwissenschaft* (1844), edited by O. Breidbach (Weinheim: VCH, Acta Humaniora, 1988).

Schlick, M. "The Four-Dimensional World," in *Problems of Space and Time*, edited by J.J.C. Smart (New York: Macmillian, 1964).

Schnädelbach, H. *Philosophy in Germany, 1831-1933*, translated by Eric Matthews (Cambridge: Cambridge University Press, 1984).

Schubert, F.T. *Theoretische Astronomie*, Vol. 3 (Physische Astronomie) (St. Petersburg: Kayserliche Akademie der Wissenschaften, 1798).

Shea, W.R. "Hegel's Celestial Mechanics," in *Hegels Philosophie der Natur: Beziehungen zwischen empirischer und spekulativer Naturerkenntnis*, edited by R.-P. Horstmann and M.J. Petry (Stuttgart: Klett-Cotta, 1986).

Simpson, G.G. *This View of Life* (New York: Harcourt, Brace and World, 1964).

Smart, J.J.C., ed. *Problems of Space and Time* (New York: Macmillian, 1964).

Sosa, E. and Dancy, J. *A Companion to Epistemology* (Oxford: Blackwell, 1992).

Stekeler-Weithofer, P. *Hegels Analytische Philosophie* (Paderborn, München, Wien, Zürich: Ferdinand Schöningh, 1992).

Stern, D. "The Immanence of Thought: Hegel's Critique of Foundationalism," *The Owl of Minerva* 22, 1 (Fall 1990): 19-33.

Strawson, P.F. *Individuals* (New York: Routledge, 1990).

Swineburne, R. *Space and Time* (New York: Macmillian, 1968).

Taylor, C. *Hegel* (Cambridge: Cambridge University Press, 1975).

Thomas, L. *The Lives of a Cell* (1974; reprint, Harmondsworth: Penguin Books, 1987).

Tuschling, B. *Metaphysische und transzendentale Dynamik in Kants opus postumum* (Berlin: de Gruyter, 1971).

Tuschling, B. "Sind die Urteile der Logik vielleicht 'insgesamt synthetisch'?" *Kant-Studien* 72, 3 (1981): 304-35.

Van Cleve, J. "Inner States and Outer Relations: Kant and the Case for Monadism," in *Doing Philosophy Historically*, edited by P. Hare (Buffalo: Prometheus, 1988).

Van Fraassen, B.C. *The Scientific Image* (Oxford: Clarendon Press, 1980).

Van Lunteren, F.H. "Hegel and Gravitation," in *Hegels Philosophie der Natur: Beziehungen zwischen empirischer und spekulativer Naturerkenntnis*, edited by R.-P. Horstmann and M.J. Petry (Stuttgart: Klett-Cotta, 1986).

Verene, D.P. *Hegel's Recollection: A Study of Images in the Phenomenology of Spirit* (Albany: SUNY Press, 1985).

Vizgin, V.P. "The Geometrical Unified Field Theory Program" in *Einstein and the History of General Relativity*, edited by D. Howard and J. Stachel (Boston: Birkhäuser, 1986).

Vlacq, A. *Tabellen der sinuum, tangentium, secantium, logarithmi de sinuum, tangentium und Zahlen von 1-10, 000* (Frankfurt/Leipzig: Fleischer, 1767).

Voigt, F.S. *Lehrbuch der Botanik* (Jena: 1808).

Wandschneider, D. *Raum, Zeit, Relativität. Grundbestimmungen der Physik in der Perspektive der Hegelschen Naturphilosophie* (Frankfurt: Vittorio Klostermann, 1982).

Wandschneider, D. "Nature and Dialectic of Nature in Hegel's Objective Idealism," *Bulletin of the Hegel Society of Great Britain* 26, (Autumn/Winter 1992): 30-51.

Wandschneider, D. "The Problem of Mass in Hegel," in *Hegel and Newtonianism*, edited by M.J. Petry (Dordrecht: Kluwer, 1993).

Wartenberg, T. "Reason and the Practice of Science," in *The Cambridge Companion to Kant*, edited by Paul Guyer (Cambridge: Cambridge University Press, 1992).

Weaver, J.H., ed. *The World of Physics*, (New York: Simon and Schuster, 1987).

Weinert, F. "Laws of Nature. A Structural Approach," *Philosophia naturalis* 2 (1993): 147-71.

Westphal, K.R. *Hegel's Epistemological Realism* (Dordrecht: Kluwer, 1989).

Westphal, K.R. "Hegel's Critique of Kant's Moral World View," *Philosophical Topics* 19, 2 (1991): 133-76.

Westphal, K.R. "Dialectic (Hegel)," in *A Companion to Epistemology*, edited by E. Sosa and J. Dancy (Oxford: Blackwell, 1992).

Westphal, K.R. "The Basic Context and Structure of Hegel's *Philosophy of Right*," in *The Cambridge Companion to Hegel*, edited by F.C. Beiser (Cambridge: Cambridge University Press, 1993).

Westphal, K.R. Review of *Übergang. Untersuchungen zum Spätwerk Immanuel Kants* in *The Owl of Minerva* 24, 2 (Spring 1993): 235-42.

Westphal, K.R. "Hegel on Political Representation: Laborers, Corporations and the Monarch," *The Owl of Minerva* 25, 1 (Fall 1993): 111-16.

Westphal, K.R. "Hegel, Idealism, and Robert Pippin," *International Philosophical Quarterly* 33, 3 (1993): 263-72.

Westphal, K.R. "How 'Full' is Kant's Categorical Imperative?", *Jahrbuch für Recht und Ethik / Annual Review of Law and Ethics* 3 (1995): 465-509.

Westphal, K.R. "Does Kant's *Metaphysical Foundations of Natural Science* Fill a Gap in the *Critique of Pure Reason?*" *Synthese* 103, 1 (1995): 43-86.

Westphal, K.R. "Kant's Dynamic Constructions," *Journal of Philosophical Research* 20 (1995): 33-81.

Westphal, K.R. "Kant's Critique of Determinism in Empirical Psychology," in *Proceedings of the Eighth International Kant Congress*, edited by H. Robinson, 2 Vols (Milwaukee: Marquette University Press, 1995), Vol. 2.

Westphal, K.R. "Kant's Proof of the Law of Inertia," in *Proceedings of the Eighth International Kant Congress*, edited by H. Robinson, 2 Vols (Milwaukee: Marquette University Press, 1995), Vol. 2.

Westphal, K.R. "Kant, Hegel, and the Transcendental Material Conditions of Possible Experience," *Bulletin of the Hegel Society of Great Britain* 33 (1996): 23-41.

Westphal, K.R. "Harris, Hegel, and the Truth about Truth," in *Hegel's Phenomenology: A Reappraisal*, ed G. Browning (Dordrecht: Kluwer, 1996).

Westphal, K.R. "Noumenal Causality Reconsidered," *Canadian Journal of Philosophy* 27, 2 (1997): 209-46.

Westphal, K.R. "Affinity, Idealism, and Naturalism: The Stability of Cinnabar and the Possibility of Experience," *Kant-Studien* 88 (1997): 139-89.

Westphal, K.R. "Transcendental Reflections on Pragmatic Realism," in *Pragmatism, Reason, and Norms*, edited by K.R. Westphal (New York: Fordham University Press, 1997).

Westphal, K.R., ed. *Pragmatism, Reason, and Norms*, (New York: Fordham University Press, 1997).

Westphal, K.R. "Harris, Hegel, and the Spirit of the *Phenomenology*," *Clio* (1998).

White, A. *Absolute Knowledge: Hegel and the Problem of Metaphysics* (Athens, Ohio: Ohio University Press, 1983).

Whiteside, D.T. *The Mathematical Principles Underlying Newton's "Principia Mathematica"* (Glasgow: University of Glasgow Press, 1970).

Winfield, R.D. *Overcoming Foundations: Studies In Systematic Philosophy* (New York: Columbia, 1989).

Witrow G.J. "Why Physical Space has Three Dimensions," *The British Journal for the Philosophy of Science* 6 (1956): 13-31.

Wolff, M. *Der Begriff des Widerspruchs: eine Studie zur Dialektik Kants und Hegels* (Königstein/Ts.: Hain, 1981).

Wright, L. *Teleological Explanations: An Etiological Analysis of Goals and Functions* (Berkeley, California: University of California Press, 1976).

Zach, F. von "Über einen zwischen Mars und Jupiter längst vermuteten, nun wahrscheinlich entdeckten neuen Hauptplaneten unseres Sonnen-Systems," *Monatliche Correspondenz zur Beförderung der Erd- und Himmelskunde* (June, 1801).

Zach, F. von "Notiz," *Monatliche Correspondenz zur Beförderung der Erd- und Himmelskunde* (April, 1802).

Zammito, J.H. *The Genesis of Kant's Critique of Judgment* (Chicago: University of Chicago Press, 1992).

About the Contributors

William Maker is professor of philosophy at Clemson University and Chair of the Philosophy and Religion Department. He is the editor of *Hegel on Economics and Freedom* (1987) and the author of *Philosophy without Foundations: Rethinking Hegel* (1994), and has published numerous articles on Hegel and contemporary philosophy. He was Vice-President of the Hegel Society of America from 1994 to 1996.

Edward Halper is professor of philosophy at the University of Georgia. He is the author of *One and Many in Aristotle's Metaphysics: The Central Books* (1989), *Form and Reason: Essays in Metaphysics* (1993), and numerous papers in philosophy journals. Most of his published work is in ancient philosophy.

Richard Dien Winfield is professor of philosophy at the University of Georgia. He is the author of *Reason and Justice* (1988), *The Just Economy* (1988), *Overcoming Foundations* (1989), *Freedom and Modernity* (1991), *Law in Civil Society* (1995), *Systematic Aesthetics* (1995), *Stylistics* (1996), and *The Just Family* (1998), as well as numerous articles. He served on the council of the Hegel Society of America from 1990 to 1994.

Lawrence S. Stepelevich has recently retired as professor of philosophy from Villanova University and concluded his nineteen-year tenure as Editor of *The Owl of Minerva*, the Journal of the Hegel Society of America. He has published on Hegel (mainly in the area of philosophy of religion) and on the Young Hegelians (especially, Stirner, Feuerbach, and Cieszkowski). He translated Bruno Bauer's *Trumpet of the Last Judgment* (1989), and is the editor of *The Young*

Hegelians. An Anthology (1983) which is being re-issued by Humanities Press. He was President of the Hegel Society of America from 1996 to 1998.

Brigitte Falkenburg is Professor of Philosophy at the University of Dortmund, Germany. She has PhD degrees in both philosophy and physics. She is the author of *Die Form der Materie. Zur Metaphysik der Natur bei Kant und Hegel* (1987) and *Teilchenmetaphysik. Zur Realitätsauffassung in Wissenschaftsphilosophie und Mikrophysik* (1995), and has also published several articles on Leibniz, Kant and Hegel. In 1995/96 she was a Fellow of the Institute for Advanced Study in Berlin.

Kenneth R. Westphal is associate professor of philosophy at the University of New Hampshire, and specializes in Kant, Hegel, and contemporary epistemology. He is the author of *Hegel's Epistemological Realism* (1989) and *Hegel, Hume und die Identität wahrnehmbarer Dinge* (1998), as well as numerous articles on the epistemologies, philosophies of science and political philosophies of Kant and Hegel.

Daniel O. Dahlstrom is professor of philosophy at Boston University, and is the author of *Das logische Vorurteil: Untersuchungen zur Wahrheitstheorie des frühen Heidegger* (1994). He is the author of several articles on Kant, the German Idealists and Heidegger and has recently published a translation of Schiller's aesthetic writings. He served as a member of the council of the Hegel Society of America from 1994 to 1996.

Errol E. Harris is John Evans Professor of Moral and Intellectual Philosophy, Emeritus at Northwestern University. He is the author of several books on Hegel and on the philosophy of science, including *Nature, Mind and*

Modern Science (1954), *The Foundations of Metaphysics in Science* (1965), *An Interpretation of the Logic of Hegel* (1983), *Formal, Transcendental and Dialectical Thinking* (1987), and *The Spirit of Hegel* (1993). He served as President of the Hegel Society of America from 1976 to 1978.

Donald Phillip Verene is Candler Professor of Metaphysics and Moral Philosophy at Emory University. He is the author of *Vico's Science of Imagination* (1981), *Hegel's Recollection* (1985), and *The New Art of Autobiography* (1991), and is co-editor of *The Metaphysics of Symbolic Forms* (1996), the fourth volume of Cassirer's *The Philosophy of Symbolic Forms*. He was Visiting Fellow at Pembroke College, Oxford in 1988 and holds a doctorate of Humane Letters, *honoris causa* from Knox College. He served as President of the Hegel Society of America from 1992 to 1994.

Mauro Nasti De Vincentis is associate professor of logic at the University of Salerno and works primarily on computational tractability, ancient Stoic logic, Boethius' logic, Newton's natural philosophy and Hegel's philosophy of nature. He is the author of numerous articles and collaborated with Cinzia Ferrini in the publication of *Guida al "De orbitis planetarum"* (1995).

Olivier Depré teaches modern philosophy at the Catholic University of Louvain (Louvain-la-Neuve, Belgium) and recently published a French edition of Hegel's Frankfurt texts (1997). He is secretary of Philosophical Society of Louvain and, since 1994, has been a research fellow at the National Belgian Foundation for Scientific Research.

Cinzia Ferrini has held research fellowships in the USA, the Netherlands, Switzerland and Germany and is the author of several articles dealing mainly with the relation between logic and the philosophy of nature in the development of Hegel's thought. She is the principal author (in collaboration with Mauro Nasti De Vincentis) of *Guida al "De orbitis planetarum"* (1995) and is the author of *Scienze empiriche e filosofie della natura* (1996).

Stephen Houlgate is professor of philosophy at the University of Warwick. He is the author of *Hegel, Nietzsche and the Criticism of Metaphysics* (1986) and *Freedom, Truth, and History: An Introduction to Hegel's Philosophy* (1991), as well as numerous articles on Hegel, Kant and Nietzsche. He served as Vice-President of the Hegel Society of America from 1992 to 1994 and was President of the Hegel Society of America from 1994 to 1996.

Index

absolute Idea (see also Idea), 30-4, 36-7, 39-42, 46, 52, 82, 126, 128.
absolute knowing, 217-18.
Alexander, Samuel, 189-90.
ambiguity, xxii, 216-19.
Ameriks, Karl, 22, 137.
Amphiboly, 148.
analogical inference (analogies), 108-9, 134, 285, 291.
Analogies of Experience, 138, 149-50, 160.
and ("andness"), 218-19.
animal, 178, 202.
an sich, 215-19, 221.
antinomies, 117, 120, 122-3, 128, 135, 170, 176.
anti-reductionism, 266, 268.
a priori (apriorism), xiv-xvi, xix, xxiv, xxvii, 5, 7, 17, 19-20, 98, 131, 152-3, 212, 273, 283, 299.
arcs, xxiii, 231-3, 235, 251.
areal law, see Newton (areal law and proof).
Aristotle, xiii, 44-5, 55, 144, 157, 174, 202, 210, 302.
arithmetic, 269, 297, 301.
arithmetic series, xxiv, 262, 301.
asteroids, xi, xxiv, 264, 283, 304.
astronomical units, 260.
astronomy, 266-7, 284, 286, 298.
atomism, 104-5, 107-8, 130, 132.
attraction, 38, 64-5, 119, 122, 142, 273.
Aufhebung, xxii, 9, 222-3.
Augustine, Saint, 67-8.
axioms, 106, 111.
Ayala, F.J., 178.

bad infinite, 270.
Bardili, Christoph Gottfried, 302.
Barrow, John, 78.
becoming, 38, 82, 191, 294, 297.
being, 33-4, 36, 53, 82, 94, 258.
being *for*, 12.
being-for-self, 38.
Bergson, Henri, 189.
Bernoulli, Johann, 231.
Berthollet, Claude-Louis, xii.
biology, xv, xxi, 145, 177-81, 186.
Bode, J.E., 259, 264, 301, 304.
body, 65, 105.
Boltzmann, Ludwig Eduard, 99, 132.
Bonola, R, 72.
Bonnet, Charles, xxi, 192, 194.
Bonsiepen, Wolfgang, 286-8, 309.
Born, Max, xviii, 77, 86.
Borzeszkowski, H.-H. von, 308.
Bourbaki, 126, 135.
Brann, Eva T., 67.
Brecht, Bertolt, 219-21, 225.
Breidbach, Olaf, 187.
British Idealism, see idealism.
Bronowski, Jacob, xi, xxiv.
Buchdahl, Gerd, xiii, xxvi, 132, 162.
Buffon, Georges-Louis, 191-2, 194.
Burbidge, John, 294, 307.

Caird, Edward, 91.
Cairns, John, 181.
calculus, 297.
Carnap, Rudolf, xviii, 72-4, 76, 79.
Cartwright, Nancy, 18.
Castel, Louis-Bertrand, xxiv, 237-8, 240-5, 250-4, 256.

categories, 34-5, 66, 124, 149, 153, 164; of logic, xvii-xviii, 30-2, 37-40, 43, 46-7, 52-3; of nature, xvii-xviii, 30-1, 33, 38-41, 43, 60.
Cauchy, Augustin-Louis, xii.
causality, 149-50; as external, 143-7.
central forces, see forces.
Ceres, xxiv, 264, 283, 304.
certainty, 76, 82.
chemism, 197.
chromosome, 204.
circular motion, 89, 274.
closure of logic, 32.
Cohen, R.S., xv.
coherence, 98, 113.
Collingwood, R.G., 21, 211, 221.
completeness, 107-8, 114, 120, 122-4, 126, 128-30.
Concept (*Begriff*, Notion), 25, 35-7, 39, 41, 81, 97-8, 126-8, 193-6, 201-3, 289.
concepts, xix, 100, 109, 114, 117-18, 129-31, 294.
conceptual schemes, 52.
concern, 85.
concrete universal, 167.
congruence geometry, 90-1.
congruency, 80-1, 93.
consciousness, xxii, 5-7, 23, 55, 60, 215-17.
conservative central force, 228, 234, 236, 248.
consistency, 78-9.
construction (constructivism), 99, 116, 122, 305.
contingency, xvi, 16-18, 25, 111, 117, 127, 129, 290, 300.
contradiction, 135.
Coolidge, Julian Lowell, 91.
Copernicus, Nicolaus, 101.
correspondence, 98, 106, 113.
Coxeter, H.S.M., 78.
Cramer, K., 134.
critical idealism, see idealism.
Critique of Judgment (I. Kant), xiv, xx, 117, 167, 169, 179.
Critique of Pure Reason (I. Kant), xx, 117, 120, 126, 137-40, 144, 148-9, 156, 158.
curvilinear arcs, see arcs.
curvilinear lines, 67.
Cuvier, Georges, xii, xxi, 192.

Dahlstrom, Daniel O., xx-xxi, 156.
Dampier, William, 191.
Darwin, Charles (see also Darwinism), 177, 179, 188-9, 191.
Darwin, Erasmus, 191.
Darwinism (Darwinian), xv, xxi, 168, 180, 196, 203.
Davy, Humphry, xii.
De Gandt, F., 232, 236, 259.
De orbitis planetarum (G.W.F. Hegel), see *Dissertation on the Orbits of the Planets*.
Depré, Olivier, xxiv.
Descartes, René, 45, 64, 105.
description, 6, 14-15.
desire, 84-5, 145, 147.
determinacy, 62-3; of thought, 9.
determinate negation (see also negation), 54, 66.
development, 194-5.
dialectic, 41, 43, 124, 152, 190, 193, 211, 215, 221-3.
difference, 207.
Differenzschrift (G.W.F. Hegel), xix, 137, 151, 153, 172, 258.
dimensions, 103.
Ding an sich, 14, 290.
Dissertation on the Orbits of the Planets (G.W.F. Hegel), xxii, xxiv-xxv, 80, 164, 236, 238, 245-6, 249-50, 256-9, 262, 266, 275, 283-5, 288, 297, 299, 300-1, 310.
divine intellect, 170.
DNA, xxi, 177, 181, 205.

Doz, André, 300.
Düsing, Klaus, 167, 183.
dynamical (dynamics) (see also quantity: dynamic), xix-xx, 102.

Earliest System Program of German Idealism (G.W.F. Hegel), 267, 269, 278.
earth, 198-202.
E. coli, xxi, 181.
Einstein, Albert, xviii, 75-6, 82, 89-90, 92, 247.
Elements (Euclid), 111.
Elsbach, Alfred C., 92.
emanation, 192.
embalming, 213.
empirical, xiii, xvi, xix-xx, xxv, 15, 17-18, 22, 24-6, 51, 97-8, 117, 122, 129-30, 151, 153, 163, 175, 284-5, 289-92, 297-301.
empiricism (empiricists), 44-5, 99, 104, 113, 115-16, 129, 303.
Encyclopedia of the Philosophical Sciences (G.W.F. Hegel), xi, xxv, 22, 35, 42, 75, 82, 100, 110, 114-15, 123, 126, 131, 137, 174-5, 192, 195, 197-8, 200, 210, 212, 222, 250, 265, 283-4, 287, 293-5, 298, 301.
epigenesis, xxi, 194-5.
epistemology, xiii.
eros, 214.
Euclid's Fourth Postulate, 80-1, 90-1.
Euclidean geometry/space, xviii, 67, 71-3, 75-6, 78, 80, 93.
Eudoxus, 101.
Euler, Leonhard, 71.
evolution, xi, xxi-xxii, 179-80, 189-94, 197, 203-4, 206.
experience, 26, 175, 215-19, 261, 289-91.
exponential series, xxiv, 262, 278.
extension (extensional), xix, 100, 103, 105-7, 112-114, 118, 121, 124, 127-9.
externality (see also self-externality), xvi, 10-13, 18, 24, 29, 32, 34, 36, 44, 46, 58, 128, 146-7, 196, 220, 288, 297, 300-1.

facticity (see also givenness), 7.
Faith and Knowledge (G.W.F. Hegel), 173, 175.
Falkenburg, Brigitte, xix, 250.
Ferrini, Cinzia, xxv, 250, 278-9.
Feyerabend, Paul, 25.
Feynman, R.P., 252-3.
Fichte, Johann Gottlieb, 185.
figure, 42.
Findlay, John N., 189, 210-11, 220.
finite intellect, 171.
finitude, 4, 14.
Fisher, K., 262.
force(s), xix-xx, 38, 64-5, 99, 102, 104, 106-7, 109, 111, 119-20, 122, 139-43, 148, 150, 158, 267, 271-5; central, 227-8, 234, 236, 248.
formalism, 286, 305.
Förster, Eckart, 138, 150, 156, 161, 163.
Foster, Michael, 49.
frameworks of reference, 52.
freedom, 19, 162, 221, 271-3, 275.
Frege, Gottlob, 114, 121, 126, 250.
Friedman, Michael, 102, 156.
friendship, xxii, 220-1.

Gaia hypothesis, xxi, 200, 204.
Galilei, Galileo, 101-2, 105, 108, 111, 114, 134, 297.
Gauss, Karl Friedrich, 72, 264.

gene, 205.
genotype, 191.
geology, 198-201, 209-11.
geometrical method, 305.
Geometrische Studien (G.W.F. Hegel), 80, 258.
geometry (see also congruence, Euclidean, n-dimensional, and non-Euclidean geometry), xviii-xix, 72-4, 269-71, 273, 297; Hegel's theory of, xviii, 75, 77-8, 80, 84, 87, 90-1, 269-71; physical, xviii, 74-7, 79-80, 82-6, 88; pure, xviii, 74-80, 82-6; of reason (speculative/philosophical), xviii, 77, 80, 84, 90.
givenness (see also facticity), xvi, 4, 10-11, 14-17, 20, 51-2.
God, 206, 273, 275, 280.
Gödel, Kurt, 78, 80.
Godron, 191.
Goethe, Johann Wolfgang von, 196, 210-11.
Görres, Joseph, 303.
Gotha congress, 260.
gravity, 38, 65, 89-90, 102, 108, 111, 123, 133, 142, 267, 273-5, 287; center of, 65.
Gross, David, 90.
Guyer, Paul, 137.

Haering, T., 258.
Haldane, J.S., 200.
Hall, Barry G., 181.
Haller, Albrecht von, xxi, 192.
Halper, Edward, xvii.
Harper, William, 159.
Harris, Errol E., xxi-xxii, 21, 212.
Harris, Henry S., 165-6, 283-4.
Hartmann, Klaus, 24.
Hegel, Christiane, 258, 276.
Hegel, Georg Wilhelm Friedrich: critique of Euclid, 80-1; critique/interpretation of Kant, xix-xx, 73-4, 115-17, 120-4, 135, 137, 139-40, 143, 153-4, 157-8, 164, 167, 172-6, 184, 258; *Habilitation*, 257; knowledge of science, xii, 29, 177, 186, 192, 211; logic, 23, 32, 124-5, 268-70, 288; on Newton/Newtonian science, xxiii-xxv, 108-10, 112-15, 164, 228-9, 232, 236-8, 242, 244-6, 248-9, 253, 258, 266-9, 271-5; theory of geometry, xviii, 75, 77-8, 80, 84, 87, 90-1, 269-71.
Heidegger, Martin, 68.
Heisenberg, Werner, 79-80.
here, 56, 59, 61, 84-6, 94.
Hermes, 214.
hermeneutics, 213-14.
Herschel, W., 260, 304.
Hertz, H., 248.
Hilbert, David, xviii, 74, 76, 78, 82, 85-6, 106.
Hinske, Norbert, 161.
Hölderlin, Friedrich, 172, 259.
holism (see also whole), 199.
Horstmann, Rolf-Peter, xvi.
Hösle, Vittorio, 307.
Hume, David, 113, 116, 127, 152.
Hutton, James, xii.
hylozoism, 145.

Idea (see also absolute Idea), xvii, xx, 12, 167, 174, 191-4, 196-8, 202, 206, 211-13, 215, 219-21; relation to nature (see also thought and nature), xvii, xxii, 10, 32-4, 36-7, 39-41, 52, 128, 192, 203, 212-14, 219-21, 261, 274, 288.
idealism, xvi, 1-8, 14, 16, 19-23, 30; British, 211; post-Kantian, 290; transcendental, 131, 151.

ideality, 292.
identity, 207, 273, 275.
Ihmig, K.-N., 250, 256.
imagination, 67.
immanence, 1, 3, 7-8, 18, 35-6, 66, 127, 137, 175, 193.
immediacy, 298-300.
indeterminacy, 5.
Indeterminacy Principle, 79.
indifference, 295.
individuals, 107, 112, 121, 125, 128.
inertia, 123, 140, 145, 159, 272.
infinite, 79, 270-1; bad, 270, 278.
ingenium, 223.
intellect, 171.
intellectual intuition (see also intuitive understanding), 171, 185.
intension (intensional), 100, 110, 114, 123-4, 126-7, 129.
interaction, 45.
Introductio in Philosophiam (G.W.F. Hegel), 257, 268.
intuition, 55, 60, 73, 83, 85, 100, 112, 118, 121, 124-5, 134, 291.
intuitive understanding (see also intellectual intuition), 173, 175, 185.
Inwood, Michael, 47.

Judaism, 270, 273, 280.

Kant, Immanuel, xiii, xviii-xxi, 55, 57, 60, 64, 72-4, 92, 98-100, 108, 112, 115-120, 124-7, 129, 131, 137-65, 167-83, 211, 215, 222, 273, 295; and metaphysics, 137-8; and Newton, 120, 139, 144, 152, 159; Hegel's critique/ interpretation of, xix-xx, 73-4, 115-17, 120-4, 135, 137, 139-40, 143, 153-4, 157-8, 164, 167, 172-6, 184, 258; second law of mechanics, 143-4, 158.
Kauffman, Stuart, 205.
Kepler, Johannes, 101-2, 108, 111, 114, 134, 164, 249-50, 258, 266-7, 272, 297, 310; first law, 229,231; second law, 164, 227-8, 234, 253; third law, 309.
Klein, Felix, 80, 90, 93.
Krug's pen, 17, 48.
Kuhn, Thomas S., xiii, 25.
Küppers, Bernd-Olaf, 181.

Lagrange, Joseph-Louis, xii.
Lakatos, Imre, xiii.
Lamarck, Jean-Baptiste, 191-2, 194.
Lambert, Johann Heinrich, 122, 132, 148.
Lardic, J.-M., 306.
laws of nature, 45-6, 109, 111, 113, 120, 297, 300.
Lectures on the History of Philosophy (G.W.F. Hegel), 174.
Leibniz, Gottfried Wilhelm, 45, 111-12, 114, 124-6, 272.
life, 145, 147, 167, 174, 195, 198, 261, 275.
light, 132.
line (see also curvilinear lines), 42, 55-8, 85-7.
Linnaeus, Carolus, xxi, 192.
literal-mindedness, 214, 223.
Lloyd-Morgan, C., 189.
Locke, John, 101, 105.
Lovelock, James, 200, 204.

Mach, Ernst, 99, 104, 106, 113, 132.
Maker, William, xvi.
Marx, Karl, 22.
mass, 88, 90, 95, 104-7, 120, 133.
mathematics, xix-xx, xxv, 75,

79, 135, 261, 266-71, 278, 286-8, 297, 299, 301, 308.
matrix algebra, 88.
matter, xviii, 38, 43, 59, 62-5, 83, 88-9, 116, 119, 122, 134, 140-2, 144-7, 267, 272-5, 280, 292; and law, 45; as lifeless, 145-7.
Maxwell, James Clerk, 99.
Mayr, Ernst, 178, 180-1, 186-7.
meaning, 100, 103-7, 117-18, 125.
measure, 261, 295-7, 298-301, 307.
mechanism (mechanics), 65, 99, 172, 176, 181, 197, 258-9, 266, 274, 279, 286, 292, 297.
medieval thought, 44.
Mendel, Gregor Johann, 177.
Mercury, 71.
metamorphosis, 196.
Metaphysical Foundations of Natural Science (I. Kant), xiii-xiv, xix-xx, 115-16, 118-22, 134-5, 138-41, 148-51, 153, 156-8, 273.
metaphysical idealism, see idealism.
metaphysics, xiii, 99, 125, 291.
meteorology, 200.
method, 274.
methodological idealism, see idealism.
Miller, Alfred E., 157-8.
Miller, Maria G., 157-8.
mineralogy, 209, 211.
Minkowski, Hermann, xviii, 82, 88, 95.
Mnemosyne, 214.
modality, 295.
modern metaphysics/ philosophy, 44-5.
momentum, 104, 120, 246.
Monatliche Correspondenz, 264-5.
Montucla, J.-E., 250.
Moralität, Liebe, Religion (G.W.F. Hegel), 278.
motion (see also circular motion), xviii, xx, 38, 43, 57, 59, 61-4, 82, 88-9, 95, 119, 140-1, 144, 157-8, 280, 292.
Münchhausen, Baron von, 125.
Muses, 214.
mutation, xx-xxii, 179, 181, 188, 203-6.
Napoleon, 210.
Nasti De Vincentis, Mauro, xxii-xxiii, 248.
natural philosophy (see also philosophy of nature), 100-1, 110, 112, 115, 126-7, 129-31.
natural selection, 204-6.
nature, xvii, 10, 12-13, 19-20, 32, 34-7, 39, 44, 128, 192, 196, 206, 213, 220-2, 261, 265, 274.
n-dimensional geometry, 90-1.
necessity, 116, 120, 127, 130, 152-3, 175, 181, 194.
negation (see also determinate negation), 59.
neo-Darwinism, see Darwinism.
neo-Kantianism, 72.
Neptune, xxiv, 265, 278.
neptunism, 210.
Neuser, W., 262, 304.
Newton, Isaac, xix, xxiii-xxiv, 71-2, 74, 89, 100-2, 104-6, 113, 120, 126-7, 133, 142-4, 152, 159, 164, 249, 256, 258, 267, 271-3, 275-6, 297; areal law and proof, xxiii-xxiv, 227-37, 239-46, 249, 252-3; definitions, 107; first law of motion, 71, 143-4; Rules, 105-8, 118, 134; second law of motion, 159-60, 239-40.
Newtonian physics/science, xix, 98-9, 101-2, 104, 107-8, 110, 112-15, 123, 126-8, 266, 269, 274.

Niethammer, Friedrich Immanuel, 257.
non-Euclidean geometry/ space, xviii, 56, 71-2, 75, 78.
non-reductionism, 114, 123.
nothing, 82.
Notion, see Concept (*Begriff*).
numbers, xxv, 261, 286, 297-302.

objectivity, 117.
Oken, Lorenz, 191.
Olbers, H.W.M., 264.
On the Orbits of the Planets (G.W.F. Hegel), see *Dissertation on the Orbits of the Planets*.
ontology, 125.
Opticks (I. Newton), 104.
Opus Postumum (I. Kant), 140-1, 143, 150.
orbital arcs, see arcs.
organism (organic), xx-xxi, 145-6, 169, 172, 176-8, 195, 198-205.
otherness (other), 8-10, 13-14, 16, 38, 42-5, 220-1.
Palmquist, Stephen, 159.
Paralogisms, 160.
Parisian foot, 262.
Peano's curve, 247.
perihelion, 71.
Petry, Michael, xii-xiii, xv-xvi, 46-7, 133, 186, 211-12, 249-50, 262-3.
phenomena, 98, 111, 113, 119, 127, 129-30, 132.
phenomenological concepts/ physics, 99, 109, 111, 129, 132.
phenomenology, 132.
Phenomenology of Spirit (G.W.F. Hegel), xxii, 5, 84, 93-4, 154, 203, 209, 213, 215, 217-18, 220, 221-3, 286.
phenotype, 191, 204-5.
Philosophiae Naturalis Principia Mathematica (I. Newton), see *Principia Mathematica*.
Philosophical Encyclopedia (G.W.F. Hegel), 297, 301.
philosophy of biology, 177.
Philosophy of Mind (G.W.F. Hegel), 55.
philosophy of nature (see also natural philosophy), 29-31, 43-4, 51, 71, 97-9, 122, 131, 175-6, 195, 197, 274, 288.
Philosophy of Nature (G.W.F. Hegel), xi-xix, xxii, 1-8, 10-11, 14, 16-20, 22, 23, 26, 29-30, 34-5, 37-8, 40, 42, 44-7, 75, 81-2, 84, 191, 197-8, 206, 211-12, 220, 272, 284, 286-8, 291-3, 296, 299, 301.
Philosophy of Right (G.W.F. Hegel), 84.
philosophy of science, 44, 51, 100, 102.
phoronomy, xx, 140-1, 143, 150.
physics (see also Newtonian physics, science), xiii, xv, xix, 18, 22, 25-6, 71, 75-6, 79, 87-8, 92, 99-104, 109-115, 126-7, 129-30, 139, 145-7, 149, 153, 163, 178, 258, 266-9, 271, 274-5, 289, 298; qualitative, 258, 267, 275; quantitative, 259, 267-8.
Physics (Aristotle), xiii, 55.
Piazzi, G., 264, 283, 304.
Pippin, Robert, 21-2, 165.
Pittendrigh, C.S., 187.
place, xviii, 38, 43, 56, 61-3, 84, 89.
plane(s), 56-8, 85-7.
planets (planetary distances/ motion/orbits), xxv, 241, 247, 260-1, 266, 271-3, 283-4, 292, 301.
Plato, xxiv, 124, 259, 262-3, 278.

Pohl, Georg Friedrich, xii.
Poincaré, Henri, 75.
point, xviii, 41-2, 55-8, 84-7.
polygonal arcs, see arcs.
Popper, Karl R., xi-xiii, 211.
positivity, 266, 268, 278.
post-Kantian idealism, see idealism.
powers, 261.
preformation, xxi, 194-5.
presuppositionlessness, xvii, 52.
Principia Mathematica (I. Newton), xxiii, 74, 101-2, 104-7, 111, 120, 152, 227, 229, 242, 246, 250, 280.
psychology, 160.
purpose (see also teleology), xx-xxi, 167-76, 178, 180, 183.
Pythagoreans, 157, 262.

qualitative physics, see physics.
quality, 105, 126, 295, 299.
quantitative physics/science, see physics.
quantity (quanta), 39-40, 49, 267-8, 287-8, 292, 295, 299-300; dynamic, 103-4, 109; extensive, 105; physical, 103, 120; spatio-temporal, 103-4.
quantum mechanics, 79.
Quine, W. v. O., 125, 162-3.

radius vector, xxiii, 227.
random mutation, see mutation.
realism, 150, 165.
reason, xxv, 79, 86, 261, 263, 265-7, 294.
reduction, 271.
reflection, 296, 307.
reflective judgment, 170, 174, 176.
Refutation of Idealism, 57, 60.
Reichenbach, Hans, 79.
relativity, 72, 89, 247.
religion, 79, 217, 278.
repulsion, 38, 64-5, 119, 122, 142, 273.
Riemann, B. xix, 89-90.
Robinet, J.B.R., 194.
Rosen, Michael, 21.
Rosenkranz, Karl, 210, 257, 266, 268.
Ruse, Michael, 186.
Russell, Bertrand, 74, 250.

Saccheri, Gerolamo, 254.
saving the phenomena, 98-102, 110-11, 113, 116-17, 128-9, 263, 278.
Scheeffer's theorem, 234.
Schelling, Friedrich W. J. von, xi, 134, 172, 185, 197-8, 206, 257, 285-6, 290-1, 303, 306, 310.
schematism, 100, 118, 138, 153, 156.
Schier, D.S., 253.
Schiller, Friedrich, xxii, 220.
Schleiden, Matthias J., xi.
Schlick, Moritz, 88.
Schnädelbach, Herbert, xi.
Schubert, F. T., 242-5, 253, 255-6.
science (see also Newtonian physics, physics), xi-xvi, xvii, xix-xx, 15, 17-18, 22, 24-6, 44, 51, 97-100, 114, 129-31, 153, 168, 172, 175-6, 211, 261, 289-92.
Science of Logic (G.W.F. Hegel) (see also Hegel: logic), xiii, xv-xvii, xix, xxii, xxv, 5, 7-8, 11, 18, 31, 34-7, 39-40, 47, 52, 64, 81, 125, 127-30, 135, 137, 167, 176, 190, 198, 212, 214-15, 218-23, 232, 242, 245, 287-8, 294-6, 298, 301.
Selbstsetzungslehre, see self-positing.
self-determination, xvi-xvii, 1-3,

7-12, 18-19, 30-1, 97, 275.
self-differentiated unity, 273.
self-externality (see also externality), 52-4, 56, 58-9, 83.
self-limitation, 8-9.
self-organization, 205-6.
self-positing, 150-2.
self-transcendence, 58-9.
sense-certainty, 93-4.
set theory, 125.
Shea, W.R., 131.
Smuts, J.C., 189.
society, 2.
Socrates, 219, 223.
soul, 202.
space, xviii, 12, 18, 24, 38-43, 45, 49, 54-62, 67-8, 72-4, 82-3, 87-90, 94, 119, 147, 269-70, 274, 287, 292-4, 297-8.
species, xxi, 112, 189, 191-2, 194; mutation, 179.
speculative sentence, 211.
Spencer, Herbert, 189, 194.
Spinoza, Benedictus de, 45, 173-4, 295, 305.
spirit, 19, 37, 46.
Spirit of Christianity (G.W.F. Hegel), 273.
Steffens, Henrik, 285, 291.
Stekeler-Weithofer, Pirmin, 135.
Stepelevich, Lawrence, xviii.
Stern, David, 24.
Strawson, Peter F., 67-8, 211.
substance, 107, 122, 125, 135, 295.
succession, logical/temporal, 60.
superstring theory, 90.
surface, 87.
Swineburne, Richard, 85.
synthetic judgments/ knowledge a priori, 72, 134.
systematicity (system, systematic thought), xvi, 1-4, 7-11, 15-18, 22, 30, 124, 151-2, 190.
System Fragment (G.W.F. Hegel), 270.

tangent, 271-2, 274.
Taylor, Charles, 21.
teleological judgment, antinomy of, 170, 176.
teleology (see also purpose), 110, 176-7, 180, 186.
teleonomy, 180-1, 187.
theory-dependence, 98.
Thomas, Lewis, 201.
thought and nature (see also Idea: relation to nature), xvi-xvii, 4, 9, 15-17, 19, 53.
Timaeus (Plato), xxiv, 259, 262.
Timaeus Locrus, 302.
time, xviii, 38-9, 42-3, 45, 49, 55-62, 67, 73-4, 82, 87-9, 269-70, 274, 292-4, 297-8.
Titius, J.D., 259.
Titius-Bode law, xxiv, 164, 259-61, 263-5, 283, 301, 304.
transcendental: arguments, 154, 158; constitution/ constructions, 52, 65; dynamics, 150-1, 154; ego, 290; idealism, 151; knowledge, 138; thinkers, 68.
transition(s), xvii, xxii, 40-1, 216, 220-1, 223, 293-7, 307.
tri-dimensionality, 42, 56, 83-4, 94.
triplicity, 215, 222.
Troxler, I.P.V., 269.
truth, 2, 6, 98, 113, 202-3.
Tuschling, Burkhard, 148-51, 156.
twoness, xxii.

understanding (*Verstand*), 7, 75, 77, 81-2, 119, 211, 263, 266-7, 269-70, 279, 294.
universal (universality), 39, 110-11, 116, 123, 126-7, 167,

220, 289.
unobservable causes/entities, 99, 106-7, 109, 118, 130.
Uranus, 260.

Van Fraassen, B. C., 113, 133.
vanishing, 294, 297.
Van Lunteren, F.H., 131.
vectors, 231.
vegetable, 202.
Verene, Donald Phillip, xxii.
Verra, V., 305, 307.
vis insita (*vis inertiae*), 246.
Voigt, F.S., 179, 187.
vulcanism, 210.

Wagner, Johann Jacob, 303.
Wandschneider, Dieter, 49, 307.
Wartofsky, Marx W., xv.
water, 199.
Weismann, August, 177.
Weldon, T.D., 211.
Westphal, Kenneth R., xix-xx.
White, Alan, 24.
Whiteside, D.T., 231, 233-7, 246, 253.
whole (see also holism), 152, 190, 193-4, 202-3, 267, 274; primacy of, 196.
Winfield, Richard Dien, xvii-xviii.
Witrow, G.J., 94.
Wolff, Christian, 151-2, 305.
Wolff, Michael, 125, 135.
Wright, Larry, 186.

Zach, F.X. von, 262, 264.
Zammito, John H., 186.